The Bluestockings of Japan

Michigan Monograph Series in Japanese Studies
Number 60

Center for Japanese Studies
The University of Michigan

The Bluestockings of Japan

New Woman Essays and Fiction from *Seitō*, 1911–16

Jan Bardsley

Center for Japanese Studies
The University of Michigan
Ann Arbor 2007

Published by the Center for Japanese Studies,
The University of Michigan
1007 E. Huron St.
Ann Arbor, MI 48104-1690

Library of Congress Cataloging-in-Publication Data

The bluestockings of Japan : new woman essays and fiction from Seito,
1911–16 / Jan Bardsley.
    p. cm. — (Michigan monograph series in Japanese studies ; no. 60)
    Includes bibliographical references and index.
    ISBN 978–1–929280–44–5 (cloth : alk. paper) — ISBN 978–1–929280–45–2
(pbk. : alk. paper)
    1. Japanese literature—Taisho period, 1912–1926—Translations into English.
2. Seito. I. Bardsley, Jan.
    PL782.E1B57   2007
    895.6′080928709041—dc22

                                                                    2007036839

This book was set in Palatino Macron.

This publication meets the ANSI/NISO Standards for Permanence of Paper
for Publications and Documents in Libraries and Archives (Z39.48—1992).

Printed in the United States of America

For my mothers,

Helen Holtby Bridges and Helen Kahl Bardsley

Contents

Illustrations

Acknowledgments

This volume about the Bluestockings of Japan (Seitō-sha) and their journal *Seitō* has been a long time in the making. I am indebted to the many teachers, colleagues, family members, and friends, and to the schools and sources of financial support, that made this possible.

Bruce Willoughby, Executive Editor of the Publications Program at the Center for Japanese Studies at the University of Michigan, and Akiko Kurita of the Japan Foreign Rights Centre deserve my thanks for their expertise and attention to this project. I much appreciate the fine copyediting work of Victoria R. M. Scott. My thanks to the families who gave me permission to publish my translations of their Bluestockings relatives' work.

I gratefully acknowledge the institutional support provided by The University of North Carolina at Chapel Hill, which has come in the form of two Chapman Family Fellowships at the Institute for Arts and Humanities as well as two University Research Council Publication grants. The Northeast Asia Council of the Association for Asian Studies and Wake Forest University both generously awarded me grants in 1993 for summer research in Japan on Hiratsuka Raichō. The 1995 National Endowment for the Humanities Seminar in Japanese history at Harvard University, led by Albert Craig and Harold Bolitho, gave me the inspiration and the time to translate Raichō's *Seitō* Manifesto.

There are many to thank from my graduate school days in the 1980s at UCLA. With admiration for his years of dedication to teaching and translation, I thank my dissertation advisor, Robert Epp. I will always be grateful to him for the challenging classes that taught me how to read Japanese, for his advice on my early studies of *Seitō*, and for his careful reading of my dissertation. Every time I see the bumper sticker that says, "If you can read this, thank a teacher!" I think of him and his patient, meticulous instruction. He and his wife Mitsuko Takeda-Epp have been a friendly presence in my life since my first days in graduate school. I thoroughly enjoyed seminars led by Professors Noriko Akatsuka, Ben Befu, Bill LaFleur, Fred Notehelfer, Herbert Plutschow, and Shirleen Wong—never was so much work also such fun. Doctoral students when I entered the M.A. program, Sucheta Mazumdar and Eri F. Yasuhara became my intellectual role models and generous *senpai*. For teaching me so much about literary analysis and translation, and for bringing such pleasure to the long process of completing the dissertation, I thank the good friends of my dissertation writing group, Aki Hirota, Leslie Pincus, and Jackie Stone. My classmates were, and still are, a constant source of support and intellectual stimulation. I would like to thank Linda Chance, Michael Marra, Stephen Miller, and especially my *Bad Girls of Japan* co-editor Laura Miller.

There are also many to thank in North Carolina, where I have enjoyed living and teaching for the past eighteen years. Colleagues at Wake Forest University—Mary DeShazer, Kevin Doak, Pat Moran, Tom Mullen, David Phillips, and Dick Sears—have been especially supportive of my research. I thoroughly enjoyed working with all of them. My friends at Guilford College, Dottie Borei and Hiroko Hirakawa, are always in supply of high spirits and good advice. Kristina Troost, Head of International and Area Studies, Perkins Library, Duke University, has helped with this project is so many ways—not the least of which is allowing me to have checked out a complete set of *Seitō* for so long. The Japanese History and Culture Study Group at Duke University and all my colleagues there have been a wonderful source of stimulation and support, as have John Mertz, David Ambaras, and Eika Tai at North Carolina State University.

The Department of Asian Studies at the University of North Carolina at Chapel Hill has been my intellectual home for the past thirteen years. I owe a great deal of thanks to my able chairs Judy Farquhar, Larry Kessler, Miles Fletcher, and Gang Yue, and to all my colleagues and students. I also would like to give a special note of thanks to my writing group friends, Altha Cravey, Joanne Hershfield, and Megan Matchinske, who saw this book in many of its stages and made so many helpful comments.

Conversations and high-test coffee with Inger Brodey, Ryuko Kubota, and Nadia Yaqub always spurred me on. In Santa Monica, Winston-Salem, and Chapel Hill, I had the good fortune to consult with Japanese teachers as I began and continued my study of *Seitō*. Yasue Harada tutored me in Japanese early on, while Kotoko Kroesen read Meiji-era novels with me. In North Carolina, Yuki Aratake, Sayoko Miyazaki Bardwell, Yuko Kato, Mari Noguchi, Akiko Yamazaki, Meiko Shimura, and Wakako Yamaguchi have been valuable consultants. I thank them for listening to my interpretations of *Seitō* essays and stories, and talking with me about my translations.

In Japan, I was able to talk, over the past twenty years, with several experts on *Seitō*. I consider myself most fortunate to have had conversations with Ide Fumiko, Kobayashi Tomie, Setouchi Harumi, Tachi Kaoru, and Yoneda Sayoko. I also would like to thank scholars of *Seitō* Melanie Czarnecki and Dina Lowy for sharing their work with me and commenting on mine. My translation of Araki's "The Letter" is much livelier for Melanie Czarnecki's suggestions. I deeply appreciate the advice that I received from Teruko Craig, whose translation of Hiratsuka Raichō's autobiography is a truly significant contribution to *Seitō* studies in English. I appreciate her references to this book in her own and apologize for giving her the overly optimistic publication date of 2006.

My first work on *Seitō* was inspired and made much easier by the pioneering work in English of Nancy Andrew, Laurel Rasplica Rodd, and Sharon Sievers. I owe a debt of gratitude to my *senpai* in the field of Japanese women's history and literature, Rebecca Copeland, Sally Hastings, Eleanor Kerkham, Phyllis Larson, Marlene Mayo, Sharalyn Orbaugh, G. G. Rowley, Barbara Sato, and Miriam Silverberg for their encouragement of my work on *Seitō*. I must not forget to thank Christine Marran for wearing long blue stockings when she lectured at UNC–Chapel Hill in 2002—"support hose" indeed.

There are many family members and friends who will share my relief at this book's completion. A big thanks to my sister Cy Bridges, my cousins, and friends Jennifer Altman, Yoko Collier-Sanuki, Penny Griffin, Diane Kaczor, Phil Kaczor, Ivonne Eiseman, Judy Kovenock, Eileen LeFever, Penny and Carl Linke, Phillip and Susan Lyons, and Jim Oliver, and to all my pals in Hikone at the Japan Center for Michigan Universities.

Phil Bardsley, New Man and lifetime partner, has been a calming presence at every step of this long project. Reading chapters, cooking meals, solving computer problems—he's been by my side through it all. Together, we decided that this book should be dedicated to the first women in our lives who inspired us with their passion for reading and their love of good conversation: our mothers, Helen Holtby Bridges and Helen Kahl Bardsley. Courageous, compassionate, and intellectual, they were New Women in their own right.

Nothing brought this writing project such good luck as the small, wriggling, sometimes slithering tokens of feline affection toted into my study from the woods outside our house. Who knows how many lines in this volume owe their inspiration to the ministrations of the Bardsley cats? Your paw prints are everywhere here. The errors, however, are entirely my own.

Jan Bardsley
Chapel Hill, North Carolina
June 2007

Introduction

There are some absolutely dreadful women in the world these days, and they're bent on causing commotion. What on earth is happening when women, who should be modest, start imitating men, visiting the Yoshiwara, and drinking sake? This is a disgrace to women all over Japan! And that is not all, students. These women carry on about things like free love— why, they act just like animals. You must never be swayed by these women. Students in Japan must defend the beautiful virtues.

Warning about the Bluestockings, as recalled in
Ishigaki Ayako, *Wa ga ai, wa ga amerika*[1]

Such commotion was a long way off in September 1911, when a Tokyo newspaper carried a brief announcement reporting the debut of a new literary magazine. Its name was *Seitō* (Bluestocking), written with the Chinese character for "blue" and an unusual one for "stocking." For the very few who would have understood the allusion, it recalled the eighteenth-century English women's salon of the same name.[2] In an era when such small publications flourished, the appearance of yet another would not in itself have stirred much excitement. But, as anyone who glanced at *Seitō*'s table of contents could see, this magazine was different. It was written, edited, and published solely by women—and not just any women. Two of the women had become famous for flaunting conventional morality: poet Yosano Akiko and Japan Women's College graduate Hiratsuka Haru, who had adopted the pen name Raichō. Writing about modern Japanese women through images of erupting volcanoes, describing them as heirs to an ancient female power, and calling on women to recover this power, the two writers signaled that *Seitō* would be a very different publication indeed. Even the journal's cover, with its display of a royal woman—perhaps even a goddess—from ancient Greece or Egypt, evoked ideas of women and antiquity, and was at once elegant and strikingly modern (see figure 1).

Few could have predicted the enormous response that the publication of one thousand copies of this first, slim volume would produce. More than

1

Figure 1. Naganuma Chieko's cover for the inaugural issue of *Seitō* presented this captivating image of a regal woman, perhaps a goddess of ancient Egypt or Greece. The characters *Seitō* (Blue Stocking) read from right to left. Courtesy of Fuji Shuppan.

three thousand letters requesting subscriptions, membership, and advice about personal problems poured into the group's makeshift office from all over Japan. The inaugural issue was sold out by the following month. The magazine *Seitō* had found an audience, the Bluestockings had been assigned a mission, and in the months to follow women and men from such varied sectors as newspapers, censors' offices, schools, and literary circles would be paying attention to their words and their actions.[3] To the delight of many and to the dismay of many more, over the next year or so the Bluestockings earned a reputation for creating styles of living that matched, or perhaps even topped, the free-thinking spirit of their writing.

Seitō prospered in its early years, giving voice to women writing in all contemporary literary forms, and to women translating European and American authors as well. The Bluestockings discussed modern plays such as Henrik Ibsen's *A Doll's House* and *Hedda Gabler*, as well as Hermann Sudermann's *Magda*.[4] The core members in Tokyo also had New Year's parties, developed friendships, and confided in one another. Newspaper and magazine reporters followed the group's activities and publications with great interest, keen to stir gossipy attention. Two events that occurred in the summer of 1912 served this function well: both the "Five-Colored Liquor Incident" (Goshiki no Sake Jiken) and the Bluestocking "Visit to the Yoshiwara" (Yoshiwara Hōmon Jiken) led to sensationalized reports of the Bluestockings as young women who freely trespassed into the masculine territory of liquor, geisha, and the entertainment quarters.[5] Before too long, the media was delighting in poking fun at the *atarashii onna* (New Woman), using the Bluestockings, other women writers, women musicians, and actresses as prime examples. Teachers, such as the one quoted by feminist critic Ishigaki Ayako in the epigraph to this chapter, were soon warning their students against being influenced by the Bluestockings. What shocked the public was that these New Women were mainly privileged young women, many of whom were graduates of the relatively new Japan Women's College.

Being the recipients of such notoriety hardly pleased all members of the Bluestockings. Ever-increasing public attention brought on all sorts of commotion, police inquiries, the fear of losing employment and marriage prospects, and the active displeasure of many of the members' parents. It also provoked tensions within the group. By 1913, many chose to quit. Still, the remaining Bluestockings—those who valued the opportunity to publish their work, who were loyal to the group, or who had elected to join precisely because the group had grown increasingly and overtly defiant—continued to publish *Seitō* monthly through February 1916.[6] Rather than shying away from all those who were attacking them as some sexually promiscuous, shallow, and unfilial kind of "New Woman," the Bluestockings of 1913—Araki

Ikuko, Hiratsuka Raichō, Itō Noe, Iwano Kiyoko, Katō Midori, to name but a few—proudly adopted the title, redefining it as the label for an introspective, rigorously honest woman who defined her own ethical code (see figure 2). While this newly configured group of Bluestockings persisted in publishing women's creative writing, they also turned more and more of their attention to what was then called the Woman Question (*fujin mondai*). Writing as if formal censorship and public censure did not exist, they questioned the importance of chastity, explored the meaning of abortion and motherhood, and debated the politics of prostitution. A few members of the group even organized a public lecture on the topic of the New Woman in February 1913.[7] Since censorship did in fact exist, some of their most controversial essays brought the Bluestockings into conflict with the police and caused whole issues of the magazine to be removed from bookstores on three occasions.

Although the Bluestockings took themselves seriously as intellectuals and as writers, they became best known for the choices they made in their personal lives, especially their love lives. Acutely aware of how scandalous these decisions would appear to the public, they nevertheless made explicit the connection between their private lives and public morality by writing frankly about their choices in *Seitō*. Gossip columnists for Tokyo newspapers eagerly reported on their ideas and activities, elaborating on tales of the Bluestockings for a wider readership. As a result, by the time *Seitō* ceased publication, the Bluestockings' highly publicized unions, divorces, and childbirths out of wedlock had virtually overshadowed the diversity and complexity of the women's writing.

And so much writing there was. The complete set of *Seitō* spans fifty-two issues—literally thousands of pages—and contains every form of writing available in the active Japanese literary world of the early 1910s. Experimental poetry, haiku, and classical waka verse are all represented here. Numerous dramas reflect the vogue for playwriting, and the excitement generated by the first performances in Japan of modern European plays. Short fiction often follows a confessional style known as the *watakushi shōsetsu* or *shi-shōsetsu* (translated as "I-novel" or "personal fiction"), which was common in that day. Influenced by Naturalism, it is a style that purports to bare the most intimate details of the author's life, even when characters in the story have different names from the author and the people in her life. *Seitō* essays, too, frequently had an intensely personal flavor, especially when they took the form of the free-flowing *kansō* (impressionistic essay) and "personal" letters. When controversies arose over such disputed topics as the New Woman, love marriages, and abortion, for example, the Bluestockings would debate each other or attack their critics in strongly worded essays published in *Seitō*, and sometimes in general-interest magazines as well. Translations of

Figure 2. This photograph of six Bluestockings shows them gathered at the home of Iwano Kiyoko, described by Ide Fumiko as a 1913 New Year's party. From the left are Kobayashi Katsu, Iwano Kiyoko, Nakano Hatsuko, Araki Ikuko, Yasumochi Yoshiko, and Hiratsuka Raichō. Courtesy of Ōtsuki Shoten.

works by Western men (Anton Chekhov, Guy de Maupassant, Edgar Allan Poe, sexologist Havelock Ellis, sociologist Lester Ward) and, later, writing by Western women (Emma Goldman, Ellen Key, Sonya Kovalevsky, Olive Schreiner) related to the Woman Question lent *Seitō* a truly modern, cosmopolitan panache.

Such attention to the ideas of Westerners indicated that the New Woman of Japan was also a new hybrid, a woman who lived in Japan and wrote in Japanese but who had an intellectual life that extended beyond the nation's borders. That the Bluestockings strove to weave these new ideas and a new morality into the fabric of their personal lives, and to communicate this publicly in their writing, made them all the more worrisome to those who believed that women should preserve the "beautiful virtues of Japan." Although men such as authors Tayama Katai (1871–1930) and Shimazaki Tōson (1872–1943) had already ventured into this creative, intellectual territory and endured criticism for it, the Bluestockings found public tolerance in short supply when women were the ones initiating philosophies of personal liberation and the awakened self. As Sharon Sievers has observed:

> Male writers, the naturalists in particular, had already encountered substantial public hostility around these same issues, but where they might use rejection to validate their art, the Bluestockings found it more and more difficult to focus solely on art, rejecting politics.[8]

Readers could become part of this challenging life, too—occasionally at their own risk. *Seitō* at its height was published in three thousand copies per month and was sold in bookstores and by subscription all over Japan. Maruzen, a popular store that sold foreign books and other imports, jumped on the bandwagon, advertising its Orion fountain pen in *Seitō* as just the ticket for a New Woman's life (see figure 3). Yet as the magazine became associated with controversial New Woman debates, girls' schools began to prohibit their students from reading it. The famous Meiji-era women's educator Tsuda Umeko (1864–1929) believed that the Bluestockings were agents of the devil and prayed that her students would not fall under their influence.[9] Discovery of a teacher's connection to *Seitō* could be grounds for dismissal.[10] Still, women teachers were some of the magazine's most avid readers and, often under assumed names, became contributors to *Seitō* as well. A short story by well-known author Uno Chiyo (1897–1996) describes how the rhetoric of the New Woman worried school administrators and captivated some of the magazine's youngest readers—schoolgirls who were especially taken with Hiratsuka Raichō's call in the *Seitō* manifesto (translated in Chapter 4 below) for women to recover their "hidden sun":

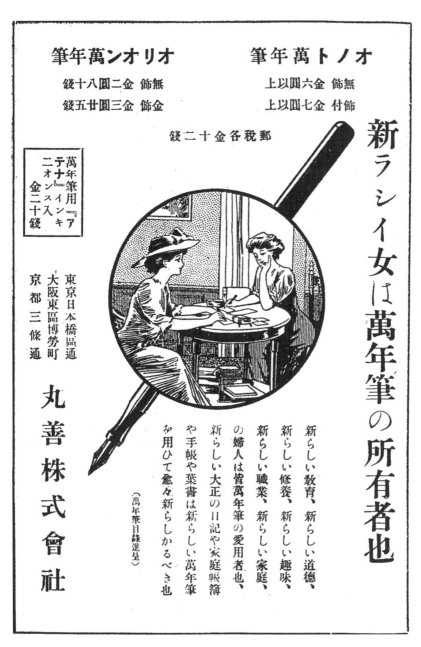

Figure 3. This advertisement for an Orion fountain pen, sold exclusively by the Maruzen Corporation, proclaims that "The New Woman is the owner of a fountain pen," suggesting that nothing goes better with new education, new morality, new work, and new homes than a fountain pen. *Seitō* 3.1 (January 1913). Courtesy of Fuji Shuppan.

At the all-girls high school I attended, we also were forbidden to read newspapers and magazines, but there it was easy to get around the rules. I read quite a few magazines—*The Third Empire*, *Bluestocking*. Deeply stimulated by a then fashionable motto, "In antiquity, woman was the sun," my friends at the school and I thought that we might really be the sun. We published a small magazine, as many literary-minded young people did in those days, featuring poems and essays of an abstract nature. This magazine was soon discovered by the teacher, and one afternoon we were summoned by the principal. "I trust this writing doesn't reflect what you girls really believe," the principal scolded us gravely in the cold room. The magazine on his desk looked pathetic, its pages flapping in the wind from the window. Someone started sobbing, and then all of us joined her. We didn't know why we were sad but the sadness seemed to belong to a sphere beyond our ordinary world; we liked words such as "exalted" and "noble." The principal's ideas about discipline proved to be no more effective than my father's; soon after this dressing-down we joined another literary group, outside the school, that published a typeset magazine.[11]

At the peak of their success, the Bluestockings had 150 subscribers as well as many more readers who bought the magazine in bookstores. Since readers would often share literary magazines with one another, it is safe to assume that *Seitō* was read by more people than those who purchased a copy. Most of the initial members of the Bluestockings were graduates of Japan Women's College and lived in Tokyo. But those who joined the Bluestockings and many *Seitō* readers could also be found in outlying provinces. What distinguished the reader reaction to *Seitō* was that so many readers seem to have felt a personal bond, as if the Bluestockings were writing directly to them. That the Bluestockings chose to write in an intimate way, as though confiding their personal problems to a sympathetic friend, must have nurtured this bond. The Bluestockings' open expressions of anger over how the family system, schools, laws, and the workplace unfairly suppressed women's freedom and ambitions no doubt rang true for women in many parts of Japan who shared those feelings and admired the Bluestockings' courage.

Evidence that readers felt a personal bond with Bluestocking writers came in different forms. Much of the mail that was sent to the Bluestockings contained requests for advice, even though *Seitō* never carried an advice column or a Letters to the Editor section. On some occasions a woman would travel to Tokyo and simply show up on a Bluestocking's doorstep, as happened to Hiratsuka Raichō and Iwano Kiyoko. And both Itō Noe and Katō Midori, who later wrote about these experiences in *Seitō*, received letters and visits from men who had become infatuated with them through their writing.[12] Once Hiratsuka Raichō remarked that so many women came to the Bluestockings' office seeking advice that it looked as if they were running a counseling center.[13]

Whether or not readers felt a bond with the Bluestockings, most of them were probably inclined to read the stories in *Seitō*, especially those with a first-person narrator or a prominent female character, as autobiography. As literary scholar Rebecca Copeland has observed, women writers in the Meiji era were often frustrated by the reading public's penchant for conflating an author with her characters.[14] By the 1910s, the vogue for the *watakushi shōsetsu* and the attendant publicity about men's confessional writing would have further supported this reading.[15] In fact, many Bluestocking authors—Itō Noe, Iwano Kiyoko, and Katō Midori, for example—were influenced by the vogue for personal fiction and did draw on the intimate events of their lives in writing their short stories. For them to do so at this time was a powerful statement, a way to use literature as the means to write into existence the New Woman, and quite literally stand behind her. Interestingly, in their comments on each other's fiction, however, the Bluestockings discuss the strengths and weaknesses of the "protagonist" (*shujinkō*), character development, and plot, showing that they also appreciated the stories—no matter how close they were to an author's life—as deliberately crafted pieces.

Other features in *Seitō* further influenced readers to equate a fictional character with the author. For instance, the Editors' Notes that discussed news of individual Bluestockings and the essays that spoke fervently about the author's efforts to become an independent person contributed to the sense that each issue of *Seitō* offered a conduit from the reader to the Bluestockings themselves. In addition, reports about the Bluestockings, their activities, and their new ideas by gossip columnists, who mined the journal for tidbits of wickedness, enhanced the feeling that *Seitō* was a direct expression of the Bluestockings' real lives. Consequently, when someone like Araki Ikuko, who was not married, wrote "The Letter," a story about a married woman planning on continuing an adulterous affair with a younger man (translated in Chapter 1), readers likely imagined that she had either committed this crime herself—for crime it was at the time—or was writing about an intimate friend.[16] As we see in Chapter 1, the story may well have referred to Araki's own quandary about whether to stay with a well-to-do patron or pursue an affair with a young student. Whether based in fact or totally fabricated, a story that even voiced such a desire was enough to provoke concern, and the perception that the Bluestockings were women determined to act on their feelings made this particular story doubly subversive. It is small wonder that the censors reprimanded the Bluestockings for printing it.

The lack of distance between readers and the Bluestockings may also have made it easier for some of those readers to become writers. As Fujita Kazumi has remarked, *Seitō* did not bill itself as an instructional magazine for women or sponsor contests for readers' essays or fiction, as did some other magazines of the era with much larger circulations.[17] *Seitō* addressed its readers as equals, and as progressives opposed to all the "other women of the world" who could not understand the Bluestockings' goals. Although not much detail is available on *Seitō*'s readers, Raichō stated that the letters from readers received at the Bluestockings' office showed a diversity of backgrounds—students, housewives, women enamored of literature, working women, and many school teachers. Fujita's investigation of this issue has led her to believe that there were many Bluestocking writers who had first been readers of the magazine.[18] To underscore *Seitō* as a magazine that sought readers' contributions, Fujita reminds us of the stipulation in *Seitō* 3.1 (January 1913) that members send in a manuscript of at least ten pages if they could not pay the membership fee.

Historical and Cultural Background

For readers unfamiliar with Japanese history, a few words on the Meiji period (1868–1912) and women's position in that period and in the early 1910s are in order. The Meiji era owes its name to the modern Japanese practice of dividing historical periods by imperial reign. The Meiji emperor reigned from 1868 to 1912; his son, the Taishō emperor, reigned from 1912 to 1926, and his grandson, the Shōwa emperor, from 1926 to 1989. The reign names of these periods are Meiji, Taishō, and Shōwa; the current (2007) reign name is Heisei. Endeavors to "catch up with the West" may be the defining theme of Meiji, as Japan came face to face with superior Western industrial and military might—and imperialist desire—in the mid-nineteenth century, after almost 250 years of relative seclusion. Translating Western philosophy, literature, medical and legal texts, and a host of other materials into Japanese became a matter of national defense as well as of intellectual excitement. Compulsory primary education for all children, military conscription, and an official abolition of feudal class hierarchies that had positioned samurai at the top and farmers as the major social base were all measures taken to strengthen the nation and the military. A unification of the written and spoken language (*genbun itchi*) that made reading easier and more accessible to the masses gradually removed writing from the province of the elite. It paved the way for mass media, and was closely connected to the rise of popular newspapers and magazines.

To encourage people all over Japan to see themselves as national subjects, the government promoted a patriarchal ideology of the family-state that positioned the emperor as father to the nation and bound by blood to all Japanese past, present, and future. Borrowing from Neo-Confucian-inspired, samurai-class models of the family, the government instituted a constitution and a civil code that made the patriarchal family the legal unit of society and gave much power over individuals in the family to the household head. Under these new laws, women's interests and activities were clearly subordinated to men and to the family. Women could become heads of households in rare cases where there was no lineal male heir, and they could inherit property if the family had no sons, legitimate or illegitimate. Upon marriage, wives saw any property they owned fall to the management of their husbands, who could sell it and reinvest the proceeds as they pleased. The samurai custom of families arranging marriages for their children, and the samurai interest in female chastity, became more and more the national norm throughout the Meiji era and into the 1910s. Adultery by husbands was condoned, but it was considered a crime for wives and could bring them a two-year prison term. Abortion was criminalized in this era, and penalties against those having abortions were increasingly enforced in the 1910s. Although women could sue for divorce, divorce itself was frowned on and divorcées returned to their family were considered a source of shame. The harshest of the Bluestockings' criticisms were generally leveled against such circumscription of female sexuality and independence.[19]

The more fortunate among women of the Meiji era enjoyed the benefits of the dramatic increase in the number of girls' schools. In 1899 the Ministry of Education initiated a plan for every prefecture to establish girls' schools, in the hopes of training middle-class women to become thrifty, domestically skilled, good wives to the nation's leaders and wise, patriotic mothers to their children.[20] The Bluestockings, almost all of whom did attend girls' schools and many of whom attended Japan Women's College in Tokyo, could certainly read, write, and manage some mathematics. Almost uniformly, they expressed frustration over the low academic caliber of girls' schools compared with boys' education, and they took vehement exception to the expectation that they should sacrifice all their ambition and personal interests to becoming "good wives, wise mothers" (ryōsai kenbo).[21]

The increase in girls' schools nevertheless advanced women's literacy, fostering an audience of readers and a market for women's magazines, novels, and newspaper columns. The canon of Japanese classical literature had long assigned a place of great importance to the work of court ladies of the Heian era (794–1185), especially to what has been termed the world's first novel, The Tale of Genji, but it was the advance in women's literacy and the advent of mass media that enabled women to become professional writers. However, such access to opportunities to write professionally was achieved largely through the women's connections to established male writers, who often had definite ideas of what and how a woman should write.[22] Nevertheless, the possibility of becoming a novelist, a magazine writer, or a reporter was a glamorous one for young women in the 1910s. More and more white-collar jobs were opening for newly educated young women by the end of the Meiji era, though much evidence exists to show that the public worried that new opportunities were taking women and students out of the home and leading them down a path to sexual promiscuity. There was a concern that girl students (*jogakusei*) and other young women, especially in the cities, were enjoying too much mobility, being encouraged to voice their desires too freely, and harming the beautiful virtues of Japanese womanhood.[23] When reports of the Bluestockings' eventful love lives and entertaining social lives became public, and censors banned whole issues of *Seitō* as "injurious to public morals," the public believed that its worst fears about educated young women had been realized. Up until then, this troublesome New Woman, as she came to be called, had seemed like one more curiosity of the West, a phantom of the large suffragist marches, radical protests, and the strange heroines of plays such as Ibsen's *A Doll's House* and Sudermann's *Magda*. With the debut of the Bluestockings, the New Woman had at last been born in Japan.

But the Bluestockings were not the first modern Japanese women to launch a protest. Women laboring under the harsh conditions of the burgeoning textile industry had already staged successful strikes. Women such as Kishida Toshiko and Fukuda Hideko had played an active role in the Freedom and People's Rights Movement (Jiyū Minken Undō) of the 1870s and 1880s, speaking out publicly on the need for women's freedom.[24] Fukuda Hideko and future Bluestocking Iwano Kiyoko had also worked to rescind Article Five of the Police Security Regulations (Chian Keisatsu Hō) of 1890, a measure that kept women out of the political process, forbidding them from joining a political party or speaking publicly on political issues. There were also Japanese women who supported socialist organizations and were actively taking part in protests.

All this was a heritage the Bluestockings could have drawn on in their own formulations of the Woman Question, but it was not an association they wished, or perhaps even considered. Nor did this avowedly women's magazine make any comment on two well-publicized and tragic women's deaths: the hanging of radical Kanno Suga (1881–1911), arrested on charges of plotting to kill the emperor and tried in a hasty trial of socialists known as the High Treason Trial of 1911, and the 1912 suicide of Nogi Shizuko (1859–

1912), the wife of General Nogi, who followed her husband in death after he committed ritual suicide upon the demise of his lord, Emperor Meiji.[25] The Bluestockings were not attracted, either, to discussion of the suffrage demonstrations in England, which were widely reported in Japan.[26] That the Bluestockings ignored momentous current events shows how intensely focused they were, especially in the magazine's early years, on their personal quests to achieve self-discovery. It also speaks, perhaps, to the repressive political atmosphere of that period, dubbed by Japanese historians the *fuyu no jidai* (winter period), and to how women were discouraged from creating a women's history, especially a history of rebels.

As we consider the hopes and frustrations of the Bluestockings, it is important to remember that the vast majority of Japanese women worked at much less exciting endeavors, in such areas as farming, textile factories, or in domestic service. Others were employed in the dangerous work of mining or prostitution. It is likely that many of them would have considered the problems discussed in *Seitō* to be emblems of privileged women of leisure who had the opportunity to trade their angst for a comfortable marriage and domestic life. But perhaps the fantasy of leading a life in the city, being writers, and having such modern problems nevertheless stirred the imaginations of some women who faced lives more restricted by the lack of financial comfort, education, and other opportunities. Although the issue of class differences among women was discussed in *Seitō*, especially in an essay by Fukuda Hideko (translated in Chapter 2) and in the Bluestocking debates on sexuality, it was not a topic that figured prominently in most *Seitō* writing on the New Woman. Most writers concentrated on gender, not class, as the barrier to women's freedom, and tended to believe that, if only brave enough, any woman could become independent. It was only as they more fully explored the Woman Question—and dealt with their own notoriety and the struggles of blending careers and motherhood—that the Bluestockings came to feel the weight of class politics and open their eyes to the plight of women less privileged than themselves.

A New Woman Legacy

The history of reception and study of the Bluestockings and *Seitō* should be the subject of a book of its own. One could make useful comparisons between junctures in the history of Japanese feminism (Occupation-era reforms, 1970s Women's Liberation movements, 1980s legislation for equal opportunity and the advent of Women's Studies, and feminist literary criticism in the 1990s and 2000s) and renewed interest in *Seitō*. The surge of scholarly work in English on Japanese women's writing, history, and feminism since

1980 would be an important chapter, too, as would the recent interest in the New Woman as an international phenomenon and an important component in thinking about constructions of modernity. Below, I provide a short introduction to some of the recent work in Japanese, which is almost entirely unavailable in English translation.[27]

Seitō and the Bluestockings have generated much scholarly attention by feminist critics in Japan in recent years. Whereas the initial and still valuable studies of the Bluestockings focused largely on biography and the dynamics of the group, and were written either by former Bluestockings or by those who interviewed them, academic interest has brought fresh perspectives. These critics consider *Seitō* in terms, for example, of its covers and advertisements, its readership, the kinds of translations included, comparison with men's writing, and how topics such as sexuality, identity, work, and marriage were discussed. Collections of this work are available in books such as *"Seitō" o manabu hito no tame ni* (For People Who Study *Seitō*), *"Seitō" o yomu: Blue Stocking* (Reading *Seitō*: Blue Stocking), and *"Seitō" to iu ba: bungaku, jendā, atarashii onna* (The Space Called *Seitō*: Literature, Gender, New Woman).[28] Iwata Nanatsu's 2003 study *Bungaku to shite no "Seitō"* (*Seitō* as Literature) is also a valuable addition to the growing interest in close readings and literary analyses of *Seitō* fiction, poetry, and drama.[29]

Biographies of the Bluestockings continue to capture readers' interest. A new dictionary of short biographies of 110 women involved with *Seitō*, written by members of a group known as the Raichō Research Group (Raichō Kenkyūkai), brings to light the stories of both the famous and the lesser known Bluestockings.[30] It is an important resource and one that I relied on often in writing the biographies in this volume. The Raichō Research Group's dictionary and their biographical work build on the pioneering books written by Ide Fumiko (1920–99) and Kobayashi Tomie (1917–2004). Ide published the first book-length history of the Bluestockings in 1961, and went on to write biographies of Hiratsuka Raichō and Itō Noe, while Kobayashi Tomie played a major role in documenting the life of Hiratsuka Raichō.[31] In the 1980s and 1990s, films, historical novels, a play, and even comic books renewed interest in the Bluestockings as colorful New Women among members of the postwar generations in Japan. Such representations of the Bluestockings in popular culture tend to celebrate the women as heroes of Japanese feminism, emphasizing their most iconoclastic moments.

The study of *Seitō* has been most encouraged by reprinted editions of the magazine and related works. Fuji Shuppan reprinted the entire magazine, including all its covers, illustrations, and advertisements, in six volumes in 1969, and reprinted this again in 1980 and 1983. This reprinted edition includes an index to the table of contents for each issue and listings of all titles that each *Seitō* contributor published in the magazine. In 1987, Kobayashi Tomie edited *"Seitō" Serekushon* (*Seitō* Selection), which made a diverse collection of fiction and essays from the magazine easily and inexpensively available in paperback.[32] In 1970, the collected works of Itō Noe were published, and in 1971–73, the four-volume autobiography of Hiratsuka Raichō, *Genshi, josei wa taiyō de atta* (In the Beginning, Woman Was the Sun), written in part by Kobayashi Tomie, appeared.[33] Ōtsuki Shoten published an eight-volume edition of the selected works of Hiratsuka Raichō in 1983–84.[34] In 1985–86, Fuji Shuppan published a twenty-volume series *"Seitō" no onna-tachi* (Women of *Seitō*); each volume features a different *Seitō* contributor, commentary on her life and writing, and some of her work, although not necessarily work published in *Seitō*.[35] All of these works are a rich source of primary materials for further research on *Seitō* and the Bluestockings.

The politics of gender, women's history, and women's writing have also been the focus of much scholarship and translation in Japanese Studies in English since the 1980s. Fortunately, as I was finishing this book, I had access to several pioneering studies in English related to Hiratsuka Raichō, *Seitō*, the Bluestockings, and early Japanese women's magazines. I was especially influenced by Hiratsuka Raichō and Teruko Craig's 2006 *In the Beginning, Woman Was the Sun: The Autobiography of a Japanese Feminist*, Dina B. Lowy's 2007 *The Japanese "New Woman": Images of Gender and Modernity*, and Hiroko Tomida's 2004 *Hiratsuka Raichō and Early Japanese Feminism*. The New Woman's relationship to late-Meiji literature, language, and theater is expertly analyzed in Ayako Kano's 2001 *Acting Like a Woman in Modern Japan: Theater, Gender, and Nationalism* and Indra Levy's 2006 *Sirens of the Western Shore: The Westernesque Femme Fatale, Translation, and Vernacular Style in Modern Japanese Literature*. The connection of *Seitō* to later Japanese women's magazines is made evident in two important books on media history, Sarah Frederick's 2006 *Turning Pages: Reading and Writing Women's Magazines in Interwar Japan* and Barbara Sato's 2003 *The New Japanese Woman: Modernity, Media, and Women in Interwar Japan*. Translation and analysis of Meiji-Taishō women's literature by Rebecca Copeland, Joan Ericson, and Laurel Rasplica Rodd, among others, provides a crucial grounding for understanding *Seitō* as literature. Barbara Molony and Kathleen Uno's 2005 volume *Gendering Modern Japanese History* and Vera Mackie's work on Japanese feminism illustrate the many ways in which *Seitō* and the Bluestockings figure as an important chapter in the history of Japanese women's movements and feminist thought.

Reading *Seitō* in Translation

This volume offers English-language readers the first anthology of *Seitō* work in translation. It is divided into twelve short chapters. Each is organized around a different Bluestocking and includes a brief biography, a translation of one or more of her *Seitō* contributions, and some commentary on the work translated. The lives of some of these women, especially Hiratsuka Raichō, Itō Noe, Fukuda Hideko, Nogami Yaeko, Yamada Waka, and Yosano Akiko, have been much discussed in English-language scholarship. The others—Araki Ikuko, Iwano Kiyoko, Katō Midori, Kobayashi Katsu, Ogasawara Sada, and Harada (Yasuda) Satsuki—may be new to English-language readers. By presenting short biographies of all these writers here, I hope to show how their personal histories may have influenced their choice to write for *Seitō*, and, for some, their choice to identify themselves as New Women. As much as the Bluestockings desired to be New Women, they were real women as well—women who had to find ways of making a living, women who suddenly found themselves pregnant, daughters at odds with their parents, and partners negotiating free-love relationships and arranged marriages. Even brief biographies show how great the distance could be between the ideal life for which these women longed and the actual life, with all its financial, familial, and physical realities, that they lived. We also see how the Bluestockings influenced one another—through their friendships and parties, the diversity of their ideas, their interaction in person and in print, and their debates.

These translations include essays, short stories, and poetry, and show some of the variety of writing found in the magazine. They also reveal the New Woman themes of a desire for independence, authenticity, creative work, and romantic love that *Seitō* essays and stories often have in common. In choosing which pieces to translate, I considered the titles most often mentioned in English-language and Japanese references as well as topics that would have relevance for readers today. I began by translating the two essays and two short stories that caused the Bluestockings to receive a reprimand and for *Seitō* to be banned in two other instances.[36] The translations in this volume represent the work of some of *Seitō*'s most frequent contributors and most active Bluestockings. Of course, there is much more work and there are many more *Seitō* authors who deserve to be represented in translation and in English-language scholarship.[37]

Most translations from Japanese state that names are written, following East Asian practice, by listing the family name followed by the given name. I also use this form. However, naming the individual Bluestockings is not as easy as it might seem. Individual women sometimes changed their given names or added the relatively new, fashionable "ko" ending. Araki Ikuko, for example, also used the names Araki Ikuo and Araki Iku. Hiratsuka Haru was known by her pen name, Raichō. Marriage, divorce, or remarriage altered all the women's family names at some point in their lives. On occasion, individual Bluestockings are mentioned only by an initial in *Seitō*; even authors of particular articles or stories are acknowledged at times with only an initial. Yasumochi Yoshiko, for instance, published her January 1912 comments on *A Doll's House* in *Seitō* under the initial "Y." In some cases, we know the Chinese characters (*kanji*) for Bluestocking writers but no longer are sure of the correct pronunciation of their names. In the individual biographies, I have tried to list all the names and, where pertinent, the multiple readings for those names, that each Bluestocking used at some point in her life. In choosing to refer to most of the women by their most common first name or pen name, I was influenced by the familiar way the Bluestockings refer to each other in much of their own writing for *Seitō* or in later accounts of the group. Immersed in their writing, I got to know them, for example, as "Raichō, Noe, and Kiyoko" rather than Hiratsuka, Itō, and Iwano, and wish to communicate here the intimacy of their world.

Another problem of naming lies in assigning authorship. In all cases, I list the author as *Seitō* gives it. In discussing individual essays, I also mention the rumors about authorship that emerged. Itō Noe's husband Tsuji Jun was said to have been the one actually responsible for the translations she published. Her later partner Ōsugi Sakae may have written his wife Hori Yasuko's single contribution to *Seitō*, just as Fukuda Hideko's partner Ishikawa Sanshirō was rumored to have been the author of her essay, "The Solution to the Woman Question." The same issue occurs with artwork: Otake Kōkichi's husband may have been the artist behind the distinctive Adam and Eve cover for *Seitō* attributed to her. In one case, Katō Midori's husband Asadori received Hiratsuka Raichō's permission to publish one of his translations under her (well-known) name in order to increase the pay he could receive for the work. It is interesting to see how a milieu that so highly prized writing for its potential to define personhood and authenticity created an environment rife with doubts about authorship. This situation may also speak to the possibilities opened up for men by writing under a woman's name and purportedly in a female voice, and to a reluctance to believe in women's abilities to do creative, intellectual work.

Appendix A is a chronology of major events in the life of *Seitō*. This chart shows when each of the translations was originally published. Excellent detailed histories of the Bluestockings are available in English, so it is not my intention to reproduce that history here.[38] Appendix B provides the Bluestockings' statement of purpose as originally composed in 1911 and as revised in 1913; it also contains the 1916 "Anti-Manifesto" by Itō Noe.

I should note that all references to Hiratsuka Raichō's autobiography, unless otherwise stated, refer to *Genshi, josei wa taiyō de atta*, originally published in 1971–73. All my citations to that work refer to the 1987 edition. Whenever I cite references to the first two volumes of this autobiography, I also cite their translation in Hiratsuka Raichō and Teruko Craig's *In the Beginning, Woman Was the Sun*. I occasionally refer to Raichō's 1955 autobiography, *Watakushi no aruita michi* (The Path I Took). There are at times discrepancies in *Seitō* volumes between page numbers cited for a given work in the table of contents and its actual page numbers; in all cases, I cite the actual page numbers.

I hope that these translations and the commentary on them serve to expand discussion of *Seitō* among English-language readers. As studies of New Women across the globe flourish, surely the Bluestockings of Japan will continue to offer a vibrant example of the life and history of the *atarashii onna*.

Notes

[1]Feminist critic Ishigaki Ayako (1903–96) remembers receiving this warning about the Bluestockings when she was a schoolgirl. She records this in her autobiography: Ishigaki Ayako, *Wa ga ai, wa ga amerika* (My Love, My America), (Chikuma Shobō, 1991), 7–8. This incident probably occurred sometime in 1912, following publicity about the Bluestockings' visit to the Yoshiwara.

[2]The character used for "stockings" originally denoted leather. Hiroko Tomida explains that the original term was *Kontabitō* (literally, "dark blue [Japanese-style] *tabi* socks"), but Hiratsuka Raichō and Ikuta Chōkō "took their hint from a new translation that Mori Ōgai produced for 'stockings.' and eventually came up with the updated term '*Seitōsha*.'" Tomida, *Hiratsuka Raichō and Early Japanese Feminism* (Leiden: Brill, 2004), 146, n. 41. According to Raichō, some mistakenly think that Mori Ōgai actually proposed the name Seitō to the group. Hiratsuka Raichō, *Genshi, josei wa taiyō de atta: Hiratsuka Raichō jiden* (Ōtsuki Shoten, 1971–73), 1: 299; Hiratsuka Raichō and Teruko Craig, *In the Beginning, Woman Was the Sun: The Autobiography of a Japanese Feminist* (New York: Columbia University Press, 2006), 145.

[3]To distinguish the magazine *Seitō* from the group Seitō-sha (Bluestocking Society), I refer to the group as the Bluestockings throughout.

[4]Excellent new analyses of *Seitō* discussions of modern drama are found in Ayako Kano, *Acting Like a Woman in Modern Japan: Theater, Gender, and Nationalism* (New York: Palgrave, 2001); Indra Levy, *Sirens of the Western Shore: The Westernesque Femme Fatale, Translation, and Vernacular Style in Modern Japanese Literature* (New York: Columbia University Press, 2006); Dina Lowy, "Nora and the 'New Woman': Visions of Gender and Modernity in Early Twentieth-Century Japan," *U.S.–Japan Women's Journal*, no. 26 (2004): 75–97; and Tomida, *Hiratsuka Raichō*, 162–70.

[5]These scandals are discussed below in Chapter 4 on Hiratsuka Raichō.

[6]*Seitō* was not published in September 1914 and August 1915.

[7]This event is discussed below in Chapter 6 on Iwano Kiyoko.

[8]Sharon L. Sievers, *Flowers in Salt: The Beginnings of Feminist Consciousness in Modern Japan* (Stanford, CA: Stanford University Press, 1983), 170. For more on art

and politics in Meiji, see also Janet Walker, *The Japanese Novel of the Meiji Period and the Ideal of Individualism* (Princeton, NJ: Princeton University Press, 1979).

[9]This anecdote comes from Yamakawa Kikue, *Onna nidai no ki* (The Accounts of Two Generations of Women), (Tokyo: Nihon Hyōron Shinsha, 1956), 157–59, and is cited in Sievers, *Flowers in Salt*, n172.

[10]Kamichika Ichiko (1888–1981), an occasional *Seitō* contributor, was fired from her teaching job at a Tōhoku girls' school when the caption to a photograph of the Bluestockings erroneously listed her name as one of the women in the photo. Kamichika had been a student at Tsuda Academy when her association with the Bluestockings was initially discovered. A fellow student once offered a prayer for Kamichika when she returned from a Bluestockings meeting. Sievers, *Flowers in Salt*, n. 172; Tomida, *Hiratsuka Raichō*, 176.

[11]Uno Chiyo, "Genius of Imitation" (Mohō no tensai, 1936), trans. Yukiko Tanaka, in Yukiko Tanaka, ed., *To Live and To Write: Selections by Japanese Women Writers 1913–1938* (Seattle: Seal Press, 1987), 190–91.

[12]Katō Midori describes this incident in her story "Obsession" (Shūchaku, 1912), translated in Chapter 7 below. Setouchi Harumi's 1984 biographical novel about Itō Noe, translated by Sanford Goldstein and Kazuji Ninomiya as *Beauty in Disarray* (Rutland, VT, and Tokyo: Charles E. Tuttle, Co., 1993), describes Noe's affair of letters with a Mr. Sōta Kimura in chap. 4, citing passages from some of the actual letters. Itō Noe wrote about the relationship in her essay "Dōyō" (Turmoil), *Seitō* 3.8 (August 1913): 87–194.

[13]Hiratsuka Raichō, *Genshi, josei wa taiyō de atta*, 2: 571; Hiratsuka and Craig, *In the Beginning, Woman Was the Sun*, 270.

[14]Rebecca Copeland, ed., *Woman Critiqued: Translated Essays on Japanese Women's Writing*. (Honolulu: University of Hawai'i Press, 2006), 1.

[15]There has been much discussion in the field of Japanese literary studies about other strategies for reading and thinking about personal fiction. See, for example, Edward Fowler, *The Rhetoric of Confession: Shishōsetsu in Early Twentieth-Century Japanese Fiction* (Berkeley and Los Angeles: University of California Press, 1988); James Fujii, *Complicit Fictions: The Subject in the Modern Japanese Prose Narrative* (Berkeley and Los Angeles: University of California Press, 1993); and Tomi Suzuki, *Narrating the Self: Fictions of Japanese Modernity* (Stanford, CA: Stanford University Press, 1996).

[16]Araki Ikuko's 1912 story "The Letter" (Tegami) is translated in full in Chapter 1 below.

[17]Fujita Kazumi, "*Seitō* no dokusha no isō," in Shin Feminizumu Hihyō no Kai, ed., "*Seitō*" *o yomu: Blue Stocking* (Gakugei Shorin, 1998), 466–88.

[18]Ibid, 471.

[19]The restrictions on married women applied much more to middle-class women such as the Bluestockings and had much less effect on the poor—especially, it seems, in the cities, where poor women were freer to change partners and had more mobility.

[20]Mariko Inoue, "Kiyohata's *Asasuzu*: The Emergence of the *Jogakusei* Image," *Monumenta Nipponica* 51.4 (Winter 1996): 431–60, cites figures showing that between 1895 and 1902 there were only 37 girls' schools but that, due to an expanding middle class after the Russo-Japanese War (1904–1905), this number had increased to 207 by 1912, with student enrollment growing from 8,857 to 64,871 pupils in that period (ibid., 434). Inoue also remarks that around 1900, more than 60 percent of the girls'

school students came from families with a samurai lineage, though samurai had made up only 5 percent of the population in 1868.

[21]The politics of the construction of the "good wife, wise mother" (*ryōsai kenbo*) ideal, which certainly influenced the reception of *Seitō*, has received much scholarly attention. For an excellent introduction to this concept, see Sharon H. Nolte and Sally Ann Hastings, "The Meiji State's Policy Toward Women, 1890–1910," in Gail Lee Bernstein, ed., *Recreating Japanese Women, 1600–1945* (Berkeley and Los Angeles: University of California Press, 1991), 151–74; Kathleen S. Uno, "The Death of the Good Wife, Wise Mother?" in Andrew Gordon, ed., *Postwar Japan as History* (Berkeley and Los Angeles: University of California Press, 1993), 293–322; and Kathleen Uno, "Womanhood, War, and Empire: Transmutations of 'Good Wife, Wise Mother,'" in Barbara Molony and Kathleen Uno, eds., *Gendering Modern Japanese History* (Cambridge, MA, and London: Harvard University Asia Center, 2005), 493–519.

[22]Chapter 9 below, on Nogami Yaeko, describes the influence of male author Natsume Sōseki on her work. Young men with literary ambitions also benefited from association with an established author.

[23]The Meiji girl student (*jogakusei*) has become the topic of much exciting new research. See Melanie Czarnecki, "Bad Girls from Good Families: The Degenerate Meiji Schoolgirl," in Laura Miller and Jan Bardsley, eds., *Bad Girls of Japan* (New York: Palgrave, 2005), 48–63; Rebecca Copeland, "Fashioning the Feminine: Images of the Modern Girl Student in Meiji Japan," *U.S.–Japan Women's Journal*, nos. 30–31 (2006): 13–35; and Levy, *Sirens of the Western Shore*.

[24]See Marnie S. Anderson, "Kishida Toshiko and the Rise of the Female Speaker in Meiji Japan," *U.S.–Japan Women's Journal*, nos. 30–31 (2006): 36–59.

[25]For analyses of these tragic events, see chap. 7, "Kanno Suga," in Sievers, *Flowers in Salt*, 139–62, and Sharalyn Orbaugh, "General Nogi's Wife: Representations of Women in Narratives of Japanese Modernization," in Xiaobing Tang and Stephen Snyder, eds., *In Pursuit of Contemporary East Asian Culture* (Boulder, CO: Westview Press, 1988), 7–32.

[26]Hiroko Tomida explains that although the Bluestockings did not mention the Pankhursts and the demonstrations they led, these were discussed in *Seitō*'s rival publication *Shin shin fujin* (The True New Woman). Tomida, *Hiratsuka Raichō*, 216. The Shin Shin Fujin-Kai (True New Woman's Association) is also discussed in chap. 5 in Dina Lowy, *The Japanese "New Woman": Images of Gender and Modernity* (New Brunswick, NJ, and London: Rutgers University, 2007

[27]Iwata Nanatsu gives a brief overview of *Seitō* reception and study of the Bluestockings in chap. 4, "*Seitō* fukken e no ayumi: kenkyūshi" (The Path to the Rehabilitation of *Seitō*: History of Research), in Iwata, *Bungaku to shite no "Seitō"* (Fuji Shuppan, 2003), 234–48. Iwata also published an extensive bibliography of relevant works in Japanese under the heading "*Seitō* o shiru tame no kōmoku kaisetsu," in Yoneda Sayoko and Ikeda Emiko, eds., "*Seitō*" o manabu hito no tame ni (Kyoto: Sekai Shisō-sha, 1999), 237–45. See the bibliography in this volume for references to English-language studies of Japanese women's history, feminism, and literature and recent publications on the New Woman.

[28]Shin Feminizumu Hihyō no Kai, ed., "*Seitō*" o yomu: Blue Stocking (Gakugei Shorin, 1998); Yoneda and Ikeda, eds., "*Seitō*" o manabu hito no tame ni; and Iida Yūko, ed., "*Seitō*" to iu ba: Bungaku, jendā, atarashii onna (Shinwasha, 2002).

[29]Iwata, *Bungaku to shite no "Seitō*."

[30]Raichō Kenkyūkai, ed., *"Seitō" jinbutsu jiten: 110-nin no gunzō* (Taishūkan Shoten, 2001).

[31]Ide Fumiko's first book on the Bluestockings was Ide, *"Seitō": Genshi josei wa taiyō de atta* (Kōbundō, 1961).

[32]Kobayashi Tomie, ed., *"Seitō" serekushon: Atarashii onna no tanjō* (Jinbun Shoin, 1987).

[33]Itō Noe, *Itō Noe zenshū*, 2 vols. (Gakugei Shorin, 1970); Hiratsuka Raichō, *Genshi, josei wa taiyō de atta: Hiratsuka Raichō jiden*, 4 vols. (Ōtsuki Shoten, 1971–73).

[34] Hiratsuka Raichō Chosakushū Henshū Iinkai, ed., *Hiratsuka Raichō chosakushū*, 8 vols. (Ōtsuki Shoten, 1983–84).

[35]*Sōsho "Seitō" no onna-tachi*, 20 vols., reprint (Fuji Shuppan, 1985–86).

[36]The four offending pieces were the two stories "The Letter" by Araki Ikuko (translated in Chapter 1 below) and "To My Lover from a Woman in Prison" by Harada Satsuki (Chapter 3), and the essays "The Solution to the Woman Question" by Fukuda Hideko (Chapter 2) and "To the Women of the World" by Hiratsuka Raichō (Chapter 4). The Harada and Fukuda pieces provoked bans, the other two earned the Bluestockings only a reprimand.

[37]Other translations of *Seitō* fiction are Reiko Abe Auestad's translation of the October 1915 story "Shiraha no ato" by Satō Kinko (1895–1949), in Auestad, "The Scar, A Story from *Seitō*," *Monumenta Nipponica* 58.2 (2003): 171–92; and Edward Fowler's translation of Tamura Toshiko's (1884–1945) "Lifeblood" (Ikichi, originally published in the inaugural issue of *Seitō*), in Rebecca Copeland and Melek Ortabasi, eds., *The Modern Murasaki: Writing by Women of Meiji Japan* (New York: Columbia University Press, 2006), 348–57.

[38]These detailed histories of the Bluestockings in English include chap. 4, "The Seitō Society and New Women," in Tomida, *Hiratsuka Raichō*, 139–219; and chap. 8, "The Bluestockings," in Sievers, *Flowers in Salt*, 163–88. See also the works by Hiratsuka and Craig and by Lowy already cited above.

Chapter 1
Araki Ikuko (1890–1943)

*In this world where so many things are but superficial formalities, none is
so bizarre as the relationship between husband and wife.*

The young Araki Ikuko had energy, drive, and a love for life in the limelight.[1] Other Bluestockings shied away from notoriety, especially the kind
that portrayed them as wicked femmes fatales or disobedient daughters,
but not Araki. She was fascinated by writer Morita Sōhei's depiction of
Tomoko, the protagonist modeled on Hiratsuka Raichō, in his novel *Black
Smoke* (Baien), and her own *Seitō* contributions featured New Women who
dreamed of adultery and flirted with prostitution.[2] Like Raichō, Araki saw
her love life become the stuff of newspaper articles, and she did not hesitate to make creative use of it. She based her 1912 short story "The Letter"
(Tegami), translated here, on her entanglement in a messy love triangle. Yet
for all her boldness, Araki Ikuko found it hard to achieve the exciting, modern life of love and work for which she longed.

Born and raised in downtown Tokyo, Araki Ikuko was the third daughter in a family of ten children. Like Hiratsuka Raichō and many other
Bluestockings, she had an energetic, striving father who saw opportunities in
the new era. Coming from an old and once-illustrious family in Kumamoto
Prefecture to Tokyo to seek his fortune around 1885, Araki's father Kanta
(1858–1910) had hoped for a position in the emerging civil service. However,
romantic involvement with Fuku (b. 1858), the divorced daughter of an innkeeper and a manager of an inn herself, changed his plans. Fuku gave birth
to their first child, a daughter named Shigeko, in 1886.[3] In 1892, Kanta persuaded Fuku to take on a new inn, one that he would call the Gyokumeikan,
and a place that he hoped would attract other travelers from the provinces.
Located in the Kanda section of Tokyo, the Gyokumeikan became a lively
meeting place for the recently arrived and ambitious, host to the development
of a hybrid culture of regional and urban Japan. The name "Gyokumeikan"
served as a proud reference to Kanta's home in Kumamoto and as a playful
twist on "Rokumeikan," the name of the imposing Victorian-style building
that stood across the street, which was the site of grand international balls
that symbolized the aspirations of the Meiji elite.[4] Not to be outdone by the

impressive neighboring establishment, Araki's father planned to make his inn a place to encourage the dreams of the common people.[5] One wonders whether or not Fuku, who had been persuaded by her father to take up inn-keeping after her divorce, found her own dreams nurtured in this environment. We do know that she managed the inn, kept the accounts, and bore nine more children.[6]

It is hard to say when the young Ikuko became aware of the public and personal politics surrounding the family business, but she did take an active hand in innkeeping at an early age. In 1906, at age 16, she graduated from a girls' art academy where she had specialized in crafting artificial flowers. According to Hiratsuka Raichō, Ikuko was seventeen years old when she began managing a branch inn for the Araki family, which also served as a student rooming-house, in the Mejiro section of Tokyo. Raichō writes that she met Araki after the branch inn had been closed and Araki had returned to helping her mother with the Gyokumeikan. Apparently Araki was a popular innkeeper among the male students from nearby Waseda University. Through this work Araki also met Japanese literati such as Mitomi Kyūyō (1889–1917), Imai Hakuyō (1889–1917), and Sōma Gyofū (1883–1950), along with Tokuda Shūsei (1872–1943) and Arishima Takeo (1878–1923), who were to write their own fiction about new kinds of women. She also came into contact with young Chinese student revolutionaries and young men involved with the Philippines Independence Movement.[7] Araki Ikuko's niece, Araki Michiko (1917–89), however, had somewhat different memories of Ikuko's participation in the family business at this time. She reported that the responsibility for the Gyokumeikan had fallen to some of Araki's sisters, and that while Araki Ikuko had often been at the inn during the early 1910s, she had been leading a rather carefree life involved in artistic pursuits.[8] Still other ideas about this time in Araki's life have been proposed, as we will see when we consider the incident of the love triangle.

Most accounts of Araki Ikuko state that she never married or had children. Yet *Seitō* scholar Iwata Nanatsu discovered some anecdotal evidence suggesting that Araki married a literary scholar, perhaps a professor several years younger than she, in the 1930s. Iwata points to a passage in former Bluestocking Ikuta Hanayo's (1888–1970) 1949 autobiography *Mibōjin* (Widow) that describes how loyal Araki remained to her young husband despite his repeated hospitalization for mental illness and the bouts of violent behavior brought on by his disease. After her husband died, apparently in the early 1940s, Araki spoke to Ikuta, whose husband had also suffered from mental illness, about her plan to establish a kind of hospice where the mentally ill could find some respite without having to be hospitalized. Ikuta reported that Araki began consulting friends here and there, including

Hiratsuka Raichō, about her plans for the facility, which she saw as a tribute to her late husband, but died without realizing this dream.⁹ Who this husband may have been, and whether or not the couple ever formally married, remain a mystery. It is most interesting to consider how tales of Araki Ikuko as a free-thinking and free-loving young Bluestocking, some of which Araki herself seems to have instigated, have taken on a life of their own, overshadowing the more sobering aspects of her later life.

During the time Araki was associated with *Seitō* and for years thereafter, rumors circulated about her several love affairs, especially those with some of the young Japanese men she met at one of the family's inns. Her liaisons led to a tumultuous emotional life, one Araki appears to have been quite happy to share with her Bluestocking friends. Raichō remembers a drunken Araki once launching into a tearful confession of her latest relationship, and how, between puffs on her cigarette, she would entertain them with gossip about the men writers she knew. A gregarious person with numerous friendships and suitors, Araki was rumored to have had a "mysterious patron" who owned a rubber plantation in Southeast Asia. It is also said that her own generosity extended to helping the children and widows of her former lovers.¹⁰ In her 1916 *Seitō* story "Starry Sky" (Hoshi no sora), Bluestocking Katō Midori (1888–1922) closely models the character Yasuko on Araki Ikuko and portrays her as a woman who clearly likes the limelight, takes pleasure in "deliberately planting the seed of rumor," and behaves in a risqué manner to capture people's attention. Iwata Nanatsu takes Katō's comments as a clue that the rumors of Araki's many love affairs may have been just that, but also that creating such a persona had great appeal for Araki.¹¹

The experiences of Araki's youth made her quite different from most of the other Bluestockings, especially the initial members who came from Japan Women's College and who had led a more sheltered life. Her involvement with the Bluestockings was linked to some of the group's sharpest conflicts with the prevailing morality. Araki's short story on adultery, "The Letter," earned the Bluestockings their first unpleasant encounter with government censorship. She also organized and attended the Bluestockings' New Year's party in 1912, which was reported as a drunken revelry (see figure 4). In fact, though Araki had been persuaded to contribute to *Seitō* by Yasumochi Yoshiko (1885–1947), she first met the other Bluestockings at that infamous party.¹² Since Araki was on good, collegial terms with the owner of the inn where the party was held, she was able to ensure that the New Year's festivities were well supplied with food and drink. The Gyokumeikan, too, provided a welcoming atmosphere for more informal and much more discreet Bluestocking gatherings, where members Raichō, Itō Noe, Iwano Kiyoko, and especially Otake Kōkichi (1893–1966) would come for conversation and

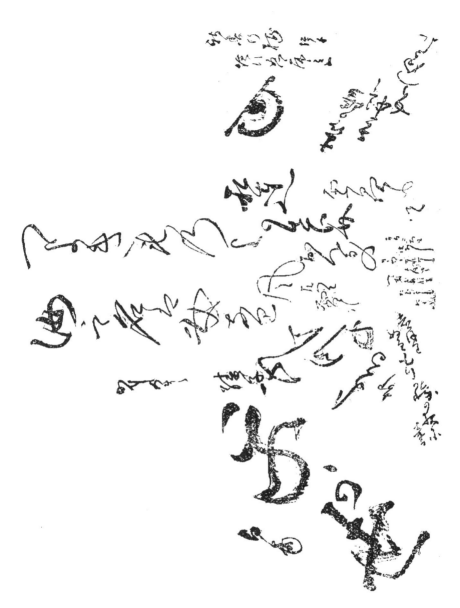

Figure 4. The Bluestockings commemorated their raucous 1912 New Year's party by signing their names and penning remarks. Hiratsuka Raichō boldly wrote "Food and Drink" *(sake meshi)* while Takeichi Aya proclaimed "Strength, thy name is woman" *(Tsuyoki mono yo, nanji no na wa onna nari). Seitō* 2.2 (February 1912): 102. Courtesy of Fuji Shuppan.

relaxation with one another.

At an early age Araki Ikuko achieved some measure of economic independence through her own efforts and became a part of an intellectual, artistic, and political world usually off limits to women. By all accounts the young Araki Ikuko was a woman who wanted to earn her own living. Newspapers followed with interest her short-lived attempts at running a small restaurant and starting a publishing business.[13] For most of her life Araki supported herself through her innkeeping, and later in life by operating a restaurant again. In the wake of her *Seitō* activity, she contributed funds to establish Shin Fujin Kyōkai (New Woman's Association, 1920) and tried her hand at starting a publishing house. As she grew older, alcoholism robbed Araki of her characteristic vitality and optimism. The disease most plagued her in middle age, ultimately forcing her to turn to her relatives for financial support. At one point during the Pacific War, she found work with the Aikoku Fujinkai (Japan Women's Patriotic Association), but her performance in this position, too, was hampered by her drinking. In February 1943, Araki Ikuko died at the age of fifty-three, the victim of a heart attack brought on by complications from pneumonia.

According to Ide Fumiko, Araki Ikuko is one of the few Bluestockings who truly fulfilled the group's original purpose of nurturing women writers.[14] She contributed nine manuscripts to *Seitō*, including two plays, some editorial remarks written with Raichō, and six short stories. At twenty-four years of age and after writing for only a little over two years, Araki published a separate volume of these, a new story, and a long novella under her own name in the 1914 collection entitled *Hi no musume* (Daughter of Fire). Although the collection boasted a brief introduction by literary giant Mori Ōgai (1862–1922) and appeared when the topic of the New Woman was generating much public attention, *Hi no musume* did not create much of a stir.[15] The novella in this collection, also entitled *Hi no musume*, is of interest here because its lead character Mitsuko resembles many of the New Women characters in *Seitō* fiction. The story begins as Mitsuko leaves the world of the girl student and the threat of an arranged marriage in Tokyo to strike out on her own by moving to Kobe to teach at a girls' art school. Love interests figure in the novella, too: Mitsuko is more intrigued with a mysterious, chronically ill young man in Kobe than with his Tokyo friend who has been ardently pursuing her. Mitsuko longs to find her mission in life, and the sentiments she expresses to her younger sister mark her as a quintessential New Woman, passionate yet in search of direction:

> What is it that I am living for? Oh, if only I could be a person who understood her mission in life, everything would be fine. But I am

just like a blind person. I don't even understand my own feelings. When I think I know what will bring me happiness, I start moving toward it. Then, I find out that it's not what I expected at all. My likes, my dislikes—I'm not even sure about those. You see what a pathetic creature I am? Sometimes when I come to dislike something that I used to like, I think I should just go all the way and really detest it, but I can't do that. That's my problem. I can't settle on any single thing as my goal.[16]

Given the censors' attention to the display of illicit love in Araki's story "The Letter," it is curious that another of her stories, "Michiko," published in this collection and in *Seitō* in November 1911, seems to have escaped criticism altogether. The story revolves around a pretty, young middle-class woman named Michiko, who is also a girls' school drop-out with a taste for adventure. Michiko is less idealistic than *Hi no musume*'s Mitsuko, and less ambivalent about going after what she wants. Michiko's initial attraction to a foreign man leads her to disobey her parents. She then tries her hand at supporting herself as a maid, at having an affair with a married man, and, finally, at trading sex for money with a Frenchman. The narrator describes how Michiko loses her innocence and becomes an adult through her work experiences, and how she comes to realize the difficulties women face in trying to support themselves. Yet the narrator does not go so far as to explain all Michiko's sexual adventures as a desperate attempt to earn money, but rather implies that they are part of her entry into a world open to her once she left her parents' home.[17]

The narrator of "The Letter" has chosen a tamer life than Michiko, having married a man who appears to be devoted to her. Whereas the narrators of many other *Seitō* stories complain of receiving too little attention from their husbands, the narrator of "The Letter" disdains her husband's overtures. As Iwata observes, her desires for the young lover Hideo are unabashedly carnal. Moreover, the narrator's association of Hideo with the "swallow song" may signal an older, even predatory woman in love with a naïve younger man—a motif that appears again in the publicity surrounding Hiratsuka Raichō and her "young swallow," Okumura Hiroshi (see Chapter 4). Despite her condemnation of marriage, the narrator does not speak of divorce, only of the fantasy of an affair.[18] Neither man is much described in the story, nor do we see the narrator having anything more in her life than her desire for the younger man. Still, the striking aspect of "The Letter" lies in the fact that it depicts a woman asserting her desire for a man, rather than seeing herself only as the object of another's love. Iwata reads the letter as an expression of self-love. She views the narrator's recreation of herself as turning her into a kind of femme fatale who will stoop to cruelty to satisfy her desires, even if that means deceiving her husband and trapping Hideo like the poor moth in the story that beats against the closed door.[19] But what government censors no doubt found objectionable was that this assertive, desiring woman was also a married one. Not only was adultery on the part of a wife legal grounds for divorce, it could also merit a prison sentence at this time. The same was not true for men.[20] As Sheldon Garon explains, the elite men who crafted this law wanted both to contain women's sexuality and to encourage women to use their energies to become modern managers of the home and family. Reading "The Letter" may have proved this point, for the censors no doubt found this narrator woefully lacking in concern for household management.

Since the censors did not issue their ban on the sale of the April 1912 issue of *Seitō* that included Araki's story until 18 April, the issue had already been distributed and had sold out in stores. The Bluestockings consequently escaped financial loss, but not without one of them experiencing the scare of being visited by reproving officials, as Hiratsuka Raichō describes in her autobiography. At the time, the Bluestockings were using the home of Mozume Kazuko (1888–1979) as their office address. On the night of 18 April, at about 10:00 p.m., Mozume was startled to hear a dog barking near her front gate and went out to see what was happening. There in the dark stood a policeman carrying a paper lantern and two men in ordinary clothes. The men had come to see the Bluestocking office, so Mozume had no choice but to take them into the house and to her room. Only one copy of the April *Seitō* was there, lying on her dresser. The visitors promptly confiscated this copy. Having no idea what was going on, Mozume could only stare at them in bewilderment. It was only when the men were putting on their shoes before leaving the house that they told her that the sale of this issue had been banned. When Mozume's father later learned of the incident, he asked that the Bluestockings find another place for their office, which they did, moving to Mannenzan Shōrinji. In the meantime, Araki Ikuko's story "The Letter" was in the hands of hundreds of readers, despite its being "disruptive of the public peace and order."[21]

But the story of "The Letter" does not end there. In her careful reading of the *Hi no musume* collection, Iwata discovered that "The Letter" appears again, although with a new title, "Michishirube" (Guidepost), and with some significant revising. Although "Guidepost" is a revision published two years after "The Letter," Araki lists the same date, 26 March 1912, at the story's conclusion—perhaps a simple oversight, or perhaps a nod to the original. The revised story is less sensual than the original, and criticism is directed at both the wife and her husband. Iwata points to the following passage as a revision made to disparage the wife as shallow and materialistic:

> I knew with all my heart how fortunate I was when I got married. There was nothing at all to worry me, nothing to struggle over. Whatever I wanted, I could have, and I was loved. And so, strangely and inexplicably, I wrestled with happiness itself. It was when I became bored by these materialistic desires that thoughts of you came back to me. I've been thinking that I should doubt my husband's feelings, and at the same time, that I should doubt myself as well. I say this because the material pleasures of my life at present are much greater than anything I could have obtained when growing up. Yet what would be left of me if I were to sweep away all this contentment? The hair ornament carved from ivory, the gem-stone ring, the lavish dinners. Were all these swept away, what would remain of my life but the existence of an insect that lacked even the glimmer of a soul? When I realized this, I knew that I must think again about what I am doing, and do so fully aware of the loneliness and shame of my present life.[22]

At the story's end, the wife is still contemplating an affair and suggesting a meeting, just as in "The Letter." Yet there is still another "version" to consider in thinking about the narrative of the adulterous wife, and that is the much-reported story of Araki's own love life. The July 1912 series on "The So-called New Woman" in *Kokumin shinbun* took a special interest in Araki's romances, particularly her relationship with a twenty-two-year-old Waseda University student, Masuda Atsuo (1891–1936). Dina Lowy summarizes this portion of the *Kokumin* newspaper series as follows:

> [Araki's] boardinghouse was in financial trouble, and a wealthy Mr. Komatsu—who happened to be the more appropriate age of thirty—agreed to take over and expected Araki's hand in marriage as part of the bargain. Araki, who had been living with Masuda at another boardinghouse, gathered her belongings and ran away. Masuda found her several days later in a disheveled state back at her own boardinghouse, seemingly having chosen the option of financial and marital security. But when she once again saw the face of her lover, she decided to flee from the city with him, disregarding personal and professional commitments in order to satisfy her own selfish passion.[23]

After sifting through this and all the other reports about this period in Araki's life, Iwata Nanatsu concludes that Araki may have left the Gyokumeikan and broken off with her family about the time *Seitō* first appeared, and ultimately left Masuda to return to Komatsu. Since she could not make money publishing with *Seitō*, she turned her attention to opening a restaurant; the enterprise failed, despite the support of writers she knew and newspaper publicity. She tried her hand at publishing but could not make a go of this, either, fell to drinking too much, and experienced continued unhappiness in her relationship with Komatsu. Finally, she left him, returned to the Gyokumeikan and her family, devoted herself to her work there, and more or less got her life in order for a time.[24]

There is a photograph (figure 5) of Araki Ikuko that appears in the September 1912 anniversary issue of *Seitō* taken the previous August at Chigasaki, a seaside town not far from Tokyo.[25] Araki is resting against Yasumochi Yoshiko, and the two are grouped together with Ikuta Chōkō and his wife and Bluestockings Hiratsuka Raichō, Otake Kōkichi, and Kimura Masako (1885–1958). Araki had likely fled Komatsu for Masuda by this time, but had come to Chigasaki by herself. It is hard to imagine the scandals dogging Araki and the other women, too, when one sees their comfortable dress and relaxed postures in this summer picture.

Reflecting on the Araki Ikuko that she knew, Hiratsuka Raichō writes that it was her nimble, passionate way of putting ideas into action, rather than anything especially new or consciously progressive about her thinking, that made Araki a New Woman. She was not often successful in bringing her plans to fruition, but she became a model of a woman who refuses the constraints of propriety in favor of living boldly and freely.[26] "The Letter" portrays the New Woman in much the same way. An older woman writes of her carnal affection for a younger man, tempting him to commit a crime. A wife confesses to the willful deception of a devoted husband. A New Woman writer entices her reader, avowing that true love and sexual desire must always trump marriage. "The Letter" gives no indication of the men's part in this triangle: Is the husband on to his wife's games? Will Hideo risk everything for this woman or leave her unfulfilled and abandoned? How far will this New Woman go to satisfy her desires? Government censors did not relish the idea of the public considering such questions.

****

The Letter
Araki Iku
Seitō 2.4 (April 1912)

I am writing this letter to you on a winter's evening, in a four-and-a-half-tatami-mat room that faces north. When you see my handwriting, I am sure you'll understand how shaky my hand is and how restless my spirit. Really, I think I have spent days and days on this letter. Every time I begin to write, I become strangely anxious and my thoughts get all mixed up. And what's more, the image of you, of your gentle innocent ways—for me, these

Figure 5. This photograph of the Bluestockings relaxing at the seaside in Chigasaki in the summer of 1912 appeared in the first anniversary issue of *Seitō* 2.9 (September 1912). Seated from left are Ikuta Chōkō, Hiratsuka Raichō, and Otake Kōkichi. In the row behind from left are Araki Ikuko, Yasumochi Yasuko, Kimura Masako, and Ikuta Chōkō's wife. Courtesy of Fuji Shuppan.

are inexplicably seductive—floats before me like an apparition, and even those dreadful words you said on the day we last parted, "Let's not see each other again," ring in my ear.

But today, no matter what, I must send this letter.

It has been almost six months since we've parted, hasn't it? It's frightening to think that I was able to refrain from writing to you all that time. What a long time it was, and what a test of my endurance! But, Hideo, please think about whether it is best to go on like this, serving only my husband and never writing to you.

In this world where so many things are but superficial formalities, none is as bizarre as the relationship between husband and wife. People treat love like a handy tool. A woman who wields that tool skillfully can earn such titles as "virtuous lady" or "wise wife." Because you haven't yet lived in this suffocating realm of "husband and wife" or "marriage," you wouldn't know this. That's why I feel I absolutely must tell you. I write this so you will understand that in the world we will create, not only must we acknowledge the happiness of lovers, we must as lovers achieve that happiness ourselves.

Perpetually smiling, my husband showers me with the requisite niceties: hair ornaments, rings, and delicious sweets, and a long kiss when I wake up in the morning. But I have never once won his heart, and he has never tried to touch mine. He thinks everything is all right simply if he sees my smiling face or my coquettish ways (these are in reality products of a man's own imagination). And so, with my fingers entangled in his collar, I brush the lint off his kimono and tie together the stitching that has come unraveled. Then I embrace him, all the while thinking of the nape of your neck and the delight of the first night your crimson lips meant mine.

In the middle of the day, when I wander to the front gate, I'm not waiting for my husband's return but hoping that I might by some chance run into you. And so for a long time I stare vacantly at the sky, calling your name. A cold, unfriendly wind whips sand at me. People in the street eye me suspiciously, as if to say, "What brings you out in this cold?" They keep staring back at me as they pass by. Also, there is a man who, perhaps thinking that I am "that kind of woman," has many a time passed back and forth in front of me, and to top it off, he even whistles at me from the shadows of the telephone pole across the street. I am well aware of what these people are thinking, but I have no desire to go back into the house. And so I sing the song about swallows, the one I learned as a child. I was pretty sure that you knew the swallow song, too. Among all these fools, I sometimes find myself looking for a tall man, a man who would remind me of you. How my heart leaps every time I see a well-dressed young man of twenty-four or twenty-five. How furiously it cries out for you. I don't know why, but even when I try to calm my heart, I am unable to do so. It gets to the point that I'm convinced every person passing before my eyes has to be you.

This room of mine is a gloomy four-and-a-half-tatami-mat room near the kitchen. But the north window is low, and the small yard in front of it reaching to the back gate has many bushes where a grown person could easily hide. When things quiet down at night, I can clearly hear the sound of water dripping from the faucet, after the voices of my neighbors and high-pitched female laughter have all subsided. So I think, "I am all alone in this room now. My husband is asleep and the maid is snoring. On a night like this I could do anything. If by some chance you came, I would seat you on my cushion and rest against your knees—something I haven't done in such a long time. My right hand would caress your neck, my lips would touch yours. We would be able to create a moment of pure happiness."

One night when I was imagining things like this, a moth got caught between the shoji screen and the storm shutter. Unable to find its way out, the moth beat its wings against the screen. Not realizing what was making this sound, I quietly held the door with my sleeve and opened the shoji. Then I noticed that if I poured some water from my inkstone onto the doorsill, I could open the door without making a sound. Try to imagine, if you will, my feelings when that door opened. I'm sure you understand how "sneaky" I felt. The pale moon peered down at my face sternly, as if it condemned my actions. I felt mortified to think I'd been made a fool of, but in my night-clothes I slipped into the deserted garden and stealthily tried to find you in the bushes. By then my whole body and soul were moving at the beck and call of your shadow, and yet your shadow wasn't even there.

Writing this down gives me such relief. Life at my home is as I have described to you. All the same, we are a married couple that lives together without any quarrels. I, too, am a "chaste lady," you see, though such words are not ones with any appeal for me. What I want instead, if indeed I am a human being, is to feel completely enveloped by an earnest and human love. Even if such love were condemned as a terrible crime, I want a life that allows our hearts to mesh as one, regardless of what form it takes, rather than endure one more anguished day of deceit.

It's all right for us to meet. Fortunately, from the beginning of next month, my husband will be away.

Hideo! Why don't we go to that room? It's perfect because it's close to your home and mine. Should we want to return to our homes, we can do so quickly. Surely you won't say you object to that room. You remember how the sleeping grass and the sea came together at the little glass window and how the pale stars of dawn shone through the dim, monochrome pane, don't you? At the time, you said, "Those stars seem to mark the trail of the two of us stealing away together." Really, that room is perfect for us.

I remember that first night from beginning to end. The stars of dawn marked the path of love. You constantly whispered sweet nothings as we embraced, gazing at those stars, spending hours and hours telling each other our secrets. How embarrassed we would have been had anybody heard us. Even the ocean waves happily sang songs of joy as they endlessly kissed the shore. Happier even than those waves were the two of us, creating unforgettable memories together.

Hideo. Please send me an answer quickly. You need only write the word "Fine," along with the date and time. In less than five days, I will be able to touch your crimson lips. I am sure that on that night, before you even hear me say one word, you will have something to place on this small forehead of mine.

Notes

[1] Araki used both Iku and Ikuko for her given name. I use Ikuko here, too, following Teruko Craig (in Hiratsuka and Craig, *In the Beginning, Woman Was the Sun*) and Dina Lowy (*The Japanese "New Woman"*), and use Iku only when Araki signed her publications as such—as she most often did when writing for *Seitō*.

[2] Morita Sōhei, *Baien* (Black Smoke, 1909), vol. 29 in the series *Gendai Nihon bungaku taikei*, reprint (Tokyo: Chikuma Shobō, 1971).

[3] Araki Shigeko made one contribution to *Seitō* herself, publishing a two-part short story about the pressures on young women to get married, especially in cases of familial financial distress. The protagonist Yoshiko ponders what rich life experiences she would forsake if she never married but remained a virgin. "Uzu" (Whirlpool), in *Seitō* 5.10 (November 1915): 70–84, and *Seitō* 5.11 (December 1915): 29–38.

[4] Araki Michiko, the daughter of Ikuko's elder sister Shigeko, cleared up some confusion about the correct pronunciation and characters for the inn when she told Horiba Kiyoko that the characters for the inn's name came from the family's native Tamana district in Kumamoto. Horiba, *Seitō no jidai: Hiratsuka Raichō to atarashii onnatachi* (Iwanami Shoten, 1988), 44. Both the Gyokumeikan and the Rokumeikan were destroyed in the Great Kantō Earthquake of 1923.

[5] As recalled by Araki Michiko in an interview with *Seitō* historian Ide Fumiko. Ide, "Araki Iku cho *Hi no musume* kaiketsu," in Araki Iku, *Hi no musume* (1914), vol. 6 in the series *Sōsho "Seitō" no onna-tachi*, reprint (Fuji Shuppan, 1986), 8.

[6] Iwata Nanatsu, *Bungaku to shite no "Seitō"* (Fuji Shuppan, 2003), 165–66. None of the biographies of Araki Ikuko consulted for this chapter gives Fuku's maiden name or the year in which she died.

[7] Ide, "Araki Iku cho *Hi no musume* kaiketsu," 7, 10; Hiratsuka Raichō, *Genshi, josei wa taiyō de atta: Hiratsuka Raichō jiden* (Ōtsuki Shoten, 1971–73), 2: 352–55; Hiratsuka Raichō and Teruko Craig, *In the Beginning, Woman Was the Sun: The Autobiography of a Japanese Feminist* (New York: Columbia University Press, 2006), 169–70.

[8] As told by Araki Michiko in an interview with Ide Fumiko. Ide, "Araki Iku cho *Hi no musume* kaiketsu," 8.

[9] Iwata, *Bungaku to shite no "Seitō,"* 161–65.

[10]After Iwano Kiyoko's untimely death, Araki raised Kiyoko's son, who died in the Great Kantō Earthquake of 1923. She later paid for grave markers for Kiyoko, Hōmei, and their son; see Yamashiroya Seki, "Araki Ikuko," in Raichō Kenkyūkai, ed., "Seitō" jinbutsu jiten: 110-nin no gunzō (Taishūkan Shoten, 2001), 35. Although Araki was also rumored to have been Hōmei's last lover, Iwata Nanatsu's research shows that this is highly unlikely. She argues that Araki's generosity toward Iwano Kiyoko's son and her arranging for the grave markers demonstrate her warm feelings for Kiyoko. Iwata, Bungaku to shite no "Seitō," 194–97.

[11]Katō Midori, "Hoshi no sora" (Starry Sky), Seitō 6.1 (January 1916): 116–39, especially 122–23, and as cited in Iwata, Bungaku to shite no "Seitō," 186.

[12]When Yasumochi Yoshiko's mother traveled from Shikoku to Tokyo for her daughter's graduation from Japan Women's College, she and Yoshiko stayed at Araki's Mejiro inn because it was near the college. During their stay Yasumochi Yoshiko had several conversations with Araki about literature, and she remembered the younger woman when plans to form the Bluestockings got underway. In their conversations about literature, Yasumochi learned of Araki's fascination with the character of Tomoko in Morita Sōhei's novel Black Smoke (Baien) and promised to introduce her to the model for the character, her friend Hiratsuka Haruko. Ide, "Araki Iku cho Hi no musume kaisetsu," 2–3.

[13]For example, Iwata reports, on 31 August 1913, Yomiuri shinbun ran an article about a New Woman opening a restaurant. Iwata, Bungaku to shite no "Seitō," 182.

[14]Ide, "Araki Iku cho Hi no musume kaisetsu," 2.

[15]Reviewing Araki's collection Hi no musume (Daughter of Fire) in Seitō in March 1914, Hiratsuka Raichō roundly criticized the book, especially its long novella Daughter of Fire, for the sentimental, old-fashioned style of its plot and writing. She mentioned that she much preferred some of Araki's other stories, ones that had already appeared in Seitō, and that despite her criticism she still believed in Araki's talent as a writer. Hiratsuka Raichō, "Hi no musume o yonde," Seitō 4.3 (March 1914): 17–24. Iwata Nanatsu conjectures that either Bluestocking Katō Midori's husband Asadori or Araki's young lover and budding writer Masuda may have introduced Araki to Ōgai. Iwata also wonders whether or not Ōgai took inspiration from Araki's "The Letter" in writing The Wild Geese (Gan), his 1911–13 novel in which a young mistress, Otama, longs for the student Okada while being obligated to the older man Suezō, who is keeping her and aiding her father financially. At one point in the novel, the narrator says of Otama, "when she submitted to Suezo, the image of Okada was behind her closed eyes. Sometimes they were together in her dreams. . . . But the moment she thought how happy she was, the man turned into Suezo instead of Okada." Ōgai Mori, The Wild Geese, trans. Kingo Ochiai and Sanford Goldstein (Rutland, VT, and Tokyo: Charles E. Tuttle, Co., 1959), 97, and as referred to in Iwata, Bungaku to shite no "Seitō," 189–90.

[16]Araki Iku, Hi no musume, 29–30.

[17]Araki Iku, "Michiko," Seitō 1.3 (November 1911): 27–37.

[18]Araki's plays Hi-gami no tawamure (Frolic of the Sun God), Seitō 1.1 (September 1911): 63–89, a comic fantasy, and Yami no hana (Flower of Darkness), Seitō 2.2 (February 1912): 52–74, also feature young wives who are unhappy with their husbands and romantically involved with young men. Declaring that people must make their own happiness, Yoshiko in Hi-gami leaves her lover after escaping with him to the mountains and returns to her husband mainly because she misses the excitement

of the city. *Yami no hana*'s Sumiko acquiesces to an arranged marriage to please her father but pledges to her sweetheart Itō that he is her true love. Some readers may have also been shocked to see the topic of sister-brother incest play a role in Araki's story "Utsukushiki jigoku" (Beautiful Hell), *Seitō* 4.3 (March 1914): 84–97.

[19]Iwata, *Bungaku to shite no "Seitō,"* 175.

[20]Sheldon Garon, *Molding Japanese Minds: The State in Everyday Life* (Princeton, NJ: Princeton University Press, 1997), 99, 102.

[21]After this incident, the Bluestockings set up a new office in Komagome in Tokyo's Hongo ward. Hiratsuka, *Genshi, josei wa taiyō de atta* 2: 357–58; Hiratsuka and Craig, *In the Beginning, Woman Was the Sun*, 171. According to Iwata, Araki took over some of the duties of running the magazine after member Kiuchi Teiko resigned in the wake of the problems with "The Letter," but was not particularly active in the group much after this. When the November 1913 issue of *Seitō* carried a special announcement inviting readers to join the Bluestockings, Araki was no longer listed as a member but as a supporter. Iwata, *Bungaku to shite no "Seitō,"* 170.

[22]Iwata, *Bungaku to shite no "Seitō,"* 177; Araki Iku, "Michishirube" (Guidepost), in idem, *Hi no musume*, 180–81.

[23]"Iwayuru atarashii onna" (The So-called New Woman), *Kokumin shinbun*, 11 July 1912, as discussed in Dina Lowy, *The Japanese 'New Woman': Images of Gender and Modernity* (New Brunswick, NJ, and London: Rutgers University, 2007), 64.

[24]Iwata, *Bungaku to shite no "Seitō,"* 187. Iwata cites, among other accounts of this triangle, comments in Itō Noe's 1916 *Osaka Mainichi shinbun* series on the Bluestockings, entitled "Zatsuon" (Noise), in which Noe recounts a conversation with Raichō about Araki on 10 April 1916, and Masuda Atsuo's story "Surrendering a Lover" (Koibito jōto no ken), published in the April 1913 issue of the magazine *Zamboa*. Iwata quotes from and comments on "Zatsuon" on pages 178–80, and mentions *Zamboa* on page 182.

[25]The photograph appears on an unnumbered page between pages 222 and 223 in *Seitō* 2.9 (September 1912).

[26]Hiratsuka, *Genshi, josei wa taiyō de atta* 2: 355; Hiratsuka and Craig, *In the Beginning, Woman Was the Sun*, 170.

Chapter 2
Fukuda Hideko (1865–1927)

Along with the liberation of women, the liberation of men, too, must be accomplished. Aren't today's men just as bewildered as women by their wretched circumstances?

Fukuda Hideko was forty-eight years old in February 1913—about twenty years older than most of the Bluestockings—when she contributed "Fujin mondai no kaiketsu" (The Solution to the Woman Question) to *Seitō* at Hiratsuka Raichō's invitation. She had long been involved in fighting for human rights, and her name was certainly well known and strongly associated with radical activism at the time.[1] Still, the Bluestockings were surprised when they learned that government censors had decided to ban the entire issue carrying Fukuda's article.[2] Newspaper reports surmised that the ban was due to an article "written by a socialist woman or one about the destruction of the family system."[3]

Raichō felt the sting of this ban in a most personal way. Her father was infuriated when he learned the story of the Fukuda essay from reading about the ban in the newspaper. Hiratsuka Sadajirō had long been tolerant of his daughter's unconventional ways, but when he assumed that she was forging connections with socialists, he angrily demanded that she leave the family home so as not to compromise his position.[4]

"The Solution to the Woman Question" is one of the most striking of all the *Seitō* essays, for it introduces the issue of class into a discussion that had until then focused almost exclusively on gender. For the privileged and educated young Bluestockings, the family system and its rigidly defined gender roles posed the greatest obstacle to their ambitions and desires in life. Fukuda Hideko could look beyond the concerns of this one privileged group to the millions of women who labored in brutal environments with little freedom or comfort of any kind. This led her to question whether the demand for women's rights was aimed toward benefiting all women or only the privileged ones. As she writes in "Solution," "Even if courts, universities, and government offices in general are opened to women, those who enter these will, of course, only be women from the influential class " In other words, daughters of privileged families would begin to enjoy the same opportunities as their brothers, while poorer children of both sexes would be equally disadvantaged. The point Fukuda makes here has become a concern in contemporary feminism internationally. It also presages, for example, criticism of (white) women's groups in the "second wave" of feminism in the 1970s by women of color in the U.S. who demanded that the Women's Movement make issues of race and class more visible.[5] Such sensitivity on Fukuda's part, however, did not mean that she was always able to surmount class barriers herself; vignettes in her autobiography about her interactions with poorer women characterize Fukuda as being in a superior, benevolent position.[6]

Fukuda's essay also broadened the Bluestockings' discussion of liberation, which had mainly revolved around individualistic introspection and creativity. For Fukuda Hideko, such definitions of liberation are attractive but incomplete. The solution she offers is equally utopian, if cast in a different mold. For her, liberation must be both less esoteric and available to everyone—men as well as women, the poor as well as the privileged. Much like Friedrich Engels and other nineteenth-century European philosophers who romanticized an imagined pastoral life that predated industrialization and the rise of capitalism, Fukuda looked back to agrarian life as the model of healthier living (a frame of reference we also see in the writing of Iwano Kiyoko and Yamada Waka; see Chapters 6 and 11 below).[7] Only when the structures of class and gender inequity were completely abolished, she believed, would true liberation be possible. Since government leaders were reinforcing at every turn a system that relied on such hierarchies and encouraged industrialization, it is not surprising that Fukuda Hideko's ideas would have been considered dangerous. Yet despite the fact that Fukuda believed in women's economic independence, her proposals that women take up such work as making embroidered silk handkerchiefs for export show how, as Vera Mackie has pointed out, "her view of women's work is shaped by dominant constructions of class and gender in Meiji Japan."[8]

Born in 1865, a few years before the Meiji Restoration, in present-day Okayama Prefecture, Kageyama Hideko was her parents' third child and second daughter. Her father, once a low-ranking samurai, became a policeman after the Restoration. Her mother became a teacher when Okayama Prefecture opened a girls' school in 1872. Hideko developed a love of learning in childhood that her parents encouraged, and for a time in her early twenties, she and her mother opened a small private school for girls. Like Hiratsuka Raichō, Itō Noe, and other Bluestockings who were to come after her, the young Hideko, as her autobiography shows, had ambitions that stretched far beyond the narrow constraints of marriage and the family system. As a schoolgirl, she, too, was dubbed a tomboy, something that concerned her parents, who tried to feminize their daughter in much the same way that Raichō's mother did hers—through music lessons. Yet, also like Raichō, Hideko found support for her individual interests and some flexibility in her parents' attitudes toward her future. After much discussion, for example, they allowed Hideko to turn down a marriage proposal in favor of letting her become a teacher as she wished. Interestingly, in her autobiography Fukuda takes an ambivalent stance toward youthful opposition to the constraints of femininity. As Vera Mackie observes, in her autobiography Fukuda describes herself as a tomboy in childhood, writing in a way that shows she is sympathetic to her own early resistance to gender constraints yet still able to feel the sting of other children's mocking her for this. But the autobiography also records how Fukuda traded her masculine style for a more feminine appearance at age seventeen, and how as an adult she advised a young woman who wished to become her apprentice to do the same.[9]

As a young woman, Hideko yearned for inspiration and direction. When a local friend (and later fiancé), Kobayashi Kusuo, drew her into political activities, he gave her his translation of a biography of Joan of Arc, a figure who was to lead Hideko to imagine becoming a courageous patriot herself, and one with whom she would later be associated.[10] Kishida Toshiko's famous speeches in the early 1880s, in the flush of the popular liberalism of the Freedom and People's Rights Movement (Jiyū Minken Undō) that called for women to break out of their sheltered lives, moved Hideko to join Kishida and speak out herself for gender equality.[11] Hideko's belief in educating women spurred her to open her first private girls' school in 1883, based on principles of freedom and equality. The closure of the school by a prefectural ordinance did not dim Fukuda's spirit; she participated in anti-government campaigns in Tokyo.[12] This active pursuit of social change landed her in jail for four years, after her romantic liaison with the radical Ōi Kentarō involved her in 1885 in what became known as the Osaka Incident, an attempt to liberate Korea from the Japanese government's increasing domination.[13]

As the only woman among 163 defendants brought to trial over the Osaka Incident, Fukuda earned a good deal of publicity, and the nickname "the Joan of Arc of the Orient" (Tōyō no Jannu Daruku).[14] Articles about Fukuda appeared in newspapers, a biographical pamphlet was published in 1887, and Fukuda herself described attending "a theatrical performance in Okayama, which portrayed her participation in the Osaka Incident."[15] This event in Fukuda's life earned her a jail sentence and made her a public figure; she became well known as "the heroic woman of the Osaka Incident" (Ōsaka Jiken no Joketsu).[16] Freed from jail in 1889, Fukuda continued to work for social change but in a different way, opening a school for working women and their children in Tokyo. Given the importance of parents' attitudes in the Bluestockings' lives, it is noteworthy that Fukuda describes in her autobiography how her father embraced his unconventional daughter. Overjoyed at the opportunity to meet his daughter after her release, Kageyama traveled to Osaka despite his ill health and joined Hideko and her comrades as they were paraded heroically through the streets in rickshaws.[17]

Another supportive man entered Hideko's life when in 1892 she married Fukuda Yūsaku, who had recently returned to Japan after graduating from the University of Michigan. Although his family strenuously disapproved of the match, hoping that their first son would take a bride of their choosing, the couple had a fairly happy relationship that ended all too soon when Fukuda Yūsaku died in 1900.[18] Alone at thirty-five years of age with four sons (one by Ōi and three by Fukuda) to support, Fukuda Hideko became ever more aware of the precarious nature of women's position in modern Japan. Persistent in romance as well as politics, she was willing to fall in love once again. In 1901, she took up with her third and last lover, a man eleven years her junior by the name of Ishikawa Sanshirō, a former servant in the Fukuda household and an assistant in the school Fukuda Hideko had established. Unfortunately, he proved to be as unreliable a mate as Ōi Kentarō, and eventually abandoned Hideko, despite the fact that she had helped him start his career in journalism and had been a source of support for him. Hiratsuka Raichō and others wondered whether it was Hideko's own suspicion and jealousy, borne from her betrayals by other men, that had ultimately driven Ishikawa away.[19]

Through the ups and downs of her private life, Fukuda Hideko never lost her ambition to work for women's rights and education. She had struggled to open schools for women, and in 1905, as she moved closer to socialist circles in Tokyo, she joined the Heimin-sha (Commoners' Association) struggle to revise Article Five of the Police Security Regulations (Chian Keisatsu Hō) that severely constrained women's political voice. As well, she contributed to the socialist newspaper *Heimin shinbun*, and in 1907 initiated a magazine for women entitled *Sekai fujin* (Women of the World). The magazine had a small circulation but its avowedly feminist, political content made it the target of government attention. Unlike *Seitō*, it had no pretensions to art or to the inner awakening of the self. From the outset, Fukuda Hideko aimed her publication toward all women broadly and called for social change. Sharon Sievers translates the *Sekai fujin* mission statement as follows:

> What are our reasons for publishing *Women of the World*? In a word, to determine the real vocation of women by extracting it from the

tangled web of law, custom, and morality that are a part of women's experience. Then, we hope to cultivate among all of you a desire to join a reform movement founded on what will be the true mission of women. . . . When I look at conditions currently prevailing in society, I see that as far as women are concerned, virtually everything is coercive and oppressive, making it imperative that we women rise up and forcefully develop our own social movement. This truly is an endless enterprise; we have not reached our goals, but our hope is that this magazine will inspire you to become a champion of this [women's] movement.[20]

What *Sekai fujin* did have in common with *Seitō* was that both publications appealed to girls' school students and college women, and worried their instructors as much as the censors. The more artistic bent of *Seitō* was probably due not only to an intellectual climate concerned with the inner self but to the chilling effects on the political atmosphere of the hasty trial and execution of several socialists, known as the High Treason Trial of 1911. By the time Fukuda Hideko wrote her essay for *Seitō*, she was certainly well aware of how close the younger women were coming to seriously offending powerful leaders, but there is no hint in her essay of warning the Bluestockings to be cautious. Rather, at the outset she wishes them well, and even places herself as subordinate to their youthful, contemporary spirit.

Mikiso Hane describes Fukuda Hideko's final years as cheerless ones. Her intimate relations with men had all failed, one of her sons had died and another had gone off to Manchuria, and she was selling piece goods to eke out a living.[21] Even her interest in politics, despite her occasional attendance at a study group, had diminished. She also expressed bitterness about her efforts to work and live with men, even with those whose beliefs she shared. Hane quotes Fukuda as saying: "Men are worthless. They are easily bought off by titles of nobility and medals. In this respect women are more reliable. Among women there are no fools who go about proudly dangling medals around their neck."[22]

Contemporary texts of Japanese women's history fully recognize the pioneering efforts of Fukuda Hideko, and many writers speak of her with admiration and empathy. Thinking back over Fukuda's sixty-one years, the many setbacks she endured, and the persistence that saw her through so much recalls the kind of heroic New Woman envisioned in Itō Noe's essay, "The Path of the New Woman" (translated in Chapter 5 below). Truly, Fukuda Hideko was a pioneer who suffered much as she opened new ground, and whose arduous efforts were only recognized years later. One hundred years after her birth, a memorial to Fukuda Hideko was erected in Okayama.

****

The Solution to the Woman Question
Fukuda Hideko
Seitō 3.2 (February 1913)

Thank you for asking me to write something for *Seitō*. Despite my earnest desire to fulfill your request, I am very sorry to say that I have been procrastinating and not writing anything at all. I sympathize very deeply with your work, your situation, and the position you have taken. I feel that if there were any way that even someone like me could help you, I'd certainly want to do so. Yet I am deterred by obstacles born from a long life of failure and am suffering in circumstances that render me unable to act. I am waiting for the sun to break through again as I endeavor to create a life that follows your lead.

I know that you are already well informed about solutions to the Woman Question, but since older people have their own peculiar views on life, allow me to express something of mine. All the same, I do not want to appear senile, despite my age. It is just that, after looking back on the pride of my own youthful days, I feel an inexpressible delight when I consider your lives today, and at the same time I am forced to realize that, just as one would expect, I myself have completely changed. This feeling of having changed—that is to say, this feeling that old people get—is, after all, the very thing that gives the old special privileges over the young. I may well be speaking like an overly cautious old woman, but I hope that you will listen anyway.

Although we talk about the Woman Question, the matter itself includes various concerns. Indeed, we must say that it is interwoven with educational, political, and economic issues, as well as with romantic concerns. It is intimately connected with every facet of human life. However, while admitting that the Woman Question is interrelated with such diverse issues, if we were to sum up all these problems, we could come back to the issue of women's liberation. Should women, in fact, be liberated? If they could be liberated, under what circumstances should that occur? And, furthermore, what is the meaning of liberation in the first place? If we take this last question as our issue and manage to resolve it, the Woman Question itself will be resolved.

First, what is the meaning of liberation? Allow me to start by presenting my modest opinions on this point. For those of us caught up in the heady days of the People's Rights Movement, the Woman Question could be summarized by the slogan "Equal rights for men and women." No doubt this was an exceedingly simple way of thinking; however, I do not believe that any new, deeper understanding of this issue has appeared even today. If we say that we shall liberate women in relation to men, then we cannot take a single step farther than to call for equal rights for men and women. Women's liberation, seen in this light, remains a relative issue. It is a way of thinking that merely contrasts women with men. The women's suffrage movement, the movement for higher education for women, and the question of women working in civil service—we can see all such movements arise from this line of thinking.

However, I believe that an absolute women's liberation must be achieved, toward which these relativistic movements shall serve simply as a means. In fact, won't these relativistic movements, too, begin to have meaning and life only if we make absolute liberation our goal? If this is the case, then what is absolute liberation? Absolute liberation does not mean liberation as women; it means liberation as "human beings." It lies in the realization of freedom for "human beings," not just freedom for women. It is not simply the destruction of legal, moral, and traditional constraints; it is the realization of a freedom that has cast off the chains within us. Therefore, it is not the Woman Question. It is the Human Question. We can also call it the Religion Question. Thus, in order to resolve the Woman Question on a fundamentally human level, I would like to establish this first essential point.

Second, if this is true, should women be liberated in this way? I say that they should. Raichō said, "I am the Sun." If only everyone could reach this awakening, things would be fine. This is not simply a problem for women; even men must be able to achieve this. Along with the liberation of women, the liberation of men, too, must be accomplished. Aren't today's men just as bewildered as women by their wretched circumstances? Though I am not familiar with the details, it seems that in the society of ancient times, women as well as men lived an abundantly free and healthy life. However, as we opened our eyes to knowledge, men separated themselves from women, those in authority separated themselves from those without authority, people separated themselves from nature, and the inner self separated itself from the outer self. The free and healthy life of the ancients was swept away by waves of class conflict and oppression, war and decay, bringing us to the sad conditions that we have today.

Because there is no mistaking this state of affairs, we need not hesitate any longer. We do not need to submit to this cruel environment forever. Isn't it our mission to sever the iron chains of delusion and realize the free, peaceful life that nature has taught us? Isn't this our destiny? And moreover, isn't this our cause? In ancient times, even when there was no science, no technology, and no machinery, a cheerful, happy, peaceful society flourished. Though many modern people may be baselessly proud of their science, technology, and machinery, with "human" life as fatiguing and debilitating as it is today, what kind of glory do we have? Isn't the saying "Possessing a gem leads to faults" the height of irony for modern people?[23]

Third, if all this is so, under what conditions must we be liberated? I believe that no matter how we may try to justify our present system, as long as a thoroughly communal system is not implemented, thorough and full liberation will not be achieved. This affects men and women equally. After a communal system has come about, both love and marriage will naturally become free. Just because these become free and natural, however, does not mean we need fear promiscuity and adultery, as today's conservative theorists imagine.

According to the leaders in the movement, in the natural society of ancient times, men's and women's sexual relations were completely free, and women enjoyed a central role in society. However, ancient society did not possess the blend of hypocrisy and adultery we see among the ladies of today's civilized society.

Many people also ask, "What will you do with the family if a communal system comes about?" But we do not need to say "We will do this" or "We will do that." Among socialists and communists, there seem to be those who are anti-family, who seek to destroy the family. On the one hand, I feel that the family cannot be so easily dismantled and that it does not need to be dismantled. On the other hand, were there a family system in which the concept of private property had vanished, marriage for money or business had been abolished, and "financially profitable" marriages no longer existed, there would be no marriage bonds other than true love. Consequently, those fortresses of egoism such as today's aristocrats and wealthy families would, of course, come to an end without leaving a trace.

No matter how many disputes there may be, one cannot doubt that the establishment of a communal system offers the surest key to women's liberation. When a communal system can be implemented, scientific knowledge and mechanical power will be utilized for the equal welfare of all. Therefore, today's meaningless, tedious, and excessive labor in the household will become extremely easy, and the household itself will become more sanitary. This will make household servants unnecessary and create for women a great surplus of time and energy. Only under such circumstances will real women's liberation come about. Unless this first step is taken, even if women get voting rights, and even if courts, universities, and government offices in general are opened to women, those who enter these, will, of course, only be women from the influential class; the majority of ordinary women will necessarily be excluded from these circles. Thus, just as class warfare breaks out among men, so class warfare will occur among women.

We will never realize a truly beautiful new paradise for both women and men until we have opened this perfect door to women's liberation. Our essential freedom will here, for the first time, send forth its true light. If we do not exert ourselves, actually striding ahead on the path leading to our liberation, then no matter how lofty the ideal, no matter how powerful the scholarly argument supporting our movement, it is no more than a mirage.

Aiming in this direction, I stand resolved to follow in your footsteps. How do my opinions strike you?

Notes

[1]Much has been written in English about Fukuda Hideko's life. See Sharon L. Sievers, chap. 6, "Women Socialists," in Sievers, *Flowers in Salt: The Beginnings of Feminist Consciousness in Modern Japan* (Stanford, CA: Stanford University Press, 1983), 114–38; Sharlie C. Ushioda, "Fukuda Hideko and the Woman's World of Meiji Japan," in Hilary Conroy et al., eds., *Japan in Transition: Thought and Action in the Meiji Era, 1868–1912* (Rutherford, NJ: Fairleigh Dickinson University Press, and London: Associated University Presses, 1984), 276–93; Mikiso Hane, ed. and trans., "People's Rights and National Rights," in Hane, *Reflections on the Way to the Gallows: Rebel Women in Prewar Japan* (Berkeley and Los Angeles: University of California Press, 1988), which includes Hane's translation of an excerpt of Fukuda's 1904 autobiography *Warawa no hanseigai* (My Life so Far) with a short biography, 29–50; and Vera Mackie, *Creating Socialist Women in Japan: Gender, Labour and Activism, 1900–1937* (Cambridge: Cambridge University Press, 1997). The most frequently cited biography of Fukuda Hideko in Japanese is Murata Shizuko, *Fukuda Hideko* (Iwanami Shoten, 1959).

[2]Fukuda Hideko, "Fujin mondai no kaiketsu" (The Solution to the Woman Question), *Seitō* 3.2 (February 1913), Supplement: 1–7. The censors did not point specifically to any one article in banning the entire issue for being "disruptive of public peace and order." Hiratsuka Raichō suspected that Itō Noe's essay "Konogoro no kansō" (Recent Thoughts), *Seitō* 3.2 (February 1913): 35–44, which is translated in Mikiso Hane, *Peasants, Rebels, Women and Outcastes: The Underside of Modern Japan*, Second Edition (Lanham, MD: Rowman & Littlefield Publishers, Inc., 2003), 257–61, and which condemned the marriage system, could have also provoked the ban. Raichō had no suspicion when she first read Fukuda's article that it would be offensive, and found it well organized, easy to read, and displaying "a masculine assertiveness." Later, Raichō conjectured that Fukuda's association with the socialist group Heimin-sha had concerned the censors more than the content of her article. She also remarks that at one point a rumor got started among the Bluestockings that Fukuda's partner Ishikawa Sanshirō had actually written the article; she does not consider why the women seemed so willing to believe this. Hiratsuka, *Genshi, josei wa taiyō de atta: Hiratsuka Raichō jiden* (Ōtsuki Shoten, 1971–72), 2: 434–39; Hiratsuka Raichō and Teruko Craig, *In the Beginning, Woman Was the Sun: The Autobiography of Hiratsuka Raichō, Japanese Feminist* (New York: Columbia University Press, 2006), 206–9.

[3]Ikeda Emiko, "'Fūzoku kairan' no onna-tachi—hakkin ni ko shite," in Yoneda Sayoko and Ikeda Emiko, eds., *"Seitō" o manabu hito no tame ni* (Kyoto: Sekai Shisōsha,

1999), 200.

[4]See "To My Parents on Becoming Independent," translated in Chapter 4 on Hiratsuka Raichō.

[5]In contrast, in an essay that had appeared in *Seitō* just one month earlier, Katō Midori criticized Fukuda and other activist women of her generation for not being more aware of themselves *as women*. Katō praised Fukuda as a pioneer but faulted her for being overly concerned about men's interests. Katō Midori, "Atarashii onna ni tsuite" (On the New Woman), *Seitō* 3.1 (January 1913), Supplement: 29–35.

[6]Mackie, *Creating Socialist Women in Japan*, 8–9.

[7]Frederick [Friedrich] Engels, *The Origin of the Family, Private Property and the State* (New York: Pathfinder, 1972), was written in 1884 but not translated into Japanese until 1922. Jean-Jacques Rousseau's famous 1762 work *The Social Contract* (trans. Maurice Cranston, Baltimore, MD: Penguin Books, 1968) was translated into Japanese in 1877 and may also have influenced this romanticization of the past.

[8]Mackie, *Creating Socialist Women in Japan*, 8.

[9]Ibid., 3–4.

[10]Hane, *Reflections on the Way to the Gallows*, 30.

[11]When Hiratsuka Raichō first met Fukuda Hideko, she found her intimidating but was also touched by her enthusiasm. Raichō writes that Fukuda's eyes would shine when she talked about her youthful involvement in the Freedom and People's Rights Movement. Hiratsuka, *Genshi, josei wa taiyō de atta*, 2: 439; Hiratsuka and Craig, *In the Beginning, Woman Was the Sun*, 208. For more on Kishida Toshiko (1861–1901), see Marnie S. Anderson, "Kishida Toshiko and the Rise of the Female Speaker in Meiji Japan," *U.S.–Japan Women's Journal*, nos. 30–31 (2006): 36–59.

[12]Hiroko Tomida explains that the school was charged with "violating the Shūkai Jōrei (the Assembly Regulation), and the law to suppress freedom of speech, which prohibited students and teachers from attending meetings to discuss political issues." Hiroko Tomida, *Hiratsuka Raichō and Early Japanese Feminism* (Leiden: Brill, 2004), 69.

[13]Fukuda Hideko soured on Ōi Kentarō when she realized he had lied to her about his several affairs, and when he showed more interest in visiting brothels than working for political change. Hane, *Reflections on the Way to the Gallows*, 31.

[14]Tomida, *Hiratsuka Raichō and Early Japanese Feminism*, 69.

[15]Mackie, *Creating Socialist Women in Japan*, 4.

[16]Mackie also states that Fukuda's "fame spread with the publication of her autobiography *Warawa no Hanseigai* (My Life So Far) in 1904, and the semi-autobiographical novel *Warawa no Omoide* (My Recollections) in 1905." Ibid., 49.

[17]Hane, *Reflections on the Way to the Gallows*, 49.

[18]Officially, Fukuda Hideko did not become Fukuda Yūsaku's wife until her name was entered in the family registry in 1896. As Sharon L. Sievers explains, a wife had no legal status in a family unless her name was entered in the family registry, and it was not uncommon to withhold this recognition from a wife until she had borne sons. By 1896 Hideko had produced two sons by Yūsaku. Sievers, *Flowers in Salt*, 116.

[19]Hiratsuka, *Genshi, josei wa taiyō de atta*, 2: 440; Hiratsuka and Craig, *In the Beginning, Woman Was the Sun*, 209.

[20]Sievers, *Flowers in Salt*, 126–27. This is Sievers' translation of, and citation from, *Sekai fujin* 1 (1 January 1907): 1.

[21]Hiratsuka Raichō's sister Taka befriended Hideko in 1918, buying kimono material from her and inviting her in for meals. The two shared grief over the early deaths of their sons. On her deathbed in 1927, Hideko asked for Taka in order to thank her for her kindness. Hiratsuka, *Genshi, josei wa taiyō de atta*, 2: 441–42; Hiratsuka and Craig, *In the Beginning, Woman Was the Sun*, 209–10.

[22]Hane, *Reflections on the Way to the Gallows*, 33. Hane is quoting and translating a citation in Marukawa Kaseko, "Fukuda Hideko," in Setouchi Harumi, series ed., *Onna no isshō: Jinbutsu kindai josei-shi* (Kōdansha, 1980–81), 6: 100.

[23]According to a dictionary of proverbs, "Possessing a gem leads to faults" stems from a passage entitled "The Tenth Year of the Emperor Kanko" (685–643 BCE) in the *Spring and Autumn Annals*. This passage says that there was once a commoner who had no faults until he came into possession of a gem, something inappropriate to his status. Owning such a valuable object upset his relations with other people and brought him calamity. By extending this metaphor to the modern age, Fukuda shows how social imbalance results when technology and other "gems" of modernity are in the hands of only a few and not used to benefit the whole. Kuramochi Yasuo and Sakata Yukiko, eds., *Kan'yoku kotowaza jiten* (Sanseidō, 1983), 609.

Chapter 3
Harada (Yasuda) Satsuki (1887–1933)

People's private concerns are their own. Humanity as a whole does not determine my personal conduct.

In June 1915, *Seitō* carried a short story arguing for a woman's right to abortion.[1] Abortion was illegal in Japan at the time, and women discovered to have had abortions were increasingly being sent to prison. In retrospect, it hardly seems surprising that government censors banned this issue of *Seitō*. In succeeding months, Bluestockings Hiratsuka Raichō, Itō Noe, and Yamada Waka wrote critically in *Seitō* of the main character's decision to have an abortion. This controversy came on the heels of another Bluestocking debate on sexuality, one on the topic of chastity, which had started in *Seitō* in January 1914. This chapter examines both these well-known debates and connects them to Yasuda Satsuki, the author of the story on abortion and an outspoken participant in the chastity debate. Yasuda Satsuki—who later wrote for *Seitō* under her married name, Harada—firmly believed in women's independence and argued for women to take financial and emotional control of their lives. That Satsuki was ultimately unable to achieve this herself proved to be the tragedy that ended her life.

Born into a prosperous family in Nagaoka City, Niigata Prefecture, Yasuda Satsuki was the youngest of four children and the only girl in her family. When her father, who was a teacher, and her mother retired to Chiba Prefecture in 1896, Satsuki went to Tokyo to live with one of her brothers, who acted as her guardian. Living in the capital, she developed an interest in literature while a student at the prestigious First Tokyo Prefectural School for Girls. About the time of her graduation in 1905, she fell deeply in love, becoming engaged to Kanno Matsutarō, a young man who had good prospects for a career in medicine. The marriage never took place because the Kanno family broke off the engagement when Satsuki contracted tuberculosis. Despondent over this unhappy turn of events, Satsuki went to stay with her parents while she recovered from her illness and the end of her romance. In the meantime, Kanno married a woman selected by his family and went on to become an army surgeon.

In 1912, Satsuki became a member of the Bluestockings. Her first contributions to *Seitō* were short stories. The scholar Ishizaki Shōko remarks on the parallel between the themes in these first stories and Satsuki's failed romance, and speculates that Satsuki's involvement with *Seitō* gave her a way to work through the pain of her broken engagement.[2] The first two stories, "Sayonara" (Goodbye) and "Hachijikan" (Eight Hours), portray a young woman who cannot completely end her relationship with a former suitor even though his family has dissolved their engagement and forced him to marry another woman. Overwhelmed by her feelings for a man and confused about what to do next, the main character in each of these stories can do nothing but pour out her unhappiness.[3] We do not know whether or not Satsuki's former fiancé Kanno, like the love-struck groom in her stories, was the unwilling suitor to his parents' choice of bride. In fiction, at least, he is depicted as equally a victim of his family's conservative attitudes toward marriage.

In 1914, while living with her parents in Chiba and continuing to take care of her health, Satsuki met and fell in love with a musician by the name of Harada Jun (whom Hiratsuka Raichō later referred to in her autobiography as an "habitual womanizer").[4] Harada was thirty-two years old at this time, but his devotion to music had not developed into much of a money-making enterprise. Satsuki realized that she would have to contribute to the family finances if the two were to become an independent married couple. In September 1914, perhaps with capital lent by her brother, Satsuki left her parents' home to open a fruit shop in the Koishikawa section of Tokyo.[5]

Every indication of Satsuki's feelings about the business shows that she felt pride and excitement about opening her shop. She even named it "Satsuki" and placed a small announcement in the December 1914 issue of *Seitō* to entice other Bluestockings to come by for some hot, fragrant Ceylon tea.[6] A photograph of Satsuki sitting at the front of her shop next to boxes brimming with luscious fruit appeared in the December 1915 issue of the magazine *Shukujo gahō* (Ladies' Illustrated).[7] As Itō Noe, who stopped by for tea and fruit, told *Seitō* readers, Satsuki in her apron and simple dress looked every inch the *okami-san*, the wife who manages the shop.[8] Raichō later remarked that, "forthright and capable, even bossy," Satsuki worked very hard at her business, doing all the "negotiating with the wholesale dealers" and "briskly issuing orders to the young male help" at her shop.[9] Ishizaki describes the store not as a place that sold fruit but as a "fruit parlor" where young people who studied the arts dropped by for light refreshments and conversation. This makes "Satsuki" sound like quite the stylish enterprise, one fitting for an intellectual New Woman living in a modern capital.

The shop did not stay open for long, however. Newly pregnant and bothered by morning sickness, Satsuki closed the shop on 8 December 1914, and married Harada the next month.[10] Despite the physical discomforts of her pregnancy, she managed to write regularly for *Seitō* until the birth of her son in August 1915. In 1916, Satsuki, Harada, and their infant son moved to Osaka because of Harada's new job with Takarazuka Girls' Opera Troupe, the first all-women's theater in modern Japan. Satsuki soon bore another child, who developed severe intellectual disabilities after suffering from dysentery. While tending to her children, she also continued to write as much as possible.

Satsuki's belief in expanding women's opportunities remained strong. As a Bluestocking she had attempted to run her own business, and she had argued strenuously in *Seitō* for women to establish financial independence. In Osaka, too, Satsuki continued to urge women to find ways to earn a living. She became active in establishing the Osaka branch of the Shin Fujin Kyōkai (New Woman's Association), and in 1921 wrote an article entitled "Josei no shokuseki to keizai-teki dokuritsu" (Women's Duty to Work and Financial Independence) for their magazine *Josei dōmei* (Women's League). Later, when her husband lost his job and the family moved back to Tokyo in the mid-1920s, she made a living by selling her services in Western-style dressmaking.

The events of Harada Satsuki's later life are sad ones, and ones for which I could find little explanation. In the late 1920s she divorced Harada, taking her eldest son with her and leaving the disabled child with her husband. Once again she developed tuberculosis and, in what must have been a difficult situation for this independent woman, had to rely on the Yasuda family for support. Sick and financially insecure, Harada Satsuki took her life in November 1933. She was forty-six years old. Authorities discovered her body in the middle of the mountains at Hakone Yumoto, a popular mountain retreat not far from Tokyo and near Mt. Fuji. About a month before she disappeared, Satsuki entrusted her registered seal and her will to Hiratsuka Raichō. In her autobiography, Raichō reports feeling honored at the time to have been trusted in this way, though she had no idea of what her colleague intended to do.[11] Apparently, Harada Satsuki is the only one of the Bluestockings to have committed suicide.

As a Bluestocking, Satsuki is best remembered for her role in two of the three major debates in *Seitō* on the topics of chastity, abortion, and prostitution. These debates related to women's sexuality, involved several of the Bluestockings, and extended to articles in newspapers and other magazines as well. The final debate, which was a dialogue on prostitution between Itō Noe and Aoyama (later Yamakawa) Kikue, is discussed in Chapter 5 below. Here, we take up the first two debates, on chastity (*teisō*) and on abortion (*datai*), with which Satsuki is most closely associated, and about which little has appeared in the English-language scholarship on *Seitō*. Examining these debates reveals key themes in Bluestocking creations of the New Woman. It also illumines much about Satsuki's own personality, especially her fervent belief in the New Woman as an independent person who exercised control over her life and her environment. The debate on chastity also introduces us to Bluestocking Ikuta Hanayo (1888–1970), a writer who believed in the New Woman just as strongly as did Satsuki, but who conceived of her position in society quite differently.

A few words about terminology are important here. Throughout the debate, words such as *teisō*, *shojo*, and *dōtei*—terms that could all be interpreted as referring to virginity and the sexually inexperienced woman—occur repeatedly. As Kazue Muta has discussed, they could even be used in this period to refer to an unmarried woman who had borne a child.[12] At times, a Bluestocking does use one of these words to refer specifically to virginity, such as when Ikuta Hanayo realizes that becoming sexually experienced has diminished her marriage prospects. Yet we can see that the discussion also struggles to define sexuality more broadly, especially when Satsuki uses *teisō* to mean a woman's "essential self." Indeed, all the Bluestockings who participated in this debate attempted to wrest women's sexuality away from its role in defining women's position in the existing family system and away from its commodification in a system of exchange. Although they disagreed about how chastity and sexuality should be defined and valued, all saw the New Woman as one who must scrutinize such definitions and act on her own beliefs.

The *Seitō* Debate on Chastity

The debate on chastity was an acrimonious exchange between Yasuda Satsuki and Ikuta Hanayo that also drew responses from Hiratsuka Raichō and Itō Noe, as well as from men writing in other journals. It took place over several months in 1914 and 1915 in at least three journals—*Seitō*, *Shin kōron* (New Review), and *Hankyō* (Echo), a publication initiated by Ikuta Chōkō and Morita Sōhei. The debate provoked disagreement about the value and definition of chastity (*teisō*), different sexual codes for women and men, and the connections between sexuality, the family, and the nation. Confessions, vows, accusations, and gossip—much of it enacted in print—all played a part in this New Woman's drama.

The changing meaning and value of virginity at this time in Japan provided important background to this debate. In her informative article on the sexuality debates in *Seitō* and the increasing significance attached to female

51

virginity in the early 1900s, Iwabuchi Hiroko calls attention to the influence of Christianity—and also to the rising popularity in the 1910s of the belief that a woman's sexual contact with one man would have a genetic effect on the child born of a later union with another man. She also points to the formation of local *shojo-kai* (maidens' associations) all over Japan beginning in about 1900. In 1918 the local associations were centralized by a national umbrella organization, linking female sexuality to propriety and service to the nation. Being a member of one these associations functioned as tacit proof that a girl was innocent of sexual experience and a patriot. Indeed, Noguchi Takenori claims that the advent of these associations marked the first public use of the word *shojo* (virgin), and that the *shojo-kai* in fact represented a deliberate effort on the part of the Meiji state to do away with other kinds of mating customs in rural villages that were now viewed as "barbaric" and "promiscuous."[13]

Yet, as Iwabuchi also points out, resistance among women to this idealization of the virgin bride was evident as well. For two weeks in September 1915, after the *Seitō* debate, the *Yomiuri shinbun* carried a special section of articles on the topic, "Seimei ka teisō ka" (Life or Chastity?). Reader responses were also run as part of the series. Many intellectuals of the day were interviewed, and almost all stressed women's vanity (*kyoeishin*) and lack of proper upbringing (*shūyō no tarinasa*) as the true barriers to the feminine ideal of maintaining chastity. They also upheld the belief that women should defend their chastity even in the face of poverty. Readers offered quite a different viewpoint. They all argued against the intellectuals' position, voicing support for such positions as the establishment of a code of men's chastity (*dansō-ron*) and the importance of a union of the physical *and* the spiritual as the ideal basis for love and marriage, with at least one reader claiming that what truly betrayed women's chastity was forced marriage. The readers' comments, as Iwabuchi says, were exactly in line with the tenor of the essays on love and marriage commonly found in *Seitō*.[14]

Consequently, in September 1914, when Bluestocking Ikuta Hanayo wrote openly about giving up her virginity in order to keep her job, we can assume that she was treading on controversial ground but was not without her sympathizers. As she said over and over, and to Satsuki in particular, one had to know her background to understand why she made the decision to give up her virginity. Hanayo had not been raised in the comfortable prosperity that Satsuki had enjoyed as a girl. A native of Tokushima, Hanayo was the eldest daughter in the Nishizaki family, a family that had lost much of its status in the community in the upheaval of the Meiji Restoration. Despite this decline in family fortunes, Hanayo was able to attend the prefectural girls' school in Tokushima. It was in girls' school that Hanayo, like Satsuki, first developed an interest in literature. The young Hanayo even submitted her first work to literary journals in Tokyo, and continued writing after she graduated and became a teacher. Although accomplished and ambitious, Hanayo felt a nagging sense of inferiority because of her unusually short stature. She later wrote in *Seitō* how much she disliked the way others treated her as a child because of this, yet vowed to turn this "weakness" into "strength."[15]

After her father's death and the family's further financial decline, Hanayo left for Tokyo in 1910, hoping for a career in writing yet briefly finding work again as a teacher. She urged her younger brother to come to the capital as well, hoping to give him the same chance for higher education that she herself had gained. After leaving her teaching post, Hanayo was in danger of running out of money until she finally got a job with a publishing company in 1912. As Hanayo later wrote in a famous essay for *Hankyō*, it was the need to support herself and her brother—and the lack of opportunities for working women in Japan—that forced her to continue working at the publishing company even after being sexually assaulted by her employer. As we will see in the Bluestockings' debate about Hanayo's decision, there is no reference to rape; the discussion is framed solely and rather euphemistically in terms of whether Hanayo was justified in acceding to her employer's demands. It is hard to say if this is due to the other Bluestockings' naïveté about rape, their misunderstanding of the nature of the event, the vague way Hanayo describes it, or their and Hanayo's assumption that a rape victim is somehow to blame for the crime. Notably, this discussion focuses on Hanayo's choice as if culpability in the matter rested with her, as if she did have a choice. Although a much-discussed problem in contemporary Japanese feminism, the issues of rape as a crime and the taboo against women reporting rape do not emerge as topics in this 1914–15 Bluestocking debate.[16] As David Ambaras writes, all young women at this time "had to deny their sexuality, and even those who were victims of sexual exploitation had to endure the unforgiving ministrations and stigmatization imposed by authorities who claimed to protect them."[17]

It was also in 1912 that Hanayo joined the Bluestockings, writing her first essay for *Seitō*'s special section on the New Woman in January 1913, under the pen name Chōsakabe Kikuko. Hiratsuka Raichō wrote of being "filled with awe and admiration" after reading Hanayo's work, commenting that Hanayo was a woman who "knew exactly what she wanted from life and was determined to fight for it." She saw Hanayo's essays as "a naked record of her life, unique and intensely lived," written with a "searing ferocity" unmatched by any other Bluestocking author.[18] In January 1914, Hanayo married the poet Ikuta Shungetsu (1892–1930) only two weeks after meeting him. As the story goes, Ikuta was so moved by Hanayo's impressionistic essays for *Seitō* that he simply had to meet her.

Reading, for example, Hanayo's "Ren'ai oyobi seikatsu-nan ni taishite" (Face to Face with Romantic Love and the Difficulty of Making a Living), one can imagine readers being rather awed by her. In "Ren'ai," Hanayo uses the term *watakushi* ("I") over and over, as if writing into existence a narrator who will have sexual passion, familial love, and adventure in her life no matter what financial difficulties the future holds.[19] Reading Hanayo's fantastic self-portrait, it is easy to imagine that many a reader, like her future husband Shungetsu, would be curious to meet this extraordinary person to see whether she actually did exist or was only a creation on paper.

Although Hanayo's emotive writing won over Ikuta Shungetsu, it did not impress Yasuda Satsuki. Indeed, Satsuki was so offended by Hanayo's September 1914 *Hankyō* essay about her response to her lecherous employer at the publishing company that she felt moved to write an angry retort of her own. Satsuki's essay appeared in the December 1914 issue of *Seitō*. The title of this essay, "Ikiru koto to teisō to" (On Living and Chastity), pointedly reworded the title of Hanayo's article "Taberu koto to teisō to" (On Eating and Chastity). The subtitle of Satsuki's essay announced that this was a response to the *Hankyō* essay. In her essay Satsuki distances herself from Hanayo at every turn, holding fast to an idealistic notion of the New Woman as one whose integrity, self-respect, and sexuality are intertwined, and condemning Hanayo for selling out. Looking at Satsuki's essay in some detail and including her quotes from Hanayo's essay shows how the debate was initially framed.

Using *watakushi* ("I") as frequently in her own essay as Hanayo had in hers, Satsuki opens by describing how she is leaving the shelter of her parents' support to open her own shop and become self-supporting:

> I am who I am. I wish to take all the responsibility for myself. I wish to live by shouldering complete responsibility for myself.[20]

Satsuki moves quickly from discussing her proud independence to launching her attack on Hanayo. Satsuki claims that one cannot "live life" by stooping to the expediency of trading on one's sexuality, selling "one's self" for food. Satsuki quotes some of the lines from Hanayo's *Hankyō* essay that she finds especially distasteful:

> "My younger brother and I had to eat. Back then . . . this is what I [Hanayo] honestly thought . . . getting the two of us enough to eat was of first importance. As for my chastity, that was second. But how I suffered over that tough and painful choice. I thought I

would die. I drank from the cup of hardship. And then I decided that I would transcend that agony. I would live by more than my virginity. That decision made even someone as naïve as I am realize that this was not necessarily impossible to do."[21]

Satsuki finds this last line appalling because Hanayo shows no criticism of her own actions but ultimately takes what she has done in stride. She faults Hanayo for reducing human life—something that Satsuki believes should be treated as an ideal—to a mere animal-like matter of survival. Furthermore, she criticizes Hanayo for thinking sexuality is something that can be separated from one's self and hence parceled out, rather than something that *is* one's self. A New Woman, Satsuki writes, should have more respect for her sexuality and, by extension, for herself and her integrity. Nor does Satsuki have sympathy for Hanayo's defending her actions as unavoidable because she lacked any trustworthy sponsor to whom she could turn for financial support. Satsuki also registers her disapproval of a woman who would give up her chastity in exchange for a marriage made for the sake of her family; she sees such a woman as just as culpable as Hanayo of selling her self-respect. Before anything, Satsuki believes, a New Woman must take responsibility for her sexuality and for her integrity, even if she starves in the course of maintaining these ideals. Satsuki promises that she would do no less. Consequently, Satsuki maintains the ideal of chastity but does not to do so in support of the family system. Rather, she argues for a woman's control over her sexuality as establishing her selfhood. Thus she writes of Hanayo:

> The author surely forgot completely what it means *to live as a person*. Or rather, I suppose, she never knew.[22] (emphasis in the original)

In January 1915, Hanayo, newly married to Ikuta Shungetsu and adopting his family name, came back at Satsuki with a blistering attack of her own in *Hankyō*.[23] Satsuki's retort had clearly injured her pride and her sense of justice. To Hanayo's mind, Satsuki's argument typified the views of many a privileged young lady. Defiant and irate, Hanayo wrote that she, in fact, was the superior (*sempai*) of the two, for she had experienced what it takes to support oneself without any recourse to assistance from others. Hanayo accuses Satsuki of being ignorant, arrogant, cruel, and infinitely less appealing to her than prostitutes or other women who know what it is like to struggle for food. Hanayo describes her own history in detail, arguing that she took control of the situation—to the extent that any choice was left to her—by doing everything she could to keep her job. She asks Satsuki to imagine what it would be like to be a woman in less privileged circumstances:

> In the middle of vast Tokyo, there is a single woman without any relatives to whom she can turn for help. Her heart and her body, too, are exhausted from work. What's more, her younger brother, who has just arrived from a remote part of the countryside, is with her. She is trying to live on only 15 yen per month, and that 15 yen is her only means of support. When she left her last job, she didn't know where she would get her next. She had no idea what to do. She couldn't even die. (On top of all that, she could barely catch her breath for the mental and physical fatigue. She was so tired she couldn't even move). So, there she was without any energy to move, without anywhere to turn, and pressed by the financial responsibility she felt for her brother, and the one and only possession she had to her name was her virginity . . . or, to put this in the most understandable way, the woman's employer sought to make advances on her chastity.[24]

Hanayo assumes that even a hard luck story such as this will not budge Satsuki from her lofty principles. She also takes a sarcastic swipe at Satsuki's now-failed attempts to operate her own "New Woman's business," remarking on how quickly Satsuki closed down the fruit shop after making such a fuss over it. In her long, emotional, and repetitive retort, Hanayo argues that she is more than her virginity, that her sexuality belongs to her, and that Satsuki should take a critical look at the forces that place hundreds of women in the situation where they must choose between selling their sexuality and starving. It is society, she writes, that turns sexuality into something artificial, that makes it a commodity, and that coerces women into either selling or preserving it to ensure their livelihoods. What's more, Hanayo argues, she has been motivated, not victimized, by love—love for her family and for herself—and she finds this a much nobler goal than "living for one's virginity." She and her husband love each other, and his sexuality belongs to her as much as hers does to him. Thus Hanayo expands the idea of *teisō* to include both men and women and to embrace fidelity. She also accepts the possibility, however, that were she and her husband forced into destitution, she might have to resort to prostitution to eke out a living. Angry to the end, Hanayo curses Satsuki in her conclusion:

> Things like understanding, liberation, self-awareness, New Woman, unawakened—these are only words, and you can't hold on to these words forever. You must come down to earth, and when you see your dreams broken one by one, that is when your own growth begins. When you begin to walk out from under the fate that has trampled you, that is precisely when, I swear, true

good fortune shall come to you. When you reach the point where you have "abandoned everything," have known true love and gone bankrupt, then please be good enough to remember me. I am disgusted and angry with you now, but these feelings will soon vanish from my breast. All that will remain will be the knowledge that you are only a person who simply does not know the world. When tears for this transient world well up in your eyes, then please remember me. I shall then for the first time want to meet you, talk with you, and confess all that is in this heart to you.[25]

More indignant than ever, Satsuki responded to Hanayo in the February 1915 issue of *Seitō*. In the meantime, Hanayo had requested a meeting with Satsuki through Bluestocking Araki Ikuko, and had visited her home. The meeting was not a success for either party. Consequently, Satsuki's February essay, "O-me ni kakatta Ikuta Hanayo-san ni tsuite" (On Meeting Ms. Ikuta Hanayo), continues her argument against Hanayo's basic position on chastity and scolds her for behaving badly at their meeting. Satsuki composes her essay as a letter to Hanayo. She admits that Hanayo's essay opened her eyes to the plight of poor women but states that she will not take back one word of her original position. She chastises Hanayo for having turned her sexuality into an ordinary commodity, for having deceived herself into believing that she could separate her sexuality from her integrity like that. Hanayo has scarred that "essential (*essensharu*) aspect of herself" and is too ignorant even to see this. What especially offends Satsuki is how Hanayo patronized her at their meeting without making any sincere effort to understand Satsuki's position. The fact that Hanayo told Araki Ikuko that Satsuki did not comprehend a word Hanayo said but seemed happy enough to be flattered only adds to Satsuki's ire.[26]

Itō Noe, who was chief editor of *Seitō* by this time, joined the conversation with an essay that also appeared in the February 1915 issue of *Seitō*. She criticized Hanayo for not truly having transcended the old morality. She writes that Hanayo had mourned her virginity only because it made her less able to marry, thus replicating an old-fashioned notion of women's sexuality. Moreover, she charged that Hanayo fairly wallowed in tears of self-pity rather than asserting herself as a woman breaking free of convention. To Noe's way of thinking, the issue of chastity had no place in a relationship between a man and a woman that was based on love. But if chastity were made a concern, she wrote, men should be held to the same standards as women.[27]

Hiratsuka Raichō, who had boycotted her girls' school class in morals because of its tiresome Confucian insistence on women protecting their chastity above all else, jumped into the debate, too. Responding in the journal

Shin kōron, Raichō defines *shojo* (virgin) as "a woman who has not had sexual experience" and states that the value of the sexual experience is something to be determined by the individual, not by society. She believes that virginity should be given up when the individual believes the time is right, and that not doing so at the right time would be as unfortunate as having a sexual relationship at the wrong time. Raichō holds that the "right time" comes when spiritual love for the other prompts physical desire and promotes a true union of two people. She condemns coerced marriages, equating women's forfeiture of their virginity in such unions as equal to impoverished women selling theirs.[28] Writing on a related topic later, in October 1916, Raichō further argues that the legal and moral borders of sexual practices have been drawn in a discriminatory way that accords maximum freedom to men, whether they are single or married, while confining women's sexuality.[29]

By April 1915, Ikuta Hanayo was reflecting on the debate from a purely personal point of view. In "Zange no kokoro yori: Hiratsuka Raichō, Itō Noe, Harada-sama ni yosete" (From a Repentant Heart: To Hiratsuka Raichō, Itō Noe, and Ms. Harada), Hanayo admits that she has learned from Raichō, been moved by Noe, and owes Satsuki an apology for having criticized her as being dishonest. Yet the real message of Hanayo's essay lies in her description of how undone she was by the experience of being roundly criticized for the first time in her life. The past year has also been her first with Ikuta Shungetsu, and while she has finally become free of financial worries, she is troubled about whether or not she has loved her husband well and truly. Hanayo also feels she has accomplished nothing in the past year except becoming a mere dependent. In the end, she adheres to the idea that confession (*kokuhaku*) remains the only way for her to make sense of her experience, and that she must strive to make her life authentic as she experiences it and as she recounts it:[30]

> I have no talent other than for recounting my experience. I do not know theory, I have no ability to argue, and, what's more, I have no discernment and I am not a clear-headed person. I suppose all I can do is confess my way of living. So, if my life is boring, my confession will be boring, too. How shall I improve myself? Because then I want to make a genuine confession.[31]

Thus at the conclusion of this debate in *Seitō*, Ikuta Hanayo pulls the conversation back to the point of personal experience, rather than pursuing her rejection of the social system that provided so few economic opportunities for women that some of them faced the choice of "eating or chastity." As we saw, this is also the realm in which Harada Satsuki places the issue. In the end, both women firmly resist more broadly examining the system that commodifies women's virginity and sexuality, its gender biases, and its connections to other social hierarchies. Yet their disagreement, conducted mostly in print, did lead to responses from several quarters that turned further critical attention toward the issue of sexuality.[32] Throughout the Bluestockings' debate, we find sexuality increasingly regarded as a matter of the contingent and the "social," rather than as something "natural." For Satsuki and Hanayo, however, the realm of the "natural" has great appeal. It is where the New Woman can attempt to live the authentic life she values, to define herself, and to speak with authority. Such a pristine space of personal freedom is hardly possible, but even imagining such a sphere threatened the social framework of their day.

Reflecting on the debate between Satsuki and Hanayo much later in her autobiography, Hiratsuka Raichō wondered whether Satsuki's uncompromising refusal to acknowledge the power of social and economic constraints was the failing that led her to suicide. Hanayo, in contrast, weathered many setbacks in her life, including her husband's 1930 suicide. She lived to the age of eighty-two, supporting herself after the war by giving classes on the Heian classic *The Tale of Genji*.[33]

The *Seitō* Debate on Abortion

Although Ikuta Hanayo criticized Yasuda Satsuki for being callous toward the poor, Satsuki displays great empathy for a woman caught in difficult circumstances in her June 1915 story, "To My Lover from a Woman in Prison." Her admiration for individual people who adopt difficult but independent stances is evident here. The story also reiterates her position that a woman must take responsibility for her sexuality and must exercise control over her body, no matter what the consequences. Satsuki wrote this story after being moved by reading the newspaper account of a woman jailed for having an abortion. Although her readers did not know it, Satsuki was pregnant at the time she wrote the story and troubled over finances herself. To appreciate why this story provoked the reaction it did, we need to broaden our perspective by understanding what it meant to have an abortion in Japan in 1915.

Although abortion was illegal at the time, this particular prohibition did not in the main stem from concerns about the intrinsic value or the autonomy of either the fetus or the mother, nor was the law defended or decried by religious groups.[34] The prohibition did build on earlier Japanese proscriptions against abortion and, like these, was guided largely by the interests of the state. Modern Japanese anti-abortion laws—influenced first by French codes in 1880, and then revised according to German law in 1907—and particularly the laws' aggressive enforcement in the 1910s, owed much to concerns for national defense. Japanese leaders sought to increase the strength and size of the population in order to build the nation's industrial and military might, making it competitive with the world powers. These goals encouraged the government to prohibit abortion, and to obligate a woman to register her pregnancy with local authorities. The registration policy enabled officials to introduce pregnant women to public health educators as well as to keep a watchful eye out lest a woman attempt an abortion. In the 1910s, when the government actively began arresting women who did have abortions, the rate of those jailed for illegal abortions rose higher each year.

Yet, as Hiratsuka Raichō mentions in her *Seitō* piece on this subject, the possibility of prosecution was not the only deterrent to having an abortion, for the procedure itself was physically dangerous.[35] The alternative of inducing miscarriages did not lead to safer methods: women were known to resort to jumping from high places, immersing themselves in icy cold water, piercing the uterus with a sharp object, ingesting poison, or using a mercury-based vaginal suppository to provoke a miscarriage. That most of the Bluestockings had only a few children suggests that educated, urban woman must have been making use of some methods to control their reproductive lives.[36]

Turning to Satsuki's story, "To My Lover from a Woman in Prison," we see that the author follows a narrative style and viewpoint common to *Seitō* fiction. Satsuki invites the reader into the narrator's private life, and accords more value to her private sense of morality than to the public values that view abortion as a crime. We also encounter in this story a representation of a kind of New Man—frequently seen in *Seitō*—who is sensitive and romantic, who loves and understands the New Woman, and who shares her devotion to creative work and independence. The love and work that the couple shares take absolute precedence over the demands of the state, and are viewed as the representation of a higher, more genuine sense of ethics. While the angry judge in the case disparages the woman as selfish and irrational, the woman believes that she holds to values that are well worth her current sacrifice. Interestingly, though Satsuki consistently argued in the chastity debate for the self as an organic physical, spiritual, and intellectual whole, and faulted Hanayo for daring to see her sexuality as something apart, she creates a character who represents the fetus as a part of the body, like the arm. What is consistent in Satsuki's thought is her belief in the individual woman's right—even obligation—to govern her own body. Sabine Frühstück summarizes the radical message of Satsuki's story as telling *Seitō* readers "to follow their own dictates, even in violation of the law, and . . . to have abortions if motherhood was going to be difficult."[37]

Government censors took exception to this position. In the Editors'

Notes at the end of the July 1915 issue of *Seitō*, Itō Noe had this to report to her readers:

> The sale of last month's issue was banned as being "injurious to public morals" (*fūzoku kairan*). It appears that the offending piece is Ms. Harada's because nothing else in the issue comes close to something that would provoke concern. I didn't find any problem with the story. . . . I published it because I found it to be an excellent treatment of a single issue, yet I was scolded for being an imprudent editor. I have heard men's opinions on the topics of abortion and contraception, but I have not heard what women think. This is what I wanted to know, and I still feel that way, even now.[38]

Such censorship did not intimidate the Bluestockings: Hiratsuka Raichō, Itō Noe, and Yamada Waka published opinions on abortion, all in the form of letters, in *Seitō* that summer. Censors did not interfere with the publication of these letters, no doubt because all opposed the position on abortion promoted in Satsuki's story. None of these three responses questions the state's right to interfere in pregnancy, as Satsuki does. Rather, Raichō, Noe, and Waka debate the issue in terms of the relationship between the mother and the fetus, and the future economic, spiritual, and psychological well-being of both. The subject was more than academic for the women involved: like Satsuki, both Raichō and Noe were pregnant at this time. Yamada Waka, having been forced into prostitution in North America for many years, was probably infertile yet valued motherhood and maternal love above all else.

Itō Noe (see Chapter 6) includes her thoughts on Satsuki's story in a rambling letter to her friend Nogami Yaeko, which she published in the September 1915 issue of *Seitō* under the title "Shishin: Nogami Yae-Sama e" (Private Message to Ms. Nogami Yae). Noe begins by considering the heart of Satsuki's narrator's argument—namely, her fears that she lacks the qualifications necessary to be a good parent. Writing that she has pondered this problem herself, Noe concludes that only someone who is seriously mentally or physically deficient can argue that she is incapable of being a parent. Women who do not want to have children for any other reason should use contraception. But Noe makes it clear that she does not extend this acceptance of contraception to approval of abortion:

> My first reaction is that abortion is extremely unnatural. At any rate, we cannot determine how the unborn child might flower or might wither and die. While none of us truly knows what fate lies in store for the unborn child, we do know for a fact that life has taken hold. No matter how many excuses one might make to jus-

tify destroying this life for the sake of one's own convenience in this or that area, is it not, in truth, a deed which insults nature? Is it not a deed which shows complete disregard for *life*?[39] (emphasis in the original)

Noe continues her remarks by taking exception to specific arguments in Satsuki's story. While Satsuki has compared the fetus with "the egg a woman gives up every month," Noe draws a distinction between the fertilized egg, which she says has a certain destiny to live, and the unfertilized egg, which does not have this destiny. To destroy the fertilized egg, according to Noe, is unnatural; the unfertilized egg, in contrast, is naturally discharged. Second, Noe objects to the comparison that Satsuki's heroine makes between her arm and her unborn child. Arguing that a child has a life as an arm does not, Noe finds ridiculous the very notion of comparing undergoing an abortion to cutting off one's arms:

> Ms. Satsuki has apparently said that while the child is inside her womb, it is one part of her body. I believe that while the child is inside me, it properly has its own *life*, and no matter how incomplete or faint its life might be, the child is indeed living. This is where my thinking and Satsuki's diverge.[40]

Tackling one of the main arguments in favor of abortion found in Satsuki's story, Noe considers the parents' poverty and lack of education as grounds for an abortion. Since Noe has personally experienced poverty, she is sympathetic to this reasoning. Yet because she found the courage to surmount worries of this sort in order to have her child, in the end Noe must attack this point also. In line with many other *Seitō* essayists, Noe refers to her personal experience in explaining why she cannot condone abortions for financial reasons:

> Every time I used to feel my first child breathing inside my body, I, too, agonized over just that problem. As you know, we were in the depths of poverty at that time. I felt distress about our financial trouble only because of the child. Yet whenever I was worried, [my husband] would say, "If it were a child who did not have the strength to fight back, who could not withstand this kind of lifestyle, then I don't expect it would have been conceived."[41]

As Noe progresses with this argument, one can see that she has extended her respect for nature to a belief in the power of (natural) fate. Although Noe does not hesitate to rebel against the conventions contrived by society, she shows a willingness to accept fate's judgment:

> I thought about how true [what my husband Tsuji Jun had said] was. And I thought about how I couldn't know if my child would come to term or not, and about how we couldn't even know what our own lives might be like the next day. In the end, the child does have his own fate. It isn't necessarily bad to be born poor, and certainly it was the child's destiny to be born into this environment. If the child had been destined to be born into wealth, then I am sure we would have miraculously escaped poverty by the time he was born. If the child could not have survived this environment, then there would have been nothing else for him to do but die a natural death.[42]

After the birth of her first child, Noe confesses that she, too, worried about not being able to educate him properly. In the end, she decided that people cannot educate one another. Furthermore, parents should worry less about educating their children and making them conform to their ideals than about impeding children's natural development. In the final analysis, Noe says that her belief in the life and destiny of the unborn child must lead her to disagree with the arguments in Satsuki's story.

Yamada Waka (see Chapter 11), who has been described as "one of the most prominent maternity ideologues of the Taishō and early Shōwa eras,"[43] contributed two pieces to the debate, both in the form of letters, which appeared in the September and October 1915 issues of *Seitō*. The letters revolve around her belief in the sacredness of nature and an idealization of maternal love, which was likely inspired by her study of the maternal feminist Ellen Key (1849–1926). Since Waka had been sold into prostitution in North America and forced to work many years before her escape, one might expect her to show sympathy for women who said that they wanted or needed an abortion. Waka makes no reference to her former enslavement and shows no compassion for poor women whose financial conditions would drive them even to an unsafe, illegal abortion. In fact, Waka sees the "lower classes" as especially in need of recognizing the wisdom both of following nature and of controlling sexual desire.

In her September 1915 letter, Waka begins by stating that the key to happiness lies in following the "laws of nature." Although Waka does not give the reader any specific idea of what such laws might be, she says that people should direct all their efforts to following them:

> By exhausting the limits of human intelligence and discovering the laws of nature, and by living obediently in accordance with those laws, we can obtain limitless happiness. Yet obeying these natural laws inevitably causes a terrific struggle for us. When we believe, "This is the way of nature," and try to go forward in that

> direction, we face the barriers of narrow views and all kinds of
> vices that we must fight and remove at all costs. Religion, philoso-
> phy, science—all are no more than tools for discovering the laws
> of nature and removing the obstacles that impede the function of
> those laws.[44]

Waka goes on to equate morality with discovering the laws of nature. As the modern world has grown complicated, she explains, this is not an easy task: concepts of morality change, and actions considered immoral one day are found to be permissible the next. Still, amid this confusion, Waka believes that there is no greater force than a mother's love for her child. For her, maternal love embodies the soul of femininity and, following Ellen Key, provides the departure point for all morality.

Waka next turns to the theme of selfishness and how a desire for one's own narrow happiness prevents people from having children. She sees this as especially dangerous among educated people because their not having children weakens the race. She realizes that the term *jiga* (self, or ego) has become very popular, and she supports respect for the individual. But Waka also says that there can be no absolute *jiga*; everyone is connected to society in some way. If it were possible for one to exist without connection to society, then one would be no more than a wild animal. She also says, but does not explain, that if society would no longer trample on *kosei* (individual personality), there would be no need to worry about *jiga*. Happiness, for Waka, lies in a blend of respect for individuality and nature, and individual responsibility to society. Having described what she sees as the basis for judging ethical conduct, Waka considers the issues of contraception and abortion. In an unusual move for a *Seitō* writer, Waka also gives weight to the needs of the state:

> Thinking this way leads me to say that both abortion and contra-
> ception are equally great crimes. They are immoral acts that de-
> stroy the happiness of the individual as well as the prosperity of
> the nation.[45]

To prevent people from resorting to contraception and abortion, Waka calls for responsible love relationships and self-sacrifice. To explain herself further, Waka introduces doubts that a "friend" of hers has raised about Waka's argument, and then answers these for her reader. First of all, the friend asks whether contraception and abortion would be permissible in cases where one does not have enough to eat. Waka coolly responds to this question by saying that one has a duty to improve one's financial situation before taking a spouse. Also, Waka says, if one's personal situation does not suit raising a child, then one must take precautions to control one's sexual desire until one can either leave the situation or improve it. She hesitates to put too much emphasis on economic preparation for child-rearing, saying that there are more important qualifications for parenthood.

Waka takes a stern line in cautioning people to control their sexual desire as a means to prevent unwanted pregnancy. She even ventures so far as to say that not exercising control should be a crime punishable by law when it results in unplanned pregnancies. Taking a particularly elitist view, Waka says that whereas educated people do not need such laws to make them aware of the need to practice self-control, the lower classes do. According to Waka, it is beneficial for the poor to learn self-control. Waka quotes her "respected friend" as arguing with her on this point:

> "Well, maybe people like us can control ourselves, but what about when we consider the lower classes of society? Simply to decide that abortion is an unqualified sin for those who lead such wretched lives—how many sad situations will that kind of thinking cause? In cases where the mother and child can get enough to eat, or when people already have several children, it would be best if the state provided certain guarantees, but because such do not exist, wouldn't it be better to permit abortion than to be left with many unsound children?"[46]

Waka responds by agreeing that the state should help mothers and children in straitened circumstances, but she also declares that the fact that no such support exists is no excuse for abortion. Similarly, Waka argues, though one can sympathize with the poor person who steals food in order to eat, the nation cannot condone stealing. In sum, Waka believes that only when the life of mother is in danger can society allow abortion.

In her second letter on the subject, published in October 1915, Waka responds to criticism by a certain Mr. Suzuki that her call for control of instinctive sexual desire runs counter to her argument that people should follow the laws of nature. What, asks her critic, could be more natural than sexual instincts? Suzuki also finds it hard to believe that Waka would expect the lower classes—which, he says, tend toward instinctual behavior because they are uneducated and overworked—to accept such an idealistic view of love and sexual behavior.

Waka answers by explaining her views on the difference between animal and human responses to instinct. Whereas animals have no choice but to follow their instincts, humans must exercise control over theirs. According to Waka, because humans live in this imperfect state of nature, they make progress—unlike animals. Thus, Waka argues, the key to poor people's own progress lies in learning how to practice self-control:

> Lower-class people remain in their wretched circumstances be-
> cause they follow irrational, unrefined instincts. Agreed, it is not
> inconceivable that given their lack of education and leisure time,
> they tend to behave instinctually. Yet can we simply say, "Well,
> they're hopeless," and forgive them for destroying something so
> immeasurably valuable as a human life? If thinking people take
> such an attitude toward poor people, when can the poor ever es-
> cape their wretched conditions? Although I know that this is not
> an easy task, I believe that there is no other way to save the lower
> classes from misery than by guiding them from their irrational
> (*irashonaru*) instincts to the rational (*rashonaru*).[47]

As for middle- and upper-class people, Waka advises that since women
are spiritually superior to men, they must guide men in controlling sexual
desire.

One can see how Waka veers in this essay from any mention of her own
background. Placing all responsibility for sexual conduct on the individual
person, she pointedly ignores discussing her enslavement. Taking this line,
Waka extends earlier images of the New Woman articulated in *Seitō*. She
envisions the individual woman—at least the educated, middle-class woman—as a virtuous and powerful individual. Her strength of character allows
her to transcend economic and social problems, and the sexual demands of
men, in order to live an ethical life. Her sexuality leads to motherhood, maternal love, and maternalist ethics. The New Woman's virtue does not arise
from merely following conventional morality, although at times she may
agree with it. Rather, her honor lies in reaching beyond the material world
to discover certain "natural" truths that she can then apply to her conduct
in everyday life.

In August 1915, Hiratsuka Raichō joined the *Seitō* discussion on abortion with an essay in the form of a letter to Itō Noe, "Kojin toshite no seikatsu to sei toshite no seikatsu to no aida no sōtō ni tsuite: Noe-san ni" (On
the Conflict Between Life as an Individual and Life as a Sexual Being: To
Ms. Noe). In this letter, Raichō begins to elaborate an idealization of motherhood—the position for which she was to become so well known in her
post-*Seitō* writing (as explained in the Chapter 4 below). At the outset of her
letter, Raichō admits to having followed Satsuki and Noe's writing on the
subject with interest, and being unsure of how to respond. Although she has
written about the Woman Question and has translated Ellen Key's work,
Raichō states that being pregnant has given her a new perspective on such
issues as abortion, contraception, and motherhood. The matter is no longer
simply academic for her:

> I am finally able to consider these issues in a truly serious way, no longer as a bystander or simply as someone thinking intellectually about the Woman Question. These are my own problems, problems that directly affect my life. Or rather, it is not so much that I have grown better able to consider these issues as that I have been forced into a position where I cannot help but think about them. Now I must evaluate these problems from the standpoint of a full awareness of myself as a woman.[48]

Raichō explains how the reality of her own pregnancy has driven her to contemplate motherhood, and she thinks back on Noe's first pregnancy as an example of how impending motherhood could change a woman. She recalls how shy Noe was about her first pregnancy, her reluctance to talk about it, and how pregnancy suddenly changed Noe, a strong-willed and self-assertive person, into an expectant mother who would not hesitate to sacrifice herself for her child. Raichō also assumes that Noe's opposition to abortion expressed in her "Private Message to Ms. Nogami Yae" reveals an unconscious maternal love for the (second) child she was carrying at the time she wrote it. (By the same token, Raichō imagines that Satsuki's acceptance of abortion stems from the fact that she has not yet experienced motherhood.)[49] Observing Noe's transformation, however, has made Raichō doubt her own ability to become a mother. It has also made her realize what she terms the contradictions between a woman's "mission for the race" and the "individual needs" of her own life and work.

Raichō sympathizes with some aspects of Noe's and Satsuki's ideas, yet she remains disappointed that neither woman addressed these contradictions. She finds that they dealt only with children's lives and overemphasized the financial burdens of parenthood, while neglecting the impact of child-rearing on the mother. In making this charge, Raichō frames her discussion in terms of the New Woman's needs for autonomy and self-expression. Raichō also shows how much she conceives of the New Woman as middle class and educated—and as far superior to the poor, "unawakened" woman:

> The two of you certainly gave me the impression that you were not much disturbed by the difficulty women face in trying to fulfill their mission for the race as *sexual beings* while attempting to fulfill their own personal needs as *individuals*. If you were traditional or average Japanese women who had no awareness of yourselves as individuals and had nothing you could call your own life, I would not expect you to consider this. Furthermore, if you were lower-class laborers who had no education whatsoever and considered eating the "be all and end all" of life, I would not expect you to think of this either. But I find it very strange that women like you would not see this difficulty.[50] (emphasis in the original)

Raichō explains the conflict that she has felt about seeing herself as a sexual being, let alone as a mother. She recalls how she has written against the practices that enslave women in the family and has expressed her indignation toward women who are satisfied with their position and lack any critical approach to thinking about the family. Rather than wanting to become a wife and mother herself, she had turned to Buddhist ideas of sexual abstinence as one path to enlightenment. Raichō further explains that after falling in love with Okumura Hiroshi, she felt a strong desire to live with him and made a choice to do so. Living with Hiroshi, she believes, has shown her that women do not always love out of obligation. This experience, combined with her reading of Ellen Key, has made her realize that love and sex are also important aspects of a woman's life, and this has changed her views on the Woman Question:

> And so, for the first time ever, I realized that not only must we liberate women as human beings and as individuals but we must also liberate women as women. At this time, the one who gave me support and provided me direction, who led me out of the impasse of my own thought, was the author Ellen Key.[51]

Life with Hiroshi has helped her mature, but even this has also conflicted with her work. Now she fears that motherhood will compound this conflict. Raichō adds that she imagines men face many struggles in their own lives, as individuals and as family men, though she wonders whether they have to struggle as much as women do to unify their work and their family life. Raichō has wanted to avoid motherhood because of her desire to satisfy the needs that she has long seen as integral to the New Woman's happiness. Here she raises some of the same concerns about parenthood voiced by Noe in her "Private Message to Ms. Nogami Yae" and by the narrator in Satsuki's "To My Lover from a Woman in Prison":

> First of all, what has always been more important for me than anything else is my own self-development and building my inner life as an individual and as a human being. For that purpose, I have always wanted to have as much time as possible for quiet thought and study as well as for my work. Also, I have wanted as much as I can have—and must have—of the strength required to pour myself into these efforts. Second, I could never find anywhere in our love even the least desire for a child or the desire to become a parent. Thus, even though this [pregnancy] may be the inevitable result of love and also chance, I have thought it was a sin against the child and against ourselves to produce a child whom we did not intend or desire; I felt we lacked the prime qualification for becoming parents. Third, I have worried that the poverty in which

we presently live will be an unsuitable environment in which to educate and support the child, and that we might not be able to carry out our responsibility as parents.[52]

Given her reservations about pregnancy, Raichō imagines that one would expect her to use contraception, and she admits to practicing contraception in the past. In explaining why she ceased to do so, Raichō exhibits a conflict between her desire for independence and a need to idealize love. Raichō states that she has no real opposition to contraception and can see where, in cases of overpopulation, nations would even want to encourage it. Yet contraception has never appealed to her personally. She feels that to deny the possibility of conception soils the sexual union of two lovers and is, in that sense, even more objectionable than abortion.

Raichō also admits that, for a very brief time, she considered having an abortion as a way to escape from her present situation. Unlike Itō Noe and Yamada Waka, Raichō does not believe abortion is always wrong. Indeed, she says that in certain cases it might be the wisest choice. In her own case, Raichō did not choose to have an abortion for fear that it might physically harm her. She was even more concerned that it might harm her emotionally. In the end, Raichō decided not to have an abortion, she writes, because doing so might cause her future regrets.

After Raichō decided not to have an abortion, she rather abruptly began to think about her pregnancy in new and positive ways. This leads her to believe that she had secretly wanted a child all along:

> I realized that even I had a hidden desire to become a mother and to have the child inside me whom I had once thought meant nothing at all. I assume that these desires had never surfaced before because I had so many other strong desires. I imagine that even from the beginning of our longing for each other's love, we have been, however reluctantly, gradually nurturing a desire to have a child. The only problem was that we were not able to sense this.[53]

Thinking along these lines led Raichō to feel as though denying her child would be equivalent to denying her love for Hiroshi. She also decided that even if she were not in the perfect situation to raise a child, she was still more qualified to do so than poor or "unawakened" women:

> I know that there are still other needs in my life that will prevent me from devoting myself to nurturing and educating my child. This will surely distress me and may be unfortunate for the child as well. Yet when one compares my child's situation with that of most Japanese children today, my child will doubtless be more

fortunate than the majority of children who are born of loveless relationships and raised irresponsibly by mothers who are completely unaware and unintelligent.[54]

Still concerned about how she will divide her time between her family and her work, Raichō explains that she is now considering plans advocated by Western women. Charlotte Perkins Gilman proposes that women continue their work by having others raise their children. Ellen Key writes glowingly of the spiritual rewards of raising a child. Unsure of which path she will take, Raichō declares that she faces a difficult problem, one that has made her see the Woman Question from a new perspective:

> Be that as it may, how am I to choose between all the possibilities in my life and all the aspects of my self? How should I integrate these choices and bring harmony to my life? Now I am confronting the Woman Question as I never have before. Or, rather, I should say that the Woman Question has become real to me, suffusing every part of my life with its complexity and its true significance. And from this time forward, I must resolve this question, using my own life as an example. But I do not face this task alone. I believe that this question weighs on the majority of today's Japanese women as our common problem.[55]

****

To My Lover from a Woman in Prison
Yasuda Satsuki
Seitō 5.6 (June 1915)

Part One

Nothing but one gloomy day follows another for me, and I have completely lost track of how many already have come and gone. When I am in here like this, I become achingly homesick for the world outside—to be near you, to be at your side. I imagine you are working at that table, aren't you? Last night I thought about how the flower in the bud vase has probably withered, its petals falling off. Nevertheless, you hadn't thrown away this tattered blossom, I imagined, but were gazing at it for me. You see, I have had some pretty strange thoughts in here, such as your hugging that nightgown of mine all full of patches as you go to sleep every night. And then these things I dream about all seem to become real. I even get the feeling that I am actually seeing them, that I know for a fact that they are true. Do tears come to your eyes when I write this kind of letter? Then go ahead and cry for me. And work with all your might to make up for my suffering like this.

I certainly worry about you. I am afraid that you may be troubled by what's happened and feeling miserable about it. However, since no matter what comes my thoughts won't change, and since the law will most likely proceed according to its own conventions, there is nothing at all worth worrying about.

The only thing that really concerns me is that you may be thinking of turning your back on the promise you once made to me in some attempt to share my distress. Being apart from you, I am no longer at all sure of what is in your heart. But if, because of your feelings for me, you let yourself fall into this same gloomy world I inhabit, then not only will you die, but I also will die.

I realize I am repeating myself here, but please leave all the responsibility in this matter to me. And please concentrate solely on your work. By saying that I am thinking only of you and describing my tender, womanly feelings, I do not mean to make you cry. For if you work as we agreed, I will live in your work. If you pity me, then please, love your work, and love me, too. Embrace my nightclothes, and my kimono or my rice bowl or my chopsticks or my comb or my powder-case—please kiss whatever is mine. And even though I am here, I will feel it all.

I imagine that you are being showered with insults. "There goes the lover of the woman who had the abortion!" You probably want to come right back at them with "What's it to you?" Imagining you doing this makes me want to laugh out loud. Whatever happens is all right though, you know. The two of us know who we are. Or, not the two of us, because the two of us are really one, aren't we? This makes me so happy.

Even when I am exhausted from the daily interrogation, I remember that at that very moment there is someone hard at work who knows me inside out. And when I think that you know all there is to know about me, then even if the whole world spits on me, I feel content.

Part Two

Furious, the judge pounded on his desk, declaring it a crime worse than nihilism, a crime that showed no thought about either the destruction of human life or the breakdown of morality. This happened after he'd asked me, "Now, then, don't you think you've done anything wrong?" and I had answered him with this: "I believe it was wrong. I really do. But what I believe was wrong was the fact that I was careless, and that was because I'd had no experience with pregnancy. It was very wrong not to have taken precautions to prevent a pregnancy, especially as I knew that I did not yet have the capacity to become a mother." I was astonished to see the judge get so angry that he turned red in the face. I had been looking at the ground, responding to the question, when the sound of his fist striking the desk startled me into looking up at his face. How threatening it seemed! I stared at that face.

"Don't you realize that you have arbitrarily destroyed a human life?" he shouted.

I responded a bit sarcastically with, "A woman's body casts away an egg cell every month. I could not feel any life or personality in that egg just because conception had occurred—I suppose because I thought of it as nothing more than a mere appendage to my body—much less could I feel anything like an instinctive love. And who's ever heard of anyone being called a criminal for cutting off her own arm?"

I bet this makes you laugh, and think, "Oh no, she's being sarcastic again!" I said several more silly things, but he asked me such ludicrous questions, like "Didn't you know that if you lived with a man you could get pregnant?" When I said, "Yes, I knew," he asked, "If you felt you weren't qualified to become a parent, then why did you move in with the man?"

How does that strike you? To tell you the truth, I thought it was ridiculous. Imagine making mathematical calculations for the subtle instincts and feelings of human beings—well, even if the judge can do that, I certainly can't. But as for having been careless in taking on a responsibility we could not carry out, we were, indeed, at fault and had not given the matter enough thought. But, given what happened, didn't I take the best way out? If I had simply admitted that I had been careless and let things take their course, I would have been doubly guilty of not giving the pregnancy enough thought. Didn't I avoid falling into the trap of such thoughtlessness by taking the action I did?

The judge's question struck me as so ridiculous that I finally laughed right out loud. And then I came back with this: "If you don't know that, sir, but wish to inquire, then I suggest you consider that the Creator knows better than I." I can't help it—even now this seems funny to me. Where is there a defendant who talks back like this? I bet you think it's funny, too, don't you? But when I saw how shocked the judge looked, I suddenly felt sympathy for him. And when I realized that this was a place where nothing other than dead seriousness is permitted, I could not laugh any longer. After this, an intense interrogation followed. The judge had taken what I'd said about my arm and the fetus being the same as some unforgivable and alarming idea. But thinking that I would really like him to understand me, I spoke at great length.

Responding to his question, "Why is the fetus an appendage?" I said, "If an arm is cut off, it has no use and no life at all of its own, but a fetus does have the potential for life, and that is where the only difference between the two lies." I knew that if I paused even a moment there, the judge would quickly try to jump in and I would lose my chance to speak, so I went on without stopping:

"Precisely because a fetus has the potential for life, I felt I had to do what I did. If, no matter how much time went by, it were to have no life and no humanity, then one would not feel particularly responsible for letting things take their course. But a fetus, as soon as it separates from my body, has already moved away from my control and has come into possession of its own precious, individual life and personality. Furthermore, it becomes the parents' responsibility to discover and nurture the abilities that sustain that personality—unique abilities hidden deep within that individual. Considering that parents must do this without any mistakes, one cannot help but feel an overwhelming sense of responsibility. The saying 'If you make a mistake, just do it again correctly' is a phrase that does not apply to our responsibilities to others."

Thus I explained that I had by no means acted rashly or selfishly in this matter. Didn't I think about it day after day, without even talking to you about it? All this I told to the judge.

"At any rate, because this had happened on account of my own carelessness—because I was pregnant—I felt I must exert all my effort for the sake of the child who was to be born. If even my best efforts should fall short, I would have to ask the child to bear with me. Anyway, I felt it would be enough to direct all my energy toward the child I was carrying."

I told the judge this was what I thought when I first learned I was pregnant. He nodded his head several times, as if to say that this would have been the right thing to do. However, when I did not continue in this vein, he no longer appeared to agree with me.

Part Three

I went on, saying, "In the beginning, I was determined to do this, but when I thought about it a bit further, I realized that while this was convenient for me, it had nothing at all to do with the child's welfare. People conceive children without being in the least aware that, from the start, they are bringing successors into this world. At least, this was true of me. And, of course, children do not ask to be born. Is there anything in the world more terrifying than thoughtlessly and without preparation bringing a precious life out of nothingness and into existence, especially when one realizes that one is not yet up to that responsibility? If the fetus had already matured and left my womb, I would have had to swallow my tears and endure whatever unsatisfactory circumstances arose. But as long as a fetus has not matured, it is still just one part of the mother's body. Therefore, I believe it is well within the mother's rights to decide the future of the fetus, based on her own assessment of its best interests.

If the mother dies, the fetus will inevitably meet the same fate. And I know that the law permits the killing of the fetus for the sake of saving the mother's life. But I did not abort this child for my sake; I aborted it for its own sake. If this were purely my own concern, I could always try to correct any mistake I might make. Even if I were to be crushed and die, the incident would affect only me. But a child, even if it is only a baby, once it leaves the mother's body, has its own life apart from the mother's. Moreover, up until a certain age, the parent who conceived and bore the child is expected to assume full responsibility for it. The parent must look after all the child's needs for a long time. After I thought things through like this, I realized that, if I wanted to fulfill my sense of my responsibility to the fetus, I had no other choice than to have an abortion. This was the only road I could take. That was my only reason. I had no other ideas apart from this."

This was generally the sense of what I said. I really put my heart into it. Even if the judge wouldn't understand me, I wanted to say all that I had to say. When I finished talking, I started sobbing uncontrollably. Remember how much I cried when I talked about this with you, too? That time, it felt like I was so moved by what I hadn't even said yet that the tears were coming before the words. I felt the same way this time. Whenever I stopped talking, tears would course down my face. But these were not in any sense tears of sadness or shame. They fell one by one, as if the reverberations of my voice had simply shaken them from my eyes. Just then I heard the judge say, "Truly appalling!"

About the only changes I notice in an entire day are the three times when meals are brought to me. The rest of the day, I exist in a grey world that makes no distinction between this hour and the hour that follows. The only things that are always working in this world are my blood and my brain. I guess you can imagine me staring at these walls every day while thinking intensely. I am literally buried in my thoughts. And when I think about the trial, I still cannot find anything wrong with what I said to the judge. I am thinking that, after all, I did not become a slave to petty sentiment.

The two of us were working as well as we possibly could, weren't we? We work so much that it's as if work were a break for us, isn't it? All the same, we often run out of food. There were even times when all we had to eat was rice cakes once a day. Remember when it got hot but we had no light kimonos around, so you had to spend the whole day in bed naked while I rushed to wash, dry, and resew the one you had? It took until midnight, didn't it? If we are together, I guess we can always get by, no matter what happens. But that doesn't give us the right to force this kind of life on a child born out of our own selfishness. Even from an ideological standpoint, this is true.

I see plenty of mothers and fathers all around, and I am not satisfied with even a one of them. But I do not have their courage; unlike them, I cannot face my child with nothing to offer but poverty. This does not mean that I have ever felt any discontent or dissatisfaction with my own parents—although here I am speaking from a child's point of view; it is not a view that parents have any right to expect. If parents cannot fulfill their obligations as parents, then they should absolutely not have become parents in the first place. I learned this when I was on the verge of becoming a parent myself. What a roundabout way I took to find this out! However, at least it was fortunate that I realized this before it was too late.

The judge said that such ideas were more dangerous than nihilism. "Truly appalling! And quite dangerous! Why, it goes beyond crime!" he exclaimed. I have no idea what will happen to me now. The judge kept saying over and over, "This would mean the destruction of the whole race!" Then he said, "Don't you realize that, if others follow you, using the same excuse, this one crime will only lead to more?" I wonder if he thinks that people can really pay attention to such large concerns as "the human race" and "other people" when they are involved in their own personal problems. I came right back at him, saying, "People's private concerns are their own. Humanity as a whole does not determine my personal conduct."

Then the judge asked, "So, do you mean that you did this never knowing that it was a crime?" What a stupid question! I answered, "Criminal law and what is right or wrong are separate issues. However, I knew that if I broke the law, I would be a criminal. And I also knew that what I was doing broke the law." This prompted him to ask why I hadn't turned myself in. I said, "It is the law that has branded this a crime, not me." Then the judge said something impressive. At least I admired these words: "Even if the authorities aren't aware of it, what do you do about the fact you've broken the law?"

He was right. Whether or not anybody knew about it, I had broken the law, hadn't I? At that point I said, "I will leave that question to the expertise of the court. All I know is that, because my beliefs were more compelling than the law, I had no other choice than to follow my conscience. However, when the law comes after me, the matter falls into your hands."

I don't know what the judge's decision in my case will be. I think about what will happen. But since my convictions will not change even in the slightest—and, what's more, what I've done won't change, either—please don't feel sad about anything. And please work with all your might. You have to do my share, too!

Part Four
Over and over today, I kept seeing our room at home. I bet you haven't swept the room at all since the day I left, right? And you never fold up the bedding either, do you? I imagine the cotton in those old quilts must be starting to come out again. Whenever I sew them up, it comes out, and then I sew them up again, and again the stuffing comes out. Soon you'll have to use a quilt that is stuffing and nothing else—I'm sure of it! But don't let this make you feel gloomy, all right?

Somehow I can't help feeling that you are sitting on one corner of that dusty quilt right now, eating cold rice on which you have poured cold water and sprinkled some salt. Am I right? I would surely like to see that. I wonder if you happened to find the salted green peas I had wrapped in paper inside my desk drawer. If you haven't, they must be all dried up by now.

I know I am repeating myself again, but if you really want to help me, please concentrate on your work. Because if, by any chance, this incident should ruin both of us, I would really hold it against you. That thought worries me so much I can't stand it. I become unbearably frightened when I think that sometime, in a state of despair, you might decide to come join me in this dark world. Sometimes I even feel that you may have already come here without my knowing it. Please, let's not waste everything.

Ah, now I can see one of your sandals upside down under the stepping stone. The other one has been tossed by the grate. The top layer on that one is beginning to peel off, isn't it?

Notes

[1]Harada Satsuki, "Goku-chū no onna yori otoko ni" (To My Lover from a Woman in Prison), *Seitō* 5.6 (June 1915): 33–45.

[2]Ishizaki Shōko, "Yasuda Satsuki," in Raichō Kenkyūkai, ed., *"Seitō" jinbutsu jiten: 110-nin no gunzō* (Taishūkan Shoten, 2001), 176. I draw largely on Ishizaki's research in writing this brief biography of Satsuki. Following Ishizaki and Hiratsuka Raichō, I most often use "Yasuda" to refer to Satsuki's family name. This was the name most associated with her *Seitō* publications.

[3]Yasuda Satsuki, "Sayonara" (Goodbye), *Seitō* 2.12 (December 1912): 117–23, and idem, "Hachijikan" (Eight Hours), *Seitō* 3.9 (September 1913): 60–82.

[4]Hiratsuka Raichō, *Genshi, josei wa taiyō de atta: Hiratsuka Raichō jiden* (Ōtsuki Shoten, 1971–73), 2: 536; Hiratsuka Raichō and Teruko Craig, *In the Beginning, Woman Was the Sun: The Autobiography of a Japanese Feminist* (New York: Columbia University Press, 2006), 254.

[5]Ishizaki Shōko surmises that one of Yasuda Satsuki's elder brothers, as the president of a shipping company, had the capital to lend her for this venture, and to help her financially later in her life, too. Ishizaki, "Yasuda Satsuki," 177.

[6]The announcement ran in *Seitō* 4.11 (December 1915): 112.

[7]This photograph is reprinted in Raichō Kenkyūkai, ed., *"Seitō" jinbutsu jiten*, 183.

⁸Itō Noe, "Henshū-shitsu yori" (From the Editing Room), *Seitō* 4.11 (December 1914): 113.

⁹Hiratsuka, *Genshi, josei wa taiyō de atta*, 2: 537; Hiratsuka and Craig, *In the Beginning, Woman Was the Sun*, 254.

¹⁰Ishizaki, "Yasuda Satsuki," 177.

¹¹Craig, "Translator's Afterword," in Hiratsuka and Craig, *In the Beginning, Woman Was the Sun*, 308–9; see also Hiratsuka, *Genshi, josei wa taiyō de atta*, 3: 283–85.

¹²Kazue Muta, "Women and Modernity in Japan: The New Woman and Moga," Lecture to the Japanese History and Culture Study Group, Asian-Pacific Studies Institute, Duke University, 19 November 2004.

¹³Noguchi Takenori, "Waisetsukan no hassei" (The Birth of the Concept "Obscene"), *Shisō no kagaku* (Sciences of Thought), no. 18 (1973), as cited in Chizuko Ueno, "The Position of Japanese Women Reconsidered," *Current Anthropology* 28, 4 (August–October 1987): 75–84.

¹⁴Iwabuchi Hiroko, "Sekushuaritei no seijigaku e no chōsen: Teisō, datai, haishō ronsō" (Challenging the Politics of Sexuality: Debates on Chastity, Abortion, and the Abolition of Licensed Prostitution), in Shin Feminizumu Hihyō no Kai, ed., *"Seitō" o yomu: Blue Stocking* (Gakugei Shorin, 1998), 312. Iwabuchi does not give names of the intellectuals featured in the series, but her discussion implies that they were men and that the readers disagreeing with them were women.

¹⁵Nishizaki Hanayo, "Ren'ai oyobi seikatsu-nan ni taishite" (Face to Face with Romantic Love and the Difficulty of Making a Living), *Seitō* 4.1 (January 1914): 70–84.

¹⁶Teruko Craig's research clarified that the employer's action should be understood as rape. Hiratsuka and Craig, *In the Beginning, Woman Was the Sun*, 252, note xxiii. For one discussion of contemporary Japanese feminist discussion of rape, see Sandra Buckley's interview with activist and writer Ochiai Keiko. Buckley, "Ochiai Keiko," in idem, *Broken Silence: Voices of Japanese Feminism* (Berkeley and Los Angeles: University of California Press, 1997), 226-44.

¹⁷David R. Ambaras, *Bad Youth: Juvenile Delinquency and the Politics of Everyday Life in Modern Japan* (Berkeley, Los Angeles, London: University of California Press, 2006), 58.

¹⁸Hiratsuka, *Genshi, josei wa taiyō de atta*, 2: 532–53; Hiratsuka and Craig, *In the Beginning, Woman Was the Sun*, 252.

¹⁹Ibid. For translations of other excerpts from Hanayo's *Seitō* essays, see Hiratsuka and Craig, *In the Beginning, Woman Was the Sun*, 251–52.

²⁰Yasuda Satsuki, "Ikiru koto to teisō to—*Hankyō* kugatsu-gō 'Taberu koto to teisō to' o yonde'" (On Living and Chastity: After Reading "Eating and Chastity" in the September issue of *Hankyō*), *Seitō* 4.11 (December 1914): 1.

²¹Ikuta Hanayo, as quoted in ibid., 3–4.

²²Ibid., 4.

²³Ikuta Hanayo, "Shūi o aisuru koto to dōtei no kachi to—*Seitō* jūni-gatsu-gō Yasuda Satsuki sama no hinan ni tsuite" (On Loving Those Close By and the Value of Virginity: Response to Yasuda Satsuki's Criticism in the December Issue of *Seitō*), *Hankyō* 2.1 (January 1915): 1–17. Perhaps Hanayo chose to place her response to Satsuki's *Seitō* article in *Hankyō* because she felt that Ikuta Chōkō was more supportive of her position than the Bluestockings were.

²⁴Ibid., 5.

²⁵Ibid., 17.

²⁶Harada Satsuki, "O-me ni kakatta Ikuta Hanayo-san ni tsuite" (On Meeting Ms. Ikuta Hanayo), *Seitō* 5.2 (February 1915): 66–73. Iwabuchi notes that Yasuda Satsuki also responded to Ikuta Hanayo in the April 1915 issue of *Shin kōron* with an article entitled "Teisō no igi to seizon no kachi ni tsuite" (On the Significance of Chastity and the Value of Existence), in which she continues to drive home her main argument equating sexuality with personal integrity and self-respect. Iwabuchi, "Sekushuaritei no seijigaku e no chōsen," 309.

²⁷Itō Noe, "Teisō ni tsuite no zakkan" (Miscellaneous Thoughts on Chastity), *Seitō* 5.2 (February 1915): 1–11. Later, Ōsugi Sakae responded to Noe in the April 1915 issue of *Shin kōron*, arguing that she needed to see the emphasis on virginity in a larger social context and understand the commodification of women's sexuality as part of capitalism. Iwabuchi, "Sekushuaritei no seijigaku e no chōsen," 307.

²⁸Hiratsuka Raichō, "Shojo no kachi" (The True Value of Virginity), *Shin kōron* (March 1915), as quoted in Iwabuchi, "Sekushuaritei no seijigaku e no chōsen," 310. Raichō quotes a lengthy excerpt from "Shojo no kachi" in *Genshi, josei wa taiyō de atta*, 2: 538–39; Hiratsuka and Craig, *In the Beginning, Woman Was the Sun*, 254–55.

²⁹Hiratsuka Raichō, "Sabetsu-teki seidōtoku ni tsuite" (On Discriminatory Sexual Morality), *Fujin kōron* (October 1916), as cited in Iwabuchi, "Sekushuaritei no seijigaku e no chōsen," 310.

³⁰Ikuta Hanayo, "Zange no kokoro yori: Hiratsuka Raichō, Itō Noe, Harada-sama ni yosete" (From a Repentant Heart: To Hiratsuka Raichō, Itō Noe, and Ms. Harada), *Seitō* 5.4 (April 1915): 19–28.

³¹Ibid., 27.

³²In addition to the Bluestockings and the *Yomiuri shinbun* article mentioned above, men writers such as Abe Isoo, Matsumoto Gorō, Ōsugi Sakae, and others also participated in the discussion through various publications. Iwabuchi, "Sekushuaritei no seijigaku e no chōsen," 307.

³³Hiratsuka, *Genshi, josei wa taiyō de atta*, 2: 537; Hiratsuka and Craig, *In the Beginning, Woman Was the Sun*, 254; also Yoneda Sayoko, "Ikuta Hanayo," in Raichō Kenkyūkai, ed., *"Seitō" jinbutsu jiten*, 36–37.

³⁴Tiana Norgren argues that the Meiji government's policies on abortion were an extension of Tokugawa national and local policies that decried abortions as "immoral acts of murder," and as robbing the state of future taxpayers. Norgren notes that in "1667 the *shōgun* (military ruler) banned the use of signs to advertise abortion services, and in 1842 a ban on performing abortions was passed as well." Tiana Norgren, *Abortion Before Birth Control: The Politics of Reproduction in Postwar Japan* (Princeton and Oxford: Princeton University Press, 2001), 23.

³⁵Hiratsuka Raichō, "Kojin toshite no seikatsu to sei toshite no seikatsu to no aida no sōtō ni tsuite: Noe-san ni" (On the Conflict Between Life as an Individual and Life as a Sexual Being: To Ms. Noe), *Seitō* 5.8 (September 1915): 1–22.

³⁶Norgren believes that practicing birth control was not common outside of elite and academic circles such as those the Bluestockings inhabited, citing a 1950 survey conducted by the *Mainichi shinbun*'s Population Problems Research Council survey in which "only 9 percent of all married couples reported having practiced birth control before 1905." Norgren, *Abortion Before Birth Control*, 25, citing Elise K. Tipton, ed., *Society and the State in Interwar Japan* (New York: Routledge, 1997), 51–52. For more on the history of the birth control movement in Japan, see Helen Hopper, *A New Woman*

of Japan: A Political Biography of Katō Shidzue, Transitions: Asian and Asian America (Boulder, Colo.: Westview Press, 1996).

[37]Sabine Frühstück, *Colonizing Sex: Sexology and Social Control in Modern Japan* (Berkeley and Los Angeles: University of California Press, 2003), 123.

[38]Itō Noe, "Henshū-shitsu yori" (From the Editing Room), *Seito* 5.7 (July 1915): 105.

[39]Itō Noe, "Shishin: Nogami Yae-Sama e" (Private Message to Ms. Nogami Yae), *Seitō* 5.6 (June 1915): 75. Much of this essay is translated in Mikiso Hane, *Peasants, Rebels, Women and Outcastes: The Underside of Modern Japan*, Second Edition (Lanham, MD: Rowman & Littlefield Publishers, Inc., 2003), 264–69.

[40]Itō Noe, "Shishin: Nogami Yae-Sama e," 76. Also translated in Hiratsuka and Craig, *In the Beginning, Woman Was the Sun*, 264.

[41]Ibid., 76–77.

[42]Ibid., 77. The sex of the child is not specified in the original. Since a pronoun is required in English and since Noe's first child was a son, I use masculine pronouns here.

[43]Frühstück, *Colonizing Sex*, 126. As Frühstück also writes on page 126, Yamada Waka published a book in 1922, elaborating her views on birth control and contraception, entitled *Katei no shakaiteki igi* (The Social Significance of the Family), (Tokyo: Kindai Bunmeisha).

[44]Yamada Waka, "Datai ni tsuite: Matsumoto Gorō-shi 'Seitō no hatsubai kinshi ni tsuite' o yonde" (On Abortion: To Mr. Matsumoto Gorō upon Reading about "The Ban on the Sale of *Seitō*"), *Seitō* 5.8 (September 1915): 31.

[45]Ibid., 34. Also translated in Hiratsuka and Craig, *In the Beginning, Woman Was the Sun*, 265.

[46]Ibid., 36–37.

[47]Yamada Waka, "Ren'ai no jiyū to honnō: Suzuki bōshi ni tou" (Love's Freedom and Instinct: A Response to a Certain Mr. Suzuki), *Seitō* 5.10 (November 1915): 78.

[48]Hiratsuka, "Kojin toshite no seikatsu to sei toshite no seikatsu to no aida no sōtō ni tsuite," 1.

[49]Ibid., 17.

[50]Ibid., 13–14.

[51]Ibid., 7.

[52]Ibid., 9.

[53]Ibid., 18–19.

[54]Ibid., 19.

[55]Ibid., 22.

Chapter 4
Hiratsuka Raichō (1886–1971)

In the beginning, Woman was the Sun.

The history of the Bluestockings and their journal *Seitō* has become nearly inseparable from the life of its most famous editor, Hiratsuka Raichō, and there is good reason for this. Much of what we know about the Bluestockings as a group has been recorded in Raichō's life histories, her short 1955 autobiography *Watakushi no aruita michi* (The Path I Took), and especially her four-volume autobiography, *Genshi, josei wa taiyō de atta: Hiratsuka Raichō jiden* (In the Beginning, Woman Was the Sun: The Autobiography of Hiratsuka Raichō), published in 1971–73.[1] Also, during the short life of the journal, Raichō's active involvement as an editor and frequent contributor and her self-proclaimed status as a New Woman closely associated her in the public eye with *Seitō*. Moreover, she developed a keen sense of ownership toward the journal and was reluctant to hand over the editorial helm to Itō Noe in 1915, even though she no longer had the energy to keep running it herself. Biographies, a novel, a recent film, and even a comic book have all contributed to sustaining Raichō's fame in Japan. These projects tend to derive most of their material from the 1971–73 autobiography and present a colorfully heroic view of her, celebrating everything about her personal choices that was once food for scandal. A controversial figure throughout much of her long, active life, Raichō has gained iconic status as one of Japan's most famous feminists, and that fame has also kept a spotlight on *Seitō*.

Recent biographies have taken a more measured view of Raichō's life and accomplishments. Yoneda Sayoko has published important scholarship in Japanese, investigating Raichō's life from new perspectives. Analysis of Raichō's understanding of eugenics, homosexuality, and her stance toward the emperor system during the Pacific War show how her life and thought continue to generate controversy.[2] Academic studies in Japanese on *Seitō* and the Bluestockings as chapters in the history of Japanese women's literature, history, and feminism have also raised new questions that expand on biographic approaches.[3]

The English-language study of Hiratsuka Raichō's life and work has been expanded by two landmark works: Hiroko Tomida's 2004 biography

Hiratsuka Raichō and Early Japanese Feminism, and Teruko Craig's 2006 translation of the first two volumes of the 1971–73 autobiography *In the Beginning, Woman Was the Sun: The Autobiography of Hiratsuka Raichō, Japanese Feminist*. Recent scholarship by Dina Lowy and Sumiko Otsubo on Raichō's interest in eugenics, and by Lowy and Gregory M. Pflugfelder on her attitude toward same-sex love, also bring new and important perspectives to the study of this influential feminist. The short biography given here, in line with the others in this volume, briefly traces Raichō's youth and her years with *Seitō*, and is much indebted to the research in Japanese and English described above.[4]

The woman who would become famous as Hiratsuka Raichō—and whom I refer to as Raichō throughout this chapter—was born Hiratsuka Haru in Tokyo in 1886 to Hiratsuka Tsuya (1864–1954), the daughter of a doctor of Chinese medicine, and her husband Hiratsuka Sadajirō (1858–1941), a highly placed civil servant in the national accounting offices and a scholar of German language and culture. Raichō had one sibling, an older sister named Taka; the Hiratsukas' firstborn child, Ine, had died in infancy. A true Edokko, or child of Edo (modern day Tokyo), Raichō's mother Tsuya had been schooled in the traditional arts and was especially adept in music. Her marriage to the straightlaced Sadajirō meant that she had to relinquish this pleasure in favor of adopting the matronly style her husband believed most appropriate to the modern wife of an up-and-coming bureaucrat. The constraints of gender and class, as evident in her mother's life, were not lost on the young Raichō. Like Itō Noe and Fukuda Hideko, Raichō was regarded by her family as a tomboy who disliked being made to conform to more feminine behavior.

As the daughter of a middle-class Tokyo family, Raichō enjoyed educational opportunities that took her through elementary school, the prestigious Ochanomizu Girls' School, and to Japan Women's College. Yet as a teenager and as a college student, Raichō made no attempt to mask her disenchantment with an educational system determined to make a "good wife, wise mother" (*ryōsai kenbo*) out of her. At Ochanomizu, she rebelled by refusing to attend the *shūshin* (morals) classes. She devoted herself to playing tennis, proud of her strength and eager to improve by challenging better players to a match. She banded together with a few of her like-minded classmates to form "The Pirates Band," and dreamed with them of forging a stimulating life of work and adventure that did not include marriage. Later, when her initial excitement over attending Japan Women's College gave way to disappointment with its femininity codes, Raichō again made no secret of her lack of school spirit. She took to spending long hours in the library reading classical literature, philosophy, and religion. Moving even farther away from "good wife, wise mother" training, Raichō began the practice of Zen, rising at dawn to walk to a temple for meditation. Even as an elderly woman, she credited her lifelong adherence to Zen principles and her youthful achievement of *kenshō* (the first stage in enlightenment) for the creativity and strength that remained with her throughout her life.

Although Raichō and her father locked horns on many occasions in her youth, mostly over his belief that she must be more conventionally feminine, they enjoyed a close relationship. Hiratsuka Sadajirō could be an exceedingly tolerant man. Nothing proved this more than his acceptance of his daughter in the wake of the Shiobara Incident of 1908, which besmirched his family's reputation and even caused some to call for his resignation from his government post. Through her participation in the Keishū Literary Society (Keishū Bungakukai), organized in 1907 by Ikuta Chōkō, Raichō had met and become involved with author Morita Sōhei (1881–1949), a married man and father whose family lived in the countryside. Raichō and Sōhei shared a flirtation with European decadent literature that culminated in a bizarre suicide attempt which led them to spend one night in the snowy mountains of Shiobara, a retreat not far from Tokyo. Obviously the suicide did not occur, the couple spent a cold night outside, and the whole event seemed a kind of risky homage to Romanticism rather than romance. Raichō's mother Tsuya and Ikuta Chōkō traveled together to Shiobara to retrieve the couple.

Newspapers had a field day with the Incident and, unfortunately for Raichō's sister Taka, initially named her (rather than Raichō) as the Hiratsukas' problem daughter. The *Tokyo Asahi shinbun* condemned Raichō, describing her as a Russian-literature-loving, cigarette-smoking, masculine kind of woman who toyed with men.[5] Japan Women's College struck Raichō's name from their alumnae rolls (and did not reinstate it until 1992). On 1 January 1909, the *Tokyo Asahi shinbun* began publishing installments of Sōhei's novel *Baien* (Black Smoke), which described the Shiobara Incident and the couple's relationship.[6] Sōhei's character Tomoko is a thinly veiled reference to Raichō, as the public well knew. Araki Ikuko, Otake Kōkichi, and Ikuta Hanayo—all future Bluestockings—became fascinated with the enigmatic character of Tomoko long before they met Raichō.[7] Although the public understood the Raichō-Sōhei relationship as one of sexual passion, Raichō later wrote that her first sexual experience was initiated after the Shiobara Incident, out of curiosity, with a Zen Buddhist priest.[8]

The next chapter in the young woman's life—her reinvention as Hiratsuka Raichō, her position as a representative New Woman, and her eventual place as editor of *Seitō*—is an eventful and well-documented one. Persuaded by Ikuta Chōkō to take on an all-women's journal, promised help by Yasumochi Yoshiko (1885–1947) her friend from Japan Women's College, and given the necessary funds by her mother, Raichō embarked on the project with some reluctance. Thus, in 1911, a core group of five Japan Women's College graduates was assembled, established women writers were enlisted as supporters, and the business of publishing a journal began.[9] The inaugural issue carried the first publication by "Raichō." It is a long poetic piece entitled "Genshi, josei wa taiyō de atta" (In the Beginning, Woman Was the Sun), translated and discussed below. Far from indicating reluctance, this essay is a fervent call for women to discover their "hidden Sun" and for *Seitō* to take up the charge.[10]

Hiratsuka Raichō made over seventy more contributions to *Seitō*, mostly in the form of original essays that reflected her interest in literature, the Woman Question, and developing a personal philosophy of life.[11] Like Itō Noe, Iwano Kiyoko, and Katō Midori (see Chapters 5, 6, and 7 below), Raichō passionately believed in self-discovery and the pursuit of an interior life from which an ethical code would follow. Even decades later, when she was criticized by a younger generation of women for not making *Seitō* more open to exploration of social problems and women of all classes, Raichō remained convinced that self-discovery had to precede social activism.[12] She held this conviction even as she, too, became more involved with social issues in her long career after *Seitō*. Under fire during her *Seitō* years to explain the New Woman, Raichō looked to the work of Ellen Key (1849–1926), the maternal feminist and eugenicist, for guidance.[13] Raichō admired the beneficial role Key envisioned for mothers, finding appeal in her references to spirituality and her call for the rights of the mother and the child to supersede the interests of the state. Once Raichō became a mother herself in 1915, with the birth of her daughter Akemi, Key's ideas had even more significance for her. Still, Raichō found combining motherhood and her writing career a challenge, and wrote about this, too, in *Seitō*. In 1917, Raichō gave birth to her second and last child, a son named Atsubumi.

Two *Seitō* Scandals in 1912

Raichō did not leave scandal behind with the Shiobara Incident, and she did not shy away from the public's view of her as a New Woman. Two incidents occurring in the first year of *Seitō*'s publication—the "Five-Colored Liquor Incident" (Goshiki no Sake Jiken) and the Bluestocking "Visit to the Yoshiwara" (Yoshiwara Hōmon Jiken)—cast Raichō once again as a figure of ill repute. The Bluestocking at the center of these scandals was Otake Kōkichi (1893–1966), a tall, gregarious, and often flamboyantly dressed teenager who had joined the group earlier that year and who was eager to talk about *Seitō*, even to newspaper reporters. Raised in an Osaka family of artists, Kōkichi had grown up in a relatively unsheltered environment that allowed her to meet many young male artists. An artist herself, she created several *Seitō* covers and also exhibited her paintings in Tokyo. She enjoyed visiting the new cafés, such as the Maison Kōnosu, where male writers and artists gathered. Even though she had little tolerance for alcohol, Kōkichi was enchanted with the concoctions being served there, once writing in *Seitō* about a cocktail of five different-colored liquors as though she had tasted it herself. In the June 1912 issue of *Seitō*, Kōkichi included anecdotes about Bluestockings drinking colorful liquours in the Editors' Notes, even as she protested that they were hardworking, serious people and not at all the New Women of popular perception. She argued that the Bluestockings should overcome their timidity and reveal themselves to the world honestly.[14] In the next issue of *Seitō*, Kōkichi playfully included this remark in the Editors' Notes, styling herself as Raichō's young boyfriend:

> Apparently, a great many doubts have been raised about the secret object of Raichō's affections. According to the report of a secret investigator, he is a handsome youth. This beautiful young man will have a drink at the Maison Kōnosu café made of five different-colored liquors and then in the evening will once again visit Raichō in her rooms.[15]

When newspaper gossip columns published reports based on such remarks, they replicated the image of Raichō entertaining a young man, a portrait that fit well with the public's idea of the New Woman as a kind of femme fatale preying on innocent youth. No one guessed that the youth was actually Kōkichi.

Soon after this, the Bluestockings sparked another scandal when Raichō, Kōkichi, and Nakano Hatsuko visited the courtesan Eizan at the Daimonjirō, a high-class geisha house in the Yoshiwara pleasure quarters, and spent the night in another room there. The visit had been arranged and paid for by Kōkichi's uncle, the painter Otake Chikuha (1878–1936), who strongly believed that the Bluestockings needed to open their eyes to the plight of women sold into prostitution.[16] The three went out of curiosity. Afterward, naïve and excited, Kōkichi told a reporter from the *Tokyo Nichi Nichi shinbun* all about their visit; the report that appeared in the newspaper in late October claimed the Bluestockings had spent three nights in the Yoshiwara. As Dina Lowy explains about the ensuing press reports, "The three women were depicted as frivolous, morally bankrupt, and out of line for crossing sexual, gender and class boundaries. Not only did they enter a world to which only men had free access, but they did so out of curiosity and not with the intent of social reform. . . . Their blithe association with loose sexuality and lower-class society allowed their demands for women's awakening and rights to be easily dismissed."[17]

A satirical cartoon that ran in *Tokyo pakku* (Tokyo Puck) on 1 August 1912 offers one interpretation of the incident. It depicts Raichō and another woman standing in front of the Daimonjirō and staring at Eizan as if they were at a zoo. Eizan, dressed gorgeously, her hair elaborately styled, and looking very feminine, shrinks back in fright from the two plainly dressed, severe looking women who have the word "Bluestocking" written on their kimonos. Raichō wears her characteristic *hakama*, and she and her Bluestocking companion both sprout whiskers on their chins.[18] Critics attacked the women's visit to the Yoshiwara as "women acting like men." They did not consider the possibility that the Bluestockings, as young women, may have been intrigued by a female role so different from their own or have flirted with imagining themselves in such a world.

As in the aftermath of the Shiobara Incident, Raichō's family stood by her this time, too. Even though some threw stones at the Hiratsuka house and Raichō was harassed with threatening letters, her parents remained calm and did not complain to their daughter at all.[19] Public disapproval, however, did have repercussions within the Bluestockings as a group. Some withdrew their membership, while others requested that their names no longer be published in the magazine. Fearing the loss of their jobs, elementary and girls' school teachers canceled their subscriptions. Mozume Kazuko's father, worried that his daughter was damaging her chances for a good marriage, demanded that she quit the group; Mozume continued writing under an assumed name. Yasumochi Yoshiko, one of the Bluestockings most dedicated to the journal, complained in a letter to Hiratsuka Raichō that the Yoshiwara visit had been a rash and callous thing to do. She wrote that *Seitō* had lost its sense of mission and dignity, and become "like a tomboy who prides herself on defying convention and doing things women never dare do."[20]

Raichō, Kōkichi, and the Scandal of "Same-Sex Love"

Kōkichi's relationship with *Seitō* and her pursuit of Raichō gradually ended as Raichō became involved with the artist Okumura Hiroshi (1891–1964). Both Raichō's relationship with Kōkichi and her later cohabitation with Okumura fueled public disapproval of her. Dina Lowy describes, for example, how the *Tokyo Nichi Nichi shinbun* began a ten-article series in late November 1912 entitled "Strange Love" that discussed the Shiobara Incident and the Raichō-Kōkichi affair as a dangerous inversion of social mores.[21] Contemporary Itō Noe later wrote about the volatility of the Kōkichi-Raichō relationship in a long essay on the Bluestockings serialized in the *Osaka Mainichi shinbun*, 3 January through 1 April 1916.[22] She remarks on how intensely attached Kōkichi was to Raichō, as if she could not bear to be away from her; how she would send Raichō two or three letters a day when she was away; and how jealous she could become. Noe observed that there was a strong bond of love between the two women, noting that their closeness became the focus of public alarm over same-sex love (*dōseiai*).[23] Noe also says that although she does not know "how far their love went," it was a fact that Raichō returned Kōkichi's affections.[24] While Noe finds Kōkichi a high-strung young woman given to dramatics, she is critical of what she sees as Raichō's capriciousness and lack of sincerity, commenting that even at the time of the Shiobara Incident, Raichō never had any intention of killing herself.[25]

It is important to note that Noe's concern is with whether Raichō had been honest and not simply toying with Kōkichi; she does not remark on same-sex love in itself as worthy of special comment. With humor, for example, she relates a time when she, Araki Ikuko, and Kōkichi went to a public bath, describing how much she and Ikuko admired Kōkichi's tall, strong body. Ikuko was so taken with Kōkichi's body that she could not resist rubbing her, making Kōkichi yelp and sending all three into a fit of giggles. As they chatted back in their room while Ikuko put on makeup, Kōkichi talked about how she liked dressing up and acting like a boy.[26] Noe recounts this incident as nothing more than good fun. Her series also described individual Bluestockings as drinking, smoking, discussing books, and confiding in each other about their love affairs and marriage problems, as well as going to a lively New Year's party and enjoying working on *Seitō*—all activities that confirmed the reputation of the Bluestockings as out-of-bounds New Women.

In her autobiography, Raichō plays down her involvement with Kōkichi, claiming that her attraction to the younger woman was not sexual. Of her own role in the relationship, Raichō writes that she "always tried to maintain some distance and made an effort to control the situation."[27] As Sharon Sievers remarks, "In this context, two issues are important: (1) the extent to which lesbianism was a spoken or unspoken source of the social criticism the Seitōsha (and earlier feminists) faced and (2) the implications of Raichō's own attitude (revealed in her comments about Kōkichi)."[28] Gregory M. Pflugfelder argues that Raichō's later disavowal of any sexual attraction to Kōkichi during their *Seitō* days reveals the influence of changing social mores. Although Raichō "had boasted of Otake as her *shōnen* in *Seitō* in 1912," "her strikingly defensive rhetorical stance [in the 1971–73 autobiography] . . . poignantly reveals the stigmatizing power that the 'same-sex love' construct would acquire over the course of the twentieth century."[29] Certainly, reports in the 1910s of the Kōkichi-Raichō relationship contributed to public perception of the New Woman as a desiring woman unconstrained by conventional mores and, through Noe's later report at least, added to Raichō's reputation as one who toyed with the affections of others.[30]

New Woman Pride

The events of 1912 did not cause Raichō to back down; if anything, they made her more determined to define herself, rather than be defined by alarmist press reports. She adopted the title "New Woman" with pride, publishing a colorful, poetic essay that Hiroko Tomida has described as "her declaration of war against public criticism."[31] Raichō's poetic essay, entitled simply "New Woman" (Atarashii onna), in which she proclaims that "I am the Sun," was published in the general-interest magazine *Chūō kōron* (The Central Review) in January 1913.[32] It was translated in full soon afterward in the English-language newspaper *The Japan Times* as "The 'New Woman' in Japan."[33] As in her earlier essay "Genshi, josei wa taiyō de atta" (the famous 1911 piece that became known as the *Seitō* manifesto, translated below), Raichō writes in "Atarashii onna" of the greatest obstacle to the New Woman's quest being an internal one—namely, a problem of self-doubt and lack of vigilance. The New Woman must be strong because the specter of the "Old Woman," who can follow a much easier, conventional path, is always waiting to invade her consciousness should she let down her guard in a careless moment. Raichō concludes "Atarashii onna" by promising that the spiritual development in New Women will radically change social institutions. As is characteristic of *Seitō* essays, she does not specify how such change will occur or what form it will take. Nor, apparently, does she think it important to envision these goals with much specificity in order to strive for them. While hoping to free women from all the rules associated with femininity training, Raichō does not want to impose new rules of her own:

> The New Woman will not merely destroy the old morality and laws created to benefit men's selfishness. Rather, with the bright virtue of a sun that renews itself each day, the New Woman is trying to build a new realm of the spirit, a realm endowed with a new religion, new morality, and new laws. Indeed, the mission of the New Woman lies in creating this new sphere. If this is so, where is this new realm? What is the new religion? The new morality? The new laws? The New Woman herself does not know.[34]

Above all, Raichō believed that the New Woman needed time to herself to read, write, and think if she were to make progress in achieving these lofty goals. Yet Raichō was clearly also a fighter who continued to brook public censure and government censorship by making public both her views and her private life, as shown in the two well-known pieces besides "In the Beginning, Woman Was the Sun" that are translated below. Her 1913 essay "To the Women of the World" (Yo no fujintachi ni) attacks conservative women educators,[35] while her 1914 publication "To My Parents on Becoming Independent" (Dokuritsu suru ni tsuite ryōshin ni) was originally a letter to her parents explaining her decision to refuse marriage but to live with artist Okumura Hiroshi.[36] Let us now turn to discussion of Raichō's famous manifesto and these two later essays.

The *Seitō* Manifesto:
"In the Beginning, Woman Was the Sun"

In one of the first postwar studies of Japanese women's history, Takamure Itsue (1894–1964) hailed the *Seitō* manifesto by Hiratsuka Raichō as the first "Declaration of the Rights of Women" in Japan. Takamure places the manifesto at the end of a feminist line of history that she sees extending from the Declarations written by Olympe de Gouges (1745–93) at the time of the French Revolution in 1789 to the eighteenth-century work of Mary Wollstonecraft (1759–97) in England, and that of the American suffragists who met in Seneca Falls, New York, in 1848. At the same time, Takamure writes that the *Seitō* manifesto was "an exceedingly Japanese" formulation of feminism and heralds *Seitō*, the first intellectual journal in Japan by and for women, as having ushered in a great new era in "the history of Japanese women's self-awakening."[37]

In fact, the manifesto is not the first declaration of feminist sentiments in Japan, and whether or not it is "exceedingly Japanese" is debatable. Yet "Genshi, josei wa taiyō de atta" is one of the foundational works of Japanese feminism and certainly remains the quintessential work of the young Hiratsuka Raichō. According to Raichō's 1971–73 autobiography, the manifesto and Yosano Akiko's poetry entitled "Sozorogoto" (translated in Chapter 12 below) were the *Seitō* pieces most mentioned in the reams of letters from young women that the Bluestockings received in 1911.[38] The poetic quality of "Genshi" may strike today's readers as surprisingly different from the overtly political documents that the term "feminist manifesto" calls to mind. There is little attention to specific conditions or demands for specific freedoms or rights. But the first lines of this essay, with their images of pale, passive "moon" women becoming as powerful and bright as the sun, are often quoted in statements related to Japanese women's movements, even when a particular work about women has nothing to do with Hiratsuka Raichō or the Bluestockings.

The manifesto begins by challenging the status quo, characterizing contemporary Japanese women as sad souls. They are neither thrifty, patriotic "good wives and wise mothers" nor the authentic, self-respecting human beings that Raichō would prefer them to become. Taking great, essentializing strides through Japanese history, Raichō compares Meiji women to the Japanese women of ancient times who uniformly, she imagines, shone with the brilliance of their own unfettered creativity and self-confidence. Many have read the image of the Sun Goddess Amaterasu, the mythic mother of the Japanese imperial line, in such references, likening the narrator to a shamaness performing a sexually charged, ecstatic dance as she channels mystic powers. Combining this image of Amaterasu and Raichō's reference to hypnosis, one can say that she, too, is trying to mesmerize her reader. Even though Raichō later denied having the image of the Sun Goddess in mind, the text certainly supports this interpretation. Others, as Hiroko Tomida remarks, have considered the influence of Raichō's reading of *Thus Spoke Zarathustra*, and the sun and moon imagery in Nietzsche's work; Raichō later denied having this reference in mind, either.[39] Yet interest in Nietzsche was certainly in the air: Yosano Akiko's poem "Sozorogoto" and Raichō's "Genshi" make reference to *Zarathustra*, and Ikuta Chōkō's 1911 translation of *Zarathustra*, published by Shinchōsha, is prominently advertised in the inaugural issue of *Seitō*.

For readers who likely read Yosano Akiko's poetry in the same September 1911 issue of *Seitō*, Raichō's opening lines may have provided a powerful transition from Akiko's melancholy verse about a woman who describes herself as a "moon flower" to the possibility of that woman retrieving her "hidden Sun." Nakashima Miyuki argues that this was not a coincidence, and that Raichō was deliberately launching an attack against a trend in the art world, favored by Yosano Akiko and Ikuta Chōkō, of associating women with pallor and the moon.[40] Raichō's use of sun imagery also reverses the ancient ying/yang Chinese mythology that similarly associated women with the moon and men with the sun. Indeed, Raichō laments the current position and "pallid" self-concepts of Japanese women. But she holds out hope as well, and what is especially potent about this hope is that it already resides in each woman herself—not in the West, not in the power of the Japanese establishment, and not even in laws or political change. Rather, it is available now, if only a woman will work fearlessly and hard to revive it.

But work she must. For Raichō, achieving liberation is a noble goal and an arduous task, and what women should be prepared to combat on their road to liberation is their own self-doubt. True, they need more and better education, and freedom from the burdens of housework and the obligations of the family, but since Raichō imagines liberation in a metaphysical sense, what she most wants for women is the time for meditation—not career opportunities, not the vote, not the mundane advantages of this world that would put women on a par with their brothers, but the passionate desire to look deep within for a genuine self, a self that transcends gender boundaries altogether.

This is especially interesting in light of how stringently the Meiji state was policing the perimeters of gender, particularly for the growing middle class. Raichō speaks in colorful language of how debilitated she felt when she realized that she was "woman," and how confining gender roles are. They are of a "lower stratum." They are a "death" to the limitless extensions of a person. In references to the reckless actions of her youth (e.g., the Shiobara Incident) that brought this realization home to her, Raichō invokes a famous play of the Noh theater, *Hagoromo*, in which an angel loses the magical robe on earth that she needs to fly in the heavens. But Raichō does not regret even this bitter experience because she has chosen her own route in life and will continue to walk it no matter what.

Yoneda Sayoko observes the central role that a longing to dissolve in nature plays in the manifesto and, in fact, in Raichō's thought throughout her life. She interprets the use of the word "crystal" in the essay as a reference to the Ōmoto religious sect founded in 1904 by Deguchi Nao (1837–1919). Deguchi "had already described her ideal equal society as a world where plants, people, mountains and seas shone, the moon and the sun gave out a stronger light, where things began to be seen through, like crystal."[41] Similarly, Raichō sees the potential for overcoming gender and other artificial social constructions by immersing or emptying the self in the power of nature.

We can imagine how many readers must have thrilled to Raichō's dramatic self-presentation and fearlessness; been impressed by the apparent sophistication of her references to science, Anton Mesmer (1734–1815) and hypnotism, and the French sculptor Auguste Rodin (1840–1917); and been struck by her casting even the Buddha as a feminist role model. Her attacks on the Naturalists—men writers of much notoriety at the time—as lacking a genuine knowledge of nature, and on those who did not want to give women more material freedoms, would have seemed quite bold. Whether or not they agreed with or felt they understood Raichō's themes, readers would not have missed her appeal to all women to find their own genius, nor the maternal imagery that enjoined them to become the mothers of their own rebirth.

Although many of the *Seitō* essays are much more direct than "Genshi" and make their arguments plainly, this 1911 manifesto stands out for its length, its lyrical style, and its free-wheeling transitions from one point to another. One of the reasons that only the first few lines are frequently cited may be the difficulty of understanding what follows. But if we think of this essay not as an exposition of an argument but, especially in its more lyrical moments, as an artistic performance of feminist aspirations, a poetic dance meant to rouse the author and her readers, then its wide appeal makes more sense. Here was the portrait of an extraordinary, real woman living an exhilarating private and nationally public life in Tokyo, and she was offering a piece of that excitement to her readers through *Seitō*, a journal to which they, too, could contribute, and also through the Bluestockings, a group open to any woman but only to women. For all Raichō's celebration of nature, it was her position as a New Woman in the capital, her personal history as the star of a modern, urban scandal, and her immersion in the intellectual and artistic world that gave her essay an added allure. The manifesto did not have to be understood on a rational level; it could be felt. Its privileging of the natural above all else even demanded the reader's sensual reaction—her passion rather than her considered thought. In a modern world that emphasized rationality, order, definition, and hierarchy, and in which gender constraints figured prominently, this irrational call to transcend gender must have seemed refreshingly creative and open.

We can also see the manifesto, the first of Hiratsuka's writing published under her pen name, as one of several efforts Raichō made throughout her life to create and promote herself as a public figure of a different stripe. Using simply the pen name for her writing in *Seitō* also enabled her to avoid directly connecting the Hiratsuka family name to her work. As her autobiographies show, Raichō was ambivalent about her notoriety. She enjoyed the attention fame brought, especially from those who approved of her actions, for as defiant as she could be, she liked approval. In her 1971–73 autobiography, for example, Raichō records her disappointment when the other Bluestockings did not comment at all on her manifesto, yet also makes constant references to her own reluctance to fully join the group and promote the journal because she valued a solitary life and craved time for herself.[42]

"To the Women of the World"

Hiratsuka Raichō, Itō Noe, Iwano Kiyoko, and other Bluestockings regularly encouraged women's self-cultivation and involvement in intellectual work. Yet some of the harshest criticism directed against *Seitō* came from those in women's education. Naruse Jinzō (1858–1919), the man who established and became the first president of Raichō's alma mater, Japan Women's College, publicly disparaged the New Women as selfish and as victims of self-defeat. He called for Japanese women to take pride in their "native virtues" rather than following "mistaken ideas" about Western women's behavior. According to Naruse, these emotionally impaired women were nothing but tomboys or tarts "who publish their writings in magazines, hold public lectures, and buy the favor of prostitutes."[43] Educators at all levels considered the Bluestockings a dangerous group, and even in the early days of criticism of *Seitō*, some of the first to retreat were students and teachers who feared reprisals from their institutions.

In a manner similar to that employed by Itō Noe and Iwano Kiyoko in some of their essays discussed or translated in Chapters 5 and 6 below, Hiratsuka Raichō reserves particular scorn for women, especially privileged women, who distance themselves from the New Woman. When she addresses "the women of the world" (*yo no fujintachi*, which could also be translated as "the ladies of today," or of "our society"), Raichō likely refers to conservative educators such as Tsuda Umeko (1864–1929) and Hatoyama Haruko (1861–1938), who saw the Bluestockings as misguided upstarts threatening the gains in women's education that they had earlier championed and achieved. Raichō explains that these women should look past what appears to be youthful rebellion to the mission of the Bluestockings to improve women's lives in substantial ways.

On 25 April 1913, Yasumochi Yoshiko and Nakano Hatsuko responded to an order for a *Seitō* representative to appear before a Special Higher Police Section at the Metropolitan Police Department in Tokyo. The authorities did not ban the April issue carrying Raichō's essay, but they did warn the young women that they would be keeping a closer eye on *Seitō* from then on. They cautioned the editors to avoid material that could in any way harm conventional morals and customs or the traditional virtues of the Japanese woman. Hiratsuka Raichō tried to republish the essay the next month in a collection of her work, but censors did not allow the book's publication until "To the Women of the World" was removed. As Hiroko Tomida explains, "The Ministry of Education and the Ministry of the Interior imposed stricter controls on women's magazines from then on, and the sales of many other women's magazines such as *Jogaku Sekai* and *Joshi Bundan* were prohibited, something frequently reported in the press."[44]

"To My Parents on Becoming Independent"

Raichō wrote "To My Parents on Becoming Independent" shortly before she moved out of her family home in January 1914 to live with Okumura Hiroshi, a man five years younger than she. To compose such a letter was at best unfilial, but to make it public was outrageous. In it Raichō offers alternatives radical for her time: the idea of pursuing romantic love rather than an arranged marriage, the possibility of choosing not to have children, the decision not to participate in a family system that failed to recognize women as independent adults, and the desire to devote oneself to creative work. Given the stern reprimand that "To the Women of the World" had inspired in 1913, it is surprising that the censors did not take action against "To My Parents on Becoming Independent."[45]

Okumura Hiroshi, too, was the recipient of a letter from Raichō that discussed their potential future together. He recounted the pointed questions she asked in this letter much later, in 1956, when he published *Meguriai* (Encounter), a novel about his relationship with Raichō. Hiroko Tomida has translated these questions as follows:

1. Whatever difficulty or trouble may happen to us in the future, will you be able to endure this with me? Whatever external pressure may be put upon us, will you never leave me?
2. Supposing that I demand marriage from you, what will you reply to this?
3. If I hate the relationship between man and woman under the existing marriage system, and do not wish to have a legal marriage, what attitude will you adopt to this?
4. If I wish to cohabit with you rather than marry you, what will you answer to this?
5. If I wish neither marriage nor cohabitation with you and wish to live separately and meet on odd afternoons and nights, what will you say to this?
6. What kind of view do you have of children? If I love you and have a sexual appetite but have no procreative desire, how will you respond?
7. Do you really intend to move out of your lodging? I am wondering whether you are ready to move out at any time if you have enough money.
8. What hopes or expectations do you hold as to our success together in the future?[46]

Tomida observes that Okumura found Raichō's blunt manner of addressing these concerns to him insensitive and bewildering. He wrote that he "wondered whether any other man had ever been thrown questions like these to answer."[47] He did, however, make an attempt to respond. He answered questions 1–4 and 7 affirmatively but was stymied by question 5, which he found impossible to answer, and also by question 8, because he did not know where his career as an artist would lead. In his answer to question 6, he expressed a love of children and a belief that sexuality without the intention to produce children was deceitful, but he also agreed that if Raichō wanted to, they could wait until their finances improved before having a child. Even though he was initially offended by her questions, Okumura's letter shows a consideration for Raichō and an idealistic view of love that make him a New Man indeed. Raichō was pleased with his reponse.[48] Tomida translates the conclusion of Okumura's letter as follows:

> As you point out, I can see that various difficulties await us. I also know that we must overcome them to fulfill our love. Whatever may happen to us, I will endure them as long as we are together. I also wish to develop our love into a more genuine, nobler and more admirable one.[49]

In the public's eye, Okumura was cast as the "young swallow" (*wakai tsubame*), a naïve and handsome young man who'd caught the eye of a notorious New Woman. The two formally married in 1941, when fearing that their son's "'illegitimate status' would bar him from taking the examinations to become an officer."[50] They were a couple for fifty years, from the time they began their life together in 1914 until Okumura's death in February 1964. Hiratsuka Raichō continued to be in the public eye as a participant in the Motherhood Protection Debate of 1916–19,[51] as one of the founders of Shin Fujin Kyōkai (New Woman's Association) in 1919,[52] and for her later involvement in domestic and international postwar women's peace movements. As an elderly woman, Hiratsuka Raichō was praised as an early leader in Japanese feminism and especially for her role in *Seitō*.

****

The *Seitō* Manifesto: "In the Beginning, Woman Was the Sun"
Hiratsuka Raichō
Seitō 1.1 (September 1911)

In the beginning, Woman was truly the Sun. An authentic person.
Now, Woman is the Moon. Living off another, reflecting another's brilliance, she is the moon whose face is sickly and wan.
And now, it is here that *Seitō* has been born.
Created by the brains and hands of today's Japanese women, *Seitō* has been born.
These days the things women do invite only mockery.
How well I know what lurks behind this ridicule.

And still I am not one bit afraid.

But what about the misery caused by the shame and disgrace women continually heap upon themselves, all of their own accord?
Is woman such that she merits only this kind of nausea? No! An authen-

tic person does not!

As women of today, we have done everything we could here. We have given our all in giving birth to this child, *Seitō*. All right—even though she may be a retarded, deformed, or premature infant—nothing more can be done. For the time being, we must be satisfied with her as she is.

But have we really exhausted all efforts? Ah, whoever shall be satisfied with her?

Here I go, another woman adding to her discontents.

Is Woman really so powerless?

No! An authentic person is not!

Yet what I shall not overlook is the fact that *Seitō*, which was created from the blistering heat of midsummer, possesses a fierce passion strong enough to scorch even the most intense heat.

Passion! Passion! We live by this and this alone!

By "passion," I refer to none other than the power of devotion, the power of will, the power of meditative concentration, the power of the Way of the Gods! Or, in other words, it is the power of spiritual focus.

Spiritual focus is the one and only gateway to recognizing mystery.

Although I have just spoken of "mystery," I do not mean to imply either something that lies beyond or apart from reality or something fashioned by one's hands or imagined in one's head or created by one's senses. I am not talking about dreams, either. Rather, I would argue that mystery is reality itself, that it lies in the farthest recesses of the human consciousness, and that it is discernible only in the depths of meditation.

I plan to search for Genius within such spiritual focus.

Genius in itself embodies mystery. The authentic person.

Genius is neither male nor female.

Categories like "Man" and "Woman," which describe sexual differences, belong to a self that has reached only the middle or even the lower stratum in the hierarchy of spiritual concentration. They belong to a false self, a mortal self destined to perish. It is utterly impossible for such categories to exist as part of the self of the highest stratum, the true self that does not die, that never will perish.

In the past, I did not know that "females" existed in this world. Nor did I know that "males" existed.

Although I had images of countless men and women in my mind, I had never seen them as "male" or "female."

Nevertheless, in the end I collapsed in fatigue from the difficulty of trying to fix and redeem the many reckless acts that had flowed from the sheer abundance of my spiritual energy.

The weakness of human character! Truly, this is what first showed me the distinctions between "female" and "male."

And thus it was in this world that I learned the word "death."

Death! The fear of death! Once, suspended between heaven and earth, I had played at the brink of life and death. Yet at the same time, I saw that the one who stumbles in the face of death, the one who must be destroyed, is what we call Woman.

Formerly living in a unified world, presently existing in a fragmented and broken one, gasping for every breath, the impure one, what we call Woman.

I break out in a cold sweat merely thinking about how close I came to trying to fall in step with that cowardly, fatalistic herd which seems unaware that our fortunes are something we make ourselves.

I cried, and cried bitterly, over the fact that the strings of the harp I'd played day and night had gone slack, its pitch grown low. When I knew that "character" (*seikaku*) had formed within me, I also knew that I was abandoned by Genius. I felt like a celestial being robbed of her heavenly robe, like a mermaid stranded on the shore.

I grieved in heartrending agony over losing the rapture that had been mine, and my last hope.

And yet, I had always been the master governing this anguish, loss, fatigue, frenzy, and collapse.

I have always claimed the right to be the master of myself, content to be a free, self-governing person. No matter what has happened in my life, without regret for having once been tempted even to self-destruction, relentlessly I have walked my own path.

Ah, the darkness of my native place! Its absolute light!

The Sun, its overflowing brightness and warmth illuminating the entire world and nurturing all things, is it not Genius? An authentic person?

In the beginning, Woman was truly the Sun. An authentic person.

Now, Woman is the Moon. A sickly, pale-faced moon, living off another, reflecting another's brilliance.

We must now recapture our hidden Sun.

"Let us reveal our hidden Sun and our dormant Genius." This is the cry we ceaselessly turn toward ourselves, the craving so hard to suppress, so difficult to extinguish. This is the sole instinct toward the ultimate completion of character, the unification of all fragmented instincts.

It is this cry, this craving, this ultimate instinct that embodies a passionate spiritual focus.

Thus it is at the peak of this spiritual focus that the proud throne of Genius shines.

In the first article of the Seitō Society's Guiding Principles, there is a statement to the effect that we aim to "give birth to the female Genius of tomorrow."

All women, without exception, are people of hidden Genius. We all have the potential for Genius. And I have no doubt at all that this potential will be realized. It is utterly deplorable when, for mere lack of spiritual focus, a life ends, its enormous abilities having been rendered forever meaningless and forever dormant, never having expressed its potential.

"The mind of a woman is shallow, it is the fickle and frivolous bubbles floating on shallow waters. The mind of a man, however, is deep, and its waters rush through subterranean caves" said Zarathustra.[53] So long ordered to tend to housework, women have had their powers of spiritual focus completely blunted.

Housework can be done amidst distractions and with no sense of purpose.

Because it is such an unsuitable environment for spiritual focus and the realization of dormant Genius, I loathe all the irritations that go with housework.

A tedious way of life fragments and complicates one's personal character. In most cases, such fragmentation and complication work in inverse proportion to the discovery of Genius.

Surely there is no one who still harbors doubts about "hidden Genius."

Hasn't even modern psychology proved its existence?

It can no longer be doubted that, even among people who have had no contact with religions and philosophies, there are those with some understanding of hypnotism. Its origins can be traced to Anton Mesmer, a mideighteenth-century Austrian through whose zeal and perseverance hypnotism has finally become a genuine research issue for today's scholars. How often wondrous events have taken place before our very own eyes. Consider how even a frail, delicate woman, upon entering a deep, hypnotic state and then responding to suggestion, suddenly reveals a stupendous strength. Or, take cases like that of an illiterate farm girl who instantly becomes fluent in foreign languages and can compose poetry. One can only call such phenomena miraculous and mysterious, revelations of a power that created existence amidst nothingness and life amidst death. Also, in times of emergency, when we have faced fires, earthquakes, wars, and other disasters, every one of us has experienced performing actions that would never occur to us in the course of our daily lives.

Scholars say the perfect hypnotic state is the psychological state of ridding oneself of all worldly thoughts (*munen, musō*), in which all self-propelled activity completely ceases.

If that is the case, then it appears to be identical to the situation I am describing, in which hidden Genius must be made manifest. Since I am not an expert on hypnotism, regrettably I cannot make unequivocal assertions, but at least I can say that it does suggest a similar state.

What does it mean to "rid oneself of all worldly thoughts?" Isn't this the point at which one reaches a state where one is able to forget the self, a state obtained only by arriving at the farthest reaches of prayer and the most intense spiritual focus? Isn't it non-action, an ecstatic trance? Isn't it emptiness? Isn't it a void?

In truth, this is the void, and yet precisely because it is so, this emptiness is the great storehouse that holds inexhaustible supplies of wisdom. It is the wellspring of all vital energy. It is the abundant field of all ability which has always passed through plants, animals, and human beings, and which must be transmitted for all eternity.

Here there is no past or future, everything is merely in the present.

Ah, hidden Genius! It is the embryo of the wisdom of Nature at the center of the flames burning deep within us. It is the child of omniscient and omnipotent Nature.

"My Rodin is in France."

Rodin is Genius made manifest. He possesses immense powers of spiritual focus. Never relaxing, not even for a moment, he lives impeccably with his mind in its state of crisis, as though this were completely ordinary. Whatever the rhythm of his spiritual life or the rhythm of this physical life, he is undoubtedly a person who can instantaneously change at will. How apt that he should have laughed at the practitioners of slavish art who would wait in vain for inspiration.

Rodin, who possesses an ever-present source of inspiration at his command, is, it must be said, one who truly holds the one and only key to becoming a Genius.

When I, who wish always to live with a sense of urgency even when taking meals or chatting in the evening cool, saw the Rodin issue of *Shirakaba*, I received many hints and suggestions. It was the first time for me, who knows so little of things, to even hear the name Rodin. And then, when I detected so much of myself there, when I found so much I could empathize with, I almost could not bear the happiness I felt.

Ever since, on the nights when I sit alone behind closed doors in my secret room, the light shining brightly from a small oil lamp, its white fire growing ever louder, droning on and on like a storm, burning without so much as a flicker—when all my five white doves, whose gentle red eyes and black eyes are veiled by the same thin silklike membranes, puff up and fall asleep peacefully atop some greenery—I awake, alone at the bottom of a wide ocean. My muscles tighten, blood coursing through my whole body. At that moment, the thought "My Rodin is in France" comes to me from out of nowhere. And then, before I know it, Rodin and I are together playing the music of Nature, that music of Nature's lost harmony.

I think of [Rodin's famous sculpture] "The Kiss," a kiss that melts everything in the crucible of passion, my kiss. A kiss that is actually *one*. Spirit! Flesh! Rapture of tranquility at the extremities of ecstasy. Repose! The beauty of rest! Tears of deep emotion surely sparkle with golden light.

It is the Sun, before sunset, burning with a scorching heat above the Japan Alps, circling round and round. It is my hushed sobbing as I stand by myself at the summit of a lone peak.

My soul shudders endlessly in the face of fear and anxiety. How weak, exhausted, indefinable, and hard to grasp it is! A trembling deep in my mind, a reverberation that would bend a silver wire, my obsession with black-winged Death that advances on me when I awake. And yet . . . and yet, once invigorated, my dormant Genius still leads me onward. It has not completely abandoned me. And then, my entire body overflows with power—I know not where it comes from—and I simply become strong. My heart becomes big, deep, tranquil and bright. My field of vision expands, and rather than seeing each and every thing as discrete objects, the whole world is reflected in one glance. My heavy spirit grows lighter and lighter, as if it had escaped from my body and become suspended in air. Or, rather, has my body become weightless and simply evaporated? I become intoxicated with an ineffable feeling of oneness and harmony in which my body and spirit are completely forgotten.

I know neither Life nor Death.

I daresay that therein lies Eternal "Life," a will of fiery steel.

At a time like this, Napoleon shouted, "The Alps? So what?" In truth, not a single obstacle stood before me.

Truly free, truly liberated, my mind and body felt not the slightest pressure, constraint, fear, or anxiety. Thus my right hand, completely numb, takes the pen and starts to write.

I have no choice but to believe in my hidden Genius. I must believe that the reason my chaotic inner life can sustain even a modicum of unity is because of this alone.

Freedom and liberation! We have long been aware of the cacophony of voices calling for women's liberation. But what does that mean? As I think of it, hasn't the meaning of what we call freedom and liberation been enormously misunderstood? Even when put more simply, as the "Question of Women's Liberation," many problems are thereby concealed. No matter how much one may escape from outside pressures and restraints, receive a higher education, be able to seek work in a broader range of fields, have the right to vote, achieve distance from the small world of the family and the hands of guardians like parents and husbands, and lead a so-called independent life, why do these define the liberation of women? I can see that perhaps these would give the space and opportunity by which women could arrive at the stage of true liberation, but they are no more than expediencies. The means, but not the ends. They do not constitute the ideal.

Yet saying this does not by any means imply that I am one of those, like so many of Japan's intelligentsia, who advocate that higher education is unnecessary for women. Males and females are born not so much of "nature" as of a unified essence. Therefore, although it has been temporarily acceptable in some countries during certain time periods to believe that what is necessary for one sex is not necessary for the other, deeper consideration shows that there is really nothing quite so irrational as this.

I am saddened by the present situation in which Japan has only one women's college and men's universities do not have the generosity to open their doors easily to women. But once the level of our knowledge equals that of men, what will that mean? In the first place, the search for knowledge exists for no other reason than to liberate the self from the darkness of ignorance and illusion. But if we rubbed our eyes and took another look, wouldn't we be surprised to find that the knowledge we had consumed, like an amoeba circling and devouring its prey, was nothing other than an empty shell? And in that case, wouldn't our obligation be to fight desperately in any we could to cast off that shell? All philosophies take us faraway from Nature, blinding us to our true wisdom. The people who live by toying with knowledge may well be scholars, but they are hardly intelligent. On the contrary, when it comes to seeing the unvarnished truth of things right before their own eyes, how close they come to a troubling blindness.

Buddha went into the snow-capped mountains, where he sat for six years until one night he attained enlightenment: "How miraculous: all creatures possess a Buddha's wisdom and virtue, and some day, throughout the universe, all plants and trees, all lands without exception will attain Buddhahood." Once he saw into the truth of things just as they are, he was enchanted with the perfection of Nature. And so Buddha became a true Realist. He became a true Naturalist. He was not a daydreamer. In truth, he became an acutely self-aware person who liberated himself completely.

In Buddha we see a true Realist whom we must regard as a Mystic, a true Naturalist whom we must regard as an Idealist.

This is also to be said about my Rodin. By penetrating reality, he discovered therein an ideal that was completely compatible with reality.

Did he not say, "Nature is always perfect. She never makes an error"?

Entirely on his own volition, Rodin chose to comply with Nature. It was in this willful compliance, in this making Nature his own, that he became a Naturalist.

The eyes of those who are called Japan's Naturalists have not yet penetrated so far as to see the ideal in untouched reality. In the hearts and minds of these men who lack the power of concentration, Nature will never reveal its entire form. The realm of the Ideal as reality which is visible only at the inner depths of human meditation has not yet opened so easily before these men. Where, in these men, is freedom and liberation? When will the shackles fall from their necks, their hands, their legs? Aren't they a pitiful lot, suffering in a slavish world of their own making, caught in a trap set by no one but themselves?

I cannot bear to see those women who blindly envy men, who imitate men, and who, though lagging behind a bit, attempt to walk exactly the same road the men have walked.

Women! Rather than building a mountain of rubbish in your minds, empty the mountain and you shall know Nature in its entirety. Given what I have said, what is this true freedom and liberation for which I plead? Needless to say, it is none other than that which makes fully manifest both hidden Genius and latent Talent. To achieve this, we must first remove all manner of impediments to our development. Are these obstacles really outside pressures or the lack of knowledge? I do not mean this at all! Of course, I cannot say that these play absolutely no role, but the main obstacle, in fact, is us. We are the owners of Genius; we will become the palaces where Genius resides.

When we separate ourselves from Self, we reveal our hidden Genius.

We must sacrifice our Self for the sake of the hidden Genius within. We must become so-called non-selves. (Non-self is the pinnacle of the magnified Self.)

There is no other Way than by believing in the hidden Genius within: from the truest instincts, earnest desires, and constant clamoring for Genius, we shall pray with zeal, we shall concentrate the spirit, and we shall forget the Self.

And then, at the most extreme point on this path, the throne of Genius shines on high.

I, together with all women, want to believe in hidden Genius. Simply believing in that possibility makes me want to rejoice with all my heart in our good fortune at having been born into this world as women. Our savior is solely the Genius that exists within us. It is not something we seek through Buddha or God, in temples or churches.

We no longer wait for Divine revelation. By our own efforts, we shall discover the secrets of Nature within us. We shall seek our own revelations of the Divine! We do not seek miracles, nor do we crave mysticism in some faraway realm. By our own efforts, we shall reveal the secrets of Nature within us. We will become our own miracles, our own mystics.

We must constantly continue our spiritual concentration and ardent prayer. Hence, we must spare no effort! Until the day on which our hidden Genius is born, until the day our veiled Sun shall shine.

On that day, we will take the whole world and everything in it as ours.

On that day, as the supreme rulers of our own existence, we will stand at the very heart of Nature. Self-aware and self-reliant, we will have no need to question ourselves, for we will be authentic people.

And it is then, I imagine, that we will finally know the innumerable pleasures and the abundance offered by solitude and loneliness.

No longer will Woman be the Moon.

On that day, Woman will once again become the Sun of ancient times. An authentic person.

And so, we shall rule the great, dazzling gold palace atop the crystal mountain in the east of the Land of the Rising Sun.

Women! When you draw your portrait, never forget to choose the golden dome!

Even if I collapse halfway, or even if I sink to the bottom of the ocean, a shipwrecked soldier, I will raise both my paralyzed hands and yell with my last breath, "Women! Advance! Advance!"

Tears and still more tears stream down my face.

It is time to put down my pen.

And yet I have something more which I want to say.

I recognize that the publication of *Seitō* provides a fine opportunity to reveal the hidden Genius within women, especially within those women who aspire to art, and that as a journal working toward those goals, it has many layers of meaning. Indeed, for as long as it casts from our hearts and minds all the dust, the sediment, and the chaff that impedes the discovery of our Genuis, *Seitō* will, in one sense at least, mean something.

I also believe that even if the day comes when *Seitō* is lost—not because of our neglect but as a result of our efforts—some measure of our goals will have been achieved.

Finally, one last point. I believe that all members of the Seitō Society [Bluestockings], young members like me, strive to manifest our hidden Genius, respect individual uniqueness, and enable all to accomplish their own divine missions in ways that do not violate others. Thus we are earnest women who single-mindedly focus the spirit. We are conscientious, serious, simple and honest, and even naive women. Still, we are not at all like the many other women's groups one is apt to see, which pass the time idly, interested in name, not in deed. We who earnestly desire not to be inconclusive do not doubt for a second how different we are.

That ardent desire is the true and certain origin that gives birth to reality.

****

To the Women of the World
Hiratsuka Raichō
Seitō 3.4 (April 1913)

I deeply regret that even now I must say this kind of thing to today's women.[54]

I frequently encounter the following kinds of questions, especially from women. They ask, "Are you and the other Bluestockings against marriage?" When contending with such odd questions—and, indeed, they are odd—I have always responded, "No." Sometimes I have gone farther, adding that "I have never once spoken in support of women remaining single, nor do I remember ever advocating the idea of marriage or the concept of the 'good wife, wise mother.' Much less have I ever indicated that the Bluestockings were proponents of any such ideas." Thereupon, the women respond simply by saying, "Oh, is that so? Since everyone says you're against marriage, we just assumed . . ." Since they do not ask me anything further, I lose the courage to go into any more detail and usually leave it at that.

I act this way because I am so completely taken aback by questions that reveal just how simple, how carefree, and how undisturbed are either these women's own inner lives or their thoughts on the inner lives of modern women such as ourselves. I daresay they have no real issue of concern in mind other than a rather idle, mindless idea such as, "Despite the fact that she's old enough, Raichō still has not married, so she's most likely against marriage," or "Since everyone says she's against marriage, I guess it must be so. I'll just ask and see if it is true or not. Besides, there are rumors that most of the other Bluestockings are also single." I can also guess from the thoughtless way these women ask their questions, and from their sarcastic tone of voice, that they have not given the matter any more thought or examination than this. If it were not so, I suspect they would hesitate to confront us with such silly questions.

Why doesn't a most basic doubt occur to most women today about such homilies as "Women must marry at least once," "Marriage is the only way for women to live," "All women must be good wives and wise mothers," and "Marriage and motherhood are a woman's whole life"? That this does not happen strikes me as strange. Why don't they make any attempt at a fundamental examination of what, by rights, a genuine life for women should be—completely apart from the accepted female virtues that have been established through the long course of history and through numerous customs, for the sake of immediate expediency and utility, and especially for the convenience of men?

We do not presume to advocate that all women remain single. We simply do not have the leisure to become involved in ideological disputes over such issues as the rejection of marriage or "good wives and wise mothers." We do, however, have fundamental doubts about women's lives as they have been led up until today, and we ourselves can no longer bear to continue such an existence. Whether women should, in fact, marry has long been at issue. Must a woman's entire life be sacrificed for the necessity of preserving the race? Is there no other vocation for women outside of procreation? Is marriage the absolute and only door to women's lives? Is being a wife and a mother the whole of a woman's mission in life? We can no longer believe in such ideas. Shouldn't there be limitless doors for women, open to each of us, besides the door to marriage? Besides meekly becoming a "good wife and wise mother," shouldn't defining a woman's mission in life be left up to each of us? Shouldn't freedom of choice be readily available to each individual? Surely this goes without saying.

For this reason, we demand as much liberal education as possible for women. Furthermore, we demand a high level of spiritual education for the sake of the women who, independent of men, shall find meaning in their own lives as women. And while I do not attempt to explain everything from a solely materialistic point of view, as many socialists do, I must say that we also demand vocational training in order to eliminate the many insecurities and obstacles that arise from a lack of economic independence. Whenever women do not depend on marriage, the issue of immediate concern is always the question of employment.

For example, the women's movement in Europe was, of course, motivated by Rousseau's theory of the natural rights of man to freedom and equality, and was based on an awakening of women that went hand in hand with the development of the concept of individualism. However, I suspect that, apart from this intellectual dimension, the women's movement was largely instigated by the actual problems of the economic conditions in European society and the imbalance of males and females in the population. It did not matter whether these women themselves questioned or disliked the idea of marriage. The fact was that many women could not get married even if they wanted to do so, and thus, for them, the question of employment was a most pressing issue.

Whether fortunate or unfortunate, we modern Japanese women are not motivated by this kind of external necessity. This is not to say that such does not exist, but rather that it is our own inner needs which make us also long to step out of the small haven of the home, take jobs, and lead our own lives.

I have heard that women's education in the United States and Europe is increasingly leaning toward vocational training. Recently, a certain newspaper carried an interview with Naruse Jinzō, the college president just returned from a trip abroad, which in essence stated the following: Naruse said that although women's vocational training was flourishing abroad, he was most pleased that women's education in Japan was entirely directed toward creating good wives and wise mothers. He also said that in England, too, the young women of the upper classes were generally educated in the home. I also noticed that he mentioned something like, "In Japan these days, although New Women might be causing quite a stir, they are nothing but worthless tarts." Because I have not had the opportunity to speak with Mr. Naruse in a long time, I may be much too hasty in criticizing him on the basis of this one article, which appeared in a newspaper that is not always reliable. Nevertheless, I am deeply saddened to hear these words from a women's educator whom I respect. Hasn't old age caught up with this zealous educator who was once so ahead of his time? It saddens me, too, to think the old must flirt with such conventional ideas.

Seen in the light of Mr. Naruse's emphasis on so-called character-building education, vocational training is, indeed, not ideal. But where does such criticism leave the pathetic "good wife, wise mother" education for girls that we have in our own country? Clearly Mr. Naruse does not understand in the slightest—nor does he even care to understand—women such as us, whom society has called New Women, or the vitality emerging within us and its needs, which are so hard to silence. Echoing the narrow views of an ignorant and excitable majority, and the insults hurled by fools who find fault with anyone who attempts something new, Mr. Naruse coolly censures us in various and unconsidered terms, calling us "tarts" or accusing us of "harming the female virtues." For the president of the only women's college in Japan to say such things is, I believe, quite unwise and most irresponsible.

Modern women who have more or less awakened as individuals can no longer feel any sense of appreciation for the so-called womanly virtues of submission, gentleness, chastity, patience, self-sacrifice, and so on that men, and that our society, have thus far forced upon us. This is because we have considered the reasons for, and the roots of, assumptions about female virtue, asking such questions as: Why have such behaviors been required of women? Why did society come to recognize them as feminine virtues, and why, in the end, did people even go so far as to believe these virtues formed the essential nature of woman? I will not give any details here about the conclusions our questions have produced. However, I can say that only one reasonable explanation exists, and that is, "for the sake of men." In short, such behaviors have absolutely no intrinsic value. However, due to irrational prejudice and to their customary antagonism to change, today's women simply do not understand such things. Rather, deluded by the slander of those today who insult anything new, they blindly oppose women such as us. Yet if even these women were to consider such issues more deeply, I believe that they would surely find many things to their dissatisfaction. But I am afraid that when I say such things, it will only make today's women immediately jump to such arbitrary conclusions as "The New Woman aims to rebel against men" and "A woman's awakening somehow seems to lead her to divorce." It is true that we might rebel against men, and at times, I imagine, divorces will occur. But rebellion itself is not our purpose, and divorce is not our goal. Indeed, the extent to which we do not even interest ourselves in questions such as whether rebellion or divorce is right or wrong shows how greatly we value our lives as individuals and our lives as women. If, thus far, women's lives have been trampled on for the sake of men's personal advantage and desires as well as their convenience, isn't it natural for us to take a defiant stance toward men at some time in order to recover what has been lost?

Were women who are lucky enough to have the title of "wife" even to rub their eyes a bit more, could they be entirely satisfied with the lives they've been leading up to now? I wonder how many wives exist today who consented to marry without love in order to secure their own livelihood, and who have given up their lives to responding to their husbands' various demands that they serve them as maids during the day, and as prostitutes by night. Sadly, I have heard that some women, believing they must be obedient, submit even to the excessive sexual desires of their husbands, and grow very weak as a result of multiple pregnancies. Even if affection should develop between husband and wife after they have been living together, in most cases such feeling represents little more than the product of self-interest and expedience. It is not a love that in and of itself transcends such considerations.

Even if we do not, for example, go so far as to oppose marriage itself, we cannot submit at all to today's idea of marriage, or to the marriage system as it presently operates. In today's social system, doesn't marriage enforce a relationship of authority and subjection that exists throughout one's entire life? Aren't wives treated in the same way as minors or cripples? Isn't it true that they have neither property rights nor legal rights to their children? Isn't it true that adultery is not a crime for the husband but is a crime for the wife? We do not wish to marry so long as it means submitting to this kind of absurd, illogical system. We do not wish to become wives.

Once our eyes have been opened, we cannot fall asleep again. We are alive. We are awake. We cannot exist without letting the vitality of our inner lives radiate outward. No matter what pressures we may face, our new vitality cannot cease finding such escape.

Now, searching for the door to a genuine life for women, we find ourselves at a loss, wondering whether to concentrate all this energy of ours. Offhand comments as to whether New Women are frivolous or serious are no longer of any consequence to us. In short, no matter how loudly or how many times we are told such superficial truths as "Live an earnest, spiritual life" or "Live in a noble, respectable, and genuine way," it does no good. Though we have only just finished the grammar school of awakening, we cannot go on living blinded by these mere silhouettes of meaning preached and defined by others. We are searching, through our own efforts, to know the meaning of our lives. While continuing to feel such insecurity from within, and while battling a great deal of unreasonable persecution from without, we shall continue our search, fundamentally doubting and fundamentally questioning what, indeed, the genuine life of a woman should be.

If, however, our inner power and awakened vitality do not find any satisfying outlet, then we are surely headed for destruction, and we shall have no other choice, I fear, but to end our lives, just as [Henrik Ibsen's character] Hedda [Gabler] did.

****

To My Parents on Becoming Independent
Hiratsuka Raichō
Seitō 4.2 (February 1914)

Actually, I have been thinking I'd tell you about this after you were feeling better, Mother. But since I've learned that your illness in fact stems from worrying that I am about to carry out something I've planned all by myself without a word to anyone, I would like to bring everything out in the open now, without another moment's delay. I would like to have you know as much as possible about me, and also about my thoughts and my lifestyle, and especially about what I am now planning and preparing to do. By doing so, I hope I can at least relieve you of needless worry and that you will be a little more at ease about me. Thus, even though you are not feeling well, I have decided to tell you about this.

In truth, we would better understand and sympathize with each other if I sat down with both you and Father and discussed this matter down to its smallest details. Yet as you know, I am not very good at explaining myself, and besides that, by nature I have trouble getting close to others. Even though we have faced one another morning and night in the same house for almost thirty years, sadly, even to this day, I have not once been able to speak in a truly revealing way to either my father, who has shown tolerance toward me and has always trusted me no matter what, or to my kind, loving mother, who has sacrificed everything for her children. Especially in recent years, though we have not discussed it openly, it has become increasingly clear that there is a gap between my thoughts and way of living and your own, a gap that cannot possibly be resolved. Because of this, ever since our thoughts and feelings about even the smallest of ordinary events have become so completely different, especially when I am at home I have closed my heart, remained aloof, and become absolutely indifferent and silent about all household affairs. Precisely because I believe that, even if I talked with you both, surely I couldn't say a tenth of what I feel, I have decided to write this letter.

Mother, it is quite true that, just as you have guessed by now and grown so worried about, sometime in the next two or three days I will leave the home in which you both have raised me for so long and start a life of my own; in fact, almost all the preparations for this have been completed. It is understandable that you will be very displeased at the way I have steadily worked to realize my plans without ever consulting you or giving you the slightest hint of my intentions until today. In fact, yesterday you even said to me, "You seem to decide everything by what is convenient for you, what suits you. But things do not work that easily. Don't you see that the family has its own concerns, and that parents have responsibilities that they must perform as parents? It's not that we won't let you do what you wish, but that there is a way to go about things. There are certain formalities. In this kind of thing, first one consults with parents and siblings, and has to determine what is best for both sides. Then one must at least talk things over with the relatives. No matter how many preparations you may have made by yourself, you cannot simply announce, 'Well, I guess it will be tomorrow or the day after.' Honestly, how can I help but worry when, no matter how serious the issue, you do whatever you like without telling us at all? I can only imagine that you take pleasure in completely bypassing our wishes, shocking us, and upsetting us as much as possible with your way of doing things. Even if you end up doing the same thing, there must be a more appropriate way of doing it. So what else can I assume but that you have decided to make your parents enemies?"

When I saw the deeply worried look on your face and your tears, Mother, I felt bad, too, and since I am a soft touch myself and started crying along with you, I couldn't say anything. But then, no matter what may be concerned or who is involved, once I have firmly resolved to do a thing, it has always been my habit never to breathe a word to anyone until I have made my plans, completed the preparations, and am ready to carry them out at any time. Painful experiences in my past taught me this over time, and thus I have found this habit the best way to manage my affairs even today. Especially considering the nature of this issue, I was afraid I would run into all sorts of problems with old-fashioned notions and feelings, and that the heart of the matter would be ignored. I was also afraid that, as so often happens, peripheral or subordinate issues would cause unexpected trouble, hindering and delaying me from carrying out my plans. Especially because of these fears, I tried to take care of everything in secret, but I had no other motive for this secrecy, so please do not misunderstand me or scold me for it. Before going on, I would like to ask you again to follow patiently what I will tell you. If only you do me the favor of reading this, I am quite sure you will understand what I am doing.

Although the idea of independence merely as an idea budded in my mind a very long time ago, it began to come alive for me in the days after I graduated from Japan Women's College. I think this all started, then, exactly eight years ago. In those days I felt that, since you had raised me to adulthood, I could no longer bear to rely on you, whether or not pressed by necessity. I embraced the thought that, somehow or other, I had to devise a way to go out on my own soon, and I even looked for a job. And yet, in the end, I never did see, in the scheme of human life, much serious or fundamental value simply in making a living per se (probably because I was born into a family that had no money worries, and so I never felt any such concerns acutely). I saw a contradiction between taking a job to make a living and working for the sake of perfecting my own inner self. The latter goal is what I live for and value more than anything else, and my greatest fear is to have this obstructed. When I felt this way, a panic would well up inside me, and I ended up thinking, "Well . . . well, if I can, I want to try to avoid the issue of making a living, and I want to use all the time I have as I wish, reading, writing, and thinking." Moreover, because an almost instinctive desire and need for the religious life in its most fundamental sense has long been stirring in the depths of my being, to this day, even though I have felt the need for a job, I have been procrastinating about getting one, and have not had enough courage to dare to leave your house and live on my own. All this has left me feeling nothing but anxiety and vague fears. Nevertheless, the need within my heart to become independent no matter what, and to change my life at once and completely, has only become more vivid and strengthened with each passing day.

I have come to feel keenly that when parents and children have different ideas, do different work, and follow different paths, yet live together in one house indefinitely, it only works to pollute their relationship and render it halfhearted. It not only does nothing to increase their happiness but actually carries the danger of destroying the feelings they have for one another. This feeling deepened particularly after I published *Seitō* and, to some extent, made public my feelings and lifestyle—which, whether or not I liked it, began my dealings with society and made me what you might even call a public figure. I have always valued and appreciated father's lenient attitude toward this work of mine and the large amount of freedom he always accords me, merely remarking, "It's because of the difference in our generations." This kind of parent-child relationship is rarely seen in today's Japanese family. And yet, precisely because of that attitude, I have felt oddly troubled. This strange feeling of constraint has just kept on, gradually building up inside me.

Only once, when *Seitō* was banned for "disrupting the peace"—probably because of the essay by Ms. F, a known socialist[55]—did Father speak to me from his position as a member of the government, as an official: "If you have no choice but to publish a socialist's work in *Seitō*, and if you feel you absolutely must associate with such people, then before you do anything else, I would like you to sever your relations with this family so that you do not compromise your father's position." (I'd like to repeat here that, the truth of the matter is, I do not have friends in socialist circles, as Father has feared, nor did I have that much sympathy for socialist thought to start with.)

Aside from this one incident, Father, you have always given me your tacit support. Even when the term "New Woman" became a kind of flippant and fashionable expression, bringing down on my head both the abusive sarcasm of the ignorant as well as the censure and pressure of the old-fashioned, so-called intelligentsia, Father did not refer to it once, and I was indeed grateful. However, Father is a middle-aged man with a certain standing in society, who values more than anything a sense of responsibility or duty to his job and who always acts with the society or public in mind. Day and night I read a look on your faces that tells me how very bothersome it is, in a sense, for Father to have a daughter like me—a young person who tries to live by new ideas, a new kind of woman who acts and thinks in a way that completely ignores public opinion and even defies convention. I also see how Mother, who stands between us, must always suffer silently and alone.

From your standpoint, I must seem to be a very selfish person who is insensitive to everything, a reckless and daring person who insists on doing whatever she decides to, no matter what, and who gives not one whit for the feelings of other people. But in truth I suffer from being more sensitive than most people, and have the unfortunate shortcoming of inevitably forgetting myself in an excessive concern for others. (At least, from my standpoint, this would be called a shortcoming. Oftentimes, this shortcoming takes the form of staying aloof from others and not easily becoming close to people. I am constantly striving to overcome this but . . .). This weakness inside me . . . the pain I inflict on you daily . . . they have become a dark shadow forever hovering over us. Furthermore, although I am a member of this household and this family, I have utterly rejected what anyone else would automatically consider the traditional sacrifices and duties within the family, and with other families especially close to ours. I myself admit that this rejection and aloofness are an essential and almost unavoidable part of my philosophy and my unsociable, "pessimistic" nature. Nevertheless, as far as the truth of my sentiments is concerned, I frequently have feelings of guilt and discomfort about being around this family. I feel deep in my heart that the presence of only one person in a family who cannot possibly get along with others causes unhappiness not only to that person but to the entire family.

There is one more point to make in addition to this—although it may be a generalized restatement of what has been said so far. What I find hardest to bear is the contradiction and disharmony between what I think and profess and my actual lifestyle. I find it distressing that this conflict has forced me to exhaust much of my precious time and energy on relatively worthless activities. Many times I have resolved to part from you and leave this house, to live on my own and start a new life, and, in order to do so, have resolved to plunge fearlessly into the task of making a living, even going so far as to broach the subject to Mother. However, perhaps partly because I am poor at explaining things, I could never convince Mother but, on the contrary, aggravated our misunderstandings. Moreover, I added to your needless worries, and matters went from bad to worse. I shrink from injuring the affection between parent and child, and besides that, it always happens that whenever I see poor Mother crying, I can no longer say anything and my courage to go through with my plan utterly fails at that moment.

However, this time for sure I have truly made up my mind. That is why this time, in view of my past failures, I have rushed ahead single-mindedly to get ready to leave without telling you any of this.

Well, then, there is something I must tell you here. Simply put, this time is different from all the other times when I said I was going to leave home and live just on my own. As you know, since early last summer, H, whom I call "Young Swallow" or "Little Brother," has been visiting me all the time.[56] This young painter, who is five years my junior, and I would like to start living together in as free and simple a relationship as possible.

Although I have made resolutions countless times, I have always lacked the courage necessary to dare to act on them. Thus I believe that what finally produced this unshakable resolve of mine and enabled me to achieve independence was the sheer strength of my love for H.

Perhaps the fact that I don't have a younger sister or brother may somehow be connected to this, but I have always wanted to befriend or take care of younger people, whether male or female. This has become very clear to me in the last two or three years. I hardly ever glance at people who are my age or older. Only those much younger ever win my affection. I kiss them like a sister, a mother, or at times like a lover. By looking after them, a part of my own life is consoled, warmed, calmed, and enriched.

And yet, among these people, the one who has most captured and moved my heart is the quiet, timid H. Gradually, I began to find H, who is half child, three parts female and two parts male, irresistibly endearing. Then, my sisterly or motherly kisses at some point changed into those of a lover. Although H, for his part, was at first afraid of me and nervous when around me, these days he feels very close to me and acts like a lover. Having first learned about love from me, he loves me with a truly pure heart. He is almost overly protective of me. Probably, Father, you have read Shaw's play *Candida* in German translation; in any case, the love H and I share reminds me of the relationship between the female heroine Candida and the young poet whose name I can't remember.

Our love has grown to the point where, if we don't see each other for a single day, we feel restless and cannot settle down to our work. Since he is experiencing all this for the first time, it is even more difficult for H. We can no longer bear to leave things unresolved indefinitely and go on with this uncomfortable situation, growing more and more ill at ease. Visiting and being visited by each other absorbs most of our time and interferes with our work, which we value more than anything else.

So, somehow, I want to resolve this quickly. That is to say, I must choose between two alternatives, letting our love thrive or killing it. Thus, having mustered all the strength within me, I have boldly determined to take the path of love. In various ways, this affirmation of love will entail a certain amount of contradiction and uncertainty as concerns my basic way of life, a life founded on my disposition and my personality. However, I have decided that even amidst this contradiction and uncertainty, I will conquer and stand firm against them, nurturing the love between us as well as possible, so that, having once budded, it does not wither. I have made up my mind to take this path just as far as it may go to see what course it takes, how it develops, and where it will lead me, to see what unknown realms will unfold before me from now on and how my life and thoughts will change.

Although H is too reserved to say so exactly, there is a strong need in his young, pure heart to live with me. I, on the other hand, know that my solitary nature does not permit me to adapt easily to people, and makes me difficult and unsuited to living with others. I also know my weak constitution causes me to tire easily. Furthermore, I have worried whether this lifestyle might not rob me of the energy I need for my work. Because of these concerns, I was not readily enthusiastic about living together. Yet in the end, I decided to try it, since if things don't work out once we've tried, then we can always live separately. However, economic considerations also contributed to my decision. (That is, even though H is still completely unable to support himself, his family has stopped sending him money because of their own troubles, putting him in a rather tight spot at present. Yet it would be a little too much for me, at least for now, to earn enough money by myself for the two of us to live separately.)

Therefore, yesterday we discovered and decided to rent the second floor of a very quiet gardener's house about one or two blocks from the Shinto shrine in Sugamo. In fact, we would like to move into that house perhaps as early as tomorrow. Although this must seem extremely hasty, it is something I have thought long and hard about for quite some time, and it is hardly a sudden impulse or a temporary whim. Because this is a very important step in my life, and because it is the first time I'll be faced with having to make a living—and, indeed, we will not be able to live if I am idle—this is truly an earnest endeavor.

Although I know you have your own opinions about this, and many of these points must surely displease you, please understand what I have said. I beg you, if you can, to consent to my carrying out my plan. As far as I can help it, I do not want to quarrel with you or argue or in any way harm our feelings for one another. Whatever you may say, I will listen quietly and think about it all. However, H and I feel we must live together at all costs, and since, after much thought, we have decided once and for all that this is the best way to meet this need, there is nothing else I can do now but carry out our plans. If by chance, after we have put this plan into action, it turns out to be a mistake, or even if it brings complete failure or unhappiness, I know that all the responsibility lies with me. Therefore, I will never trouble you with my problems or blame anyone else for them. Also, I cannot help but think how much closer I will feel to you by living separate lives in separate homes and visiting each other occasionally than by living separate lives in the same house.

And then, though I almost forgot to mention it, yesterday Mother said it would look bad to live in the same house with a young man without marrying him, and asked me what I would do if I became pregnant. Because of my dissatisfaction with the present marriage system, I do not want to go along with that system, nor do I want a marriage that must receive such legal recognition. In fact, I can't even tolerate the title of "husband" or "wife." While it may well be strange for a man and woman who don't love each other to live together, and in such a case particularly, I can imagine they would need some recognition by others, there is nothing more natural than a man and woman who do love each other living in the same house. As long as a couple has an understanding between themselves, I think, a formal marriage is really immaterial. Also, because, for a woman, marriage consists of an extremely disadvantageous system of rights and obligations, I am all the more opposed to it. Not only that, but the old-fashioned morality of today's society does a good deal of harm by imposing unreasonable restraints, forcing a woman to carry out unnatural obligations such as to treat her husband's parents as her own and other sacrifices, as though they were a matter of course. There is no way I shall ever willingly place myself in that kind of situation. Because H understands this reasoning very well, he, too, has no desire to marry.

But it is not only logic that's important; simply as a matter of taste, that kind of thing repulses me. That is why I am not attracted to the idea of calling H my husband, and I don't even like thinking about it. When H and I are out walking together, he gets very angry when people call us "Mr. and Mrs." He always says he prefers "Older Sister" and "Younger Brother."

As for children, as things stand now (I don't yet know what the future will bring), we are not planning to have any. I would like you to understand that those who value themselves and live for their work are not the kind to rush into having children. In truth, at the present time I feel almost no desire to have children or become a mother, and since H has not yet established himself, even common sense tells us he is not ready to have children. Also, the present state of our lives, both financially and spiritually, does not afford us the capacity to raise a child were we to have one, so we don't plan on it. So please don't worry about this. But I would like to add that this is not because we share Mother's idea that it is improper or shameful for a man and a woman who have not been formally married to have a child.

Now, I think I have generally outlined what I had originally intended to say. I beg you with all my heart not to get angry and think I am being "selfish as usual." Since I have made up my mind, I would like to carry through with this plan as soon as possible; since all the preparations have been made, all I am doing now is eagerly waiting for your consent.

—January 10, 1914

Notes

[1]The first two volumes of *Genshi, josei wa taiyō de atta: Hiratsuka Raichō jiden*, 4 vols. (Ōtsuki Shoten, 1971–73) expand on the autobiography Raichō wrote in 1955, *Watakushi no aruita michi* (Tokyo: Shinhyōronsha, 1955), giving a detailed account of her childhood, education through Japan Women's College, her entanglement with author Morita Sōhei, and her involvement with *Seitō* and the New Woman's Association (Shin Fujin Kyōkai). Although volumes three and four continue the first-person voice, they were written after Raichō's death by her longtime friend, secretary, and biographer Kobayashi Tomie (1917–2004). For literary analysis of Raichō's autobiographies, see Livia Monnet, "'In the Beginning, Woman Was the Sun': Autobiographies of Modern Japanese Women Writers," *Japan Forum* 1.1 (April 1989): 55–81, and 1.2 (October 1989): 197–233.

[2]Raichō's 1955 autobiography skips over her life during the war. In the latter half of the 1971–73 autobiograpy (see note 1 above), Kobayashi Tomie portrays Raichō's evacuation to the countryside in the 1940s as a refusal to participate in the war effort. Yet Yoneda Sayoko and Teruko Craig point to essays Raichō wrote in the 1930s lauding the emperor system. See Yoneda, *Hiratsuka Raichō: Kindai Nihon no demokurashii to jendā* (Tokyo: Yoshikawa Kōbunkan, 2002), 220–23, and Hiratsuka Raichō and Teruko Craig, *In the Beginning, Woman Was the Sun* (New York: Columbia University Press, 2006), 330–31, n6.

[3]See the Introducton for a discussion of this work.

[4]Hiroko Tomida, *Hiratsuka Raichō and Early Japanese Feminism* (Leiden: Brill, 2004), Hiratsuka and Craig, *In the Beginning, Woman Was the Sun*; Dina Lowy, "Love and Marriage: Ellen Key and Hiratsuka Raichō Explore Alternatives," *Women's Studies: An Interdisciplinary Journal* 33.4 (January 2004): 361–80; Sumiko Otsubo, "Engendering Eugenics: Feminists and Marriage Restriction Legislation in the 1920s," in Barbara Molony and Kathleen Uno, eds., *Gendering Modern Japanese History* (Cambridge, MA and London: Harvard University Press, 2005), 225–56; Dina Lowy, *The Japanese "New Woman": Images of Gender and Modernity* (New Brunswick, NJ and London: Rutgers University, 2007); Gregory M. Pflugfelder, "'S' Is for Sister: Schoolgirl Intimacy and 'Same-Sex Love' in Early Twentieth-Century Japan," in Molony and Uno, eds., *Gendering Modern Japanese History*, 133–90.

[5]"Koi no gisei" (Victims of Love), *Tokyo Asahi shinbun*, 26 March 1908, 6.

[6]Morita Sōhei, *Baien* (Black Smoke, 1909), vol. 29 in the series *Gendai Nihon bungaku taikei*, reprint (Tokyo: Chikuma Shobō, 1971).

[7]Tomida, *Hiratsuka Raichō*, 135.

[8]Hiratsuka, *Genshi, josei wa taiyō de atta*, 1: 283–87; Hiratsuka and Craig, *In the Beginning, Woman Was the Sun*, 137–39.

[9]The original core members of *Seitō* were Hiratsuka Raichō, Kiuchi Teiko, Mozume Kazuko, Nakano Hatsuko, and Yasumochi Yoshiko.

[10][Hiratsuka] Raichō, "Genshi, josei wa taiyō de atta" (In the Beginning, Woman

Was the Sun), *Seitō* 1.1 (September 1911): 37–52. Partial translations of this essay are also found in Tomida, *Hiratsuka Raichō*, 156–57; Hiratsuka and Craig, *In the Beginning, Woman Was the Sun*, 157–59.

[11]Hiroko Tomida analyzes many of Raichō's publications in detail in chap. 4, "The Seitō Society and New Women," in Tomida, *Hiratsuka Raichō*, 139–219.

[12]Hiratsuka, *Genshi, josei wa taiyō de atta*, 4: 300–302.

[13]For more on Raichō's interest in Ellen Key, see Lowy, "Love and Marriage," and Otsubo, "Engendering Eugenics." For an extended discussion of the relationship between eugenics and the New Woman, see Angelique Richardson, *Love and Eugenics in the Late Nineteenth Century: Rational Reproduction and the New Woman* (Oxford: Oxford University Press, 2003).

[14]Attributed to Otake Kōkichi, "Henshū-shitsu yori" (From the Editing Room), *Seitō* 2.6 (June 1912): 121–25.

[15]Attributed to Otake Kōkichi, "Henshū-shitsu yori" (From the Editing Room), *Seitō* 2.7 (July 1912): 110.

[16]Tomida, *Hiratsuka Raichō*, 172.

[17]Dina Lowy, *The Japanese "New Woman": Images of Gender and Modernity* (New Brunswick, NJ and London: Rutgers University, 2007), 62–63. Lowy's book has excellent analysis of the newspaper articles that followed the *Seitō* scandals, including reports of Raichō's relationship with Kōkichi.

[18]This cartoon is reproduced in Raichō Kenkyūkai, ed., *"Seitō" jinbutsu jiten: 110-nin no gunzō* (Taishūkan Shoten, 2001), 43.

[19]Ibid.; Hiratsuka, *Genshi, josei wa taiyō de atta*, 2: 376–77; Hiratsuka and Craig, *In the Beginning, Woman Was the Sun*, 181.

[20]Hiratsuka, *Genshi, josei wa taiyō de atta*, 2: 377; Hiratsuka and Craig, *In the Beginning, Woman Was the Sun*, 181.

[21]Lowy, *The Japanese "New Woman,"* 64–72.

[22]Itō Noe, "Zatsuon" (Noise), *Osaka Mainichi shinbun*, 3 January–1 April 1916; reprinted in Itō, *Itō Noe zenshū* 2: 7–120.

[23]Ibid., 16.

[24]Ibid., 87.

[25]Ibid., 90.

[26]Ibid., 28–29.

[27]Hiratsuka, *Genshi, josei wa taiyō de atta*, 2: 368, as cited and translated in Sharon Sievers, *Flowers in Salt: The Beginnings of Feminist Consciousness in Modern Japan* (Stanford, CA: Stanford University Press, 1983), 225, n. 26. Also translated in Hiratsuka and Craig, *In the Beginning, Woman Was the Sun*, 176.

[28]Sievers, *Flowers in Salt*, 225, n. 26.

[29]Pflugfelder, "'S' Is for Sister," 167.

[30]For analysis of stories in *Seitō* and by other women writers of the day related to same-sex love, see Watanabe Mieko, "*Seitō* ni okeru rezubianizumu," in Shin Feminizumu Hihyō no Kai, ed., *"Seitō" o yomu: Blue Stocking* (Gakugei Shorin, 1998), 269–84. As for Kōkichi, she remained a lifelong friend of Raichō, married artist Tomimoto Kenkichi in 1914, had three children, and separated from Tomimoto in 1946; see Lowy, *The Japanese "New Woman,"* 72. In 1914, Kōkichi initiated the short-lived magazine *Safuran* (Saffron).

[31]Tomida, *Hiratsuka Raichō*, 179.

[32]Hiratsuka Raichō, "Atarashii onna" (New Woman), *Chūō kōron* (January 1913),

reprinted in Hiratsuka Raichō Chosakushū Henshū Iinkai, ed., *Hiratsuka Raichō cho-sakushū* (Ōtsuki Shoten, 1983–84), 1: 257–59.

[33]*The Japan Times* translation is reprinted in *Seitō* 3.2 (February 1913): 101–2.

[34]The essay is translated in Hiratsuka and Craig, *In the Beginning, Woman Was the Sun*, 203-4; Lowy, *The Japanese "New Woman,"* 82–83; and Tomida, *Hiratsuka Raichō*, 177–79.

[35][Hiratsuka] Raichō, "Yo no fujintachi ni" (To the Women of the World), *Seitō* 3.4 (April 1913): 156–64.

[36][Hiratsuka] Raichō, "Dokuritsu suru ni tsuite ryōshin ni" (To My Parents on Becoming Independent), *Seitō* 4.2 (February 1914): 102–16.

[37]Takamure Itsue, *Josei no rekishi* (1953; reprint Kōdansha, 1972), 2: 277–78.

[38]Hiratsuka, *Genshi, josei wa taiyō de atta*, 1: 327; Hiratsuka and Craig, *In the Beginning, Woman Was the Sun*, 156.

[39]Tomida, *Hiratsuka Raichō*, 159; Hiratsuka, *Genshi, josei wa taiyō de atta*, 1: 334–35; Hiratsuka and Craig, *In the Beginning, Woman Was the Sun*, 160–61. Tomida also mentions that some of the esoteric flavor of the manifesto is due to Raichō's use of "uncommon terms: *nessei* (devotion), *seishin shūchū* (power of spiritual concentration), *munen musō* (rid oneself of all worldly thoughts), *shinkū* (vacuum), and *kyomu* (nothingness)"; Tomida, *Hiratsuka Raichō*, 158.

[40]Nakashima Miyuki, "Shi to kaiga ni miru *Seitō* no joseizō," in Iida Yūko, ed., *"Seitō" to iu ba: Bungaku, jendā, atarashii onna* (Shinwasha, 2002), 138–39. Nakashima's theory is discussed below, in Chapter 12 on Yosano Akiko.

[41]Yoneda Sayoko, "Hiratsuka Raichō's Idea of Society: Nature, Cooperation and Self-Government," translated by Hiroko Tomida, in Hiroko Tomida and Gordon Daniels, eds., *Japanese Women: Emerging from Subservience, 1868–1945* (Folkestone, Kent : Global Oriental, 2005), 26. Yoneda remarks that Raichō's interest in the sect intensified in the 1930s.

[42]Hiratsuka Raichō, *Genshi, josei wa taiyō de atta*, 1: 327; Hiratsuka and Craig, *In the Beginning, Woman Was the Sun*, 157.

[43]Hiratsuka Raichō, *Genshi, josei wa taiyō de atta*, 1: 463; Hiratsuka and Craig, *In the Beginning, Woman Was the Sun*, 221.

[44]Tomida, *Hiratsuka Raichō*, 188. Raichō's original book was entitled *Marumado yori* (From the Round Window); the revised book, provocatively titled *Tozashi aru mado nite* (At a Locked Window), was published 10 June 1913; ibid., 187–88.

[45]Similar sentiments were voiced by Bluestocking Okada Yuki (1895–1996) in her brief essay, "Kekkon ni tsuite ryōshin e" (To My Parents on Marriage), *Seitō* 4.10 (November 1914): 109–10, also cited in Iwata Nanatsu, *Bungaku to shite no Seitō* (Fuji Shuppan, 2003), 154–55.

[46]Tomida, *Hiratsuka Raichō*, 190–91. Tomida cites Okumura Hiroshi, *Meguriai* (Encounter), (Tokyo: Gendaisha 1956), 171–72. For Raichō's account of these questions, see Hiratsuka, *Genshi, josei wa taiyō de atta*, 2: 489–90; Hiratsuka and Craig, *In the Beginning, Woman Was the Sun*, 231–32.

[47]Tomida, *Hiratsuka Raichō*, 191.

[48]Ibid., 191–92.

[49]Ibid. 191.

[50]Hiratsuka and Craig, *In the Beginning, Woman Was the Sun*, 311.

[51]For more on the Motherhood Protection Debate (Bosei Hogo Ronsō), see Barbara Molony, "Equality versus Difference: The Japanese Debate over 'Motherhood

Protection,' 1915–50," in Janet Hunter, ed., *Japanese Women Working* (London and New York: Routledge, 1993), 122–48; Laurel Rasplica Rodd, "The Taishō Date over the New Woman," in Gail Lee Bernstein, ed., *Recreating Japanese Women, 1600–1945* (Berkeley and Los Angeles: University of California Press, 1991), 175–98; and Hiroko Tomida, *Hiratsuka Raichō and Early Japanese Feminism* (Leiden: Brill, 2004), 221–61.

[52]For the story of the Shin Fujin Kyōkai, see Tomida, *Hiratsuka Raichō*, chap. 6, "Hiratsuka Raichō and The Association of New Women," 263–330.

[53]Friedrich Nietzsche, "Of Old and Young Women," in idem, *Thus Spoke Zarathustra*, trans. R. J. Hollingdale (New York: Penguin Books, 1961; reprint 1984), 90. This translation of the same passage from the German reads: "And woman has to obey and find a depth for her surface. Woman's nature is surface, a changeable, stormy film upon shallow waters. But a man's nature is deep, its torrent roars in subterranean caves: woman senses its power but does not comprehend it."

[54]This essay by Raichō is also translated in Pauline C. Reich and Atsuko Fukuda, "Japan's Literary Feminists: The Seitō Group," *Signs: Journal of Women in Culture and Society* 2.1 (Autumn 1976): 280–91.

[55]"Ms. F" is Fukuda Hideko. Her essay is translated in Chapter 2 in this volume as "The Solution to the Woman Question."

[56]"H" refers to Raichō's lifelong partner, Okumura Hiroshi.

Chapter 5
Itō Noe (1895–1923)

The New Woman has her own path.

Among the youngest of the Bluestockings, Kyushu-born Itō Noe was to become one of the most famous of all. She contributed sixty-one pieces to *Seitō*, including poetry, stories, essays, opinion pieces, and Editors' Notes. In her essays, Noe writes passionately about what kind of person the New Woman should be, while rebuking more conservative women as mired in convention and incapable of comprehending the New Woman's mission. Yet in some of her stories Noe speaks in a far less confident voice, picturing her main character as paralyzed by indecision or consumed by jealousy. Noe's zeal to make a name for herself as a New Woman, her bravado together with her fears of not measuring up, motivated her request to take over the helm of *Seitō* from Hiratsuka Raichō in January 1915, when she was only twenty years old. Under Noe's leadership in its final fourteen months, the magazine broached even more controversial topics, such as abortion and prostitution, than it had done in the past. But the novelty of *Seitō* had worn off by this time, most members had gone on to other projects, and many found their lives filled by their new responsibilities as mothers. Compounding the problem was the news that *Seitō* was not selling well and that its finances were shaky, just when the core of the Bluestockings Society was losing whatever group cohesiveness it had once had. Divorce, a new partner, and motherhood complicated Noe's private life as well. When Noe published the final issue of *Seitō* in February 1916, she, too, was ready to move on.

Regrettably, Noe had few years left to accomplish all she wanted to. She was murdered in September 1923—along with her last partner, the anarchist writer and activist Ōsugi Sakae (1885–1923), and his seven-year-old nephew—in the wave of police brutality that was directed against leftist radicals in the wake of the massive destruction and chaos wrought by the Great Kantō Earthquake. She was only twenty-eight years old and the mother of seven young children, two by her second husband, the musician, Dadaist writer, and translator Tsuji Jun (1884–1944), and five by Ōsugi, her third partner. Her eventful life has inspired several biographies, a novel, a play, and at least two films.[1] Her writing received renewed attention in

1970, when *The Collected Works of Itō Noe*, including all her essays and stories for *Seitō*, was published.[2] In his 2003 edition of *Peasants, Rebels, Women and Outcastes: The Underside of Modern Japan*, Mikiso Hane includes translations of several of her essays.[3] A few photographs of Noe as a young woman have no doubt also played a part in dramatizing her legacy as a New Woman of Taishō Japan. A portrait of Noe that captures her as a determined young woman is often used, as are smiling, relaxed family portraits of Noe, Ōsugi, and some of their children.[4]

The first translation of Noe's writing in this volume is her "Anti-Manifesto" (translated in Appendix B).[5] Noe directed this statement to all *Seitō* readers in July 1916 by printing it boldly on the cover of the journal itself (figure 6). She avows that the journal will no longer represent an exclusive group but remain open to any and all women who wish to contribute. She reveals more than a hint of defensiveness about her ability to manage the journal, despite her concluding resolve to fight on. In fact, the remaining Bluestockings—including Hiratsuka Raichō, who had been Itō Noe's mentor in many ways—doubted that Noe could successfully edit *Seitō*. Various comments in and about *Seitō*, although phrased in polite language, leave the impression that several members had always found Noe a bit rustic for their tastes and given to overly impulsive action. Remarks in the Editors' Notes of the 1915 issues show that Noe had her own worries about undertaking this responsibility. In issue after issue, she apologizes for the journal's tardiness and poor quality, resolving to "do better next time" and pleading for help and patience from other members. She admits to having trouble getting both advertisements and manuscripts.

The lack of confidence that the other Bluestockings express in Itō Noe's work raises the question of how this relatively unsophisticated Kyushu teenager came to play so large a role in a group initially comprised of the privileged daughters of the Tokyo elite, and why, when so many of them faded from the limelight, her life has continued to command attention. To understand what brought her to the Bluestockings and to notoriety in the first place, we have to go back to Noe's roots. Born in 1895, Noe grew up in a small fishing village near Fukuoka in northern Kyushu. Like Fukuda Hideko and Hiratsuka Raichō, Noe was regarded as boyish; she easily got into fights with other children and loved to swim in the ocean. Such activities were forbidden by her parents as inappropriate for a girl. Although Noe did well in school, her parents' meager income would not allow for advanced schooling, and after her six years of compulsory education, Noe went to work for the local post office. Although this was considered quite a good job for a country girl, Noe was far from satisfied. Finally, she persuaded a well-to-do uncle who lived in Tokyo to finance her continued schooling there. Noe's

青鞜

讀者諸氏に

私は自分で編輯するこの雜誌を、出來る丈け、立派なものにしたいと思ひます。けれども如何に、私が自惚れて見ましても本當に貧弱な內容しか持つことが出來ません。私一個の微力では勿論どうしても讀者諸氏を滿足させるやうな大家の執筆を乞ふことは出來ません。目次にならんだ人達はまだ世間の表に立つてゐない人の方が多數を占めて居ます。私は每號々々かうして貧弱だとかつまらないとか云ふ非難を耳にしながらも何時もねうちのない雜誌ばかり編輯して居ります。けれども私の考へではそれにも相當の理屈はつくのです。私自らはこの雜誌自身に單なる苗床としてより以上の何の價値をも求めやうとはしません、私はこの雜誌を引きつぐ際に、一切の規則を取り去つて無規則無方針、無主義無主張と云ふことをお斷はりしました。一切の規則のなくてはならない方は各自におつくりなさるがいい。何の主義も主張もない雜誌を凡ての婦人達に提供いたしますから各々に自由勝手にお使ひ下さい。お用ひになる方のまゝに出來るやうに雜誌そのものには一切意味を持たせません。と云ふことも其の際に申しました。この雜誌は苗床卒この貧弱な價值より他には何にもありません。どの苗がどう育つてゆくか――未成品――と云ふことに芽を出した苗がどんな處に育つてゆくか――此處に芽を出した苗がどんな處に下さる方に初めてこの雜誌は雜誌自らの存在の意義を明らかにするのです。私はかう云ふ負け惜しみな理屈を楯に何ど非難されても相變らず貧弱な雜誌を倦きずにこしらへてゐるのです。

――編輯者――

貳月號

Figure 6. In lieu of a graphic design, Itō Noe printed her "Anti-Manifesto" on the final covers of *Seitō* in January and February 1916. Courtesy of Fuji Shuppan.

parents depended on her income to help with family expenses and tried their utmost to dissuade her from going to Tokyo. In the end, however, Noe left home, forcing her younger sister to quit her own schooling in order to work and compensate for Noe's lost income.

Noe thrived at Ueno Girls' School, enjoying her studies and school activities. In the meantime, unbeknownst to Noe, her parents were planning for her marriage. In the summer before her senior year, Noe's parents informed her that they had arranged for her to marry a hometown boy, Suematsu Fukutarō, an émigré temporarily returned from the United States, after her graduation from Ueno Girls' School. Since the wedding plans were all arranged, the young man's family would pay the remainder of Noe's educational expenses. Noe felt trapped. She had fallen in love with Tsuji Jun, her English teacher at Ueno, enjoyed living in Tokyo, and had no desire to return to Kyushu. Yet if she were to rebel against the arrangement, no one would pay for her to finish school. Furthermore, a refusal to accept marriage would be an insult to her family—both to her parents and to the uncle to whom she was so obligated. Noe saw no other choice but to agree to the match.

After her graduation came and went, Noe dutifully returned to Kyushu for her wedding. The troubles with this union, her choice to divorce Suematsu and marry her former teacher, Tsuji Jun, and the problems that developed in their "love marriage" were the subject of three autobiographical stories Noe wrote for *Seitō*. In her 1913 story "Wagamama" (Willfulness, translated below), Noe describes the frustration the character Toshiko feels as she returns home for an arranged marriage.[6] The story ends without the reader knowing whether Toshiko will escape her family, all of whom seem like villains who want to rob Toshiko of her future and her will. In her own life, Noe did go through with the wedding and saw her name formally entered in the family register of her husband. She soon fled her husband's home without telling anyone in either family, an act that was not only unconventional but illegal. With very little money in her pocket, Noe made her way to the island of Shikoku to stay with a girlfriend and some days later arrived at Tsuji Jun's Tokyo apartment. This experience became the topic of her story "Shuppon" (Flight).

The Toshiko of "Flight" is a much-chastened character. She no longer speaks bravely about standing up to the world, as in "Willfulness," but hesitates to think about her situation at all. Running away from her husband's family without money or a plan of action has led Toshiko to seek shelter at a friend's house. She begins to doubt the wisdom of having left home impulsively, like some Japanese Nora (in Ibsen's *A Doll's House*), with no thought of the trouble that might lie in store for her. Toshiko tries to find the courage to tell her friend why she has come to Shikoku:

Every day Toshiko would think, "Today I will explain everything, no matter what." She would plan what she might say. But since even making this effort was very painful for her, Toshiko would once again end up saying nothing. She didn't want to think about all the things that had happened to her since she had set out on this long road. Nor did she want to think about what had moved her to leave home, to abandon everything. When she dredged up thoughts like these and remembered the agony of the last week, she could no longer calmly decide how to talk about her predicament. Toshiko imagined the confusion at home since she had left without telling anyone. All her thoughts turned to the people back home—her father would be perplexed by it all, her uncle and aunt would be worried. At times like this, the joy Toshiko had felt when she'd made it through her first ordeal by striking out on her own completely evaporated. She would fall into a dark mood, aware of how much she'd like to just run crying home to her father. There were even days when, deep in thoughts like these, Toshiko felt she had no other choice but to kill herself.[7]

Toshiko receives word from her sweetheart Mitsuo, a character modeled on Tsuji Jun, that her husband believes that the two of them are together in Tokyo. The husband has gone to the capital—with his father and a policeman—to find her. Mitsuo urges Toshiko to come to Tokyo and confront everyone openly. Toshiko decides to leave for Tokyo immediately, using funds that another teacher has sent her. Once again, the reader is left not knowing what will happen to Toshiko or how her story will turn out. We do see how the experience has affected this New Woman's sense of self, however. Toshiko has placed herself in a precarious and illegal situation that frightens her. Although support from sympathizers helps restore her courage, ultimately she must depend on her own resources and assume responsibility for her life. Noe leaves her reader thinking that to acquiesce to an arranged marriage and parental demands is certainly the easier route, and that Toshiko is an unusually courageous woman.

In Noe's own life, quite a bit happened next. When officials at Ueno Girls' School learned of the romantic relationship between one of their teachers and his former pupil, they promptly fired Jun. The abrupt loss of the comfortable income he had earned at Ueno Girls' School left Jun adrift and also meant that he could no longer support his mother and sister. On top of this, Noe moved into their crowded apartment. Nevertheless, Jun resisted getting any permanent job. He did some translating but generally worried very little about money, spending hours playing the *shakuhachi* (Japanese flute). He believed in Noe's abilities, encouraged her to continue her studies on her own, and introduced her to *Seitō*. Taken with the defiance and idealism of the magazine, Noe immediately wrote to Raichō, describing her marriage problems, for she was still legally bound to the Suematsu family. Eventually, Noe returned to Kyushu to divorce her husband. Once in Kyushu, she found matters more complicated than she had expected and again wrote Raichō for advice. Raichō responded with a 5-yen note, enough money for a return trip to Tokyo. She assumed Jun was kindly helping out as Noe's teacher, having no idea that he had lost his job over his personal involvement with her. Noe seized the opportunity to return to Jun and her life in the capital. Fortunately, both her family and the Suematsu family consented to annulling the hapless marriage in February 1913, leaving Noe free to remain with Jun, whom she formally married over two years later, in July 1915.[8]

Realizing that Noe needed a job to support herself in Tokyo, Raichō arranged for her to work in the *Seitō* office, paying her 10 yen a month. In her 1971–73 autobiography Raichō recalls how Noe, as the newest and youngest Bluestocking, brought a new energy to the *Seitō* office. She describes her as "ebullient and full of energy" as well as "efficient, practical, and reliable."[9]

Noe joined the group in the second year of *Seitō*, just when the Bluestockings were experiencing their greatest criticism. Meeting these attacks head on, Noe wrote essays in *Seitō* rebutting the journal's critics, who were mostly rather well-known educators such as Shimoda Utako (1854–1936). Although other members cautioned her not to write so impulsively, Noe was fearless and single-minded in her defense of *Seitō*. She also used *Seitō* as a means to vent her anger against the traditional marriage system, writing essays outlining her own views about love and marriage. One of Noe's shorter essays is translated below as "The Path of the New Woman." Translations also appeared in *Seitō* under Noe's name, although Noe actually lacked ability in foreign languages and relied on Jun to translate for her.

Although Noe was a tireless worker for the Bluestockings, she never seems to have formed close relations with other members of the group, except for her friendship with contributor Nogami Yaeko (see Chapter 9 below). Perhaps her background and her personal habits were just too different from theirs. Raichō recounts that Noe initially struck her as a country girl who lacked an urban sophistication. She also remembers how Noe's habits could irritate the other Bluestockings. For example, after Noe had borne her first son, Makoto, she would bring him to the *Seitō* office with her. Others were rather annoyed at the crying baby, but Noe seemed quite undisturbed. She did not make much of an effort to keep the baby clean. Yasumochi Yoshiko, in particular, was annoyed at the sight of Noe holding the infant on the verandah so that he could relieve himself into the garden.[10] Raichō also comments on Noe's lack of cleanliness—one reason for the end of the communal dinners that the two women and their partners had briefly enjoyed. However, Raichō also remarks that Noe had great powers of concentration and vitality, and describes a memory of the young Noe nursing her child at a casual gathering while alternately arguing and laughing. In addition to behaving differently from other Bluestockings, Noe had more radical views. A keen admirer of Emma Goldman, whom she met at an anarchists' meeting in Japan in 1913, Noe long sought to push *Seitō* in more overtly political directions.[11]

This apparent distance from the other Bluestockings had a deleterious effect on Noe's leadership in 1915. By the time Noe assumed responsibility for *Seitō*, membership in the organization and subscriptions to the journal had decreased for various reasons: the younger members were marrying and having children, political essays on the Woman Question had alienated many, and circulation, especially in the provinces, had decreased since the publishing house Tōundō had withdrawn its services. If the journal were to survive, the small core of remaining members clearly had to work together. As we have seen, Noe's Editors' Notes in 1915 reveal that few if any members had faith in her leadership.

In the early Editors' Notes, we see the twenty-year-old Noe trying to persuade the membership that she is not too young for the job, as "many seem to think." Yet her performance was less than convincing. Whereas she had begun her tenure as *Seitō* editor with many grand ideas, such as publishing pamphlets of essays as well as the monthly journal and opening the group to all women, she had failed to realize the enormity of the task before her. Soon overwhelmed by the work, Noe could not keep up with even the usual publication duties. She decided to discontinue what she called the "ineffective" practice of arranging exchange advertisements with other publications. Noe also complained that few manuscripts were coming to the office and that she had no time to solicit contributions herself.

Problems in Noe's personal life compounded the problems with *Seitō*. By this time she and Tsuji Jun were desperately poor, she was pregnant with their second child, and her "free love" relationship with Jun was failing quickly. The third story about their relationship, "Mayoi" (Perplexity), published in *Seitō* in April 1914, describes Noe's reaction at learning that Tsuji Jun had saved a love letter from an old acquaintance, a classmate of Noe's at Ueno Girls' School who had had a schoolgirl crush on Jun when he was her teacher.[12] Machiko, the main character of "Perplexity," is disillusioned, angry, and jealous. Noe later learned that Jun had been having an affair with her cousin Kimi—the model for the character Makiko, the cousin of Toshiko, the protagonist in her earlier story "Willfulness"—an event that further weakened their marriage.

In 1918, Noe wrote about this period in her deteriorating relationship with Jun, her mother-in-law, and her sister-in-law, as well as her struggles with being a good mother to her young, much-loved son in a long story called "Kojiki no meiyo" (Beggar's Honor). The lead character in the story, Toshiko (the same name as in three earlier stories on this topic), feels torn between her duties as a mother, the demands of her intellectual work, and her desire to live a meaningful life. She has devoted so much energy to battling convention through the magazine "S" but ironically finds herself leading a conventional life in a conventional home. She fears that all the efforts of the women involved in "S," although igniting public debate, have had little effect on society. Most of the story dwells on how inspiring the beleaguered Toshiko finds the writing of Emma Goldman, the battles she withstood and her brave determination; the title "Beggar's Honor" comes from one of Goldman's works. The reader learns that "what captivated Toshiko more than anything else was Goldman's courage," and Toshiko, too, resolves to lead a meaningful life. Thus a story that begins as an expression of a woman's despair over her personal life turns into a rousing call to regain energy by working for social justice.[13]

In July 1915, Noe left *Seitō* in the hands of Ikuta Hanayo (on whom see Chapter 3 above on Harada Satsuki), and went back to her hometown in Kyushu with Jun and her first son to have the second baby. She stayed in Kyushu much longer than expected, not returning to Tokyo until December. Back in Tokyo, she tried to rescue *Seitō* by printing the new anti-manifesto on the cover and gathering many articles for the 1916 New Year's issue. Repeating a theme she had discussed when she first took over the magazine, Noe boldly proclaimed an anarchist future for *Seitō* in her new manifesto. She declared that *Seitō* would no longer have any guiding policy. Each member was to use the journal as she saw fit; if any members needed doctrine, then, according to Noe, they could create it on their own. By this time, however, it was too late to save the journal. World War I had already caused a rise in prices in Japan, making paper and ink more expensive. Furthermore, despite Noe and Jun's six-month vacation in Kyushu, the registration of their marriage in July, and the birth of their second son Ryūji in August, their relationship was over. Noe abruptly closed down *Seitō*'s publication after the February 1916 issue appeared and, at about the same time, began an affair with Ōsugi Sakae.

Raichō has characterized Noe's affair with Ōsugi as one of the "last chapters in the life of *Seitō*." A firm believer in what he called "free love," Ōsugi was already married to Hori Yasuko (1883?–1924), and was having an affair with Kamichika Ichiko (1888–1981), a newspaper reporter, when he became involved with Noe. Ōsugi's multiple relationships became a matter of public scandal in November 1916, when Kamichika Ichiko stabbed him in the throat one night while both were staying at the Hikage Inn in

Hayama, a seaside town near Kamakura. Itō Noe had been at the inn the previous two days, and the threesome had spent an uncomfortable night sharing one room. Following the event, Ōsugi recovered but was shunned by other leftists. Hori Yasuko wrote publicly that she had severed all connections with him. Kamichika Ichiko went on trial, ultimately serving two years in jail. Itō Noe remained with Ōsugi, who made no further attempts to put his theories of free love to the test.[14] Hori Yasuko, Kamichika Ichiko, and Itō Noe were also linked by their association with *Seitō*.[15] Consequently, media attention turned once again to the Bluestockings as advocates of modern sexual mores as articles appeared on the "Hikage Teahouse Incident" and at the same time, on Bluestocking Iwano Kiyoko's suit against her husband Iwano Hōmei (see Chapter 6 below).[16] In the aftermath of the scandal, Hori divorced Ōsugi, and Noe divorced Tsuji Jun in September 1917. Together, Noe and Ōsugi continued their passion for anarchist publications and the movement itself while Noe had five more children. The couple never married, nor did they register their children's births. After their deaths, the children were registered in the family of one of Noe's relatives.

Noe's New Woman Essays

Noe's essays, thickly brushed and in big characters, were often of a personal nature and took a strong tone. The essay translated below, "Atarashiki onna no michi" (The Path of the New Woman), which appeared in the January 1913 section of *Seitō* devoted to the Woman Question, is no exception.[17] In this essay Noe responds to those who see the New Woman as a frivolous young woman bent on selfish pleasures. She writes that, far from being self-indulgent, the New Woman risks everything to break new ground, an effort that most women are too soft or too scared to contemplate. The metaphor of the New Woman's journey as a "path" or "way" calls to mind the image of the Zen priest who pursues the religious "way" (*dao/michi*). Noe's choice of Chinese characters for describing the self (*jiko, onore*) would have struck her readers as bold and rather masculine.

To counter the Bluestockings' image as frivolous women, Noe imagines a route to liberation that recalls all the arduousness of a mythic pilgrimage. She casts the New Woman as the brave pioneer who will forge her new path through much suffering and determination. All those who oppose the New Woman are mere "followers" or "stragglers" who cannot understand where the New Woman is headed, much less have the strength to follow in her footsteps. Reminiscent of Yosano Akiko's initial poem "Mountain Moving Day" (translated in Chapter 12 below), which warns readers that even if they don't believe it, "All the women who were sleeping / are awake now and moving," Noe tells her readers that even the straggler will one day follow gratefully in the footsteps of the very pioneer whom she now castigates. Emphasizing the nobility of the New Woman's mission, Noe will grant no credit to the straggler who belatedly realizes how much has been done for her by the misunderstood pioneer. As in several other *Seitō* works in support of the New Woman, "The Path of the New Woman" does not call for any specific legal or social changes. This lack of specificity allows readers their own interpretations. More importantly, the repetition, dramatic imagery, and florid style evident here make the New Woman's path exciting—a new way realized in language and emotion, if less easily achieved in specific social changes. One can imagine Taishō schoolgirls sneaking a peek at the forbidden *Seitō* and becoming fascinated by Noe's visions of the extraordinary New Woman.

The *Seitō* Debate on Prostitution

In the last issues of *Seitō*, Noe became involved in a debate on prostitution with Aoyama Kikue (1890–1980, best known by her married name, Yamakawa Kikue), who is remembered for her long career as a socialist-feminist critic and as the first director of the Women's and Minors' Bureau (Fujin Shōnen Kyoku) established in 1947 within the Ministry of Labor. The debate, couched in letters written back and forth between Noe and Kikue, has been categorized as the last of the three major debates on sexuality published in *Seitō*.[18] (For discussion of the first two debates, on chastity and abortion, see Chapter 3 above on Harada Satsuki.) Their letters are frank and strikingly different: Noe writes in a dramatic, highly emotional way, whereas Kikue, as many scholars have remarked, takes a more measured tone, brings in facts and figures, and chastises Noe for fuzzy thinking and for publishing work that Noe herself had later admitted was not her best. Most interestingly, the debate takes the discussion of prostitution past any simple division between "degenerate" and "virtuous" women to an understanding of its causes, how it is protected by those in power, how laws against it aim to punish the women it employs rather than their male customers, and what can be done to aid women who wish to escape it.

Providing background to the *Seitō* debate on prostitution, Iwabuchi Hiroko points to the furor that arose among women's groups such as the Japan Women's Christian Temperance Union (Fujin Kyōfūkai; literally translated as Women's Moral Reform Society, here referred to as JWCTU) over the decision to have geisha dance at the 1912 accession ceremonies for the Taishō emperor.[19] Much of the opposition stemmed from a fear that Westerners would disapprove of the Japanese government including geisha in a public ceremony.[20] Concerns about prostitution did not end there, however, for the topic continued to rouse the JWCTU for years to come. The organization continued to lobby for the abolition of licensed prostitution and geisha houses as well as on behalf of such causes as women's suffrage.

Itō Noe took aim at the JWCTU and other women's groups with her initial article on prostitution, the title of which is translated by Mikiso Hane as "Arrogant, Narrow-Minded, Half-Baked Japanese Women's Public Service Activities."[21] The long, rambling, and often vitriolic essay was published in the December 1915 issue of *Seitō*. In it Noe lambastes both the vain "aristocratic ladies" of organizations such as the Women's Patriotic Association (Aikoku Fujinkai) and what she calls the intolerant "Bible women" of Yajima Kajiko's (1832–1925) JWCTU[22] for the ways in which their characterization of prostitutes as "shameful women" magnifies their own position as virtuous ladies. Noe attacks the JWCTU for ignoring unlicensed prostitution while calling for the end of licensed prostitution largely because the latter will make Japan look uncivilized in the eyes of the West. She asks why unlicensed prostitution should not be regarded as equally shameful, especially since it contributes more to the spread of venereal disease. Noe also demands that these supposedly concerned, privileged women take a more compassionate view of the conditions of poverty and the lack of education that force women into prostitution in the first place. She also states that prostitution has a long history that is rooted in "men's inherent needs."

It was Noe's line about "men's inherent needs" that motivated Aoyama Kikue to write a response. The January 1916 issue of *Seitō* carried Kikue's "On the Social Work of Japanese Ladies: A Response to Ms. Itō Noe" (Nihon fujin no shakai jigyō ni tsuite: Itō Noe shi ni atau).[23] Kikue agrees with Noe's low opinion of the conservative, wealthy women's motivation for joining charity organizations, and adds her own scathing criticism of what she sees as their ignorance and vanity. But she supports the JWCTU, which she admits to knowing little about, in their fight against the system of licensed prostitution, which she finds more despicable than unlicensed prostitution. She argues that it is a kind of slavery that is neither natural nor inevitable and must be stopped. Kikue cites specific problems with the system of licensed prostitution, such as the constraints on women's mobility, the poor living conditions, the high rate of venereal disease (Kikue states that 70 percent of Japanese prostitutes are afflicted), and especially the practice of indenturing women through usurious loans. She also takes issue with Noe's implication that men's desires make prostitution somehow natural or inevitable, charging that such a position only serves to mask the abuse of power and male selfishness that truly sustain prostitution and does not provide any basis for effecting change. To Kikue's mind, recognizing how social systems are created by people—not nature or fate—motivates change rather than resignation. Although Kikue agrees that women's self-awareness (*jikaku*) is needed, she states that a "reform of various systems" is also necessary. In a much lighter tone, Kikue concludes her letter saying that she is looking forward to meeting Noe and imagines how busy she must be as the mother of two children.

Noe's response to Kikue was also published in the January 1916 issue, placed immediately after Kikue's letter. Noe opens by gratefully acknowledging Kikue's letter, agreeing with her position on the necessity for the abolition of licensed prostitution, and apologizing for her own lack of knowledge about the system, which Kikue's critique has revealed. She emphasizes that her initial essay was intended as an attack on the arrogance of the JWCTU and on its lack of the kind of reasoned and compassionate arguments Kikue marshaled. But Noe still has disagreements with Kikue's position, and while she states that she would like to present these in a civil fashion, it becomes evident that she cannot resist adopting a sarcastic tone about the way in which Kikue has made some of her remarks. Noe's main points include: that the abolition of licensed prostitution will not lead to a decrease in unlicensed prostitution; that prostitution cannot end until other kinds of livelihoods are found for former prostitutes; and that promoting sexual abstinence to young men will not abolish prostitution.[24] Most importantly, Noe wishes to challenge Kikue's belief that social systems are made by people alone. Noe believes that the "inevitable" forces of nature—the forces that create human beings—determine the environment in which people can construct or dismantle systems.

The February 1916 issue of *Seitō*, which proved to be the magazine's last issue, carried a second response from Aoyama Kikue and one in return from Itō Noe, who concludes by calling for an end to their debate. By this time, the two women had met each other in person. As Kikue's letter makes clear, they remained in agreement about ladies' charity societies while continuing to disagree about whether the forces of nature or human agency alone can change the structure of society. For Kikue, women's self-awareness is not an end in itself (as much *Seitō* writing would imply) because individual people do not exist independently of one another. Thus self-awareness must be accompanied by a critical awareness of social systems. In thinking about prostitution as a social system, Kikue calls for the state to provide financial support, education, and job training so that women can leave prostitution and escape the extremely low-wage work that pushes them into prostitution in the first place. To end prostitution, there must also be reforms in education and in sexual mores. Kikue affirms that disagreement and discussion are the keys to individual maturity and ultimately to social progress, and ends by scolding Noe for publishing her initial essay the previous December, in which even Noe herself had little confidence. Public figures, Kikue advises, must be more responsible. Noe spends most of her final response reasserting her belief in the forces of nature and concludes by stating that, even though she shares Kikue's quarrels with their society, she must concentrate on her responsibilities as a parent and an individual. If others find inspiration in her work, that is fine, but she does not have the energy to try to save anyone.

Hiratsuka Raichō added her own thoughts on prostitution in June 1917, in an article in the review *Shin shōsetsu* (The New Novel).[25] Raichō credits Yajima Kajiko with being a reformer, but does not view her as acting in concert with Raichō herself or with others working on behalf of women. Raichō also takes issue with the basic premises of Aoyama Kikue's philosophy, arguing that as long as marriage is not based on love but on economics, there is no real difference between the wife and the prostitute. What Raichō believes is needed is that women be empowered and marriages be based on romantic love. Without this, even if licensed prostitution is abolished, unlicensed prostitution will continue. As Iwabuchi points out, Raichō's emphasis on women's empowerment and on the idealization of love moves the discussion of the abolition of prostitution from the rhetoric of morality and the nation-state to the sphere of individual human rights.

Itō Noe's passionate, personal engagement in the prostitution debate illustrates her readiness to take a stand on public issues. She made her private life, too, in all its excitement and despair, the public record of a New Woman's journey to find herself and a new way of life. The drama of her life, its tragic end, and her prolific writing have made Noe one of the most legendary Bluestockings. The mother of seven children, an editor of *Seitō* at age twenty, and an outspoken social critic, Noe experienced much in her short twenty-eight years. For many, she did achieve the dream described in "The Path of the New Woman" of being recognized as a pioneer in advancing women's rights.

****

The Path of the New Woman
Itō Noe
Seitō 3.1 (January 1913)

The New Woman does not trudge in endless search of the dusty footprints left by the women who have walked before her. The New Woman has her own path. The New Woman will advance beyond the point where so many other women have stopped and, as a pioneer, will dare to tread an entirely new road.

Those who wend their way on old roads and those who stand stock-still on well-traveled paths will never know this new way. Even the pioneer who attempts the new path has no idea what she will find.

She does not know where this new path originates nor where it leads. Consequently, she understands the danger and the fear that attend the unknown.

The pioneer must walk this unexplored road all on her own. Cutting away thickly overgrown and thorny brambles, she must make her way forward. Chiseling through massive rocks and losing her way through remote mountains, she must rove. Stung by poisonous insects, hungry and thirsty, she must cling to the roots of weeds as she climbs over rocky passes, scales high cliffs, and crosses valleys. In feverish prayer she wails, knowing that she must wring out every last anguished tear.

Unexplored, unknown, eternally silent, the path stretches on and on. It has no end. Yet the pioneer cannot possibly live forever. She will struggle against all the torment and she will finally succumb to it. Once she falls, she can walk no farther. Then and only then will the one who follows recognize the strength of the pioneer and begin to follow in her footsteps. Only then will the one who follows appreciate the one who has led the way.

But the path that was new to the pioneer and the footprints that she left as she explored it can only be new once. Thus, for those who follow, the path will already have become an old way and walking it will carry no significance whatsoever.

Hence it remains for new pioneers to take up where the old pioneers have fallen. They shall walk farther on the path. They, too, will suffer grievously as they move on, opening up the way.

For the word "new" to express any meaning at all, it must remain the exclusive term for this small band of pioneers because only those who have lived in agony and died in agony—only those who have truly struggled to know the self, to believe in the self, and who have blazed the way to the self—deserve this word. Those carefree women who would follow after, who have done absolutely nothing of importance, should never be described with this word.

First of all, the pioneer strongly believes in herself. Next, she possesses strength. Then, she has courage. All these qualities force her to realize the responsibility that she alone has for her own life. No matter what the situation, the pioneer will not permit others to interfere with her work. Nor will she associate with those who only seek to follow. Those who merely follow lack any qualification whatsoever to make even the smallest criticism of those who lead. They have no right to do so. Indeed, those who follow can do nothing else but give thanks to the pioneer and walk behind in the footprints she has left. They have no idea how to move forward on their own. All they can do is take after the pioneer's progress, tentatively following from behind.

First and foremost, the pioneer needs to develop her inner self. After this, gathering all the strength and all the courage that have slowly built inside her, she must rise. She must stand up and take responsibility for this self and for an unwavering confidence in this self.

All the while the pioneer struggles to open the new way, she denies herself even the smallest of worldly comforts. From beginning to end she is alone, and every second is one of hardship. There is torment. There is fear. At times even she feels overcome with deep despair. Yet the only words that she utters are ardent, passionate prayers for the strength to believe in herself. This is why one who searches for happiness, for comfort and for sympathy, can never become a pioneer. One who would be a pioneer must be a powerful person, a person who gives life to a sense of self that will not crumble.

How could anyone imagine that the way of the New Woman, the way of this pioneer, is anything less than one continuous, tortuous struggle?

****

Willfulness
Itō Noe
Seitō 3.12 (December 1913)

Toshiko had been lagging far behind her companions Makiko and Yasuko ever since they had all gotten off the connecting ferryboat at Shimonoseki. While Makiko and Yasuko strolled cheerfully ahead, Toshiko had straggled dolefully behind. On summer vacation the year before, when Toshiko, her aunt, and Makiko had all come off the boat together, Toshiko had felt as if she were climbing out of a carriage at the front gate of a much-loved home. To sense herself back in Kyushu had truly given her the happiest feelings of belonging. But where were those feelings now? She felt as though she literally had to force herself to move forward. In five or six more hours she would be back in that wretched house, even though she had vowed never to return there and knew full well how uncomfortable she would be. There were many who stood in her way, but worst of all was her uncle, the man whom she regarded as her bitterest enemy. He would be at the house. Then there was that fellow who everyone forced on her, who was in every way her inferior—her fiancé. Even thinking about this second enemy made her stomach churn.

Imagining the face of each and every one of her relatives as if all of them were lined up right before her eyes heightened Toshiko's agitation. She felt her teeth clenching. Trying to shake off the dreadful anxiety that threatened to consume her, Toshiko quickened her steps until the sensation passed. She continued walking, almost unaware of what she was doing. When she entered the train station, she flung her luggage on a nearby bench. Makiko and Yasuko kept hold of their belongings as they looked happily about the train station.

"Say, when does the next one leave? Do you think we still have to wait a long time?" her older cousin Makiko asked in a buoyant voice when she saw Toshiko staring absentmindedly at the timetable.

"I suppose so," Toshiko managed halfheartedly, and immediately took a seat nearby. Whenever Toshiko heard Makiko's voice, what inevitably came to mind—and called forth the most disagreeable feelings—was the image of Makiko's father and his high-handed way of deciding everything all by himself. Sitting perfectly still, Toshiko willed herself to remember the painful separation that had taken place last night at Shinbashi station, gazing on the imagined scene as if it were directly before her.

No longer able to bear the agony of thinking about how she was going to feel in another four or five hours, Toshiko searched her mind for all the things that had happened to her in Tokyo through last night, gathering these up to camouflage the present. Yet even among these memories were disturbing ones that cast further shadows on Toshiko's mood. She tried with all her might to evade these painful recollections. But a few moments later, Toshiko's gloominess gave way to an all-enveloping vision of the man who had so passionately kissed and embraced her on their last day together. Neither of them had known at this parting whether or not they would meet again. It was this all-encompassing vision of him now that weakened Toshiko's ability to decide what to do. She was being dragged along in a direction that absolutely repelled her. Yet at the same time she felt as though she were being pulled in quite another direction, too—one that she sought for herself.

At Shinbashi station, when Toshiko had felt as if it were to be their final parting, she had looked into the man's eyes as he stood there, hugging his chest as it trembled ever so slightly. She did not know if she would ever be able to see him again. If she were not able to do so, this moment would become one of the most painful memories of her entire life, something that she would probably never be able to forget. When she thought that this might well turn out to be the case, Toshiko no longer had the courage to look into his eyes.

She had been about to leave Shinbashi station, giving as an excuse that her younger brother back home had asked for a model airplane and so she was going to Ginza to buy him one. She'd mentioned that there should be plenty of time for her to do this and still make the train.

"I'll go with you." The man had followed right after her as if nothing were amiss. The two of them had walked side by side through the brightly lit town. They had passed by many stores until they had finally come to one that seemed to have what they wanted. When the man had inquired for her, however, the store had turned out not to have the model they were looking for. At that point, Toshiko had decided that making this purchase did not matter much after all. She had not harbored any hope that the two of them would be able to hold hands and be alone together, so now, when the chance to do exactly this came so unexpectedly, how delighted she felt. And yet how sad it made her, too.

"If we headed farther up the road, there might be something up there, but I'm not sure that we have time."

"Yes, well, that's all right. Let's turn back. By now everyone will probably be waiting for us." Walking close by each other's side as they went up the stone steps of the train station, they held each other's hands so tightly it hurt. Near the ticket gate, they could see Makiko with her back to them. Next to her stood the teacher who had been so kind to them, and next to him was Tanaka, one of the meddling friends of Toshiko's relatives. As soon as he caught sight of Toshiko, Tanaka started scolding her, complaining that it was all her fault that they had missed the daytime train. Unsettled by the violent waves of emotion that pounded against her, Toshiko flashed with anger at Tanaka's reproach. To be criticized by one who had not the slightest qualification to say anything at all to her was supremely insulting. Her lips feverish and trembling and her eyes filled with tears, Toshiko snapped back at the man.

Scenes like these, so fresh in Toshiko's mind, kept coming to her one after another. After looking back on them for awhile as she sat here now, in this station, Toshiko became deeply aware of how the one dearest to her, the one who had most consoled and sympathized with her, had been left behind in Tokyo. Just last night. It had been just last night that she had been there, looking at him and talking with him. Then she had boarded the train and been carted off to this place. They were beneath the same wide sky, breathing the same air—and yet all was hopeless. Toshiko felt dazed. Her vision blurred.

Excitement began stirring inside the station, making Toshiko vaguely aware of her surroundings again. Many people were tidying themselves up or hurrying over to the ticket taker to see if anything was happening.

"We only have fifteen minutes left, Toshiko-san." Hearing her name called startled Toshiko to her feet. Yet when she realized that there were, after all, fifteen minutes more to wait, she settled down again. Just then, as she glanced at the others around her, Toshiko was struck by an inexpressibly sad sense of her own helplessness. She had considered escaping from everyone on the way here by giving them the slip at Osaka and then entrusting herself to her friend on Shikoku Island, who would conceal her whereabouts. Thinking back on this now, as she sat in this train station searching through her thoughts and feelings, Toshiko could well imagine how bewildered and forlorn she would have felt had she been in the station of that unfamiliar place.

Toshiko felt herself becoming discouraged all over again. All her thoughts led to the same conclusion: she had no choice whatsoever but to give everything up as "hopeless." Just thinking of that word prompted a sudden, deep sigh from Toshiko. Startled by her own voice, Toshiko jumped up. She had let her emotions get the best of her without even being aware of what was happening. What most annoyed her about this slip was not only that it exposed her to Makiko, who had not one ounce of sympathy for her and was ignorant anyway, but also to Yasuko, with whom she had almost no connection in the first place. Exasperated with herself, Toshiko walked toward the exit in a state of frustration.

When Toshiko spied a red postbox directly left of the driveway in front of the station, she turned and walked in the opposite direction as if she had just remembered something. She took a postcard and pencil from her handbag. Then, standing with her back to the direction where Makiko stood, she concealed the postcard with her face, scribbled the man's name and address, and flipped the card over. What should she write? She could not write a single thing. Hot tears spilled down her cheeks.

"I have finally arrived here." As she wrote this, her glasses fogged up, making it impossible to see. She could not write. The feeling that she must write quickly was making her nervous, and then, the instant she looked over her shoulder, she heard someone trying to rush her: "They've started taking tickets! Let's get going right away."

She wrote the last five or six words barely conscious of what she was doing. Even after she had boarded the train and it had begun to move out, Toshiko would not budge from where she sat next to the window on the right. She gazed determinedly out this window. Even after the train had picked up to its normal speed, she found that she still could not think at all. Her mind had nearly stopped working altogether. Even Toshiko herself, feeling stiff and empty, had no idea of what was going to become of her.

Despite the fact that Yasuko could probably understand nothing of the magazine Toshiko had brought, she had it spread out before her and was reading it merely to stave off boredom. Makiko, however, was romping about like a child who hadn't been home in four or five years. Occasionally the mere sound of her cousin's voice would get Toshiko to thinking about how the two of them compared.

At twenty-two, Makiko was two years older than Toshiko. Nevertheless, since she had been spoiled by her father and raised to have her own way, Makiko had never once tried looking at things as an adult woman. Even when comparing Makiko to herself, Toshiko could only think of how terribly immature her cousin was. Watching the kinds of things that Makiko would do and the way she thought irritated Toshiko no end. From morning until night they had lived in the same room and sat behind the same desk in the same class of the same school. Not a single thing that Makiko had done had escaped Toshiko. What loathing Toshiko felt when she remembered how this so-called elder cousin of hers was, in fact, two years older than she.

Toshiko kept all her contempt for Makiko to herself. Yet she directed such contempt not only toward her elder cousin but also toward Makiko's father—Toshiko's uncle—whom she absolutely despised. From the time they were both very young, Toshiko had trained a skeptical eye on her aunt and uncle, watching how they treated her and how they treated Makiko. She noticed that while her uncle had displayed something close to an instinctive, almost blind feeling of love toward Makiko, he had shown Toshiko nothing but the authority of a strict supervisor. To Toshiko's observant eyes, both ways had always appeared extremely inappropriate, as well as exceedingly unnatural and even comical. Toshiko secretly snickered whenever she saw her uncle affecting this absurdly serious manner, as if he were some sort of fine moralist. One certainly could not see the evidence for any such authority in anything either he or her aunt said.

Yet Toshiko did not have the courage to take on these contemptible people, to tell them what she thought or to hear what they might have to say back to her. No matter what they told her and no matter what she heard from them, she remained silent. But what she always said to herself was, "Sooner or later . . . sooner or later, when I am able to live as I want, I shall not be silent. I will shout my disgust and laugh out loud at the lives of my uncle and all the rest, at that which I now scorn in silence. If only I could live on my own, I would never practice such hypocrisy. I would never let myself sink to such low and despicable behavior."

Such thoughts consumed Toshiko's attention. She lay in wait for the day when, yelling at the top of her lungs, she would finally lock horns with her uncle.

But when had all this happened to her? She knew about her uncle, and yet she had been ensnared by his craftiness and her precious Self was about to be sacrificed for his gain. To Toshiko's naïve and uncomplicated way of seeing things, nothing she could imagine would ever appear as dishonest and superficial as society. What was all this fuss about making a living? True, if one were intent on getting rich, then the ingenious, rather shrewd conduct of her conniving uncle would be an indispensable talent. How well Toshiko knew his special abilities in this area. Even though she abhorred his actions, she herself had fallen prey to his skillfully wrought deception. Persuaded by his "indispensable talent," she had been tricked before she had even realized what was happening.

"What sort of idiocy is this? The truth of the matter is that, in order for my uncle and his lot to have a comfortable life, I've been forced to be of use." Toshiko grew irritated all over again. This vile uncle of hers had left Nagasaki for Hakata, and would arrive there fifteen minutes before they were due. This meant that he would be waiting for them there when they arrived. Toshiko let out a long sigh, her face registering the disillusionment she felt inside. It was simply beyond her to think about all this any further now. Nevertheless, the train raced on.

And what a dismal direction Toshiko was being dragged toward. Something deep inside her unexpectedly came welling up. It pierced through her head and seemed to make a clean break from her miserable self. The sensation was quite pleasant, yet it also made her fearful of falling once more into that terrible state of bewilderment. Suddenly, she pressed against her stomach, shutting her eyes.

The sound of the familiar words of the dialect that she was so used to hearing on this train had always sparked a sense of happiness and belonging in her. But today this was far from the case. She could not afford to pay any attention to whatever Makiko and the others were doing or saying. Her face pale, she kept her head directed firmly toward the window, leaning against it.

"Oh, we've arrived! We've arrived at Hakozaki. Next is Yoshizuka, and then Hakata, right?" Makiko bounced up energetically and began to get her luggage together. This put Toshiko even more on the alert. The moment that she had made every effort to avoid had arrived. It was right before her and closing in.

"Whatever concerns I may have don't matter anymore. What will be, must be. I have come to the end of the road." Choking back the tears that inexplicably sprang to her eyes, Toshiko vigorously rose to her feet. The train sailed on through a grove of pine trees, a place she immediately recognized. The head of the statue of Nichiren suddenly loomed large over the tops of the pine trees. "I've come. I've come to Hakata. At long, long last."

The train made the ground tremble as it pulled into the station and moved down the length of the platform. The instant the train stopped moving, Toshiko was overcome by intense feelings of dread and confusion.

Makiko made quite a commotion as she got off the train. Toshiko quietly got off after her. Once off the train, Toshiko caught sight of something in the midst of the people waiting for them on the other side, a little ways away. She recognized this as the sleeve of her uncle's coat. He came rushing over to her in no time. When she got a look at the face of the young man who came following after him, Toshiko could not help but shudder. "That man is here. That awful man. Oh, how I hate this! I hate this!"

She wheeled around and gazed off toward the left, though there was nothing there. She looked toward the windows of the train that they had just come in on, noticing the figure of a tall man surrounded by a swarm of girl students. Toshiko strained to get a better look at the retreating figure.

"Toshiko-san." The animated voice of her cousin brought Toshiko back to reality. Nagata . . . this husband of hers . . . was nodding, taking care of his greetings to her despised uncle. Viewing the face of her uncle as he assumed his haughty posture, and spotting the meek Nagata at his side, made Toshiko feel utterly mortified.

"What became of all the happiness I should feel at coming home? The person who has made this so terribly painful for me, who has made everything so hard for me, is my uncle. He is the one who has done this to me. And will this Nagata, this man I know nothing about, will he steal my freedom? Who allowed this to happen to me? To me? Who gave permission for this to happen? There is no way I will ever throw myself—my precious Self—recklessly down in front of that sort of man, a man I don't even know. I . . . I will never value myself so cheaply. Not I!" Toshiko swallowed the desire to cry that rose within her by keeping her eyes riveted to the tip of her umbrella. Nevertheless, the tears came little by little, misting her eyeglasses and falling against the hard surface of the station platform.

"Toshiko-san. Let's be going." Toshiko heard Yasuko's voice calling her. It seemed as if she had forgotten all about Yasuko. At this point, Makiko and her uncle were already walking toward the stairs two or three paces ahead of Yasuko and Toshiko. As Toshiko started to go up the stairs, she heard someone running up behind her, a man calling her. It was Tajima, the man she had glimpsed shortly before.

"It is Toshiko-san, right? You've just arrived, haven't you? Congratulations on your graduation!" Toshiko was caught completely off guard by Tajima congratulating her here in this unexpected way. Last year Tajima had graduated from high school and had taken an appointment as a teacher in the area. While he had been in high school, Toshiko had somehow fallen into the habit of addressing him as "older brother." Sometimes he would come over to Toshiko's home to visit and would help her, since she was behind in English and math. After he had come home and assumed his teaching position at the girls' school, however, it had been inappropriate for Tajima to contact her and thus their communication had ceased. He had not known of Toshiko's graduation and her return, but had met her quite by accident at the train station.

Although this was a chance encounter, Toshiko felt nothing but happiness at meeting Tajima. At last there was someone here who would sympathize with her if she told him all her troubles. But Toshiko could not bring herself to say a single word. When she tried to talk, all the tears she had been holding back threatened to spill forth. Yasuko was watching her. Tajima had no idea what was going on. What's more, all of his students, who clung together in one big group as they walked, were exchanging glances with each other while they stared curiously at Toshiko and at Makiko, who was walking ahead of them, ascertaining that from quite a distance the pair seemed to be girl students.

Toshiko had no idea what she should say. It wouldn't do to say nothing at all. After a bit, and while trying to affect a laugh, she squeezed out a few words: "Yes, thank you. I finally somehow made it through."

"Is something wrong? You look so pale. Are you not feeling well?"

"I'm just a little tired. That's all."

"Oh, I see. Are the people in front there Makiko-san and your uncle?"

"Yes."

When they had gone down the stairs and were about to exit the station, her uncle and Tajima exchanged greetings. Tajima once again expressed his congratulations on their graduation to her uncle. Her uncle's face shone with satisfaction: "Yes, well, somehow we pulled through without any mishaps. Though I have to say it was really quite an effort, you know."

"I'm sure it was. But all has turned out well. You can relax now. You've done very well," he said, glancing toward Makiko.

In a cheerful mood, her uncle began busily getting the luggage together. Toshiko stood by, speechless. The thought of Nagata talking to her disgusted Toshiko, so she simply stood there, making no effort either to look at him or to allow their eyes to meet. Nervous, she hoped to speak only with Tajima. Their eyes met many times. Each time the other seemed to want to say something, but they both remained silent. Finally, Toshiko could stand this no longer. Choking back the urge to cry, Toshiko grasped the handle of her Western-style umbrella, wishing that she could somehow be by herself. Yet she knew full well that there was virtually no possibility of this.

With a promise to drop by her house for a visit when he had some free time, Tajima went on home. Now Yasuko, Nagata, and Toshiko were left alone together. Toshiko hated hearing Nagata's voice so much that even the sound of it could send shivers all over her. She had tried as best she could to avoid talking with him but finally the inevitable opportunity to do so was upon them. Maybe she should try talking with Yasuko, but once she did Nagata would no doubt join in, so Toshiko decided to remain silent. The three of them stood there, absolutely quiet. This in itself aggravated Toshiko, making her even more distressed as she waited anxiously and expectantly for the silence to break. But there wasn't a thing she could do about it. She hoped that Makiko would hurry back and looked around for her, but Makiko was nowhere to be seen.

"You must be terribly tired."

Toshiko was startled. Yet upon hearing Yasuko's quick and easy reply, she felt relieved. Nagata had not been trying to talk with her.

Just then her uncle finished taking care of the hand luggage and came over to them. Makiko followed after him. Toshiko breathed a sigh of relief. But when she realized that sooner or later, whether she liked it or not, she would have to speak to this dreadful man, Toshiko felt her whole body tighten up once again. She felt even worse when she remembered that in ten or twelve days she was to move into this horrible man's house and set up housekeeping with him. Toshiko could not imagine how she would ever be able to do such an appalling thing.

"So why did I come home?" Over and over, she kept asking herself this same question.

The place to which Toshiko and Makiko were returning was a little more than 3 *ri* from the bus stop. Even on the way there, Toshiko continued to feel tormented, as if bound by an anxiety so great that she wanted to writhe in frustration. She longed to rid herself of this feeling. When she saw Makiko talking in an excited and lighthearted fashion, she could not understand why her cousin did not at least show some sympathy, as she was certainly not unaware of Toshiko's plight. If only Makiko would show some consideration for her, grumbled Toshiko to herself, her irritation stirring renewed displeasure within her.

All of them dropped off their luggage at Makiko's home. After visiting with everyone briefly there, Toshiko headed out in the direction of the houses of the town next to the pine grove. Since Yasuko was going to stay at Makiko's, Toshiko and Nagata went back to her home together. As soon as she said her goodbyes, Toshiko left Makiko's house and without a glance behind her, walked as fast as she could, kicking up the hem of her *hakama* as she went. She was fully aware that her attitude was making Nagata uncomfortable. But even the thought of hearing his voice made Toshiko feel as if her whole body would tremble. There was no way she could walk alongside him, so Toshiko kept walking as fast as she could. Nevertheless, the meek Nagata followed her, plodding on behind. But Toshiko moved on even faster, making it difficult for him to keep up.

Finally, Nagata could take no more of this. He said, "Toshiko-san, what is all this foolish rush?"

Toshiko could not bring herself to answer.

At home, her mother had been wandering in and out of the house, waiting expectantly for her daughter's return. When Toshiko came rushing into the house as though she were on a mad dash, her mother and grandmother were there beside each other, their dear, smiling faces welcoming her home. As the sheer warmth of the house suffused Toshiko's body, her tormented heart finally eased. Yet as soon as she realized that Nagata was there, Toshiko wanted to cry. Everyone was talking to her, but she couldn't hear anything they were saying.

"I'm exhausted. I'm going to bed for awhile, until evening." Toshiko flung off her *hakama* in a willful manner. Taking in the sight of her granddaughter who had arrived home looking pale and listless, Toshiko's grandmother raised her eyebrows in tender concern.

"Oh, I imagine so," her grandmother said. "Even on a long trip, it is impossible to sleep well on the train. Let's get your mother to put out your bed." She stood up, placing her hands supportively behind Toshiko.

Toshiko's aunt and mother both felt sorry for Nagata, who was sitting there in obvious discomfort.

"Her grandmother is like that, you see, so she's become truly willful," said Toshiko's aunt, forcing a laugh and trying to apologize in a way that would placate Nagata. Having no idea what to do, Nagata laughed in response, then fell silent and looked nervously about the room.

Keenly observant, Toshiko's grandmother had been beside herself with worry ever since noticing how fiercely her granddaughter's willfulness had grown after she had been so displeased by her engagement last summer. She was well aware of how Toshiko was feeling when she came home today. She could sense Toshiko's attitude without even having to look at her, and she could certainly tell from the way Toshiko acted as she came into the house that her granddaughter had not the slightest inclination to give in to Nagata. She obviously detested the man. Toshiko's aunt, on the other hand, who sat facing the quiet young man, felt only anger at the willfulness of her niece. To her mind, Toshiko was behaving in a disgracefully argumentative and impudent manner.

"Why on earth is she acting like that? This willfulness of hers is terrible. This is certainly not something that her family approves of, you know. After you two are married, you'll have to take a firm hand with her right away, that's for sure."

As soon as Toshiko got into bed, she buried herself beneath the quilt. Realizing that she was finally alone, she began crying as if the tears would never stop. She felt numb, but still the tears kept coming. She was hollow, yet still the tears came. Dulled and spent, void of all feeling, her heart fixed on the tears flowing from within as Toshiko sank into a deep sleep.

Notes

[1] The first volume of Setouchi Harumi's two-volume novel based on Itō Noe's life, *Bi wa ranchō ni ari* (Bungei Shunjū, 1966; reprint 1984), has been translated by Sanford Goldstein and Kazuji Ninomiya as *Beauty in Disarray* (Rutland, VT, and Tokyo: Charles E. Tuttle, Co., 1993). Wakatsuki Setsuko's play *Netsujō: Itō Noe no seishun* (Passion: Itō Noe's Youth) was published in 1996 by Shuppan Purojekuto. The films are *Erosu + purasu gyakusatsu* (Eros + massacre, 1969), directed by Yoshida Yoshishige, which tells the story of the Hikage Inn Incident; and Fukusaku Kinji's 1988 film *Hana no ran* (Chaos of Flowers), which is about the Taishō artistic world. An early biography of Noe is Ide Fumiko's *Jiyū: Sore watakushi jishin* (Freedom: That Is I), (Chikuma Shobō, 1979).

[2] Itō Noe, *Itō Noe zenshū* (The Complete Works of Itō Noe), 2 vols. (Gakugei Shorin, 1970). In 2000, Gakugei Shorin brought out a four-volume edition, *Teihon Itō Noe zenshū* (The Standard Edition of the Complete Works of Itō Noe), and in 2001, a collection of selected works edited by Mori Mayumi, entitled *Fukeyo areyo kaze yo arashi yo: Itō Noe senshū* (Howl, Wind! Rage on, Storm! The Selected Works of Itō Noe), which includes a long section of letters exchanged between Noe and her third partner, Ōsugi Sakae.

[3] Mikiso Hane, *Peasants, Rebels, Women and Outcastes: The Underside of Modern Japan*, Second Edition (Lanham, MD: Rowman & Littlefield Publishers, Inc., 2003). His translations from Itō Noe's essays in *Seitō*, with the month of their publication, are: "To My Cousin" (March 1914); "The New Woman's Road" (January 1913); "To [Women's Higher Teachers College professor] Mr. Shimoda Jirō" (July 1914); "Recent Thoughts" (February 1913); "To the Readers [Anti-Manifesto]" (January 1916); "To [Educator] Lady Shimoda Utako" (September 1914); "On Chastity" (February 1915); "Arrogant, Narrow-Minded, Half-Baked Japanese Women's Public Activities" (December 1915); "Private Message to Ms. Nogami Yae" (June 1915), and "To Ms. Aoyama Kikue" (January 1916). Hane also includes translations of some of Noe's later essays.

[4] Several photographs of Itō Noe can be found in Ikeda Michiko, "Itō Noe," in Setouchi Harumi, series ed., *Onna no isshō: Jinbutsu kindai josei-shi* (Kōdansha, 1980–81), 6: 103–40.

[5] Itō Noe, "Dokusha shoshi ni" (To All of You, My Readers), *Seitō* 6.1 (January 1916), cover.

[6] Itō Noe, "Wagamama" (Willfulness), *Seitō* 3.12 (December 1913): 51–67.

[7] Itō Noe, "Shuppon" (Flight), *Seitō* 4.2 (February 1914): 85.

[8] Hanmura Shinobu, "Itō Noe," in Raichō Kenkyūkai, ed., *"Seitō" jinbutsu jiten: 110-nin no gunzō* (Taishūkan Shoten, 2001), 40–41.

[9] This is the only mention of a Bluestocking being paid for working on the maga-

zine. Hiratsuka Raichō, *Genshi, josei wa taiyō de atta: Hiratsuka Raichō jiden* (Ōtsuki Shoten, 1971–73), 2: 407; as translated in Hiratsuka Raichō and Teruko Craig, *In the Beginning, Woman Was the Sun: The Autobiography of a Japanese Feminist* (New York: Columbia University Press, 2006), 194.

[10]Hiratsuka, *Genshi, josei wa taiyō de atta*, 2: 494–98; Hiratsuka and Craig, *In the Beginning, Woman Was the Sun*, 234–36.

[11]Noe was so impressed by Emma Goldman that she decided to translate her essay "On the Tragedy of Women's Emancipation." Although Tsuji Jun did most of the actual work on this translation, it was published in March 1914, by Tōundō, under Noe's name. Ide, *Jiyū: Sore watakushi jishin*, 96.

[12]Itō Noe, "Mayoi" (Perplexity), *Seitō* 4.4 (April 1914): 192–203.

[13]Itō Noe, "Kojiki no meiyo" (Beggar's Honor), *Bunmei hihyō* 3 (April 1918), in idem, *Itō Noe zenshū*, 2: 255–81.

[14]For more details about this scandal and Noe's life with Ōsugi, see chap. 7, "Scandal and Eclipse," in Thomas A. Stanley, *Ōsugi Sakae, Anarchist in Taishō Japan: The Creativity of the Ego* (Cambridge, MA: Council on East Asian Studies, Harvard University, 1982), 91–110; and Stephen S. Large, "The Romance of Revolution in Japanese Anarchism and Communism during the Taishō Period," *Modern Asian Studies* 11.3 (1977): 441–67. I thank Stephen Filler for helpful information on the couple's life.

[15]The Bluestockings approached Hori Yasuko, asking her to write something for their special issue on the New Woman from the perspective of a socialist woman. The resulting essay, entitled "Watakushi wa furui onna desu" (I Am an Old-Fashioned Woman), was published in *Seitō* 3.1 (January 1913), Supplement: 61–65, under Hori Yasuko's name, although there has been some suspicion that the author was actually Ōsugi Sakae; see Kawahara Aya, "Hori Yasuko," in Raichō Kenkyūkai, ed., *"Seitō" jinbutsu jiten: 110-nin no gunzō* (Taishūkan Shoten, 2001), 148–49. In the short essay, the author complains about the police harassment she suffers because of her partner's political involvements, assuming that she may end up following him in death much as General Nogi's wife, Shizu, famously followed her husband in 1912. She admits that, as an "old" (*furui*) woman, she would like to marry her partner and take his name. Hori chides the Bluestockings for addressing her as "Mrs. Ōsugi" and for expecting her to share her partner's political beliefs. However, she concludes by applauding the New Woman as one who follows her own path. Hori wrote about her life with the radical in her March 1917 *Chūō kōron* article "Ōsugi to wakareru made" (Until Separating from Ōsugi). Adept at English, Kamichika Ichiko translated an essay by Havelock Ellis (1859–1939) on Walt Whitman, publishing this in four installments in *Seitō* 3.1 through 3.4. She also published a translation of a Guy de Maupassant story, "Journey to Corsica," in *Seitō* 2.12 (December 1912): 70–85. She contributed one long and very interesting story in the form of a letter, "Tegami no hitotsu" (One Letter), which was published in *Seitō* 2.9 (September 1912): 100–120. The story describes an ambitious student who seeks true love and self-awakening. Her first love, a man who does not support her intention to write an outstanding senior thesis, is a disappointment, but her second relationship seems to be working out. She directs the letter to "H" (Hiratsuka Raichō), approving of Raichō's work but reminding her that there are many definitions of the awakened self. Kamichika published only this story under her own name; the translations appeared under a pseudonym.

[16]Shocked and dismayed at the Hikage Incident, Hiratsuka Raichō believed that it "could only hurt the cause of those who opposed feudalistic morality" and criticized Noe in an article in *Osaka Mainichi shinbun* on 4 January 1917: "One of the so-called New Women has completely lost sight of the fact that free love in its true sense must be accompanied by a desire to live permanently with one's partner and a desire to take responsibility for the children of that union." Hiratsuka, *Genshi, josei wa taiyō de atta*, 2: 609–10; as translated in Hiratsuka and Craig, *In the Beginning, Woman Was the Sun*, 284–85.

[17]Itō Noe, "Atarashiki onna no michi" (The Path of the New Woman), *Seitō* 3.1 (January 1913), Supplement: 20–28.

[18]The prostitution debate in *Seitō* between Itō Noe and (Yamakawa) Aoyama Kikue occurred in five essays published from December 1915 through February 1916. Itō Noe wrote three: "Gōman kyōryō ni shite futettei naru nihon fujin no kōkyō jigyō ni tsuite" (Arrogant, Narrow-Minded, Half-Baked Japanese Women's Public Service Activities), *Seitō* 5.11(December 1915): 1–18; "Aoyama Kikue shi ni" (To Ms. Aoyama Kikue), *Seitō* 6.1 (January 1916): 154–65; and "Futatabi Aoyama shi e" (A Second Response to Ms. Aoyama), *Seitō* 6.2 (February 1916): 80–85. Aoyama Kikue published two responses: "Nihon fujin no shakai jigyō ni tsuite: Itō Noe shi ni atau" (On the Social Work of Japanese Ladies: A Response to Ms. Itō Noe), *Seitō* 6.1 (January 1916): 142–53; and "Sara ni ronshi o akiraka ni su" (Further Clarification of My Argument), *Seitō* 6.2 (February 1916): 69–79.

[19]For a short history of the JWCTU in Japan, see chap. 5, "The Women's Reform Society," in Sharon Sievers, *Flowers in Salt: The Beginnings of Feminist Consciousness in Modern Japan* (Stanford, CA: Stanford University Press, 1983), 87–113.

[20]In her discussion of this incident, Kelly Foreman argues that diverse interpretations and misunderstandings of who geisha were generated the controversy: "The result of such a highly unique, insular society, visible to or understood by few, is that the social status of geisha varies greatly depending on perspective and context. Those with no knowledge of the arts world often interpret geisha to be fancy bar hostesses with little talent; the geisha career would not be the profession of choice for one's daughter. For example, when the Emperor Taishō was to take the throne, the Shimbashi geisha association wanted to celebrate with a colorful parade, and held a press conference to announce the details of this plan. Many women's groups protested, claiming that geisha were 'vulgar' (*iyashī*), and tried to prevent this parade from taking place (Iwabuchi, *Danna to Asobi to Nihon no Bunka*, 44). The strongest negative reactions came from housewives, and the key supporters for the Shimbashi geisha parade were poet Yosano Akiko and progressive educator Yamawaki Fusako (both women) (Iwabuchi, 44–45). Therefore, the symbol of what geisha represented possessed within it a component of volatility, indicative of the divergent views of women (and by women) present during Taishō-era Japanese society." Foreman, "The Role of Music in the Lives and Identities of Japanese Geisha" (Ph.D. diss., Kent State University, 2002), 68. The embedded citation is for Iwabuchi Junko, ed., *"Danna" to asobi to nihon bunka: Tatsujin ni manabu sui na ikikata* (PHP Kenkyūjo, 1996).

[21]Itō, "Gōman kōryō ni shite futettei naru nihon fujin no kōkyō jigyō ni tsuite," partially translated in Hane, *Peasants, Rebels, Women and Outcastes*, 277–82.

[22]For an excellent analysis of Yajima Kajiko's work and the JWCTU, see also Elizabeth Dorn Lublin, "Wearing the White Ribbon of Reform and the Banner of Civic Duty: Yajima Kajiko and the Japan Woman's Christian Temperance Union in

the Meiji Period," *U.S.–Japan Women's Journal,* nos. 30–31 (2006): 60–79.

[23] Aoyama, "Nihon fujin no shakai jigyō ni tsuite."

[24] Arguments about providing a reasonable livelihood for former prostitutes and evidence of similar class tensions occurred in the 1950s. See G. G. Rowley, "Prostitutes against the Prostitution Prevention Act of 1956," *U.S.–Japan Women's Journal,* no. 23 (2002): 39–56.

[25] Hiratsuka Raichō, "Yajima Kajiko-shi to Fujin Kyōfūkai no jigyō o ronzu" (Comments on the Enterprise of the Women's Reform Society and Ms. Yajima Kajiko), *Shin shōsetsu* (June 1917), as cited in Iwabuchi, "Sekushuaritei no seijigaku e no chōsen," 326.

Chapter 6
Iwano Kiyoko (1882–1920)

We are women of the human species. We are not a species called woman.

Iwano Kiyoko liked to think of herself as a rational woman, one who did not let her emotions get the better of her no matter what the occasion.[1] Like most Bluestockings, Kiyoko wrote frank autobiographical essays. Indeed, one of her favorite topics was the exploration of how she and Naturalist writer Iwano Hōmei (1873–1920) intended to develop their ideal, modern marriage based on individualism. Yet even her most personal essays portray a first-person narrator who takes an objective view of herself and who can consider her life in a broader context. Kiyoko's essays are not as lyrical or enigmatic as Hiratsuka Raichō's or as impassioned as those of Itō Noe (see Chapters 4 and 5 above), but rather straightforward and occasionally playful. The self-assurance reflected in her writing underscores her years of commitment to seeing political and legal changes made to advance the rights of women. The composure displayed in her essays, however, belies a personal life marred by loss, betrayal, and deep despair, feelings that Kiyoko does dramatize in her short stories that appeared in *Seitō*.

In her autobiography, Hiratsuka Raichō records several impressions of Kiyoko, with whom she became good friends. Although she found her fastidious to a fault and cold at times, Raichō enjoyed Kiyoko's forthright manner. Their approaches to feminism differed, with Kiyoko pushing Raichō to become involved in efforts to improve the legal status of women in Japan. Perhaps this is why Raichō found Kiyoko to be a stubborn "by-the-book feminist" (*keishiki-teki na jokenronsha*) with a "legalistic turn of mind."[2] Yet she also recognized in Kiyoko "a sentimental streak and a genuine concern for others."[3] The two first met through letters and by reading each other's work. Kiyoko's "firm and bold handwriting" led Raichō to imagine "a woman of sturdy build, healthy and full of life." But the sad heroine of her story "Karekusa" (Withered Grass), described in detail below, made her wonder if Kiyoko herself was "pale, emaciated, and worn down with misery." When she finally met Kiyoko in April 1912, Raichō was completely surprised by her appearance:

Small and thin, with thick makeup and hair gathered up in a voluminous marumage, she looked like a housewife with a taste for
flashy clothes. Even more surprising was her dark green mantle,
which clashed with her Japanese-style hairdo. Perhaps I was struck
by how exhausted she looked even with a layer of makeup because
of the contrast with Hōmei, who exuded health and vigor. . . . As
Chōkō said, she had a beautiful voice, her speech was crisp and
clear, and she had a habit of breaking out in high-pitched laughter.
And yet, seeing the cigarette tremble in her slender, veined fingers,
I could not help thinking of the woman in "Withered Grass."[4]

Raichō also recorded that Kiyoko was always proud of her roots in old
Tokyo.[5] Born in Kanda on 11 March 1882, Kiyoko was the second child and
first daughter of Kimura Nobukura and his wife (whose name is unknown).
When Kiyoko was only two years old, her mother died, and Kiyoko was
made the heir of her maternal grandmother, Endō Wasa.[6] As a teenager she
dropped out of a respected Tokyo girls' school when her father's business
failed. At age fifteen Kiyoko completed training at a teaching academy, and
she worked at three different elementary schools over the next five years.
She later worked temporarily for the railroad offices until she joined a tele-
graph company in 1905. Kiyoko left this position when she fell in love with
one of her colleagues there, a married man by the name of Nakao Gorō, and
turned to working as a newspaper and magazine reporter. Kiyoko was so
enthralled with Gorō that when he refused to divorce his wife and wanted
to end his relationship with Kiyoko in 1909, she tried to commit suicide
by drowning herself in the ocean. This attempt was foiled by a fisherman
who happened to spot Kiyoko and pulled her to safety. Although she had
resolved to forswear any further love affairs, Kiyoko's six-year involvement
with Iwano Hōmei began later that same year, in December, upon their introduction by a mutual friend, socialist Imai Utako.

The couple's relationship—from their initial decision to live together to
their tumultuous divorce—was played out in the public eye. It was certainly
an unusual match. Hōmei had just established himself as a Naturalist writer after publishing his novel *Tandeki* (Debauchery) in the journal *Shinchō*.[7]
The narrator of this comic tale comes "to realize that debauchery is the *rai-
son d'être* of life" through a lusty affair with a geisha.[8] Soon after meeting
Kiyoko, Hōmei proposed they move in together and get married. Kiyoko
would not be rushed into romance. She insisted that friendship must come
first, followed by a genuine spiritual connection, and only then should a
sexual union and marriage occur. She agreed to live with Hōmei, but only if
they had separate rooms and treated each other as friends. Although Hōmei
asserted that it was artificial to make such distinctions between body and

spirit, he agreed to Kiyoko's conditions. He had had a complicated love life of his own, having separated from his first wife and broken off with a lover after failing at a crab canning business on Sakhalin Island. Less than ten days after they met, Kiyoko and Hōmei took up residence together.

Once it became clear that newspapers had gotten wind of their unusual arrangement, the couple decided to come out with the story on their own. They gave separate interviews, first to a *Yorozu shinbun* reporter. The newspaper ran a humorous story, asking whether "the flesh or the spirit" would ultimately win in what seemed to be a tug-of-war between the author of *Debauchery* and his virtuous girlfriend. In the end, Kiyoko felt misunderstood, believing that newspaper reports took her to be advocating celibacy when in fact she was arguing for a profound emotional connection as the basis for sexual relations. For the reading public, the story must have seemed like one more bizarre example of attempts to change social mores. For Kiyoko, it was the beginning of her life as a public figure as well as the start of a difficult relationship. It was also a way for her to make a statement about how she valued true love above all else—above material gain, convention, and sexual desire alone.[9]

In the midst of her eventful romantic life, Kiyoko had also become associated with the socialist group Heimin-sha (Commoners' Society), and from 1905 through 1909 worked alongside Fukuda Hideko and other women members for the revision of Article Five of the Police Security Regulations (Chian Keisatsu Hō), which restricted women from participating in any political group or speaking in public on issues of a political nature. In her 1913 essay translated below as "On Intellectual and Economic Independence," Iwano Kiyoko reflects on this campaign, reserving a special bitterness for all the women who distanced themselves from her and her colleagues, and expressing gratitude to the men who supported the revision efforts.[10] Her own work on behalf of this project included gathering signatures on the street for petitions and visiting the Diet on a daily basis. She retreated from all activity for a time after her previously mentioned failed suicide attempt. Perhaps it was Hōmei's enthusiastic encouragement of her writing career and her association with the writers and publishers in his world that helped Kiyoko regain her strength and jump into the fray once again.

The possibility of writing for *Seitō* opened up a new opportunity for Kiyoko to involve herself in the Woman Question. At Ikuta Chōkō's suggestion, Raichō invited Kiyoko to join the Bluestockings. In 1911 Kiyoko and Hōmei, who had taken a job as a reporter for the *Osaka shinpō* (Osaka News), were living in Osaka. Kiyoko began contributing to *Seitō* in the journal's first year, and was to publish twenty pieces in it before its cessation. Her first attempts were short stories, tales of selfish and insensitive men partnered with women yearning for romantic passion or, at the very least, honesty. They consistently show a painful clash between a New Woman's ideals, nurtured by reading modern fiction and philosophy, and the reality of her love life. One of her characters even wishes she could escape her humdrum marriage for the thrill of being "the female protagonist" of a romance like *Black Smoke*, the famous novel based on Hiratsuka Raichō's involvement with Morita Sōhei (see Chapter 4).[11] Considering three of these stories will help us understand how Kiyoko empathized with women's dissatisfactions, especially in their intimate relationships with men. And when we discuss Kiyoko's divorce from Hōmei below, we will learn how much her characters' frustrations mirrored her own.

The story "Otaka," published in the second issue of *Seitō*, features a young working-class woman named Otaka who loyally befriends and becomes romantically involved with Masao, an aspiring theater owner. Masao, who pretends to be a widower, does not have the courage to tell Otaka that he is married, but instead sends her to his home, where he tells her that his older sister awaits her. Otaka eagerly goes to the home that she expects will one day be hers. She suffers a crushing blow when she comes face to face with her lover's wife. Scolded for having caused the wife to suffer for the last two years, Otaka feels miserable, realizing she, too, has been duped.[12] Another story, "Antō" (Secret Feud), published in the April 1912 issue of *Seitō*, is probably closely autobiographical and somewhat similarly depicts the character Kimiko's surprise at opening the door to her husband's former lover, the prostitute Otori.[13] In both cases, women must adjust as they learn about their partners' love lives.

At the invitation of Bluestocking Araki Ikuko (see Chapter 1 above), Kiyoko followed "Otaka" with an autobiographical story in February 1912 entitled "Karekusa" (Withered Grass), a piece that she found difficult to write and with which she was not entirely satisfied.[14] Sayoko, the main character of "Karekusa," works so hard around the house that her soft hands have toughened. Cooped up all day by herself at home, she is bored, lonely, self-pitying, and full of resentment toward her husband, who perpetually ignores her. She has given up everything for his love, yet he refuses to spend any time with her and stays out amusing himself until the early morning hours. Misunderstanding Sayoko's unhappiness, her husband assumes she is dissatisfied because he doesn't make much money. He also feels that working all day entitles him to have fun away from home at night. An excerpt from their conversation describes the tension in their marriage:

> "There's no way I'm going to sacrifice myself to the family and become somebody who wants to cling to the house all the time.

No way am I going to turn into such an Average Joe (*heibon na ningen*)."

"Well, then, what am I supposed to do? From morning to night there's no one around to talk with. Should I be like some dog who's satisfied as long as she's kept fed? Except for when we're in bed or having a meal, you're always out somewhere. Am I supposed to stay here, content with this lonely life, without being given even one word of comfort?"[15]

In the end, Sayoko mourns her husband's lack of understanding and his inability to become close to a woman who does not resort to coquetry:

Men just can't understand a woman's feelings. They take no account of the tender affection for which women long. They seem to think that as long as they give a woman physical satisfaction and guarantee their livelihood, that alone is enough. They don't understand that women can't be satisfied with that. But no matter how hard she explained this to her husband, when she saw that he wasn't going to give an inch, she no longer felt like harping on it to him.[16]

Although Iwano Kiyoko's fictional women suffer from untrustworthy, selfish men, in her essays she maintains that a much different, much happier married life is possible. The key to this is the practice of individualism, which for Kiyoko means that partners—and in fact all members of a family—should respect each other as autonomous human beings and communicate openly. With such ideals in mind, Kiyoko returned to Tokyo with Hōmei in 1912 and set up housekeeping in what was then the suburb of Shita-Meguro ward. The couple legally married in 1913, and Kiyoko gave birth to their son Tamio in 1914. Although Kiyoko eventually became close to Tamio, she did not greet impending motherhood with relish. Short essays published in *Seitō* document her frustration with the "parasite" taking up residence in her body and, later, her budding love for her newborn son. Kiyoko writes of her intentions to raise her son in a way that nurtures his independence without sacrificing her own dreams. Like other Bluestockings, Kiyoko wants the New Woman to be a New Mother as well.[17]

As far as Kiyoko was concerned, their home life was happy until Hōmei began his affair with Kanbara Fusae (1890–1944), a young woman who came to their home to work as a copyist. Kiyoko had suggested Kanbara for this job, having met the younger woman in Tokyo when she asked to become a full-fledged member of the Bluestockings.

Thinking about Kanbara Fusae's connection with the Bluestockings and her entry into Iwano Kiyoko's life gives us an idea of how the public may have regarded the whole affair. Kanbara Fusae's essays for *Seitō* show that her sympathies for the New Woman had much in common with Kiyoko's own. The fourth daughter of the chief priest of a temple in Niigata Prefecture, Kanbara was educated at the prefectural girls' school, becoming an elementary school teacher upon graduation. She continued working after bearing her first child and marrying in 1910. Much like a character in one of Iwano Kiyoko's stories, Kanbara found her work and home life so frustrating that she left for Tokyo in 1914, leaving her child with her husband and later obtaining a divorce. Like Kiyoko, Kanbara Fusae apparently felt a special affinity for the Bluestockings almost as soon as the group formed. Her name first appears on the list of Bluestocking members and supporters in the February 1912 issue of *Seitō*. She contributed two short articles to the journal in 1914, one describing her contempt for the sexism of the men teachers with whom she had worked, and another lashing out at the woman educator Kaetsu Kōko (1867–1949) for being "ignorant, incompetent, and foolish" and a self-described "old-fashioned woman" (*furui onna*). She reviles Kaetsu for the way she condemns young women for disregarding the "special, feminine virtues of Japanese women" in favor of chasing after outmoded Western fashions, and finds Kaetsu typical of the conservatives who make no attempt to understand the young women of Kanbara's own generation.[18]

Kanbara's youth, fiery criticism, and her abrupt departure from home recall the writing style and actions of Itō Noe, and perhaps it was this dramatic personality that drew Iwano Kiyoko's husband Hōmei to her. Interestingly, Kanbara and Kiyoko had in common their dislike of Kaetsu Kōko. Kiyoko had also criticized the educator in a much earlier issue of *Seitō*, in a more restrained but even more damning manner. She takes apart, point by point, Kaetsu's argument in favor of men taking concubines in order to continue the family bloodline, faulting Kaetsu for hypocrisy at every turn.[19] Although Kanbara Fusae and Iwano Kiyoko agree in spirit in this case, their ways of arguing their position could not be more different.

How much Iwano Kiyoko knew about Kanbara when she hired her is not recorded. What Kiyoko does report is how shocked and betrayed the relationship between her husband and Kanbara made her feel. Kiyoko gives a candid account of the affair and its effects on her life in the short 1915 essay translated below as "Thoughts on Separation." Later in 1915, she published an entire book on the sad tale of her failed marriage, which had, from first to last, been a matter of public curiosity.

One of the most curious aspects of the Kiyoko-Hōmei marriage was its controversial "modern" end (a topic explored in more detail below). A firm believer in women employing the law and asserting their rights rather than bemoaning their fate, Kiyoko sued Hōmei, demanding that he come home to her, their son, and his son by a previous marriage for whom Kiyoko was caring. Hōmei, in turn, responded by suing Kiyoko for divorce. In the end, Kiyoko won what the newspapers termed "a paper victory" in both suits, and the couple jointly agreed to divorce in 1917. Kiyoko resumed her position as head of the Endō family and adopted her own son Tamio as its heir; Hōmei's first son was sent back to live with his birth mother. Hōmei continued to live with Kanbara Fusae, who divorced her first husband, Watanabe Kanji, in 1915. Kanbara had two children with Hōmei, and married him in 1918. When Hōmei died suddenly in 1920, Kiyoko wrote a piece over one hundred pages long about their life together and published it in the journal *Shin shōsetsu* (The New Novel).[20] As for Kanbara Fusae, she was left to raise three children from her two marriages. She published Homei's collected works, continued writing, among other activities to make money, and eventually went to China with her children in 1934. She died there after an illness in 1944, at age fifty-three.

Although shaken by her troubles with Hōmei, Iwano Kiyoko did not give up her public life or circumscribe her personal one. A newly single mother at thirty-five years of age, Kiyoko developed yet another romance. She began living with Endō Tatsunosuke, an artist in his twenties who enjoyed Western-style painting. Ever determined to contribute to the family income, Kiyoko opened a flower shop that, unhappily, did not prove profitable. In fact, the family fell into such financial straits that she once again considered suicide. This was another dispirited chapter in her life that Kiyoko wrote about for the women's magazine *Fujin kōron* (Ladies' Review).[21] When Hiratsuka Raichō and others established the Shin Fujin Kyōkai (New Woman's Association) in March 1920, Kiyoko joined, speaking out on protection for working children, advocating women's participation in politics, and once again taking a stand against Article Five. Soon after, in June of that year, she gave birth to a daughter. On a trip to Tatsunosuke's family home in Kyoto at the end of 1920 to broach the topic of the couple formally marrying, her chronic problem with gallstones suddenly worsened. Endō Kiyoko died in a Kyoto hospital on 18 December 1920, at the age of thirty-eight. Thereafter, her daughter was raised by Tatsunosuke's mother while her son was taken in by Bluestocking Araki Ikuko. On 10 May 1922, partial revision of Article Five of the Police Security Regulations took effect, enabling women to attend and participate in political gatherings.

In 1935 Hiratsuka Raichō and Araki Ikuko persuaded other former Bluestockings to join them in contributing funds to erect a memorial at the Yanaka Temple graveyard in Tokyo dedicated to Kiyoko and her son Tamio, who had died in the Great Kantō Earthquake of 1923. It was the first memorial established to honor a woman who had been both a member of the Bluestockings and a pioneer in the women's movement of Japan.[22]

"Men and Women Are Equal as Members of the Human Race"

The first two of Iwano Kiyoko's essays translated here suggest that Iwano may have been familiar with the work of New Women writers Charlotte Perkins Gilman (1860–1935) and Olive Schreiner (1855–1920). Gilman's 1898 *Women and Economics* was translated and published in Japan in February 1912; a Japanese translation of Schreiner's 1911 *Woman and Labour* was published in 1914. Though both authors' writing is related to the language of the eugenics movement, like Iwano Kiyoko they see gender roles not as immutable but as contingent, and argue against seeing women's subservience or inferiority to men as natural.[23] Iwano Kiyoko's essays differ from their books in her occasional use of a playful tone and, of course, in her specific references to women and events in Japan. Her invocation of the primitive, however, resembles Gilman and Schreiner's visions of the past as a kind of timeless time when people lived in a state of nature.

Iwano Kiyoko's essay "Jinrui to shite dansei to josei wa byōdō de aru" (Men and Women Are Equal as Members of the Human Race) appeared in the special section of the January 1913 issue of *Seitō*, a supplement devoted to discussion of the New Woman.[24] In it Kiyoko raises issues commonly used to argue for women's inferiority and proceeds to refute them one by one. Her references to zoology are rather startling, and probably unfounded, but they do show how she moved to separate biological distinctions of sex from socially constructed gender roles. In another move to disrupt convention, Kiyoko's use of old proverbs prods her audience into reflecting on how language has served to naturalize gender hierarchy; Gilman also makes use of this strategy. Whereas the poetic writing of Yosano Akiko (see Chapter 12 below) and Hiratsuka Raichō opened up new ways of speaking about gender and liberation that were highly individualistic, Iwano Kiyoko's essay unfolds in a way that invites further argument.

Iwano Kiyoko expanded on these ideas in later essays in *Seitō*, holding fast to the notion that an individual's growth must not be impeded by outmoded notions of biology, gender, family, or nation. In November 1913, she writes proudly of how she and her husband are trying to live this new life in the suburbs of Tokyo, even with the addition of her father, his mother, and, soon, a new baby living with them. Kiyoko wants to build a family by honoring the individual freedom of each member, and avoid relations based on sacrifice or subservience. In September 1914, she laments how often people forget that individuals do not exist for the sake of the family or the nation, writing that everyone must understand that these alliances are useful only insofar as they nurture the individual.[25]

"On Intellectual and Financial Independence"

Iwano Kiyoko originally wrote "Shisō no dokuritsu to keizai-jō no dokuritsu" (On Intellectual and Financial Independence) as a speech to present on 15 February 1913, at the first (and last) Bluestocking public lecture (figure 7). She published a summary the following month in an untitled appendix in *Seitō*.[26] In her autobiography, Hiratsuka Raichō includes a lengthy article on the event published in the *Yomiuri shinbun* on 16 February 1913. The reporter is as taken with Kiyoko's fashion as her ideas:

> Dressed in a silk crepe kimono and satin obi, her hair piled up in a towering marumage, [Mrs. Iwano Kiyoko] was greeted with enthusiastic applause as she mounted the stage. . . Her ideas were clearly reasoned and delivered with great aplomb.[27]

Kiyoko's remarks to the audience explained how a woman's financial independence enables her freedom of thought. Having worked as a teacher, an office worker, and a journalist, she spoke from experience. Her own background made Kiyoko well aware of the problems even educated women could face in the workplace. Nevertheless, she fully believed that women could achieve intellectual freedom if they first obtained the tangible freedoms afforded by financial independence. Without their own money, Kiyoko believed, women would inevitably become reliant on their parents and husbands. If economic independence could force even men to live fractured lives in which reality warred with aspirations, how much more so, asks Kiyoko, is this true for women. For Iwano Kiyoko, the true New Woman is a gainfully employed or entrepreneurial woman.

But what kind of "working woman" does Kiyoko envision? The majority of Japanese women were already laboring on farms, in textile mills, as domestic servants, or in numerous other occupations. Work did not often guarantee many of them a living wage, let alone the leisure to develop their intellects. Kiyoko is clearly speaking to the increasing number of girls' school graduates who have a choice of new white-collar positions, though certainly not an array of highly remunerative career possibilities. Vehement in her call for women to take care of themselves, she finds no fault with gender discrimination in the marketplace but assigns all the responsibility to women for developing sufficient initiative. Moreover, she derides those women who distanced themselves from her Meiji-era fight to revise Article

Figure 7. This photograph captures Iwano Kiyoko speaking at the Bluestockings' public lecture event at Kanda Youth Hall on February 15, 1913. Courtesy of Ōtsuki Shoten.

Five, considering them probably too numbed by convention and their own lack of ambition to imagine either intellectual or financial independence. To her mind, the fault for women's dependence lies within women themselves, and only New Women such as the Bluestockings can head in new and freer directions.

"Thoughts on Separation"

In her September 1915 essay "Bekkyo ni tsuite omou kotodomo" (Thoughts on Separation), Kiyoko admits to feeling thrown by her own lingering illness, her husband's affair, and his attempts to rationalize his infidelity.[28] She makes an effort to gain perspective and a sense of control by speaking with her friend and fellow Bluestocking Ikuta Hanayo (1888–1970), who serves as her amanuensis. Above all, Kiyoko does not want to wring her hands in despair and give Hōmei an easy victory. But what should a New Woman do in this instance? She had not chosen an arranged marriage sanctioned by their families and was presumably loath to call on family members to help resolve their differences. In her *Seitō* writing, Kiyoko had made public her hopes for their new-style marriage based on a union of the flesh and the spirit—a marriage that she believed would enrich each partner's individualistic, "natural" development. Now she felt a need to confide her feelings about the failure of this marriage to her readers as well.

Iwano Kiyoko's decision to challenge Hōmei by going through legal channels was an act that took the Bluestockings in a new direction. Thus far, liberation had been styled as something interior, a kind of meditative path, and as a refusal—a choice not to marry, not to follow convention, and not to obey. Yet Kiyoko wanted the Bluestockings to engage with the law and work for change in a more overtly public way, too. Certainly she was not afraid of confronting officials. For example, in August 1914, she and Hiratsuka Raichō walked into the Ministry of the Interior and requested an appointment with Chief Internal Security Officer Yasukawa, who had reportedly defamed the Bluestockings in an interview in the *Tokyo Asahi shinbun*. Yasukawa had referred to the Bluestockings as "famished demons of lust" (*shikiyoku no gaki*). They were able to meet a lower-level official, a Mr. Gōtō, whom they questioned sharply until he ended up admitting that there had been no evidence for such remarks.[29]

Yet, as we have seen, the question of how far to go in pressing for legal reforms was something that divided Kiyoko and Raichō. In an October 1914 letter to Raichō (later published in *Seitō*), Kiyoko explains why she cannot accept Raichō's invitation to write an introduction for her second collection of essays. Although she admires Raichō's work on behalf of women and finds her attention to praxis increasing, Kiyoko faults Raichō for not "going out into the streets" with her message:

> This may be a bit cruel to say, but while you have expended great effort on awakening women through focusing on their interior lives, you have underrated that aspect of the movement that would raise the position of women in a formal sense. At the very least, you have thought that it was premature. Isn't this exactly like my first romance, in which I valued the spiritual too much and despised the physical? If I have the chance, I would like to revise the legal position of women, even to the extent of reforming the rights of wives and mothers. As we address the Woman Question, this kind of movement, too, absolutely must be involved. My hope for you is that you will leave your study and go out into the streets. This means that I would like you to put both your head and your hands into action.[30]

Hiratsuka Raichō, however, did not express much sympathy for Iwano Kiyoko's legal pursuit of her husband that followed her essay "Thoughts on Separation," and found it odd that her "individualism" extended even to labeling all the possessions in the Iwano household that were hers as "Property of Kiyoko." [31] Nevertheless, she and Kiyoko respected each other as intellectuals, and evidently discussed much about their lives and philosophies with each other. In her autobiography, Raichō records her memories of her conversations with Kiyoko at this time:

> Kiyoko explained the situation like this. The reason she had not filed for divorce was not because she believed there was any love left between her husband and herself or because she hoped, or expected, that Hōmei would come back to her. Nor was she motivated, as so many women were, to tolerate a faithless husband for financial reasons or for the sake of her children's welfare. Her real reason, she said, was to defend the legal "position of wives." She told me she was not doing this just for herself but for all unhappy wives. For the sake of all women, she would advocate the rights of the wife.[32]

In "Thoughts on Separation," Iwano Kiyoko writes about how betrayed she feels by her husband's affair, yet locates the heart of this betrayal in her husband's lack of integrity rather than in his sexual infidelity. As she says, his actions countered everything he had written. In this way Iwano Kiyoko reserves the moral high ground for herself, as someone who is not unable to free her husband for another romance but who requires that such a liaison be based on a sincere love and respect, a sexual passion based on mutual friendship. Nowhere in her essay does Kiyoko mention that the great love affair of her own youth had been with a married man.

This short essay was only the first volley in what became an even more public exchange when Hōmei and Kiyoko each published lengthy books. In October 1915, Hōmei published a 280-page volume with Shinchō-sha entitled *Danjo to teisō mondai* (Men, Women, and the Issue of Chastity), in which he zealously defended himself as an honest practitioner of the "new morality." Kiyoko's 508-page book, *Ai no sōtō* (Conflict of Love), published a month later by Yonekura Shoten, purports to be a brutally honest confession of her entire relationship with Hōmei, and is in the form of a diary that begins with their first meeting, describes how they came to live together, and continues until the day Hōmei moved out of their home in Tokyo.[33] It includes prefatory remarks by Tanaka Ōdō (1867–1932), Ikuta Chōkō, and Hiratsuka Raichō. Advertisements for both books about this "now-famous separation" tout them as explorations of the new morality of modern Japan, and evidence of a case that has "gone beyond the level of the individual to become an issue of social concern."[34] Kanbara Fusae also published her version of the affair in 1915 in the journal *Shinchō* (New Tide), entitling her essay "Iwano Hōmei to dōsei shita jiken no shinsō" (The Truth about Iwano Hōmei and I Living Together).

As Ogata Akiko states in her essay appended to a 1985 reprinted edition of Kiyoko's 1915 book *Ai no sōtō* (Conflict of Love), there is little recorded for those years other than Kiyoko's love for Hōmei, and as a result, the words that most often appear are those such as "love," "spirit," and "flesh."[35] After reviewing Kiyoko's confident essays and stories in *Seitō*, it is surprising to find such a different voice in *Conflict of Love*. The figure of Iwano Kiyoko that emerges here seems less like a New Woman actively engaged in the conflicts of modern Japan and more like the bitter writer of the famous Heian-era *Kagerō nikki* (Kagerō Diary/The Gossamer Years), whose whole life narrowly turns on the lover who has long since lost interest in her. Ogata points out the contrast between Kiyoko's obsession with Hōmei and what he records in his own diary of their years together. Kiyoko is mentioned only occasionally, whereas his writing projects, conversations with friends, dealings with publishers, and physical ailments are described in detail. When he does mention Kiyoko, it is often to record some displeasure with her or to make note of some mundane incident.[36]

The public controversy over Kiyoko and Hōmei's separation kept their relationship in the public eye for some time. Editorials on the subject appeared in all the major Tokyo newspapers and in special issues of the prominent intellectual journals *Chūō kōron*, *Shinchō*, and *Shin shōsetsu*. Indeed, Hōmei's main reason for writing a book on the subject seems to have been to fend off the criticism that was largely directed at him. While her Bluestocking friends offered tacit support to Kiyoko, they were too involved with the dramas of their own love lives in 1915 to offer much help. For the public, the incident became one more case of the extraordinary personal lives of people in the literary world becoming the catalyst for a discussion of modern life and mores.

****

Men and Women Are Equal as Members of the Human Race
Iwano Kiyo
Seitō 3.1 (January 1913)

I do not deny that, in this day and age, men display a greater knowledge and a greater ability than do women, and so I respect the men of our day as those who are more advanced than I. Nevertheless, I cannot subscribe to the notion that women are absolutely inferior to men, as do those pundits who like to expound on the role of women in our society, nor can I abide by the supremely facile, hollow arguments they mount to compare men and women. Speaking in the most inane fashion, these critics point to the relative physical strength of both sexes, or they draw attention to biological factors, or they line up examples from mythology that present men as good and women as evil. They even boast about how men's intellectual abilities have become genetically innate, cultivated over time by their environment.

When I paid a visit recently to the home of a certain acquaintance and spoke with her husband, he put the comparison this way: "The physical strength of two women equals that of one man. Man is thus naturally the superior of woman."

At this, I burst out laughing!

If, for the sake of argument, we were to say that the one with the greatest strength is the superior being, then in our nation, a sumo wrestler would necessarily be superior to everyone else. Indeed, even a sumo wrestler would not be the most superior, for bears and great snakes would place ahead of any human. Taking this argument still farther, I suppose that we would have to say that tigers, elephants, and crocodiles would be by far the most superior animals of all!

Comparing the relative strength of these fearsome creatures with men will never elaborate the difference between women and men. Moreover, human beings always like to say that, in comparison with these beasts, we are much the superior animal. In other words, it is quite clear that the superiority or inferiority of animals has nothing to do with issues of simple brute strength. Yet, in drawing comparisons about men and women, men violate this basic principle by calling themselves naturally superior to us because of their greater might.

Men speak in the same quite contradictory ways concerning matters of a biological nature. They reason that since women's periods of activity are so often restricted by pregnancy and other infirmities, women cannot keep up with men in the public sphere. Thus, the argument goes, women have a divine mission to care for the home. Yet the truth of the matter is that women do wish to attempt to be every bit as active in society as men are, and this silly view ignores women's actual biological condition. Men dare to say that it is women's brains that are immature, and that is we who are lacking in logic. When we give thought to something, they say, we simplify and our emotions get the better of us, and this proves that we are the inferiors of men. How those who comment on women's role in our society enjoy saying just this sort of thing!

There is a certain proverb, rather stale and old now, but it goes like this: "Man is the carrier of disease." Being male does not guarantee that you will not get sick, for no one can predict a life free of disease. Nor is the untimely attack of an illness the only issue. Given the conditions in our present society, disease itself is becoming increasingly prevalent. Our world has advanced, and along with this advancement have come diseases both complicated and diverse, diseases that were largely unknown to people of primitive times. Even in an era when we permit ourselves to be called civilized, we run the risk of catching such diseases. Each of us does. Yet the civilized person, with all this risk of disease, could not imagine having lost some sort of competition with primitive people simply because they lacked modern illnesses.

Women's reproductive functions should hardly be considered a disease. Processes like menstruation are a natural part of our biological condition. Healthy women do not experience the sort of pain that would require them to give up their jobs or professions. That so many women in our own country do have jobs and are active as individuals proves this. As for pregnancy, simply because it is an issue largely limited to women, and also because it usually occurs only once in two or three years, is not sufficient reason for viewing it as a major impediment to a woman's employment. Granted, some disruptions of a biological nature will occasionally transpire, but this is no reason to limit the right to free thinking that must be equally allowed women as human beings.

Coming to the problem of intelligence, as I outlined at the outset, men are generally superior to women. However, when we compare the women of our day, who are forbidden from entering the kingdom of knowledge and forever cloistered in the home, to today's men, who have been able to enter that kingdom freely, I believe it is a mistake to conclude that women have no intellectual ability. Despite their clear advantage over us, men persist in their unfounded denigration of women, taking no account of the fact that we are their subordinates because we have not had the same advantages. In the days of the Meiji Restoration, our people were regarded as an inferior race by the countries of England, the United States, Germany, Russia, and France. But we, too, had the ability to understand a level of knowledge equal to theirs. Haven't the last forty-five-odd years proved that? The same is true for today's women. To argue that they are an inferior breed to men is to make the same hasty judgment that the people of several Western countries did when they assumed that the Japanese of the Meiji Restoration were an inferior people.

Some critics talk about women by premising their arguments on the way that Buddhism conceives of women as devils or by taking the myth of Adam and Eve as entirely true. To do this is to mimic the simpleton who thoughtlessly keeps reciting some old fairy tale or one of those vile stories that men in the past created simply as an expedient to oppress women.

"In the shadow of wickedness, there is woman."

We hear this saying repeated all the time. Yet the events of this world, whatever they may be, are not wrought only by men. No matter what the field, society is composed of the communal life of both sexes, of men and women. As all the myriad things of society are brought about by men and women together, so, too, is it a fact that even good things cannot be brought about only by men. Thus, to change the expression, we could say, "Behind every good deed, there is always a woman."

Advocates of women's inferiority should at least glance at studies in Zoology. Their mistaken opinions do not carry much weight in their present form. It is a shallow view that draws absolute distinctions between the male and female sex, and it is a fundamental mistake. Of course, I am no scholar of Zoology, nor do I have any deep knowledge of this subject. However, what I have gleaned from the little reading I have done confirms that the male and female sexes are not absolutely different. While I am hesitant to get into a discussion of this, I would like to say a word about it.

A certain middle-aged lady experienced a transformation in her reproductive organs, brought about by a change in her physiology, and is said to have become a man. This is what I read in a certain physician's book. The book also discussed an instance where one who possessed male and female sex characteristics had a purely female character after a certain aspect was amputated. Don't even these examples prove that, although there are clearly differences in the reproductive organs of both sexes, the difference is not so great as to warrant discrimination?

My purpose here, however, is not to try to explain Zoology. Suffice it to say that men and women are not born with any innate distinction of superiority and inferiority between them. It is enough if we can enlighten the ignorant among those who debate women's position today to this fact. They distinguish between men and women as if they were comparing the differences in knowledge and talent between the civilized and the primitive. Therefore I would like to state that when we are in our mother's womb, before we receive the distinctions of sex, we dwell there simply as members of the human race. It must be said that we receive distinctive sexual characteristics after that.

We are women of the human species. We are not a species called woman.

This is a truth that cannot be denied and that should guarantee us freedom of thought as human beings. Even though our way of thinking does not recognize the old morality, who has the right to stop us from believing so?

The ancients themselves had a saying for this: "No matter how lowly he may be, a man's spirit should not be broken."[37]

****

On Intellectual and Economic Independence
Iwano Kiyo
Seitō 3.3 (March 1913)

To stand before you at this moment and on this stage, after we have heard from such celebrated figures, makes someone like me feel quite inadequate. All the same, I humbly request the favor of your attention for just thirty minutes. The matter which I should like to address is intellectual and economic independence, and I would also like to say a few words about the progress in women's thinking as I have witnessed it from the final years of the Meiji era until today.

Prior to Meiji 38 or 39 (1905–6), the women of our country had not the slightest awareness of intellectual matters. Ever faithful to convention and the old morality, they had remained as ignorant as newborn babes. Thus, when the women of Europe and the United States advocated equal rights, Japanese women, too, blindly adopted this position without ever defining one of their own. Or, when there were certain men who said that women must sacrifice themselves to the family for the sake of preserving the race, women meekly obeyed without giving this matter any thought whatsoever. Pulled this way and that by puppeteers, they were like lifeless dolls that lacked the spirit to move freely on their own.

It was precisely at this time that I sought to press for women's awakening, and therefore lodged a petition with the Diet to dissolve the legal prohibitions that were unjustly restricting us. My reasons for doing this were not due to a simple desire to elevate the status of women. Rather, they originated in my hope to see women, too, come to have an appreciation and an understanding of law and politics, as individual members of the nation. I also wanted women to train their vision on human life and society as they exist outside the home.

Yet what was the result of all this? Despite the fact that, with the exception of a bigoted few, men gave their enthusiastic support to our petition as something both reasonable and appropriate, the women who scoffed at us as presumptuous were more numerous by far. Or, even if they did not find us so alarming, there were still many women who pointedly refrained from supporting us. They withheld their support for the rather base but quite calculated reason that women who are seen as meddling in the workings of society are likely to incur men's hatred to no useful end. Such women did not wish to jeopardize their own exploitive attempts to rely on men for their livelihoods. For them, remaining pliant offered the greater profit.

Yet all the time women were sleeping, a revolution was occurring in men's thought. I am referring to the Naturalist Movement, which arose from one group within the new literary circles. These men had grown bored with the novels that were formulaic, simplistic morality tales, and with the entertaining fiction that had no relevance whatsoever to real life. Their assertion that true art must be human life itself gave birth to a new literature, one free of the shackles of the old morality, religion, and such that have been influential to this day. As men's views of life began to alter in this way, the expectations they held for women and for the family also changed. No longer could these men admire women who spent one day after the next in the most submissive and banal manner, caring about nothing more than the necessities of food, clothing, and shelter, and raising their children. No longer could they respect such women as their wives. Life within the formal family structure grew tedious for them. Yet despite the fact that men had lost all interest in the kind of woman who behaves like an ignorant slave—a living yet spiritless doll—and found themselves needing a fully human, vibrant woman, women themselves remained as somnolent as ever. Unaware that times had changed, unaware of the revolution in the intellectual world, and unaware of what the men of this new age expected in a woman, they indulged themselves in a sweet dream world, believing in obedience and convention as the solitary creed of their lives.

In the end, men could no longer fathom the views of life expressed by these women—their own wives and the mothers of their children—so they took to ignoring their families in favor of finding stimulation elsewhere. At the same time, each and every family was thrown into turmoil as new ideas clashed with the old. And what did all those women who had been cosseting themselves in peaceful slumber do at this point? Completely panicked, they lamented their hard lot and made a great display of blaming the men. But that was all they did. They did not go forward with any attempt to open their own eyes to life, nor did they try to consider the point of the men's requests. Finally, these old-fashioned women could conceive of no other resolution than to resign themselves in a halfhearted way that was itself a form of self-deceit. No matter how provoked they were by the men, these women would not open their eyes to their own sense of self. Since even those women writers who faced life with relative frankness were doing no more than changing their writing style to suit the trend of the times, their basic ideas did not break free from the usual pattern, in regard to either their attitudes toward life or toward the self.

Yet even within this female world of dulled nerves, there finally was one group of young women who did awaken, spurred on by the endless stimulation of the larger social environment.

This was the Bluestockings, the literary society that formed in the fall of 1911.

I was in Osaka at that time and received a notice about the Bluestockings from Hiratsuka Raichō. I remember feeling so happy that at last women had awakened, that women of genuine spirit had been born. Of course, I sent my approval right away and joined the group at the same time.

Even though this group was a small one, I took a keen pleasure in the effort and courage displayed by these young women. They were trying to look at life through their own eyes and trying to interpret it with their own minds. They were struggling to clear a new path with their own hands. How surprisingly the world had changed in the five or six years since I and a few kindred spirits had labored to awaken the women of this world but had failed so miserably! The birth of this group of young women, even though it differed in form from our own movement, made me feel that we had at last won the successors who would redeem all our failures, and that we would achieve the same ends after all. Thus I felt the same sense of happiness one feels when recovering something that was once utterly lost.

The Bluestockings, as a group newly born, will not leap ahead to grappling with the harsh realities of law and politics as our group tried to do, but will forge ahead only by working to elevate women and to spur on our progress through a fundamental awakening that rests on thinking about the interior life. Naturally, one cannot see the full flowering of this work in such a short time, but the foundations of this effort are strong.

Of course, even those of us in the Bluestockings are as yet inexperienced in the ways of the world and in life. Our intellectual preparation, too, lacks

165

the most elementary education in many areas. Henceforth, we shall whole-heartedly devote ourselves in all spheres, for we want to become women who have lived in truth. To this end, we have made many plans. Since Ms. Hiratsuka will speak about these, I will not elaborate on them here.

All things considered, however, we have at least started on the path that will take us closer to life. We understand that women, too, possess the right to freedom of thought and independence, and we know that each must create her life in her own way. At the same time, we face pressures from all around us and we must fight against them. We must battle against terrible suffering both materially and psychologically. To realize our beliefs, we must strengthen our position of independence in all areas because if we do not accomplish this, no matter how independently we may think, we will have no way of putting our thoughts into action but will inevitably be forced into compromises in order to sustain ourselves. Therein lies the necessity of financial independence. Insofar as women have failed to reconcile their beliefs and their actual lives, they have been subdued by pressures of a financial nature. Thus, when they happened to encounter situations that threatened their intellectual independence, since they could not support themselves and had made no preparations to leave, women had no other choice but to rely on their husbands and parents. In such events, one must make numerous concessions to others, no matter how disagreeable we find this. When this happens, something of one's own intellectual independence is destroyed in the process. One's beliefs and one's actual life become two quite different things.

There is an old expression we often hear that goes, "One does not live by bread alone." Yet I would like to say that the opposite is also true, that "One cannot live by ideas alone." Because one's intellectual life and livelihood are bound together, recognizing one's intellectual freedom as a woman and gaining the ability to support oneself are equally important. That is to say, we must find the courage to be financially independent. Without this, we have no authority to stand and defend our independence of thought. We often see in the real world cases where even men sometimes bow to financial pressures, doing things that inevitably betray their beliefs. How much more often is this the case for women who can only survive by depending on men? I would like the women who believe in freedom of thought and independence to be able to walk their own paths, free of interference from the others in their lives. I would like them to be prepared to support themselves and to ready themselves to gain financial autonomy. Then women shall be able to stand for the first time as truly free, independent individuals, with the qualifications and authority of true women.

One reason I have decided to become an actress is so that I can attempt to live my life in accord with art and at the same time attain the financial independence that will enable me to try to build my own independent life with my own strength. This is generally what I intended to say when I gave my speech this title, so now I will close.

****

Thoughts on Separation
Iwano Kiyo
Seitō 5.8 (September 1915)

Iwano Hōmei and I are presently living apart.[38] He now resides with a woman by the name of Kanbara Fusae, a copyist who was employed in my home. As for me, I have been ill and should be under the care of a doctor for one more month or so. I have remained at home, however, because this sudden turn of events has brought on all sorts of things for me to settle, or to mull over in terms of matters both inside and outside the household. Even though I still cannot get a good night's sleep, I am not able to get proper medical care now. This does not imply that I am a woman who becomes hopelessly emotional over such things. Indeed, I have always thought about things in a levelheaded way, and now, too, wish to act calmly and rationally. Since I am not yet able to collect all my thoughts in writing, what I say may sound scattered. Even so, I do want to press forward with what I have to say.

On the 25th of last month, Iwano confessed to me that he was having a relationship with that woman. The gist of his confession was that he was now in love with Kanbara Fusae. He told me, "Nothing has changed in the respect I have for you. The thing of it is that there is something I cannot obtain from you, and I compensate for this by getting what I need from another woman. There is really nothing at all to be excited about. So as long as you do not insist that I love you, I can live with things as they are now."

What Iwano Hōmei said in this confession diverges to an absolutely astonishing degree from everything that he has ever written. So then and there, I cross-examined him about these blatant contradictions. I pointed in particular to the way he had plainly lied to a certain newspaper reporter when he was first asked about his relationship with that woman, how he'd said that the affair had only begun when, "after hearing Kiyoko's decision on the matter," he had "started to live apart from her." In truth, I had suspected what was going on back in June. I asked him how he could be so dishonest as to be involved with two women at the same time.

But all Iwano said in return was that his ideas had changed of late. He no longer believed what he had said in the past. He repeated that he could see nothing wrong in having one woman supply what he could not obtain from another. He said this without any sense of shame whatsoever.

As I said before, I listened to Iwano's confession on the evening of the 25th. I told him that I would need to take ten days to come to a firm decision about all this, and that in the meantime I would not make any special move to interfere with his relationship with Kanbara. Nevertheless, I did think I should have a word with her, and so when she came in as usual on the morning of the 27th, I called her in for a talk. I assumed that she had already heard from Iwano that he had confessed everything to me, but I wanted her to hear what I had to say. What I said was this:

"I do not intend to reproach you as women normally do, nor do I intend to interfere in your relationship. Above all, I will not fight with you over love. But I will have you know that you have destroyed my home life, a life that until now has been genuine and undisturbed, and that this has caused me a sorrow so great that it can never be undone. But what's done is done, so there is nothing else I can say. You were a weak woman. Oh, of course, this happened to you because a man chose to tempt you, but because you were weak, you consented. What a pity that you did not give more thought to things when you encountered temptation in the first place. But it appears that with all that has happened, there is nothing much that can be done. I know that you have been trying to avoid me lately, but you needn't be so solicitous. I will come to a firm decision on this matter in my own good time."

The woman did not say anything for some time, but then she began making apologies. "If only I hadn't come to Tokyo! Then, this misfortune would never have occurred," she said.

It was agonizing for me to decide how to resolve this, but I did feel that I must come up with my own solution in my own way. I could not take any of this lightly, and so I thought about everything a great deal. About the time that I had come to some decision, I went to see Ms. Hiratsuka, and told her the gist of it.

The reason I had not said anything before Iwano's confession to me, even though I knew what was happening, was to give the two of them plenty of time to reflect on what they were doing. When I told Iwano this, he replied: "This is about my needs, so there is no room for introspection. Of course, it isn't a sin!" He said that he had not been thinking about his family or anything else in the beginning, but had simply felt that his life must be provisioned in two ways. As long as he could satisfy this need, he said, he did not feel compelled to disrupt the outward appearance of his life at all.

Five years have passed since Iwano and I became a couple and started living together. Back then, I believed that before anything else, our love must be spiritual. I expected that as we lived together, our spiritual and physical love would unify as one in the natural course of things, and that when that happened, for the first time our love would be pure and sincere, and would lead us to maintain a way of living genuinely. Following this, if it happened that he were to fall in love with another woman, whether an ordinary woman or a prostitute, and if he were to share his love even a little by doing this, then our romantic life together would have reached its end. We both promised that we would tell the other if that time ever came.

One is free to choose whomever to love, but if this takes no thought and no self-examination, then love becomes a vulgar thing indeed. Acting blindly in the name of absolute freedom is to desire as animals do. Accordingly, such behavior will not be assigned much value, because to whatever extent love is blind, it is unworthy of respect. To my way of thinking, it is the spiritual bond that should call forth the union of the flesh. A union that begins with the flesh and gradually awakens to a spiritual relationship is a wholly unthinking and conventional association. As one who felt that we two could never bear anything so insensible, I cannot condone a romance that was initiated in that manner.

This means that if I found the love between Iwano and that woman to be truly genuine and serious, and to be a conscious and spiritual bond, then I would not begrudge them my respect. But after thinking long and hard about this, I can say that theirs is not such a union. Especially after they moved out of this house, they behaved in ways that robbed me of my heartfelt respect and affection for them. The problem was not only that I doubted that their life together had any authority, conviction, merit, or seriousness, but that things happened which made me feel contempt for them.

Iwano's son by his first wife is now thirteen, although we are the ones who have been taking care of him. When all the trouble started, I told the boy that he could decide if he wanted to live with me or Iwano. After all, as an individual human being, he has the ability to judge things for himself. He asked to remain with me. The child is not close to his father.

I have not divorced Iwano. I am afraid that there has been some misreporting that says that I have, but I am not seeking a divorce. I have gone so far as to separate from him, but I will not remove my name from the official family registry.

As I became more and more certain that the resolution to this would mean that Hōmei would leave, I felt how terribly cruel it was to rob children of their father. Yet there is another perspective from which one can view this. I believe that for children to learn life's true colors, it is far better that they be raised by my love alone than in a home where their father's dishonesty and insincerity have cast a pall over everything.

I absolutely will not compromise. Nor will I yield. Were I like the women of old who had no keen sense of Self, I would probably have reacted to my lover's infidelity by crying myself to sleep. But I was armed with the knowledge that my Self was strong, so even if I were to come to ruin in the end, I would live the life I must as a human being. Isn't this the truest way? I resolved that, come what may, I would fight with my own strength, whether I proved weak or powerful. Motivated by my own desire to fight back, I realized that there were things that I must think about, and that I must say to men, as a woman.

After coming to this conclusion, I find myself in a peaceful, even cheerful mood, for all I have to do now is fight. Both in my financial life and in my personal life, I want to be as energetic and active as I was five or six years ago.

I have not been to Iwano's new home even once. Nor have I been through his neighborhood much, either. Since I would hate to cause some trivial misunderstanding or create confusion about my own attitude toward this matter, I shall practice prudence in everything.

August 18th

Ms. Ikuta Hanayo, who kindly paid a visit to Ms. Iwano Kiyo[ko]'s home in Sugamo, has written this piece for us based on their conversation.

Notes

[1]Iwano used both Kiyo and Kiyoko as her given name. Since much of the secondary literature in English and Japanese refers to her as Kiyoko, I use that version throughout this book. Most of her publications in *Seitō*, however, appear under the name Iwano Kiyo and are cited as such here—except in cases where she used Kiyoko (as in the case of her story "Otaka").

[2]Hiratsuka Raichō, *Genshi, josei wa taiyō de atta: Hiratsuka Raichō jiden* (Ōtsuki Shoten, 1971–73), 2: 523, 577; as translated in Hiratsuka Raichō and Teruko Craig, *In the Beginning, Woman Was the Sun: The Autobiography of a Japanese Feminist* (New York: Columbia University Press, 2006), 247, 272.

[3]Ibid.

[4]Hiratsuka, *Genshi, josei wa taiyō de atta*, 2: 358–59; as translated in Hiratsuka and Craig, *In the Beginning, Woman Was the Sun*, 171.

[5]"For some reason, whenever I think of Kiyoko, I think of [Bluestocking] Yasuda Satsuki. As natives of downtown Tokyo—Kiyoko was particularly proud that she was born in Kanda—both were stubborn and assertive, yet surprisingly fragile." Hiratsuka, *Genshi, josei wa taiyō de atta*, 2: 579; as translated in Hiratsuka and Craig, *In the Beginning, Woman Was the Sun*, 273.

[6]Orii Miyoko, "Iwano Kiyoko," in Raichō Kenkyūkai, ed., *"Seitō" jinbutsu jiten: 110-nin no gunzō* (Taishūkan Shoten, 2001), 44–45. Much of the biographical infor-

mation here comes from Orii, "Iwano Kiyoko" and Ogata Akiko, "Iwano Kiyo cho, *Ai no sōtō*: kaisetsu," in Iwano Kiyo, *Ai no sōtō* (Conflict of Love, 1915), vol. 4 in the series *Sōsho "Seitō" no onna-tachi* (Fuji Shuppan, 1985), 1–21. According to Ogata, her grandmother's death made Kiyoko the family head at age fifteen (Ogata, "Iwano Kiyo cho, *Ai no sōtō*: kaisetsu," 10).

[7] It was published in book form in 1910. Iwano Hōmei, *Tandeki* (Debauchery), (Tokyo: Shinchosha, 1910).

[8] For a brief description of *Tandeki*, see "Introduction," in Mori Ōgai, *Vita Sexualis*, trans. Kazuji Ninomiya and Sanford Goldstein (Rutland, VT, and Tokyo: Charles E. Tuttle, Co., 1972), 12. An excellent description of Hōmei's life and work can be found in Donald Keene, *Dawn to the West: Japanese Literature of the Modern Era, Fiction* (New York: Holt, Rinehart, Winston, 1984), 288–95.

[9] Kiyoko includes some of these newspaper articles in her 1915 autobiography, Iwano Kiyo, *Ai no sōtō*. On page 19 of the autobiography, Kiyoko expresses her idealization of love.

[10] Iwano Kiyo, "Shisō no dokuritsu to keizai-jō no dokuritsu" (On Intellectual and Economic Independence), *Seitō* 3.3 (March 1913), Supplement: 1–7.

[11] Iwano Kiyo, "Uranai" (Fortune-telling), *Seitō* 3.9 (September 1913): 99–116.

[12] Iwano Kiyoko, "Otaka" (Otaka), *Seitō* 1.2 (October 1911): 52–63. It is unclear to what extent this story may have roots in Kiyoko's relationship to Hōmei's first wife, but the character Masao's callous treatment of his wife sounds familiar. As Keene points out, Hōmei's description of the wife in his autobiographical novel *Hōrō* (Roaming, 1910) casts her "as a superstitious harpy incapable of understanding her husband's need for incandescent pleasure." Keene, *Dawn to the West*, 295.

[13] Iwano Kiyo, "Antō" (Secret Feud), *Seitō* 2.4 (April 1912): 82–93. The prostitute Otori also figures prominently in Hōmei's autobiographical novel, *Hōrō* (Roaming, 1910); see Keene, *Dawn to the West*, 293-95.

[14] Iwano Kiyoko talks about this in her diary, "Nikki no dampen" (Odds and Ends from My Diary), *Seitō* 2.5 (May 1912): 65–75; see especially 72–73.

[15] Iwano Kiyo, "Karekusa" (Withered Grass), *Seitō* 2.2 (February 1912): 49.

[16] Ibid., 50.

[17] See "Omotte iru koto" (Ruminations), *Seitō* 4.5 (May 1914): 105–9 for Iwano Kiyoko's feelings about her pregnancy, and "Sugamo-mura yori" (From the Village of Sugamo), *Seitō* 4.7 (July 1914): 114–15, for her thoughts on her changing feelings toward her baby and her intentions to be a new kind of mother.

[18] Kanbara Fusae, "Saikin no kansō" (Recent Thoughts), *Seitō* 4.8 (August 1914): 97–100. This article, "Recent Thoughts," was actually written by three Bluestockings: Hiratsuka Raichō, Itō Noe, and Kanbara Fusae. Kanbara's remarks discuss how all the women teachers in a study group wanted to read the 1913 special issue of the journal *Taiyō* (Sun) devoted to the Woman Question (*fujin mondai*), despite the disinterest expressed by the men teachers in the group. For the article attacking the educator Kaetsu Kōko (given name also romanized as Takako), see Kanbara Fusae, "Kaetsu jo-shi no seiyō no haibutsu ni tsuite" (With Respect to Mme. Kaetsu's "Obsolescence of the West"), *Seitō* 4.9 (September 1914): 169–70. For more details about Kanbara's life, see Shimizu Kazumi, "Kanbara Fusae," in Raicho Kenkyūkai, ed., *"Seitō" jimbutsu jiten*, 82–83.

[19] Iwano Kiyo, "Henshū-shitsu yori" (From the Editing Room), *Seitō* 4.1 (January 1914): 141–42. This section of the Editors' Notes also contains comments by Hiratsuka

Raichō and Itō Noe. Kiyoko's comments are explicitly directed to Kaetsu.

[20]Iwano Kiyo, "Wakaretaru otto Iwano Hōmei-shi no shi no kyōgaku o mae ni okite" (Remarks on the Sudden Passing of My Former Husband, Mr. Iwano Hōmei), *Shin shōsetsu* (June 1920), as cited in Orii, "Iwano Kiyoko," 45. Ogata Akiko, "Iwano Kiyo cho, *Ai no sōtō*: kaisetsu," 19, notes that Kiyoko wrote the article because she urgently needed money for the care of her infant daughter. Ogata also praises the essay as an excellent analysis of Iwano Hōmei.

[21]Iwano Kiyo, "Binbō no ichi-nen" (A Year of Poverty), *Fujin kōron* (May 1918), as cited in Orii, "Iwano Kiyoko," 45.

[22]Ogata, "Iwano Kiyo cho, *Ai no sōtō*: kaisetsu," 19; Orii, "Iwano Kiyoko," 45.

[23]Charlotte Perkins Gilman, *Women and Economics* (Boston: Small, Maynard and Company, 1898), translated by Ōtawa Take as *Fujin to keizai* (Dai Nihon Bunmei Kyokai, 1912); and Olive Schreiner, *Woman and Labour* (London: T. Fisher Unwin, 1911), translated by Takano Jūzō in *Fujin mondai haya-wakari: Fu: Fujin to rōdō* (Guide to the Woman Question: Appendix: Women and Labor), (Keisei-sha Shoten, 1915).

[24]Iwano Kiyo, "Jinrui to shite dansei to josei wa byōdō de aru" (Men and Women Are Equal as Members of the Human Race), *Seitō* 3.1 (January 1913), Supplement: 23–28.

[25]See Iwano Kiyo, "Kita no kōgai yori" (From a Suburb to the North), *Seitō* 3.11 (November 1913): 73–77 (this is Kiyoko's second essay under this title; the first appeared in *Seitō* 3.8 [August 1913]: 66–71); idem, "Kojinshugi to katei" (Individualism and the Family), *Seitō* 4.9 (September 1914): 1–6.

[26]This appendix includes two other speeches given on the occasion of the Bluestocking public lecture, Iwano Hōmei's "Danshi kara suru yōkyū" (What Men Require), *Seitō* 3.3 (March 1913), Supplement: 8–32, and Baba Kochō's "Fujin no tame ni" (For the Sake of Women), *Seitō* 3.3 (March 1913), Supplement: 33–45. After each of the two men's essays, but not after Kiyoko's, the word "Applause" appears in parentheses. Kiyoko's essay is seven pages long, Hōmei's is twenty-five pages, and Kochō's is thirteen. Both men encourage women to develop their intellectual abilities, condemn the current educational system as well as men who treat women as inferiors, and approve of the Bluestockings' endeavors. There is more than a little self-serving sentiment here: the men admit to being bored with conventional and unawakened women like Hōmei's former wife, whom he had to divorce for this reason, and Kochō's current one, whom he admits to being too lazy to divorce. Hōmei predicts great things for the Bluestockings: "Today, it's gotten so that a woman does not really become a woman (*onna*) unless she is a graduate of a women's college. Clearly, the day is coming when a lady (*fujin*) cannot truly be called a lady unless she is a member of the Bluestockings, or at least a lady who understands that Movement"; Iwano Hōmei, "Danshi kara suru yōkyū," 29. He sarcastically refers to the current ideal of *ryōsai kenbo* (good wife, wise mother) as *gusai akubo* (stupid wife, evil mother); ibid., 14. For a description of the ruckus that ensued when Hōmei gave this speech, see Dina Lowy, *The Japanese "New Woman": Images of Gender and Modernity* (New Brunswick, NJ, and London: Rutgers University Press, 2007), 102–4.

[27]Hiratsuka, *Genshi, josei wa taiyō de atta*, 2: 445; as translated in Hiratsuka and Craig, *In the Beginning, Woman Was the Sun*, 212. In her research on the rise of the female speaker in Meiji Japan, Marnie S. Anderson observes a connection between fashion and the publicly vocal woman, finding that reporters dazzled their readers first with accounts of the women's clothing and then with the content of their

speeches. Kishida Toshiko (1861–1901) became famous for her vibrant stage presence and her resplendent outfits. Marnie S. Anderson, "Kishida Toshiko and the Rise of the Female Speaker in Meiji Japan," *U.S.–Japan Women's Journal*, nos. 30–31 (2006): 36–59.

[28]Iwano Kiyo, "Bekkyo ni tsuite omou kotodomo" (Thoughts on Separation), *Seitō* 5.8 (September 1915): 23–29.

[29]Iwano Kiyo, "Yasukawa naikeiho kyoku-chō no iken ni tsuite" (With Regard to the Opinion of Bureau Chief Yasukawa), *Seitō* 4.9 (September 1914): 150–51. This interview also reveals that officials mistakenly thought of the Bluestockings as a big group, rather than as the handful of women who actually published the journal *Seitō*. True to form, Kiyoko also took this opportunity to press her opinions on the need for the revision of Article Five.

[30]Iwano Kiyo, "Raichō-shi no dai-ni ronshū hakkan ni tsuite" (On the Publication of Raichō's Second Essay Collection), *Seitō* 4.11 (December 1914): 13–14.

[31]Hiratsuka, *Genshi, josei wa taiyō de atta*, 2: 523; as translated in Hiratsuka and Craig, *In the Beginning, Woman Was the Sun*, 247.

[32]Hiratsuka, *Genshi, josei wa taiyō de atta*, 2: 579; also translated in Hiratsuka and Craig, *In the Beginning, Woman Was the Sun*, 272. Kiyoko bluntly criticizes Raichō for privileging the interior life over public action in another essay as well: Iwano Kiyo, "Omotte iru koto" (Ruminations), *Seitō* 4.5 (May 1914): 105–9.

[33]Kiyoko's book is dedicated to "G. N.," apparently a reference to her first lover, Nakao Gōrō. The dedication reads: "Offered at the grave of Mr. G. N."

[34]Ogata, "Iwano Kiyo cho, *Ai no sōtō*: kaisetsu," 1.

[35]Ibid., 4–5.

[36]Iwano Hōmei's writing career was going very well during these years, and he was quite prolific. A later entry in his diary reveals Hōmei's thoughts on reading Kiyoko's *Ai no sōtō*. There he notes how surprised he is to realize how completely Kiyoko misunderstood him—a lament that prompts Ogata Akiko to ask whether Iwano ever considered how little he had understood Kiyoko; see Ogata, "Iwano Kiyo cho, *Ai no sōtō*: kaisetsu," 16.

[37]As translated in the proverb dictionary: Ikeda Yasuburō and Donald Keene, eds., *Nichi-ei koji kotowaza jiten* (Hokuseidō Shoten, 1995), 105.

[38]*Seitō* did not appear in August 1915. Consequently, issue no. 8 of vol. 5 appeared in September.

Chapter 7
Katō Midori (1888–1922)

What a terrible obsession! They had almost separated on countless occasions, yet here they were, still together. The power of this invisible obsession was not ever going to let them go.

Katō Midori's 1912 story "Shūchaku" (Obsession; translated below), like most of her *Seitō* stories, draws on her actual experiences with courtship and marriage.[1] It tells the story of a romance initiated and developed through love letters, strongly associated with the literary tastes of the times, and as thrilling as any novel. It is a romance in every way different from the staid matches that many middle-class families sought to arrange for their daughters. Here was a New Woman on her own in the city, being pursued by a stranger madly in love with her. What today might seem like an unhealthy example of stalking could have been read in 1912 as an exciting tale of the perils and pleasures of urban life.

But the problem with this modern romance is that it can only come alive through the drama and distance of writing. Unfortunately for both partners, the everyday realities of marriage, and especially parenthood, pale in comparison to the excitement of their literary courtship. Once married and a father, the New Man misses his modern partner, the intriguing woman who cared more about following her own ambitions than following him. He also misses his former identity as the bachelor who recklessly pursued her. All the same, he expects the convenience of a full-time homemaker. As Katō Midori sees it, such expectations place the New Woman in an untenable situation. She cannot fulfill her husband's dreams, nor can she obtain the love and support she desires. The only way to recapture the romance is through reading old letters, and the only way to face her present situation is through writing about it.

Katō Midori's biographer, Iwata Nanatsu, looks to Midori's early stories for evidence of her idealistic notions of love and work. Two of Midori's stories for the magazine *Joshi bundan* (Women's Literary World) consider the important role a successful marriage plays in a New Woman's happiness. Her January 1907 story, "Ai no hana" (Flower of Love), written about ten months after Midori arrived in Tokyo, describes how the visit of a well-

dressed school chum, now married to a wealthy man, gives the main character Ayako pangs of envy. In the end, Ayako decides she is the happier of
the two for having married a poor man who shares her love of literature and
ambitions for a career as a writer. Midori was the first *Joshi bundan* contributor to receive the magazine's newly established prize of a silver watch for
this story. Her May 1909 *Joshi bundan* story, "Haisha" (The Defeated), takes
up the same theme in reverse, depicting the regrets of a young woman who
married a man (who turned out to be fickle and authoritarian) for money
and status, and who envies her schoolmate Teruko's happier, freer life and
relationship of equality with her mate. Teruko gives an impassioned speech
on how the meaning of life lies in following her literary ambitions, not in
material gain or status, making her friend, the narrator, feel as though she is
"the defeated" one. As Iwata points out, these stories show how the young
Midori idealized love, work, and the artistic life—and, I would add, romanticized financial difficulties.[2]

Although Midori's *Seitō* stories were written only a few years later, they
reflect the reality of the changes in her life in the interim. Now the artistic
husband is not a dream but modeled on her real mate, who brings his own
struggles to their marriage. The demands of young children and the financial burdens they bring complicate the couple's life, often making the woman
writer nostalgic for the freedom of girlhood. Together, these stories and her
short reflective essays present multiple perspectives and a range of feelings
about the New Woman's life. Midori's October 1913 *Seitō* story, "Geijutsu to
haru" (Springtime and Art), is based on her experience performing the role
of Queen Dectora in William Butler Yeats's (1865–1939) *The Shadowy Waters*
(1900) in Osaka the previous April. Midori describes the rush of excitement
her protagonist "Etsuko" feels from being on stage: she feels young again
and immersed in art, as though she has no children, no family.[3] In the May
1914 issue of *Seitō*, her story "Bokusha no kotoba" (What the Fortune-Teller
Said) describes how newspaper reporter "Tsuneko" is assailed by fear after
a fortune-teller asserts that she and her husband were never meant for each
other and that no child can survive if raised by the two of them. In a short
essay at the end of the same issue, Midori also writes of how happy she is to
come home to her children after a busy day of work outside the home. After
stating her opposition to the extremes of individualism, she compares herself to an "old-fashioned knight" (*kishi*) who works for the love of husband
and children as well as for herself, and says she feels deeply grateful for the
"family" she has cursed as a burden.[4] In "Tada hitori" (All Alone), published
in *Seitō* in December 1915, Midori's character "Yumiko" has nightmares,
imagining that everyone in her life is out to get her, even her own child,
whom she tries to kill; she wakes up and, sobbing, clings to the hands of her

husband and son.[5] In Midori's last *Seitō* story, "Hoshi no sora" (Starry Sky), "Fumiko" worries about money, worries about her marriage, and worries that there is no easy way for a woman to combine life in a family with a life in art; in the end, she hurries home to finish her novel, resolving to treat herself with more respect.[6] All in all, Katō Midori creates the New Woman as idealistic yet vulnerable and not always sure of what direction she should take. Her New Woman is brave and—like the New Women celebrated by Hiratsuka Raichō, Itō Noe, and Iwano Kiyoko—values her struggles as she walks an uncertain path toward self-awareness and creativity.

Midori began her own journey toward becoming a New Woman in 1906, when she left her hometown in Nagano Prefecture to move to Tokyo at age seventeen, four years after graduating from girls' school. She had developed a passion for reading after her mother died in 1899, perhaps as way to compensate for the loss and as an escape from the responsibilities of caring for her younger siblings. Her father, a doctor, strenuously disapproved of Midori's fascination with literature, and would probably have forbidden her move to Tokyo had she not been needed to chaperone her younger siblings who were in school there. Yet life in the city offered Midori more than a chance to be with her siblings and away from a strict father; it gave her the opportunity to be close to the literary world and to experiment with new ways of life. She once wrote about the day of her arrival in Tokyo, remembering how, "breathing the air of the eastern capital of civilization for the first time in my life, I felt as though I had become a person of the twentieth century."[7]

Eager to try her hand at something new in the big city, Midori decided, with the help of an uncle, to open a small shop that would sell items such as cosmetics, ashtrays, and other notions. Inexperienced at running a shop, Midori had problems with petty thieves and swindlers, yet later looked back on this project as one that brought her out of her sheltered life. Another new enterprise was to try her luck at writing. When Midori met and became a student of author Tokuda Shūsei (1872–1943) in 1906, she embarked on her career as a writer. As Iwata describes it, the decision to write also represented a defiance of her father's disapproval of her fascination with literature.[8] Writing provided Midori with a sense of purpose, with money, and even with a new name. Born Takanaka Kikuyo, she chose the pen name Midori in 1909, and adopted her husband's family name, Katō, upon marriage.

In the course of a fifteen-year writing career that included marriage, motherhood, and, finally, a losing battle with cancer, Katō Midori produced more than ninety works. A versatile author, she wrote in such diverse forms as serialized newspaper novels, newspaper interviews, short stories, critical pieces, plays, translations, poetry, and children's stories. Midori once commented that what she liked best about writing was seeing that which was "born of the subjective transformed into the objective," a comment that may refer to the stories she wrote for *Seitō* about her stormy marriage to the writer Katō Asadori.[9]

In fact, Midori's entire relationship with Asadori, a graduate of the English department of Waseda University, was intimately connected to the literary world and is well documented both in her own writings and by others. For example, *Seitō*'s father-figure Ikuta Chōkō served as their go-between, and their union had the blessing of such literary lights as Midori's mentor Tokuda Shūsei; one newspaper reported that Asadori had won Midori's heart by writing a long proposal of marriage to her; and after Midori's death in 1922, Asadori wrote an article about her in *Fujin kōron* (Ladies' Review) in which he described her battle with cancer and confessed that he had once wanted to leave their marriage.[10] Opposed to the family system, the couple initially lived together for some time but participated in a wedding ceremony with many writers in attendance in July 1909; they officially married on 5 July 1910 and filed their marriage papers on 1 September 1910, after the birth of their first child (a son who grew up to win acclaim as a painter).[11]

In 1911, the couple moved to Osaka, where Asadori worked as a newspaper reporter and Midori began contributing to *Seitō*. In 1912 Midori bore a second son and, as mentioned above, she briefly took to the stage in 1913 in the role of Dectora as part of the Osaka Women's Exhibition. Later that year, the Katō family moved back to Tokyo. By this time Midori was well known among some of the central figures in the Bluestockings, and they gave her a party in November 1913 to welcome her back to Tokyo. The next month her younger son died, and the first of forty-one installments of her novel *Curse* (Noroi) appeared in *Sagishirō shinbun*, where they continued through January 1914. Although she started working as a reporter for the *Tokyo Nichi Nichi shinbun* in March 1914, ill health forced her to give up the job. She must have recovered to some extent by 1915, because she then began taking archery lessons with another Bluestocking, Kodera Kikuko. Through all the hardship she endured in these years, Midori kept writing, and in 1917 gave birth to her last child, a daughter. Toward the end of her career, she became interested in children's fiction.

In September 1920, Asadori left for Borneo and Java on a reporting assignment. Shortly thereafter, Midori developed cancer. After having an operation, she went to her father's home to recuperate. Asadori did not return to Japan until August 1921. By September of that year, Midori was back in the hospital. All the couple's friends rallied around, including Hiratsuka Raichō and other Bluestockings, helping to sell one of Asadori's translations to raise money for Midori's care. Asadori rented a house in Tokyo where he and Midori spent their last months together. When Katō Midori died at age thirty-three in May 1922, her death was reported in both the *Yomiuri shinbun* and the *Asahi shinbun*.

Another portrait of Midori and Asadori is found in Hiratsuka Raichō's autobiography. Raichō remembers Midori, whom she describes as "energetic and efficient," as "so determined to achieve her goals as a reporter and writer that for a while she had sent one of her children out to nurse."[12] She recalls Asadori as a "gifted and productive" man with an "innate sense of humor . . . who always looked as if he were enjoying life" even though he was perpetually in need of money. While Araki Ikuko, who was friends with the couple, apparently scolded Midori "for not being more supportive of her husband," Raichō believed that "Midori was a practical person" who "must have felt frustrated being married to a man with the romantic sensibilities of a poet." In the end, Raichō assumed that it was Midori's efforts to be "writer, reporter, and mother of two small children" that caused her to die at the young age of thirty-three.[13]

Although Katō Midori figured prominently in the Bluestockings and was the only member to stay with *Seitō* from its inaugural issue to its last year, her involvement in the group never attracted the attention later paid to Hiratsuka Raichō and Itō Noe. In 1993 Iwata Nanatsu published a biographical novel about Katō Midori in which she weaves aspects of Midori's life and her stories into a dramatic recreation of the artist, casting her as a star equal in ambition and talent to any of the other Bluestockings.[14] As her *Seitō* essays and fiction show, Midori wrestled with what it meant to be a New Woman, and encountered her greatest frustrations when the power to direct her life threatened to slip from her hands. She seemed at her happiest when lost in the reverie of possibilities, and saddest when failing to meet the realities of others' demands on her and her own high ideals. Above all, she believed in facing these challenges. Near the end of her 1913 essay "Atarashii onna ni tsuite" (On the New Woman), Katō Midori wrote:

> Perhaps in another fifty or one hundred years, women will be able to bask in the bright, hopeful light of good fortune, but as for us, we have no choice but to spend our whole lives anxiously immersed in doubt.[15]

Writing nonfiction essays offered Midori another way to think about who the New Woman could and should be. In two essays for *Seitō*, one about Ibsen's *A Doll's House* in 1912 and another on the New Woman in 1913, Midori adopts the position of a critic, stating her ideas in a clear, confident voice. In *Seitō* scholar Dina Lowy's excellent analysis of the Bluestockings' essays on

A Doll's House, she describes how Midori sympathized with Ibsen's heroine Nora's position, imagining that Nora's childish behavior "was literally all an act, a mask she wore out of love for husband" and feeling that the play revealed "a gradual unfolding of Nora's inner personality, not a sudden awakening."[16]

Midori's 1913 essay "On the New Woman" is also relevant here not only because it offers another window on Midori's thought but because it provides comparison with the ideas of the other Bluestockings included in this volume. In "On the New Woman," Midori argues that whether women are demanding social change or change in their personal lives, they must always speak from their position as women. The defining power of gender over women's lives in the 1910s, she believes, cannot be ignored or wished away. In this respect Katō Midori sees the New Woman as different from the politically active women of Fukuda Hideko's day (see Chapter 2 above):

> Pulled along by the trends of their times, these women took part in political activities, unaware of their identity as women. They may have been passionate, but they did not seem to consider things objectively from their position *as women*. But nowadays, the woman who aspires to become a true "New Woman" is acutely aware of the anguish of the era. She has serious concerns that men, who criticize her only on the basis of their observations of her behavior, will never be able to understand.[17] (emphasis in the original)

In this essay, Midori describes the true New Woman as one who is financially independent and self-supporting, and who has the same kind of self-awareness exhibited by characters in modern drama, such as Nora, Magda (in Hermann Sudermann's play *Magda*), and Hedda (in Ibsen's *Hedda Gabler*).[18] The New Woman must be able to view both her self and society critically, not hesitating to look at even the most shocking aspects of the world. Similar to many of the ideas that Raichō voiced in *Seitō*, Midori advises that the New Woman cannot be satisfied by romantic love alone but needs "spiritual fulfillment."

What most worries Katō Midori—and perhaps this is a fear that stems from her own experience—is that the New Woman's freedom may be only a temporary state associated with girlhood. Is it possible, Midori asks, for a New Woman to marry, and if so, what kind of marriage will she have? Won't marriage and motherhood radically alter her identity?

> While she is single, a young woman can do whatever she likes with enthusiasm. She is filled with ambition and imagination. Her girlhood shines with her hopes and ideals. But when once

she takes a husband and ventures out into the real world, oh, how the contradictions between dream and reality will make her cry. Although she has lived thus far for herself, now, no matter what, one part of her must live for another, that is, for her husband. Even if she is so fortunate as to have a husband of the new age who understands her feelings and thus permits her a degree of freedom, her life will not be satisfying. If she has children, she cannot give in to self-fulfillment or to her newfound spirit. What's more, if she must then identify herself not as a *human being* but rather as a *woman*, as someone's wife and another's mother, in the end she will have to heed that painful curse, "Your name is Woman."[19] (emphasis in the original)

Midori continues by saying that even if both husband and wife work and share equal rights in their home, they cannot escape problems because the worlds of men and women are completely separate and prevent them from understanding each other. What will make this painful for the New Woman is that she is no longer satisfied with superficial relationships and constantly searches for something more. But since the new era has not completely replaced the old, the New Woman will inevitably become caught in clashes between the new and the traditional, clashes that will confuse even her. Although Midori imagines that in fifty or a hundred years women will not face these problems, she feels that her generation is destined to agonize continually over women's lot in life. She closes her essay with the hope that all women will work for the advancement of their sex.

One sees in Midori's essays—perhaps even more dramatically than in those translated in this volume by Iwano Kiyoko—how much the word "human" (*ningen*) signifies the province of men. Throughout Midori's writing, she struggles with a definition of self that is torn between, and cannot unify, an awareness of oneself as a female and as an individual human being. In speaking of the importance of women's financial independence, Midori urges women to realize their "humanity." She says that when a woman works, she will instantly realize she deserves the same freedom and privileges men have: "One who has been chained to the name of Woman awakens as a human being."[20] Yet Midori criticizes earlier activists for insufficient awareness of themselves "as women." In the end, Midori sees remaining single as the only hope for women to retain their newfound freedom, and their humanity; the duties of the wife and mother inevitably mold women into self-sacrificial non-humans. Consequently, according to Midori, over the course of most women's lives, gender becomes an inescapable burden that neither internal nor external changes can ease completely.

****

Obsession
Katō Midori
Seitō 2.4 (April 1912)

She held the exquisite card to the light, mooning over its beauty as if she were lost in a dream, and letting her fingertips run gently over the indentations left by the handwriting. She had been nineteen years old the spring she had received the card. It had a pale, flesh-toned background and a crown of laurels embossed at the top. The script was small, and had even been penned in violet ink. The letter was a mixture of sentiments such as "I promise that someday you are bound to trust me" and "The stars shall sparkle forever on all the faith and love in my heart."

Hisako sat at her desk, her elbows splayed out in front of her, framing a bouquet of white violets. She had picked the flowers when walking in the neighborhood yesterday with her sisters and had replanted them in an empty face-powder container. Poetry collections, their titles inscribed in gold, as well as half-written pages in her own childish hand lay strewn everywhere else on the desk. Her whole body—her face, her hands, her breasts, and even her knees, falling slightly apart as she sat there—pulsed with youthful energy and felt warm to the touch. Her heart beat gently like the quiet sea tides of spring.

Oh, that card! That card was what had brought her to this life that she and her husband were leading. When Hisako had first received it, the card had rather bewildered her. She had never met the man who wrote it; in fact, she did not know him at all. Still, she'd been so charmed by the lovely seductiveness of art itself that she had sent a card of her own three or four days later. She could hardly dismiss the power of the man's writing style as whimsical infatuation, for the strength evident in his hand never failed to stir her. Was this in itself an omen of the fate that lay in store?

A recent illness had left Hisako's face gaunt. Closing her tired eyes, she turned toward the direction of the sweet, innocent face of her sleeping child. That is when all the old memories came back to her.

Hisako had been far too troubled by all the anxieties in her life of late to feel as if she had any time at all to contemplate her youth. Yet today, as she was straightening one of the closets, she had happened upon a big packet of old love letters. When Hisako opened the packet and looked at the letters inside, she recalled with absolute clarity the course of love that she and her husband had pursued together as a married couple.

The refined handwriting, the intoxicating language, the lovely card, the pale gray of his small name card, and the sky-blue envelope he'd used—how these things had become the stuff of dreams and fantasy for the two of them!

And yet eventually they had fallen into their present fate. At this thought Hisako could not hold back a rueful smile.

The changes of going from the many hopes and pleasures of girlhood to becoming a wife and mother were not all of the flesh. Indeed, there was nothing more heartbreaking for Hisako than reflecting on all the emotional changes that marriage had wrought. What truly pained her was that she had not even enjoyed being courted by Sawano, the man who had become her husband. Although she had been a young woman then, Hisako had not been able to indulge herself fully in the romance or take any pleasure in being in love. Rather, she had hated all of it, suffering immeasurably as she tried to run away from this man who nevertheless harbored such an obsession for her. After Hisako had finally become his wife, how well she had understood the coldness of men. At that point, even the womanly feelings of love that had taken hold in her own heart had caused her pain.

Four years had passed since they'd married. Nevertheless, Hisako never stopped retracing the footprints they had made on the path that fate had determined for them.

The way Sawano had acted toward her, sending letters and being so intent on winning her, had made Hisako suspicious from the start. Could a man fall head over heels in love? Once, a man who occasionally participated in the Akebono Literary Society had seen her name printed in the society's literary magazine. Knowing nothing else about her, he had been able to talk of devoting his entire life to her, and had whispered words of love. But Hisako had found this odd, and had felt not the least bit of faith in his protestations. She had imagined that he was a devil enticing her affections. On another occasion, Hisako had even received a letter from a young man pretending to be a woman. When this man had actually appeared at her door, Hisako had scolded him and sent him home.

Since Hisako had had such experiences before ever receiving the letter from Sawano, she had remained quite aloof from him, too. Yet it was this coldness of hers that had fanned the flames of Sawano's ardor all the more. Finally, a letter had come from Sawano asking if he could meet her.

On the day they did meet, Hisako was at home by herself. Her sisters and brother had all gone to school, and her housekeeper had gone back to her own home, saying that she had some things to do there. Alone in a quiet room, Hisako had lost herself in a book. The end of spring was fast approaching, and the leaves on the trees in the small garden had grown luxuriant. The shoji screens were shut, and completely darkened by the shadows cast from the lush leaves outside. Now and then, children's voices could be heard from the home of the military man next door. Afternoon in the *yamanote* was truly peaceful.[21]

All of a sudden, Hisako heard the front door sliding open. Her first thought was that the housekeeper must have come home, but then she heard a deep male voice outside the front door.

"Is this where Miss Ōtsuki Hisako lives?"

Assuming that this was the mail delivery, Hisako didn't respond but slid back the *fusuma* and went to the entryway.

"Is it the mail?" she asked, opening the door.

Standing there was a man who appeared to be a ricksha driver.

"Yes, I am Miss Ōtsuki, but may I ask . . ."

"Some young fellow is waiting for you out here."

"What? A man?" exclaimed Hisako in surprise. The blunt way the driver spoke to her was so offensive that Hisako felt herself prickle with anger.

"And just who is this man?" she asked tersely, as if cross-examining the driver.

"He says his name is Sawano."

Hisako's heart skipped a beat when she heard the name Sawano.

Here she was, miles away from home, living with her younger siblings who were still in school and employing an older woman to help with the housework. Nothing much ever happened in Hisako's quiet life. It was her duty to run the house and act as guardian to her younger sisters and brother. Whenever she thought about these responsibilities, Hisako was reminded that she must never do anything rash, and so she had behaved with a single-minded sense of purpose, not once doing anything that would incur others' disapproval. Having been raised in the old-fashioned ways of traditional morality, Hisako had respected and defended her chastity like a saint. But these days, the spirit of the times was so different! Chiefly in literature, now that Naturalism had become so popular. Hisako had to admit that she felt more than a little derailed by that philosophy, but then, that was only insofar as it influenced literature. When it came to matters of everyday life, she had no doubts in her mind whatsoever.

Nevertheless, here she was, being paid a visit at home by a man. She thought it rather cowardly for the man to have called on her in the way that he had, and for that reason, too, she did not immediately go out to greet him. Still, there was something about all this that had finally made Hisako lose her reserve. Slipping on her sandals, she followed the driver out of the entrance. As soon as she turned the corner, a young man came out from the shadow of an electric-light pole.

"Are you Miss Hisako?"

Hisako stared at the young man abruptly before her.

"Yes. I am Hisako. Right now . . . as it happens . . . I am here alone, so . . . would you like to come in?

What a quandary Hisako was in! Any number of letters had come from Sawano asking whether it would be all right for him to visit her, but she had always concocted some excuse to refuse him. Hisako had naturally had some curiosity about Sawano, but she certainly was not in love with the man. Nevertheless, the thought of keeping up their lyrical correspondence without ever actually meeting delighted Hisako's young heart. She feared that if they were to meet each other, this poetic fantasy might vanish into thin air. But Sawano persisted in his requests to meet her, and this provoked a sort of terror in Hisako. It was the passionate style of his writing, and the conviction displayed in his words right from the start—it was particularly things like these that made Hisako sense she was going to suffer forever. How she longed to escape his grasp before it was too late! But he had finally paid his visit, and in the end Hisako was powerless to do anything in the face of such a strong obsession.

Hisako's manner showed how fearful she was of being caught doing this. Still, she invited Sawano into the parlor room. She sat down diagonally across from the desk where she'd been sitting only a little while ago, and seated her guest in front of the large bookcase. Sawano seemed just as nervous as Hisako, but simply kept quiet, his head bowed. The two sat for awhile in an awkward silence.

There were things that Hisako wanted to say to him. She wanted to ask why he hadn't come to visit in a more open way. Being summoned by a ricksha driver was the sort of behavior that shamed a woman. What would have happened if her younger sister or servant had been about? Surely there was no reason for such cowardly methods if one was meeting a literary companion, thought Hisako, as she coolly trained her eyes on the man.

What an appearance! His kimono lacked a proper collar. The print of his soiled *hakama* was so faded that one could hardly make it out, and it was awfully tattered and dirty at the hem. His hair fell long and unkempt, resembling a black hat pulled down around his head. His face alone was white, and his eyes were sparkling in a rather excited, nervous way.

As she took in Sawano's appearance, Hisako sensed that he was somehow different from ordinary men. One would expect a young man who came to call on a woman to dress nicely, just as the young woman would want to look her best for him. Understandably surprised by Sawano barging in on her looking as he did, Hisako thought this made his behavior all the more perplexing. She also felt very uneasy. Was he plotting something?

After staying only a short while, Sawano announced that he would leave her, but promised that neither of them would ever forget this first time they'd met.

Upon leaving Hisako's home, Sawano went straight back to his boardinghouse and sent her a note on Western-style lined paper describing his feelings at having met her that day. Reading his letter, Hisako understood the reason he had visited her and why he had intended to look so ragged. And at the same time, she understood that he embraced ideas about love, and feelings about her, that were wholly different from those held by any ordinary man.

And then it happened that he sent her an even warmer letter. But the nicer his letters were, the more Sawano frightened Hisako and the more she wanted to run away from him. For his part, Sawano realized that while Hisako did not dislike him, she was not especially enamored of him, either. His first meeting with her had all been part of a test of Hisako's feelings as a woman. After all, that was why he had purposely arrived in such shabby dress. It was all because he felt like destroying what it was that a woman hoped for in a man. The whole process had made him rather uneasy, but since Sawano felt a desire for Hisako that surely would last forever, he could easily dismiss his initial anxiety. He had made up his mind that nothing would stop him from making Hisako his eternal love, so the more Hisako tried to flee, the more doggedly he pursued her.

But Hisako knew that she could not fall in love with any man. Her responsibilities to her father and to her younger siblings shackled whatever freedom to love Hisako might otherwise have had. There was also her fear of what others might think. She had an overwhelming desire to live an idealistic life, to be the woman of a new era, and yet the sad fact of the matter was that her heart was not free. Without having any joy of her own, she had been respectful of chastity, and had made her lonely passage through girlhood like a nun. All this she had told to Sawano, but he would hear none of it. What's more, he said that he was coming to visit again. Hisako gathered all her courage in an attempt to avoid this happening. For some reason or another, Sawano always struck a kind of fear in Hisako. Everyone in the household soon knew that letters from Sawano were arriving almost every day. Her housekeeper and others were telling her younger brother and sisters all kinds of rumors behind her back.

And there was, after all, the fact that Hisako was a woman who had already been unlucky in love once before. She explained to Sawano that to be loved by her would be worthless to him. Yet no matter how she tried to cool his ardor, she only succeeded in making him feel all the more sympathetic to her.

Since Sawano wrote her so many letters, Hisako was always anxious when her housekeeper or younger siblings were home, lest he make an unexpected visit. She had a certain authority as the eldest sister, and an authority and trust as the head of this household, but wasn't all this being injured by Sawano's continuing interest in her? At the very least, a household head-ed by a woman attracted notice, and if her relationship with Sawano became common knowledge, who knew what sort of rumors that would spawn? Still, all Hisako could muster was a meek fear of Sawano.

Spring had already passed, the green leaves of June were delightful-ly lush, and the weather was far too warm for flannel. It was about this time that Sawano sent her a single photograph. When the package arrived, Hisako's pulse quickened, but she simply took it from her sister and placed it on the bookcase.

"That's a photograph, isn't it, Sister? Let me see it," pleaded her young-er sister.

When they heard this, Hisako's younger brother and her other younger sister all gathered around and finally she tore open the package.

"It's a man's picture."

"Oooh, he's a young man, isn't he?'

"Gee, what a scary face."

As one would expect, her brother was content with one glance at the photograph, and left the room.

There was nothing Hisako could do at this point.

"Is this person someone you know, Sister?"

After a pause, Hisako answered, "He's a member of the Akebono Literary Society."

Despite Hisako's discomfort, her sisters were innocent, too young to care about any of this. They soon forgot all about the photograph and went off to play. Hisako looked furtively at the photograph. It was an anxious face that bore the evidence of a strong will, that spoke of a determination to win one's heart's desire no matter what the cost. Hisako felt all the more apprehensive as she looked at it.

"This sort of thing should definitely be sent back. Why on earth did he mail it to me?" Frustrated, Hisako threw the photograph to the back of one of the drawers in the bookcase. She lacked the courage to dare return it to Sawano.

Even though Hisako distrusted Sawano, she was still a maiden who yearned to be in love. Like any other young woman who hoped for an af-fectionate verse, and longed for romance, Hisako did not find it unpleasant to listen to Sawano's dreamlike whispers of love or read letters from a man who had such a way with poetry.

Then had come the time for changing into her white summer clothing. By now, Sawano had visited her twice. Hisako had been in the middle of writing a long novel, which he even borrowed and took home with him.

About that time, Hisako's father sent her word about a marriage proposal back home. An acquaintance in Tokyo had brought this up with her once or twice, too, but Hisako had turned a deaf ear to the matter. Still, as one who knew what fate had in store for her, Hisako realized that she could not avoid marriage forever. Seeing that her girlhood was finally coming to an end made Hisako feel so despondent that all she could do was shut herself up in her room. She no longer had the strength to look at the letters that came from Sawano, for she had lost the ambition to break with all forms of convention and live in a free realm. One by one, the muggy days of summer slipped by while Hisako sadly bowed her head before the God of Fate.

Hisako had been a young girl when her mother died. She'd seen her father worry over having to raise his children all by himself, and she'd felt such sympathy for her younger sisters, bereft at no longer having a mother to rely on. There had been no time for her to think only about her own interests. Now Hisako resolved that, if fate would also have her marry without love, then she would break off with Sawano once and for all.

She explained the import of all of this to Sawano, but he was a young man already driven mad with love. He couldn't help cursing this woman who was like none he had ever met before, who hated him so much that she kept trying to avoid him. He would call her a "bewitching princess" one moment, and in the next breath resolve to give her up completely. Yet, every once in a while, when Hisako thought about his letters—their erratic alternation between a terrible desperation and loving sentiments—she felt she could sense the man's heart at fever pitch.

It was not long before Sawano had had more than enough of this separation, and came over to ask Hisako to take a stroll in the neighborhood with him. Feeling powerless to resist his determined pursuit of her, Hisako simply refused to respond to him, and even made efforts not to read any more of his letters. It was as though she were being persecuted by a man possessed. Hisako became so unnerved by Sawano that she made it a point to avoid having anything to do that would take her out of the house at night. Certainly she would not dream of going for a walk with the man.

It was in the middle of that summer, about the beginning of August, that talk of the marriage proposal that had been buried for a time suddenly surfaced once again. A friend of Hisako's father had agreed to be the matchmaker, and before she knew it, Hisako was having an *omiai* at an art exhibition in Ueno Park.[22] The young man was a student at X University, and would graduate in another year, but this did not make any particular impression on Hisako. She passed these sad and lonely days well aware of herself as a woman who bowed to the God of Fate, and left everything up to her friend who spoke so enthusiastically of the arrangement.

Her two younger sisters went back home for the summer festival.

Presently Hisako received a message from her father ordering her back home immediately. Since she was suffering from a bout of beriberi, Hisako decided to go ahead and return home, too. She arranged for her aunt to come from the country to mind the house in her absence.

Thinking she could at last flee from Sawano, Hisako wrote him a melancholy letter explaining that, since the plans for her marriage were proceeding, she could no longer see him, nor should she receive any further letters from him. Leaving things like this, she went home.

As she relived these old memories, Hisako was startled even now by her dreams of what might have been. Would she be living as she was now if she had broken off with Sawano back then and married the young man from X University? "Fate determines all," she thought, and closing her eyes, Hisako traced her past once more.

Her child breathed gently, dreaming pleasant dreams. The sound of a nightingale singing made it seem like spring. Two or three sparrows were chirping, too. A train came speeding by, rumbling like a great storm.

In the end, all the talk about Hisako's marriage went nowhere. The negotiations had been too drawn out, and what's more, her father did not agree with much of what had emerged in these discussions. Yet returning to the peaceful countryside had calmed Hisako, and had also given her time to think about who she really was. How pathetic it would be if she died accomplishing nothing at all, having made a sacrifice of herself like this. There would be no point to her having been born. Her education would count for nothing. She must do everything in her power to rouse and expand herself. If she had any mission in life as a human being, then she must fulfill it. Surely there was no reason she had to rot away like this, chained to some narrow expectations for "woman," "daughter," or "older sister"! As Hisako thought over her situation anew, her heart became full, suffused with the shining light of self-awareness. At last Hisako confessed her feelings to her father, requesting that, if she absolutely must marry, she be allowed to find someone who conformed more to her own ideals. Fortunately her father agreed, and suggested that she ask her old teacher for introductions.

Hisako returned to Tokyo full of hope. When she got back, it was the middle of September, and another letter had come from Sawano. All the uneasiness she had put behind her asserted itself once again. Since Hisako had never expected to marry Sawano, when she spied his letter she felt like a one-time runaway who was being pursued all over again. Still, she opened the envelope and read the letter.

Anguished by his romance, Sawano had exchanged some of his precious books for money and had simply gone wandering, traveling as far as Sado Island. It was on that small isle, while listening to the sound of the ocean, that he had tried to stop crying. But then Hisako's letter had been forwarded to Sado from his address in Tokyo. When he read the letter, he felt as if he were perched on a cliff and that the sadness of the letter itself would hurl him off. His despair was profound. He wandered the beach that evening, praying for Hisako's future happiness. He was apologetic about having followed Hisako everywhere she went, but promised that he had done this because he loved her so much and had never meant to cause her any harm. All the time he had been weeping over his failed romance, he had been praying that only good fortune would come to Hisako.

It was the end of August by the time he had returned to Tokyo, after wandering for some time more on Sado. He had immediately gone to see how things were at Hisako's house. Though he did not expect Hisako to be there, he noticed that the nameplate and the house were just as before. This made him wonder whether Hisako had not gone home after all. Had it all been a ruse to deceive him? He had trusted Hisako and sympathized with her, but feeling betrayed, he could not stop himself from cursing her now. His letter went on and on with lines such as "Why did you want to run away from me like that? I'll go after you no matter where you are."

When Hisako read the first part of the letter, learned about Sawano's drifting about on Sado, and imagined him walking along the beach at twilight praying for her good fortune while crying over the death of his own love, she couldn't help but shed a few tears for him herself. But when she read to the end of it, Hisako felt an overwhelming sense of outrage at the deeply suspicious heart of this man.

Two months after this, at the end of October, a certain magazine reporter suddenly showed up at her door saying that he was a friend of Sawano and bringing a letter for her from him. Earnestly pleading Sawano's love for her, and giving assurances about their future happiness, the man encouraged them to marry. Both the man's impassioned speech and hearing about Sawano's present situation sparked feelings of sympathy in Hisako that had not been there before. Hisako began to feel that, if everything this man said were true, then perhaps she would not mind marrying Sawano.

In the end, this feeling turned into the fuse that ignited their relationship, and their fate was sealed.

Hisako heaved a great sigh and opened her eyes. How bitter her life had been since she had become Sawano's wife. His passion for her had cooled with time, and was eventually buried by marriage, the graveyard of romantic love. Yet as his wife, she had seen her feelings for him glow softly at first, but shine ever more brightly as time passed.

Hisako had ended up with a lifelong obsession from which she could never escape. As for Sawano, he had been thrust out of the youthful world of fantasy into the realities of everyday living. He was learning how very difficult it was to be saddled with a wife and still have to make one's own way in the world. He showed no mercy as he vented all his worry and frustration on Hisako until they would both collapse in tears. Once he had even tried to shake off this woman he had so labored to win, but she was just like a piece of candy. There was nothing he could do about the way she stuck fast to his hand.

Hisako was no happier. To think that she had once been awakened to her self!

This made it all the more absurd that she was now miserable, bound by the shackles called "wife." There were times when Hisako thought about showing a woman's pride and standing up for herself, but she had not been able thus far to take such decisive action.

The child opened his eyes wide. Blinking, he caught sight of his mother's face and sat halfway up.

Glancing at the clock, Hisako realized that it was past three. Outside the sun was shining warmly and small birds were keeping up a steady chirp. The boy always had such an easy time of waking up. Hisako picked him up and put him on her back, then went outside.

Ah, spring. Spring would indeed be here soon. With this hope in mind and with her face bathed in warm sunlight, Hisako turned her feet toward the footpath running between the rice paddies. The child on her back was happy and gleeful.

Youthful blood was suddenly coursing through Hisako's veins again. There had been a time, before her marriage to Sawano but after she had received her father's permission to marry him, when she and Sawano had been able to meet each other freely and would go walking about the outlying areas of Tokyo together. How young she had felt then! She was not only infatuated with literature but as enchanted as ever with nature. Oh, how the rural area of Musashino had captivated her![23] There was nature, indescribably expansive and pure.

Embraced by the warmth of early spring, Hisako had tasted even more deeply from the wellspring of love. Recalling that sensation refreshed her spirit even now. She had been so gloomy over her inability to give herself over to nature anymore, and yet now her heart was soaring, buoyant as the clouds in the sky. Hisako felt calm at last.

A thick haze enveloped the mountains on all sides. Branches of a plum tree in bloom could be seen over the thatched roof of a farmer's home. Perched on one of these branches, a bird was singing for all it was worth. Sleepy cows followed ruts in the road made by the cart jostling up ahead.

The sound of their mooing faded softly into the distance as they trod on.

Hisako wanted to grab tight to all the emotions she was feeling now and hold them close to her forever. If she could at least keep them to her until her husband came home, if she could retain this youthful gaiety toward nature and life, how she would like to take a stroll in the moonlight with him this evening! Wouldn't plum-blossom viewing at night be fine? Yes, they would go. Tonight, they would definitely view the blossoms. Together with her husband, just as before, she might even dine at a Western-style restaurant, and perhaps sip some red wine.

Crossing the ridges of the rice paddies, Hisako came to the bank of a clear stream. She broke off a branch of sprouting flower buds from a river willow and gave it to her child to hold. She stared absentmindedly at the flow of the stream. A school of tiny river-fish darted in and out of the shadows cast by the grass in the stream. Bits of green were already starting to sprout on the ridges of the rice paddies.

Hisako finished dinner and went outside. Seven days old, the moon sparkled, throwing off brilliant rays of light. It was a peaceful evening, without even the slightest breeze blowing. Hisako had waited expectantly for her husband to return, but it was already eight o'clock and he had still not arrived. A short time later, perhaps a little before nine, he finally came back home.

"How about dinner?" she asked.

"I've eaten," he replied, going straight over to the foot warmer and sticking his feet under it.

"But tonight I had a real feast prepared," complained Hisako, the resentment in her voice clear.

With her child in her arms, Hisako, too, put her feet under the warmer. She considered speaking about all that she had thought of that day, but when she saw her husband looking so tired and aloof, the calm in Hisako's own heart vanished, too. Yet in the same instant, all the usual misgivings she had about him flared up as well.

Usually, when he came home and found the child still up, her husband would start talking with her about one thing or another. But tonight he was silent, his face buried in one of the cushions.

"I'm going to sleep."

"You want to go to bed as soon as you get home these days, don't you?" Hisako smiled sadly as she said this.

"Well, when I get home, there is nothing else to do."

"But . . ." All Hisako's feelings of dissatisfaction finally came to the surface. She demanded to know why her husband did not enjoy their home life.

She complained that he started scowling as soon as he got home. Hisako's list of grievances went on and on: "If you don't look after the boy for me, I can't put out the beds."

"So dump him!"

"What an awful thing to say!"

"You have no pride whatsoever."

"Why do you say that?" Hisako shot back with a frosty glare. "Because you have no determination to become financially independent of me. Look how you've let yourself become completely preoccupied with the child."

"I do have determination. And if the time comes when I need to . . ."

"You said you were going to be a newspaperwoman, but you haven't made any effort to do that at all."

"But becoming a newspaperwoman takes a good deal of thought. If I did decide to become independent, I would certainly have all the strength I needed. But if I didn't consider everything ahead of time . . ."

"You're simply weak-willed. That's the problem."

"Well, why is it that you are telling me to become a newspaperwoman anyway?"

"It's so that you can cultivate yourself."

"Cultivating oneself is fine if it is genuine, but . . ."

"You're hopeless, because you don't know anything about the real world. Just look at that long piece you're writing now."

Hisako listened to her husband, her mouth clamped tight in anger. Her lips trembled.

"Look, there's an opening for a reporter now. All you need to do is make up your mind and the job is yours."

"What about our child?"

"You don't have to worry about the child. The only question is whether or not you've got any backbone."

"You're saying that you'd like to divorce me, aren't you?"

"I'm not saying that we have to get a divorce, but wouldn't it be better if both of us worked?"

"No, no, no! That will only cause other problems to come up. Men are always making impossible demands on women! On the one hand you tell us, 'Be like a man,' and on the other you say, 'Be like a woman.' You demand that I involve myself in activities outside the house, but you still want me to do everything around the house that women have always done. No one can do that! Why should a person of one sex be asked to take on the qualities and the work of both sexes?"

"All I'm saying is that if you're not more active, things are not going to go well. Isn't there something you can do?"

Being spoken to in this fashion so provoked Hisako that she felt as though all the blood in her body had reached its boiling point. Who had gotten her into this situation in the first place? None of her youthful energy remained, and what was left in its stead was only a deep pain. Who had been the one to pursue his own ideals while interfering with her life? He made more than the ordinary demands on her as a wife and mother, and on top of that, he was now seeking his ideal of a single woman in her, too. He criticized her morning and night for not being able to satisfy these demands. It was simply too cruel, thought Hisako, tears welling up in her eyes.

"But even if I don't become a newspaperwoman, I know there is a path to self-cultivation for me. Why, I, too, have my own ideals. What's more, if you're going to keep on about how I must cultivate myself, then please sever our relationship as husband and wife once and for all. If this doesn't happen, I won't be able to do anything freely, no matter what it is, as someone's wife."

Hisako stared back at him, her eyes filled with despair and resentment. All the recollections of their past that had been on her mind that day suddenly came to her again. What a terrible obsession! They had almost separated on countless occasions, yet here they were, still together. The power of this invisible obsession was never going to let them go. Rather, Hisako sensed, it was making them suffer in any number of ways.

Notes

[1] Katō Midori, "Shūchaku" (Obsession), *Seitō* 2.4 (April 1912): 9–26.

[2] Iwata Nanatsu, *Bungaku to shite no "Seitō"* (Fuji Shuppan, 2003), 125. Iwata summarizes the plots of Katō Midori's stories "Hana no Ai" and "Haisha" on pages 124–27. This kind of plot also figures in Katō's story "Kaigi" (Doubt), *Seitō* 2.9 (September 1912): 56–81, in which Shimako, who is about to enter an arranged marriage to a wealthy man, envies her sister Yaeko, whose love marriage has rendered her poor and estranged from her father, but happy. Shimako feels like some kind of doll whose feet and hands are bound, and thinks wistfully of her brief romance with a young reporter.

[3] Katō Midori, "Geijutsu to haru" (Springtime and Art), *Seitō* 3.10 (October 1913): 105–25.

[4] Katō Midori, "Bokusha no kotoba" (What the Fortune-Teller Said), *Seitō* 4.5 (May 1914): 5–21.

[5] Katō Midori, "Tada hitori" (All Alone), *Seitō* 5.11 (December 1915): 47–53.

[6] Katō Midori, "Hoshi no sora" (Starry Sky), *Seitō* 6.1 (January 1916): 116–39.

[7] As quoted in Iwata, *Bungaku to shite no "Seitō,"* 123. I draw most of the biographical material in this chapter from *Bungaku to shite no "Seitō."*

[8] Ibid., 123.

[9] [Hiratsuka] Raichō, [Katō] Midori, [and Itō] Noe, "Yonda mono no hyō to saikin no kansō" (Comments on Things We've Read and Our Thoughts of Late), *Seitō* 4.5

(May 1914): 114.

[10]Yasumoro Yasuko, "Katō Midori," in Raichō Kenkyūkai, ed., *"Seitō" jinbutsu jiten: 110-nin no gunzō* (Taishūkan Shoten, 2001), 74–75; and the earlier version of this essay in Yasumoro Yasuko, "Katō Midori," in Hiratsuka Raichō o Yomu Kai, ed., *"Seitō" no go-jūnin* (Hiratsuka Raichō o Yomu Kai, 1996), 38–39.

[11]Iwata, *Bungaku to shite no "Seitō,"* 128–29.

[12]Hiratsuka Raichō, *Genshi, josei wa taiyō de atta: Hiratsuka Raichō jiden* (Ōtsuki Shoten, 1971–73), 2: 413; Hiratsuka Raichō and Teruko Craig, *In the Beginning, Woman Was the Sun: The Autobiography of Hiratsuka Raichō, Japanese Feminist* (New York: Columbia University Press, 2006), 197. Craig notes that the practice of sending children out to nurse "was not uncommon, especially when there were too many children or the mother was in poor health." Ibid., note xxv.

[13]Hiratsuka, *Genshi, josei wa taiyō de atta*, 2: 593–94; Hiratsuka and Craig, *In the Beginning, Woman Was the Sun*, 278. Raichō also recounts how in 1919 Asadori published his translation of Ellen Key's *The Renaissance of Motherhood* under Raichō's name because he was desperate for money. Raichō had suggested the work to him as a good one to translate but had objected to his using her name. Asadori did receive recognition years later from the Polish government for having been instrumental in introducing Polish literature to Japan. Ibid.

[14]Iwata Nanatsu, *"Seitō" no onna: Katō Midori* (Seikyūsha, 1993).

[15]Katō Midori, "Atarashii onna ni tsuite" (On the New Woman), *Seitō* 3.1 (January 1913), Supplement: 35.

[16]Dina Lowy, "Nora and the 'New Woman': Visions of Gender and Modernity in Early Twentieth-Century Japan," *U.S.–Japan Women's Journal*, no. 26 (2004): 87.

[17]Katō, "Atarashii onna ni tsuite," 30.

[18]Dina Lowy observes that Sudermann's play is titled *Heimat* in the original German, was translated as *Kokyo* in Japanese and *The Home* in English, and is commonly referred to today in Japan, Europe, and the United States as *Magda*. Dina Lowy, *The Japanese "New Woman": Images of Gender and Modernity* (New Brunswick, NJ, and London: Rutgers University, 2007), 140, n. 1.

[19]Katō, "Atarashii onna ni tsuite," 34. Perhaps Midori is thinking of the line from Shakespeare's *Hamlet*, "Frailty, thy name is woman!"

[20]Ibid., 31–32.

[21]Yamanote, sometimes translated as "uptown," refers to the hilly, residential section of Tokyo and is distinguished from the city's older "downtown" (*shitamachi*) areas associated with entertainment and shopping.

[22]An *omiai* is a first meeting, often arranged by a matchmaker (*nakōdo*) at the request of a young person's parents, that introduces a woman and man to each other as potential marriage partners.

[23] Musashino, incorporated in 1947 as one of the cities in Tokyo, was a rural farming area at this time.

Chapter 8
Kobayashi Katsu (1894–1974)

The woman thought how much it would mean to be assured of a monthly salary. At the same time she was ashamed to see how thrilled a naïve young woman like herself could become over money.

Born in Tokyo, Kobayashi Katsu was the fifth daughter of noted Meiji woodblock artist Kobayashi Kiyochika (1847–1915) and his wife Yoshi (d. 1912). She grew up in Kyobashi and Asakusa, the lively downtown areas of Tokyo where the artistic world of Edo-style painters, geisha, and actors still flourished. Kobayashi herself must have absorbed some of the atmosphere of these quarters, since the writer Tamura Toshiko once described her as having the appearance of a young geisha. Despite such associations with an older Japanese sensibility, Kobayashi enjoyed a girls' school education that was both privileged and modern, graduating from a school that specialized in teaching French, English, and Japanese. If one of her *Seitō* stories is as autobiographical as it seems, the young Kobayashi, much like Hiratsuka Raichō and Fukuda Hideko, impressed her neighbors as a tomboy. O-Chiyo, one of the main characters in Kobayashi's 1913 story "Kashi" (Riverfront), remembers inspiring gossip for dressing and acting like a boy when she was fifteen. When adults asked her as a child what she would become when she grew up, O-Chiyo responded that she wanted to be a "woman who fights for the underdog" (*onnadate*) and to "kill all the bad guys," just like a hero she had once seen on stage.[1] Perhaps it was this same desire for adventure that motivated Kobayashi Katsu to join the Bluestockings in November 1911, becoming one of the group's youngest members. While active in the group, she also continued to study at the language school, even though she had already graduated.

By all accounts a vivacious and fun-loving teenager, Kobayashi brought cheerfulness to the Bluestockings, and energy, too: she worked at editing and proofreading, and contributed twenty-three pieces to *Seitō*, including plays, poems, and short stories, while writing occasionally for other publications as well. From 1912 through 1915, Kobayashi experienced major changes in her personal life: her mother died in 1912; she married the Japanese-style artist Kobayashi Shōsaku (1892?–1956; no relation) in 1914;[2] and in 1915, one month after her father died, she bore the first of her eight children at age twenty-one.

Child-bearing and child-rearing, the demands of her husband's active professional life, and the calamity of her husband's family suffering a devastating fire all conspired to leave Kobayashi little time to pursue her own artistic work. Nevertheless, she occasionally published stories and translations, and during the war years sometimes worked as a teacher of Japanese in Tokyo. She was widowed in 1956, when her husband Shōsaku died at age sixty-four. Kobayashi continued to write short pieces, especially biographical essays about her father, and she painted until her death at age seventy-nine. In 1960 she was appointed to the committee that awarded the Tamura Toshiko prize for fiction, and in 1962 she was made a member of the advisory board for Meiji Village, a kind of historical theme park near Nagoya for presenting Meiji-era architecture and lifeways. In 1973, at age seventy-eight, Kobayashi appeared in an NHK television program, "The Last Ukiyo-e Artist: A Daughter's View of Kiyochika."[3]

Kobayashi Katsu's *Seitō* stories and plays bring in the lives of geisha, Kabuki actors, and others depicted in Ukiyo-e prints, but also the world of young girl students, movies, and modern city life. "O-Fuyu-san no hanashi" (O-Fuyu's Story), for example, is a story recounted in a beauty parlor, and tells the tale of O-Fuyu, a woman who leaves home for the love of an actor, ends up becoming a geisha, and later opens a restaurant to support herself.[4] In Kobayashi's play, *Onna bakari* (Women Only), a mother takes her young teenaged daughter Mitsuko to visit a Christian girls' boarding school run by foreigners. Mitsuko detests the nuns' garb, finds the school unfairly strict, and resists her mother and the nuns' plans for her, concluding that "whether they're old ladies from the West or Japanese old ladies, they're still old ladies" who do not understand young girls.[5] Mother-daughter conflict plays a role in these and some of Kobayashi's other stories, especially when the mother's bitterness over her own failed romance makes her urge her daughter to forswear love. For example, in "O-Fuyu's Story," O-Fuyu's mother has acquiesced to an arranged marriage, giving up her love for the actor Risuke; O-Fuyu, in love with Risuke's son, leaves home to be with him, but later separates from him. And in "Fukeyo kawakaze" (Blow on, River Breeze), young Onou, who has a boyfriend, becomes angry at her mother for urging her to master some kind of artistic practice so that she can become self-supporting and remain single her entire life.[6] In "Masui" (Anesthetic), however, the 1912 story translated below, Kobayashi depicts the problems of a young woman who does wish to work and who encounters trouble with a man, not her mother.

"Anesthetic" portrays the kind of barriers a young and ambitious New Woman could face in her attempts to be taken seriously as an intellectual. The man in this story cautions Mitsu, a young woman hoping to find a position as a tutor, that further study will make her overly serious and rigid, not lead to much pay, and hurt her chances for marrying well. To her further dismay, Mitsu soon realizes that all these excuses serve only to camouflage the man's true intent to persuade her, or even trick her, into becoming his mistress.

Dressed as a serious student in her shabby *hakama*, Mitsu sees herself as socially and personally distant from Omachi, the woman who has actually been the man's mistress. She imagines that an uneducated woman like Omachi merely resigned herself to this man's mistreatment and to her "fate" as a kept woman. Even the two women's names position them on opposite sides of a cultural divide: Omachi is an old-fashioned name one might associate with a geisha, whereas Mitsu (or perhaps Mitsuko) is the fresh, new-style name of a girl student. One way the man tries to diminish Mitsu's status is by abbreviating her name and using the diminutive *chan*, calling her "Mitt-chan" as if she were a little girl.[7]

Everything about this situation—the location of the man's secret house in an industrial section of the city, the tawdriness of its furnishings, the vulgar conversation, and even the sight of impoverished women sweating over grim piecework—repulses Mitsu. Yet what bothers her most are the twin problems of her own desire to have a good position and her willingness to enlist this unsavory man's influence to achieve this. The abrupt break in the middle of the story and the way it continues with the man more overtly harassing Mitsu suggest that, despite her discomfort, she has remained in the room a fairly long time in the hope that they will leave soon for the appointment with her prospective employers. Only when Mitsu concludes that the man is plotting to sedate and rape her does she flee the house.

"Anesthetic" was not unusual in broaching the topic of sexual harassment. Anecdotes about how working women, especially factory workers and servants in private homes, frequently became the victims of sexual harassment and rape were well known in Japan at this time.[8] There was also the suggestion that young women leaving the protection of the home were inviting sexually charged attention. In describing sexual harassment in this melodramatic story, Kobayashi Katsu takes the opposite tack, clearly defining the man in power as the harassing figure while painting the protagonist, the New Woman, as a determined young person who is only seeking a job and who is repulsed by the man's attention. As in many other *Seitō* stories, the New Woman, though not always sure of how to react to such an uncomfortable situation, does see that she has a choice and, in this story at least, acts on it.

****

Anesthetic
Kobayashi Katsu
Seitō 2.12 (December 1912)

They were in a part of the city that was home to many marine transportation businesses and other shipping enterprises. The noonday sun blazed a bright reddish-yellow, its light suffusing the narrow streets where old packing rope flew about, giving off the smell of dust, and where the pounding of hammers beat into one's head. Sullen, the young woman followed behind the man as he wound through these narrow back streets. They passed by a carpenter's house beneath whose soot-covered, jet-black eaves stood a pole wrapped in faded red paper, a celebratory gesture from days long past. They could see through rattan blinds to a crowd of women whose fat shoulders were half-bared as, dripping with sweat, they labored at their piecework of tying thongs on sandals. The man stopped in front of a newly made lattice door at the third house from the corner.

"Auntie, are you there today?" called the man, raising his voice.

"Yes, yes. Oh, Mr. Tanaka! I had given up on you, you know. And who have you brought with you?" About fifty years old, the woman had the sort of appearance that one frequently saw in this part of the city. She directed a rather crude look at the young woman, her eyes running all over her as she took in everything from the sweat showing through around the young woman's chest to her discolored, salt-stained *hakama*.

"What? Oh, she's my protégée. Well, would it be all right to stop in for awhile? Mitt-chan, don't you want to come in and rest?"

It was a cheaply built place. Reluctantly, the young woman made her way up scuffed stairs to the room above. The room held some inexpensive furniture clumsily shoved together. There was a chest of drawers with a façade of pawlonia wood, another chest similar to it, and a long hibachi with a fake copper brazier inside. Without a moment's hesitation, the man removed his jacket. Then he took a candy dish out of a small cupboard in the dresser. He produced something that looked like Western-style candy wrapped in paper and offered it to the young woman.

"Is this why you've brought me here? For this sort of nonsense?" she demanded, bristling with indignation.

"What? I've only brought you here because we'll be taking the Yamanote Line and it leaves from this neighborhood. Our appointment is for four o'clock and, well, we still have an hour and a half until then, so I thought we might as well take it easy for awhile. But please, just relax and make yourself comfortable. I rent this place, so it's no trouble at all."

The young woman had a vague memory of hearing once from the man's wife that he kept a woman who'd worked in a yakitori bar somewhere around Asakusa.

"So, then, you must have been renting this for your mistress?"

"Mistress? You've got to be joking!" the man replied, but the look on his face showed that he was barely repressing a smile.

The woman who had been his mistress must have sat in front of this long hibachi, too. The young woman had the odd sense that she had even seen her face somewhere. She wondered how the mistress must have felt, doing nothing all day except sitting here and staring blankly into space as she waited for the man. The young woman couldn't even begin to understand what was going through the mind of a man who would enjoy bringing her—one of his wife's own relatives—to the home where he had kept his mistress. She couldn't get the tawdriness of all this out of her mind.

The man had left the room to get hot water for tea. He returned shortly, carrying a tray on which he had placed two cups of steaming hot tea. He sat down very close to the young woman.

"What has you so deep in thought?" he asked, his large, ugly face looming uncomfortably close to her.

"What happened to the woman who used to live her? Omachi-san was her name, wasn't it?"

"Oh, so you even know her name, do you? . . . Well, well, you're quite informed, I see . . . The trouble was that she had no education, you know . . . so . . . I ended up having to send her back home."

The young woman found it utterly absurd to think that a woman would need any education at all to become a mere plaything for this man. She wondered whether the man had simply let the woman go back home or whether there had been some reason he'd felt that he must send her back. Perhaps she had decided to run back home on her own?

"Is it still too early to leave?"

"Ah, well, let's leave in a little while, shall we? Now let me tell you about the position. The family to whom I will introduce you live in Nishi-Ōkubo. They are quite well off and very well known in the area. Their second eldest daughter is . . . I think she's twelve or thirteen years old. At any rate, they said that they'd like to have her learn English and Japanese literature. Then—and this is the mother's one request—if it is at all possible, they would like to have the tutor live at their house and also teach their daughter good manners. If this suits you, Mitt-chan, I will help you make the necessary arrangements as soon as I can."

"If I have at least three or four hours to myself each day, then I wouldn't mind staying there."

"Really? What would you want to do with all that time to yourself?"

"I must study, of course."

"What sort of study? You're already plenty familiar with foreign languages. What on earth do you have to study now?"

The young woman assumed a smug expression, as if to say, "How could an oaf like you possibly understand?" The man responded by smirking at her haughty demeanor, making it clear that he did not take her seriously.

"Quite a few things actually."

"Quite a few things? What a pity that is! If you become all that educated . . . well, it isn't really all that becoming in a woman, now is it? You should think about getting married instead. You know that would be a relief to your parents, too. My wife keeps saying the same thing. How old are you anyway?

"I'm twenty-five."

"Twenty-five! You're young. Three years younger than I am . . . Why, I could introduce you to many suitable families."

The young woman fell silent, making it clear that she did not see this man as someone to confide in. Indeed, she found herself irritated by his each and every word. Who needed an introduction to those people wanting a tutor if it meant relying on this lout? Every time this dull, ugly dolt of a man turned his eyes on her, a creepy sensation would come over her, making her flesh crawl. She imagined she was a mouse cowering before the glare of a cat.

Finally, she simply blurted out, "If you cannot introduce me to the family today, I suppose I'd better be going."

"Now, please, just a little bit longer. We'll be leaving very shortly. Please, wait just a little more."

The woman thought how much it would mean to be assured of a monthly salary. At the same time she was ashamed to see how thrilled a naïve young woman like herself could become over money. Listlessly, she sank down on the cushion.

The sound of the man's footsteps grew fainter as he went farther down each step of the stairway. The young woman sensed the strain of every muscle in her face and especially the tension pulling at her cheeks. She wanted to shout every single angry thought she was thinking, but she could not say anything. An inky black rage raced throughout her mind, yet it would not let any sound escape from her. Unable to speak, the woman felt horribly trapped.

Since it was nearly sunset, the sunlight coming through the window cast a harsh, dusty light on the room. She could hear the deep voice of the man coming from below, and the curiously playful voice of the older woman alternately becoming high-pitched and then low, at times mixed with laughter.

The man's voice still rang in her ears, and the sight of his ugly face stayed with her just as strongly. The woman couldn't help but shiver as she broke out in goose bumps.

"Stop being so rigid," he'd said. "In the long run, that's only going to make matters worse for you. This way, rather than becoming some stuffy, straightlaced teacher, you'd be able to do whatever you pleased. At most, you would get only a mere 12 or 13 yen a month as a teacher, but this way you could make plenty of money much more easily. Your mother wouldn't have to know anything except that you were working somewhere, right? You see, it just won't do to be so inflexible. Everyone, no matter how high and mighty, has one side they present to the world and one they keep hidden!"

When the young woman had understood that the man was saying, "So let's create a 'hidden side' together," she'd become so enraged that she'd felt like clawing at him, like ripping apart his big, fleshy face.

"How dare he treat me this way!" Burning with resentment, the young woman had kept telling herself that the man was treating her like a fool. But he had persisted in trying to win her over, pleading that since his wife was sickly, things weren't too interesting for him at home, and wouldn't she please comfort a man who was exhausted from all the fast-paced, high-pressured life of his company, since, after all, he would give her at least what she would make as a teacher.

The young woman had been so furious that she had wanted to lash out at the man, to give him a real dressing-down. Yet strangely, her voice remained completely blocked and not a sound emerged from her. She clenched her teeth and shook her body from side to side in sheer frustration. Then she poked her fingers through the shoji screens and ripped a hole in the brand-new paper. Next, she spun the teacup around the table. Every single object in the room became a target for her rage.

The man came back up to the room. He said something, but the woman didn't register what it was. Her face taut with anger, she glared straight into the man's lecherous gaze.

"Well now, you don't have to get all that angry, Mitt-chan. If you find my proposal that awful, it's all right. Have some candy and then let's leave. Please don't be mad any longer. Okay? . . . Okay? Go ahead and grab one. Then, let's head out for Nishi-Ōkubo."

In the man's hand was a jar filled with Western-style sweets that looked like black candy. The young woman had keen eyesight and from the corner of her eyes she could make out the red horizontal letters on the label. It wasn't English and it didn't seem to be French. Suddenly, a scary thought stopped her short. These must be filled with drugs to make her sleep! She imagined what would happen if she swallowed one. She felt as if she could see the man laughing, and hear the older woman calling up to him from the first floor. Then and there, the young woman knew that this candy had to be an anesthetic.

"How about it? It has a lemon flavor."

The man unwrapped a piece on the woman's hand. With her other hand, the woman yanked the sticky candy from the palm of her hand and threw it full force right over the man's shoulder. It flew straight out the window that opened onto the alley below, in sight of the windows of the row houses next door.

The man's face fell in disappointment and sank into the darkening shadows of the room. The woman leapt to her feet and stomped down the stairs.

—October 31, 1912

Notes

[1] Kobayashi Katsu, "Kashi" (Riverfront), *Seitō* 3.5 (May 1913): 125.

[2] Kobayashi Shōsaku was a disciple of Otake Kōkichi's uncle, the famous artist Otake Chikuha (1878–1936).

[3] Inoue Mihoko, "Kobayashi Katsu," in Raichō Kenkyūkai, ed., *"Seitō" jinbutsu jiten: 110-nin no gunzō* (Taishūkan Shoten, 2001), 92–93. I draw much of the biographical information for the notes here on Kobayashi's life from Inoue's essay.

[4] Kobayashi Katsu, "O-Fuyu-san no hanashi" (O-Fuyu's Story), *Seitō* 3.4 (April 1913): 93–103.

[5] Kobayashi Katsu, *Onna bakari* (Women Only), *Seitō* 4.7 (July 1914): 73.

[6] Kobayashi Katsu, "Fukeyo kawakaze" (Blow on, River Breeze), *Seitō* 3.2 (February 1913): 45–52.

[7] In this story, Kobayashi often refers to Mitsu as "the woman" (*onna*). I call her "the young woman" here in order to distinguish Mitsu from two other women in the story, the mistress Omachi and the older "auntie," who are also referred to simply as *onna*.

[8] E. Patricia Tsurumi, for example, documents how the young women working in the thread mills sang songs of protest against sexual harassment. See Tsurumi, *Factory Girls: Women in the Thread Mills of Meiji Japan* (Princeton, NJ: Princeton University Press, 1990), 89, 98, 144–45. The many young women who worked in this period as domestic servants were also vulnerable to harassment. Few had any way to protect themselves or vent their complaints; when the *Asahi shinbun* began an advice column in 1931, the editors published countless sad and angry letters from harassed women servants; see Okuda Akiko, "Jochū no rekishi" (The History of Maids), in Kōno Nobuko and Tsurumi Kazuko, general eds., and Okuda Akiko, vol. ed., *Onna to otoko no jikū: Nihon joseishi saikō* (Time Space of Gender: Redefining Japanese Women's History), (Fujiwara Shoten, 1995–98), 5: 389–92. Sexual harassment became a major

target of feminist advocacy, media attention, and litigation in Japan in the late 1980s. See Hiroko Hirakawa, "Inverted Orientalism and the Discursive Construction of Sexual Harassment: A Study of Mass Media and Feminist Representations of Sexual Harassment in Japan" (Ph.D. diss., Purdue University, 1998).

Chapter 9
Nogami Yaeko (1885–1985)

What an enviable person the Buddha's mother Maya was! She was the only one ever blessed in childbirth.

Long celebrated as one of Japan's most distinguished and prolific women writers, Nogami Yaeko died in 1985, only a few weeks short of her hundredth birthday. Over the course of her career, Nogami wrote in many different modes, publishing more than 150 works of fiction, criticism, drama, children's literature, and translation.[1] Even at the time of her death, Nogami was writing yet another novel, *Mori* (The Forest), a story that drew on her experiences as a young female student at the center of intellectual life in Tokyo in the early 1900s. Although her name appears on the first roster of Bluestockings published in *Seitō*, Nogami withdrew formal membership from the group shortly thereafter, preferring the status of occasional contributor. This kind of stance accorded with her lifelong reputation as an independent thinker who remained aloof from the factionalism of the Japanese literary world even while she paid attention to its intellectual trends and borrowed from them.

Nogami Yaeko was only twenty-six years old at the time of *Seitō*'s debut, yet she had already married, borne her first child, and published her first short story, "Enishi" (Ties That Bind), in the magazine *Hototogisu* (Cuckoo) in 1907. Her writing career began most auspiciously, for she won early encouragement from one of Japan's most respected novelists, Natsume Sōseki (1867–1916). Sōseki first noticed Yaeko's promise when her husband, Nogami Toyoichirō (1883–1950), a literary scholar and student of Sōseki, brought her writing to his attention. Although Toyoichirō remained a supporter of his wife's writing, her achievements and the attraction she inspired in other male writers in his circle caused him no end of jealousy. He, too, had a successful career, in his case as a scholar of the Noh Theater and Greek drama, and as a professor of English literature at Tokyo University, but his accomplishments did not bring him the fame his wife achieved.[2]

Nogami Yaeko's successful writing career was aided and inspired by the privileged education she enjoyed in childhood and as a young adult. Born into the wealthy Kotegawa family, which owned and operated a sake brewery in Kyushu, "Yae" studied the Japanese and Chinese classics, becoming a voracious reader. As a teenager she traveled to Tokyo in 1900, at her mother's suggestion, to study at the prestigious, Christian-inspired Meiji Women's School, where she learned to think freely and was encouraged to read widely in Western literature. According to Yukiko Tanaka, Nogami later reported that the demanding curriculum of Meiji Women's School removed her completely from the kind of "good wife, wise mother" training and nationalism promoted in public schools of the day.[3] However encouraging they were of her intellectual development, Nogami's parents nevertheless expected her to marry soon after she graduated in 1906. Her father did not especially approve of her choice of Toyoichirō, and Yaeko herself, as she later wrote, did not love the young scholar. But marriage to him meant that she could remain in Tokyo and live in an intellectual environment, rather than having to return to Kyushu. Thus Nogami acquiesced to her parents' request that she marry in a way that both fulfilled the expectations of her class and allowed her to embark on life as a modern woman. Yet such acquiescence should not be taken as unquestioning support of the marriage system; as Eleanor Joan Hogan has discussed, some of Nogami's fiction demonstrates a keen distrust of how women were pushed into marriage and out of careers.[4]

As a young wife and mother, Nogami enjoyed an intellectual and financial freedom that few women in Japan could have imagined. She had maids to help care for her three sons; a husband who supported her creative work even though he was jealous of her talent and success; and an increasingly national reputation as a writer and translator. Perhaps it was for these reasons that Nogami never fought against the family system, despite her misgivings about it, with the same virulence that the other, more outspoken Bluestockings did. In fact, accounts of Nogami's career make special mention of how much she valued her private life with her family. Perhaps, too, it was Nogami's contentment with her life and her independent way of thinking that drew some of the younger Bluestockings to her. Fellow Kyushu native Itō Noe, in particular, sought Nogami's advice when the two women were next-door neighbors during Noe's troubled marriage to Tsuji Jun. When Noe left her husband and children for the radical activist Ōsugi Sakae, this impulsive action destroyed her friendship with Nogami Yaeko.

One of the most interesting of Nogami Yaeko's contributions to *Seitō*, aside from the story "Atarashiki inochi" (New Life; sometimes romanized as "Atarashiki seimei") translated here, is her lengthy translation of the life of Russian mathematician Sonya Kovalevsky (1850–91).[5] Published in English in 1895, the book is part autobiography and part biography written by Kovalevsky's friend Anna Carlotta Leffler (1849–92).[6] According to Iwata

Nanatsu, it was widely read among intellectual Japanese youth around 1912, and Nogami Toyoichirō published an article about it in the magazine *Hototogisu*.[7] The book takes the reader through Sonya's childhood and her friendship with Fyodor Dostoyevsky (1821–81) as a girl, to her study of mathematics in Germany and her position as the first woman employed as a professor in Sweden. Replete with rich descriptions of upper-class Russian family life, the cosmopolitan world of European intellectuals, and the international friendships among progressive women, *Sonya Kovalevsky* concentrates on Kovalevsky's competing desires for academic fame and romantic love. In the introduction to a 1933 edition of her translation, Nogami expressed how intrigued she was by the similarities she saw between the Bluestockings and the Russian women of Kovalevsky's generation.[8]

Nogami's lifelong fascination with this account of Kovalevsky's life seems to have owed much to her own hopes of maintaining an elite professional life and a family life as well, a mission she accomplished with much more success than did the mathematician. "New Life," however, shows that Nogami Yaeko, for all the value she accorded motherhood, did not sentimentalize childbirth. Indeed, several aspects of "New Life" qualify it as the kind of modern story the public might expect of a New Woman. The main character, Kaneko, is clearly a New Woman herself: she is an educated, urban woman involved in the solitary highbrow occupation of translating Western mythology into Japanese. Kaneko's privilege and her modernity are further marked by the fact that she is giving birth in a clinic and is attended by a pair of doctors and several nurses, rather than having a midwife and female relatives assisting her in her own home. Still, Kaneko's repeated references to one of these physicians as a "woman doctor" point up the surprise that even a New Woman could feel about women having high-status medical careers.[9]

The telling of this story, too, makes it a modern New Woman's tale of childbirth. Kaneko's unflinching, graphic description of her physical pain, her anxiety, and her ambivalence about the birth create a narrator-centered story with all the hallmarks of the "I-novel" (*shi-shōsetsu*) so popular at this time. In true I-novel style, the story's emphasis on personal experience counters prevailing customs: rather than following the feminine code of hiding the hugely pregnant female body and the pain of childbirth, Nogami makes the entire experience visible and distinctly unappealing.[10] Consequently, Kaneko is neither the stoic samurai woman who bears her pain silently through clenched teeth, nor the "good wife, wise mother" who welcomes her new child unconditionally.[11] Rather, she is a woman full of doubt, trying to understand, even if she cannot control, the event she is experiencing. Yet after the infant's birth, Kaneko feels dazed, as if there is no way to express or explain what has just happened.

Despite all the features that qualify "New Life" as a modern story, it is the author's numerous references to ancient tales that are most striking. Why would a New Woman rely on the themes of ancient stories to tell such a modern one? To answer this question, we might consider first of all that Nogami Yaeko, like her character Kaneko, was pregnant with her second son while preparing her translation of Thomas Bulfinch's *The Age of Fable, or Beauties of Mythology* (1894), which she published in 1913. The fact that she draws parallels between a contemporary childbirth experience and mythologized ones is not a coincidence. We also need to consider that Nogami's use of modern European literature, and especially her references to obscure figures such as Wendla or Ann, would likely have been no more recognizable to most readers then than now.[12] Such references would, however, surely have contributed to creating the character Kaneko as a New Woman—not as the brash New Woman of tabloid journalism, but as the New Woman the Bluestockings preferred to promote: namely, the New Woman who was well-read, intellectual, urban, and free-thinking.

Mythology also adds yet another dimension to "New Life." As Kaneko says, the ancient myths dramatize all human emotions, from the base to the idealistic, as extraordinary characters. Myth provides a framework, too, for making the particularities of individual experience universal. Given that childbirth is a nearly universal event for women yet one that is uniquely experienced by each mother, employing mythology enables Nogami to invoke both the universal and the particular. Reading "New Life" in the context of other *Seitō* writing and the history of the portrayal of women's bodies in Japanese literature also brings to mind intriguing comparisons with ancient Japanese myth. Recalling how Yosano Akiko and Hiratsuka Raichō, writing in the inaugural issue of *Seitō*, associate women's liberation with a remarkable, almost mystical power enjoyed by ancient Japanese women, we see that Nogami's story might elicit a similar reading, even though she refers to Western rather than Japanese myth.

Take, for example, Kaneko's characterization of herself as being reduced to the level of a wild beast yelping with pain. Although Japanese folk literature includes many instances of women being transformed into jealous demons or devious foxes, this scene is most reminiscent of one of the oldest tales in Japan, that of the Sea Princess from the *Kojiki* (Records of Ancient Matters, 712 CE). Having fallen in love with a man, the Sea Princess has ascended to Earth, and when the delivery of the couple's first child draws near, requests that her husband not look upon her while she gives birth. Unable to control his curiosity, the man does peek into the parturition hut, only to see his beautiful wife transformed into a writhing, thrashing, fearful dragon. So ashamed is the Sea Princess to have been seen by her husband in this form that she returns to the sea, and, as the story goes, from that time forward the sea and the land have been forever separate.[13] Though encoding such display of the female body as shameful, this ancient tale nevertheless conveys an image of pregnancy and childbirth that is magnificent and powerful—and one that reduces even a brave prince to fear and shock at the sight of it.

In contrast to the *Kojiki* myth, the birth in "New Life" takes place in a clinic where Kaneko's husband is kept well away from the scene and permitted to see his wife only after all the commotion is over. Giving birth has left Kaneko tired and anxious. Her husband coaxes her to relax, trying to relieve her anxiety by talking happily about the vitality of "the Life Force." And even though Nogami herself later claimed that she had not married for love, this autobiographical story presents a husband and wife who certainly are on good terms and care for each other. In the vocabulary of Japanese marriages of the 1910s, the man's affectionate words to his wife present him as a New Man, one concerned about his partner and able to communicate with her on an equal plane. Although Nogami keeps the conversation between husband and wife light and mundane, she crafts their relationship as a loving friendship, a modern marriage.

In a prose poem that Nogami published in the next month's *Seitō*, she presents a sweet and humorous portrait of family life with her children.[14] A child pesters his father with questions about nature, such as why peach trees produce red flowers. The father tells him to ask his mother, who in turn tells him to ask Iiya (perhaps a servant), who suggests that he ask the baby. The boy objects, saying that the baby doesn't say anything and just laughs no matter what he's asked. Iiya responds that the baby knows the answers, all right, and that's why he's laughing. Here Nogami writes in a much different tone than in "New Life," though she keeps a sense of mystery about life all the same.

****

New Life
Nogami Yaeko
Seitō 4.4 (April 1914)

Kaneko was still half asleep, and so drowsy. She had the strangest sense of being in pain but didn't have the faintest idea where the pain was coming from. Sometimes this sensation became so acute that Kaneko felt as if she were going to start crying out loud. But when she tried to think about where or how badly she hurt, drowsiness overcame her, confusing everything.

At that point Kaneko would drift back into a shallow, fitful sleep, imagining herself drenched in sweat, as though making the most agonizing climb up some steep, steep slope. Yet as her sleepiness gradually abated, Kaneko sensed that the pain was in her abdomen. The realization startled her awake, and she became fully conscious. And in that instant she suddenly realized that the moment she'd long been expecting had likely arrived. "I wonder if this means the baby is finally coming."

"You live so close by that there will still be plenty of time if you come after you start showing signs of labor. Just don't panic, all right? Call for a rickshaw and take your time coming here." Kaneko remembered these words of advice, with which the friendly woman doctor at the clinic had reassured her so often. Wearily Kaneko raised her heavy body and sat up under the mosquito net. Before worrying about calling anyone, she felt like testing her body on her own. She wondered what time it was, but felt that it was too much bother to go look at the clock in the next room. The pain subsided for a bit, but came back in an ever so subtle way.

Suddenly feeling an attack of diarrhea coming on, Kaneko got up and went to the toilet. Afterward, she felt pleasantly relieved. It was as if every bit of the pain had evacuated her body in one enormous bowel movement.

"So maybe it was only a stomach ache after all," mused Kaneko, recalling how many roasted chestnuts she'd consumed before going to sleep. Since the festival celebrating the local Shinto deities had taken place the night before, Kaneko had let their maid Shige go to see the old comedies that were performed as part of the festivities. She had also asked her to buy a bag of roasted chestnuts on the way home. The fragrance of the nuts had so tantalized Kaneko that she had not been able to stop eating one chestnut after another.

"What if I had fled to the clinic in the middle of the night and it had turned out that my only problem was that I had eaten too many chestnuts? I would have looked utterly ridiculous!" Giggling to herself, Kaneko made her way back to her room at the other end of the pitch-black corridor.

But soon the pain returned. After the first wave of pain, another came racing behind it. Anxious and bewildered, Kaneko concentrated on the pain in her abdomen, trying to ascertain whether it was only a simple stomach ache or the first pangs of labor. Since Kaneko was already the mother of one boy and had experienced a painful labor with him fours years ago, one would naturally expect her to know the difference now between a mere stomach ache and labor. Nevertheless, Kaneko couldn't be at all certain which kind of pain she was feeling. Just then the wall clock in the next room struck one o'clock in the morning. The sound stirred Kaneko into action. She went to rouse her husband, who was sleeping in the study. As he went to wake up their maid, Kaneko lit the gaslights in the sitting room and in the parlor.

"Shige! Shige, please get up." The sound of Kaneko's husband's loud voice at the door of her tiny room startled Shige, who immediately got up. She tied an obi over the white cotton kimono she slept in. "The mistress is going to the clinic. I'm sorry to have to trouble you, but would you go to Yoshikame to call for rickshaws? Since you'll be going with her, we'll need two carriages. She's feeling a little queasy, so please tell them to hurry. You're not afraid, are you? If you are, you can go wake up old grandpa in the back and ask him to do this."

"No, I'm fine, sir."

"Light a lantern to take with you."

"Yes, sir." Carrying an old round lantern that she had taken out from a closet in the back, Shige rushed out into the darkness at the front of the house.

The stinky, waxy smell of the lantern being lit struck Kaneko as strangely repulsive. She went back to the parlor and was about to change her clothes when she realized that all her kimono had picked up the same nauseating odor of burning wax. "Ugh! I must be overly sensitive." Kaneko took some perfume from her dressing table and doused her kimono with it.

"Put on plenty of layers. It will be cold in the carriage."

"I'll wear a coat."

Her husband had dragged the rattan chair from the corridor half onto the tatami and was sitting there in his nightclothes. "Why don't I go over tomorrow about noon and see how you are doing?"

"Fine."

"Mommy!" Tomo-o, who had been left alone in bed under the mosquito net, had awakened and was now calling for his mother.

"Why don't you wake up and come over here, dear?"

As the child lifted up the net and started to come out, he asked, "Is it still nighttime?" He looked around at the bright lights in all the rooms as if this bothered his eyes.

"Yes, it's still night," said Kaneko. Gently taking his hand, Kaneko explained that she wasn't feeling very well and would have to go to the clinic. She asked him to be good and look after the house while she was gone.

"I will," agreed the child.

"You're here with Father, so you're going to be just fine, right?" Her husband lifted the boy to his lap. Kaneko became terribly anxious, afraid of how her son might react. She knew that the boy was used to her routinely leaving the house during the day, but she worried about his putting up a fuss now. Contrary to her fears, the boy did not express the slightest concern about being left behind. Ironically, it was this unexpected nonchalance that caused his mother to feel wistful.

Suddenly the bell at the front door rang. Shige had returned with the rickshaws. Perhaps fearing that someone had taken seriously ill in the middle of the night, the owner of the rickshaw business himself had gotten everything together and come over with one of his men. His demeanor respectful, he made the proper courtesies.

"Good evening. We heard that your wife was not feeling well. You must be terribly concerned."

"Why, no, I . . ." Kaneko's husband was temporarily stunned by the men's misunderstanding of the situation. Unable to say anything else, he stood silently in the entryway.

Kaneko, whom the rickshaw men had assumed was desperately ill, came out the front door in great haste, slipping on her overcoat. The rickshaw owner, his face registering surprise at the speed with which this supposedly sick woman moved, hurried over to his rickshaw, which stood at the front gate. With the help of the other driver, Shige piled quilts and baggage into the second rickshaw and then climbed in herself, wedging herself next to them.

"Well, please pull the rickshaw gently," said her husband, cautioning the men as he remained standing at the entrance to the house. Kaneko peered through the curtains of the rickshaw to catch a glimpse of the child seeing her off, too, standing to the right of his father. The sight of that little hand waving as the boy yelled, "Good bye," stayed with Kaneko for some time.

Kaneko had been very agitated, concerned over whether or not everything at home was taken care of, yet as the rickshaw wound through the streets in the dead silence of night, she gradually calmed down. Once she had fully collected herself, Kaneko was able to see that the specific intervals at which the waves of pain were hitting her could only mean that she had gone into labor. This led Kaneko to think back to the long, hot days of summer and the clumsiness of her slow, heavy body. More than once she had lost her balance. Kaneko remembered feeling then as though she couldn't wait for the day when these labor pains would come. How she had hoped for an easy birth that would take away all that suffocating heaviness! Yet her first experience with childbirth had been a fairly difficult one, and one that had left Kaneko with a great and fearful aversion to the pains of childbirth.

"What an enviable person the Buddha's mother Maya was! She was the only one ever blessed in childbirth. Even Pandora or Eve could not achieve that." This was the refrain that played in Kaneko's mind every time she thought of childbirth, for the topic never failed to remind her of the legend of Maya. As the tale went, it was in the middle of spring when Maya went strolling through the lush garden known as Lumbini Grove, where tropical flowers and trees and exotic birds brought forth every imaginable color, song, and fragrance. Maya stopped beneath a tree with big scarlet flowers that shaded her like an umbrella. When she reached out with her left hand to break off a branch of these flowers, the little Prince Siddhartha was born from her armpit.

"I won't covet the glory of being the mother of the Buddha! The only thing I envy about that woman is that she had such an easy time of it in childbirth." Thinking over and over about this legend had made Kaneko start grumbling to herself like this. Not only did Maya's easy childbirth irritate her, but to make matters worse, she found herself nagged by what she knew to be a bizarre and superstitious fear about this fetus in particular. Unfounded though this fear was, it had the effect of intensifying Kaneko's trepidations about labor, which in turn kept her in a state of almost continual anxiety. But an explanation did lie behind all this.

Since late last fall, Kaneko had been reading and translating from a large book of Western mythology. In these myths every facet of the universe, from the very depths of hell to the highest reaches of the heavens, was transformed into a human personality. Powerfully creative, the ancients had wrought a human personality for everything—for Absolute Beauty, Strength, and Light, and for Fear, Darkness, and Ugliness as well. As Kaneko had immersed herself day after day in this world, the myths had made an indelible impression on her. And how could she not be strongly affected by these tales, with their way of turning one extreme after another into a symbol? Beauty, Pathos, and Bravery, on the one hand; Tragedy, Horror, and the Macabre, on the other. What an extraordinary power these tales possessed!

The myths had had an even stranger effect on Kaneko than they normally might have because of the changes taking place just then in her body. Indeed, what most threatened to unsteady her already frail nerves were the supernatural transformations that appeared in these tales. Medusa, whose black hair was changed into snakes by the rage of Minerva, the flame-breathing Chimera. The Harpies, with female faces and birds' bodies. The poisonous snake Hydra. Monsters like Argus, which had a hundred eyes all over its body. All these monsters invariably haunted Kaneko's imagination. What's more, the books about painting and sculpture that Kaneko had gathered about her desk at the time were filled with photographs of ancient art that naturally featured plenty of such monsters, too. At times these images all conspired to make Kaneko feel the oddest sense of confusion, as if even her own body were being enveloped by a whole host of these ghostly figures. And whenever she happened to think of all the references to snakes in those myths, Kaneko could truly feel goose bumps rise on her skin.

"Could it be normal to have these kinds of feelings? I wonder if I won't have a deformed baby?" There were times when Kaneko would be startled awake in the middle of the night by a strong fetal movement. Once again she would find herself convulsed with worry about producing a deformed child, until she ended up beside herself with fright. "I must not think like this. It simply will not do! I've got to drive away these kinds of wild ideas."

Then Kaneko would make an effort to think only of the beautiful gods and goddesses. This didn't work any better, though, because she became taken with the tale of the twins Apollo and Diana, and thought also of the twins Castor and Pollux, who had been born to the gods Leda and Jupiter after Jupiter had come to Leda in the form of a white swan. There had even been a time when Kaneko, with an intensity that verged on hysteria, had pleaded with her woman doctor, "Doctor, if I am going to have twins, please, please tell me ahead of time. It wouldn't surprise me at all!"

Yet now that her labor pains had at last begun, Kaneko felt an unusual sense of calm and none of her past anxiety. It was as if all the fears and feelings of apprehension that had assailed her had become a dreamlike, fleeting shadow. But it still did not seem real to her that a new life was emerging from all this pain. A new life, just like that born in the stable in Jerusalem, was on its way. Yet one more life would soon join this world. Her child. This tiny human being known as her child would be born from her own flesh and blood. Strange that none of this had any resonance for her whatsoever. Rather, Kaneko felt as if the whole thing were an incredible lie. This sense of unreality made even the act of going to the hospital in a rickshaw in the middle of the night seem like nothing more than going in for an ordinary exam for some minor illness. In a dazed, disoriented state, Kaneko, who had not been out of the house for a long time, gazed in wonder at the condition of the road, which had recently been widened. Amidst the unfamiliar scene of the homes all neatly in a row and the sight of the lonely, sleeping town, Kaneko had the sensation of going on a trip, as if she were running off to a faraway railway station by setting out at night in a rickshaw. Kaneko noticed that she could also hear the sound of crickets somewhere.

Those working at the clinic had all been startled by the shrill sound of an electric bell coming from the front gate. Suddenly, the late-night activity began. Four or five nurses, all having changed into their white uniforms but looking as if they were just barely awake, began rushing about, getting Kaneko and her things into the clinic. The woman doctor had also awakened immediately and had come out to meet her, too. Her husband, the head doctor of the clinic, had changed into his surgical uniform and was present as well. Surrounded by all these people from the clinic, Kaneko could not imagine feeling any safer or more secure than this. Even the voice of the woman doctor, which usually sounded so jovial, had a high-pitched, urgent quality to it as she ordered various preparations. Her voice struck Kaneko as both authoritative and reliable.

"Now, please come this way," said the woman doctor, adopting a purposeful, masculine gait as she led Kaneko toward the operating room. Grimacing in pain, Kaneko followed her. As she approached the door that opened into a brightly lit room, she smelled the faint odor of Lysol.

"Are you in pain?" asked the woman doctor.

"Yes," said Kaneko, producing a smile through her still pained expression.

"You're not going to have the baby yet. In fact, there's still a fair amount of time. Relax and try to get some rest." Despite the woman doctor's advice, the pain had progressed too far to allow Kaneko any sleep. Walking down the corridor from the operating room to her own room in the clinic, Kaneko had stopped short, recoiling in pain two or three times. Even when she was lying down on the white hospital bed, she could not make herself comfortable but clenched her teeth. One nurse, who came in to tidy things up, drew near Kaneko's side and asked in a very polite way, "Is the pain very severe, Ma'am?" The nurse started to give her a massage, but soon Kaneko could sense that the hands rubbing her lower back had gone limp and had stopped moving. It seemed that the nurse was starting to fall asleep.

"Press a little harder!" said Kaneko, becoming more exasperated every time she had to tell the nurse to do this. The pain was so intense that she felt she could not stand another second of it. At the same time, Kaneko could feel what seemed to be a mass of frenzied strength thrashing about inside her, as if it were crying, "Let me out! Let me out!" There were moments when it pressed against her throat with all the energy of a ball of fire, making Kaneko feel that it was difficult to breathe, as if that frenzied mass were actually going to suffocate her. Dripping with sweat, Kaneko cried out in pain, howling like some great beast.

Before she knew it, there were two nurses pressing down against her, trying to restrain her as she writhed in pain.

"What time is it?" asked Kaneko, her eyes still shut tightly against the pain.

"It's five o'clock. It's already dawn," echoed the voice of a new nurse. In less time than it had taken for this brief exchange, fresh waves of pain attacked Kaneko one after another. At that point the shoji screen opened:

"How are you doing? You seem to be in quite a lot of pain," said the head doctor as he entered her room. Two or three nurses followed him in, and Kaneko caught a whiff of the strong smell of Lysol again. The high-pitched voice of the woman doctor ordering something, perhaps hot water, came closer and closer to Kaneko's room. Even though she was right in the middle of all these people, Kaneko could no longer keep up her guard or endure this distress, but screamed in pain, moaning and crying.

The pain came in great, violent spasms, each attack swift and sharp, like a rod being whipped smartly through the air. Kaneko was startled to discover that the few seconds between each spasm afforded her complete respite from even the slightest pain. The difference was dramatic, just as if water brought to a rolling boil had instantly turned to ice water. Kaneko felt dazed by all the pain and confusion, yet each time the respite came, her mind immediately regained clarity.

"Who does this person remind me of? Who does she look like?" Perplexed and intent, Kaneko scrutinized the face of the nurse, all the while clinging to her with both hands. Then, another attack of pain.

"It hurts! It hurts! It hurts!" Kaneko cried, as if she were going to faint at any moment. "Ann said that she would bear a genius. But who cares if one is having a genius or any other kind of remarkable child? Nothing can be worth this much pain!" Somehow Kaneko still had the presence of mind to come up with all kinds of odd ideas. In other moments, she would see the rectangular portrait of Shaw, the one with laughing eyes, before her.[15] How utterly strange, thought Kaneko, that thoughts like these should come to her in the middle of such distress.

"It hurts. It hurts. It hurts." Kaneko yelled at the top of her lungs. "This is labor pain for sure. Oh, how dreadful I must look lying here like this! How disgracefully I am behaving." Such feelings, too, swept through Kaneko's mind.

"It hurts, hurts, hurts. Doctor, please do something."

"It's coming soon, so bear up, please," said the woman doctor soothingly.

"You mustn't breathe too heavily. Please try to calm down."

Kaneko was aware of the voices of the woman doctor and the head doctor. They spoke one after the other.

"Oh, the band of musical sandwich-board men is passing by." Kaneko was in agony, crying and thrashing about, and yet in the moment she noticed the band's passing, she experienced an instant of complete relief, as if cut off from her torment. Then the pain started in again.

"It hurts! It hurts! Oh, how it hurts!" Even while Kaneko yelped at this fresh attack of labor pain, she could sense the lower half of her body being soaked with warm water. She also became keenly aware of the nurses hurrying in and out of her room. And then, all of a sudden, it happened. In one of the brief intervals that came between the alternating hells of excruciating pain and dull respite, the frenzied, powerful spirit at last tore free of its confinement in her body.

Kaneko let out a deep breath, and immediately after this she concentrated on greedily lapping up the cold, delicious medicine from the spout cup the nurse held up for her. Yet even while she was drinking, Kaneko began to think that something was wrong. The infant was not crying.

"There's no crying, is there? Why don't I hear any crying?" demanded Kaneko. Her voice rang out, clear and insistent.

No reply came from anyone in the room. Rustling sounds indicated that something was going on at the foot of Kaneko's bed, but none of the activity was visible to her. After some time the infant finally started to cry, but in a rather feeble little voice. Gradually this voice grew louder and louder, until it turned into one very impressive and spirited wail.

"It's a boy." This was the first time that the woman doctor had spoken since the birth.

"It's a very big boy. No wonder your wife had to make all that effort." When Kaneko heard someone out in the hallway exchanging pleasantries with the doctor, she knew that her husband had come.

"How was it?" asked her husband, entering the room where his wife had just given birth. "Was it painful?"

"Oh, yes, that it was." Looking up at her husband, Kaneko managed this rather energetic reply. The birth had been terribly, terribly painful, yet when she tried to sort through her recollections to explain this, Kaneko realized that all she had left were the dazed feelings of having awakened from a bad dream. No matter what part of her flesh she searched or what muscle she questioned, none seemed to have any memory of the anguish that only a short while ago had truly made her think that she was about to die. Her entire body, from head to toe, felt nothing but dog tired. But like some happy imbecile stuffed from overeating, Kaneko felt herself submerged in an agreeable fatigue.

How could she have so completely forgotten it all? The inexplicability of this left Kaneko dumbfounded. When she told her husband this, he said, "That's just the way it is. If you'd always had to endure the memory of that kind of pain, you'd never want to have another child."

His comment made Kaneko wonder if she had ever truly intended to bear another child. When she looked back in time, there had never been any point, any instant at all, when she had consciously thought about having another child. Kaneko described to her husband how she tried to make sense of this.

"But it's the *Life Force* making you give birth! There is nothing you can do about it. In that sense, all babies are Children of the Gods." Her husband laughed as he said this.

"'Children of the Gods' sounds pretty good, doesn't it?" Kaneko laughed, too. Talking and laughing like this, Kaneko realized that she had not the slightest sense of herself as one who had just accomplished a major feat. After everything was said and done, she had begun to separate herself from the birth process, in much the same way that she had felt apart from the events in all those books in her library, or from a rumor about another person. Just then the baby, who had been taken into the room in front to be bathed, was brought back, all wrapped up in a colorful *yūzen* baby robe.

"This is quite some baby. He weighs nearly eight and a third pounds." The nurse held the baby so as to give his father and mother a first look at their new child. His round face was beet red beneath a tuft of jet-black hair. Then the nurse explained to them why the baby had not cried when he was first born. Apparently the umbilical cord had been wrapped about his neck, threatening to asphyxiate him.

From birth to death and back again. This tiny, new being, who had turned about in the space of a few minutes, seemed both miraculous and pitiable.

"Thinking of everything that happened scares me somehow." Kaneko said this as though absorbed in her thoughts.

"Well, I guess it's time for me to be heading home," said her husband, putting his overcoat back on. "You need to stop ruminating and just be a dunce for awhile, so you can get some sleep."

"I know."

"Oh, I forgot this," said the husband, untying the cloth wrapper at his side as if he had just remembered what was in it.

"What is that?"

"It's the present for the boy."

"Oh, of course, " thought Kaneko. Out of the cloth wrapper came some Western-style candy, a set of colored pencils, and some notepaper that had been packed into a makeup box. Her husband explained that if everything continued to go well, he would have the maid bring their older son to the hospital that evening. He suggested that Kaneko give the boy his present at that time. Then he left for home.

The present was supposed to be given to their son as a gift from his new baby brother. Tomo-o had been told that sometime soon he might have a new little friend, a baby who would come down from the heavens. His parents had promised that when the baby arrived, it would surely bring Tomo-o candy, colored pencils, and notepaper as presents.

"What will the baby ride to get here from heaven?" Tomo-o became obsessed with this question. He tried listing all the winged things he knew: cranes, peacocks, geese, pigeons, sparrows. Tomo-o felt certain that the baby would ride in on some kind of bird.

When asked if he thought the baby would take an airplane, Tomo-o looked horrified. "No!" he protested, "An airplane is for me to ride!"

This evening, her son would at last see this new little human being. If he were to ask how the baby had arrived, or where it came from, Kaneko would have to answer that, just as they had told him all along, the baby had flown from heaven upon a crane. She certainly did not mean to lie to the boy or intentionally deceive him, but for the time being this seemed like the most appropriate answer. In truth, even Kaneko herself had absolutely no idea where new life came from.

"We know not from whence we come or whence we go." A line from the Bible, the dialogue between Wendla and her mother in *Spring's Awakening*.[16] One after another such thoughts rambled through Kaneko's mind, but only for a very short time. Soon she dozed off to sleep.

Notes

[1]For more in English on Nogami Yaeko's life, writing, and synopses of some of her major works, see entries about her in Donald Keene, *Dawn to the West: Japanese Literature of the Modern Era* (New York: Holt, Rinehart, Winston, 1984), 1115–24; Michiko Aoki, "Nogami Yaeko," in Chieko I. Mulhern, ed., *Japanese Women Writers: A Bio-Critical Sourcebook* (Westport, CT: Greenwood Press, 1994), 247–83; Sachiko Schierbeck, *Japanese Women Novelists in the 20th Century: 104 Biographies, 1900–1993* (Copenhagen: University of Copenhagen, Museum Tusculanum Press, 1994), 29–33; and Yukiko Tanaka, ed., *To Live and To Write: Selections by Japanese Women Writers 1913–1938* (Seattle: The Seal Press, 1987), 145–58. Although "New Life" originally appeared in *Seitō*, Nogami later published the story in a separate volume, also entitled *New Life* (Atarashiki inochi), (Iwanami Shoten, 1916), which included other stories she had written from the point of view of being a mother of small children; Schierbeck, *Japanese Women Novelists*, 30.

[2]Michiko Aoki writes that Nogami's diaries reveal the extent of her husband's professional and sexual jealousy, as well as how Nogami's strong feelings for the author Naka Kansuke (1885–1965) provoked her husband's insecurity. Aoki, "Nogami Yaeko," 275.

[3]Tanaka, ed., *To Live and To Write*, 148.

[4]Eleanor Joan Hogan considers, for example, Nogami's story "Meian" (Light and Dark), written in 1906, which was criticized by Sōseki and hence not published until 1988, in which the main character, Sachiko, turns down marriage proposals to pursue art. Similarly, Machiko, the lead character in *Machiko* (1928–30), objects to the idea that a woman must marry at all costs. These anti-marriage sentiments are diluted, however, in that Sachiko appears to think she made the wrong decision because her art is poor and Machiko seems to look forward to marriage at the novel's conclusion. Interestingly, the fact that Machiko's father had died allows her a certain freedom in her choice of mate. Hogan, "When Art Does *Not* Represent Life: Nogami Yaeko and the Marriage Question," *Women's Studies: An Interdisciplinary Journal* 33.4 (January 2004): 381–98.

[5]Nogami Yaeko, "Atarashiki inochi" (New Life), *Seitō* 4.4 (April 1914): 9–27. Nogami published twelve installments of her partial translation of *Sonya Kovalevsky: Her Recollections of Childhood* (New York: The Century Company, 1895) in twelve issues of *Seitō*, from November 1913 through February 1915. According to Donald Keene, *Dawn to the West*, 1115–17, Nogami published a full translation in 1924, and saw the translation reissued in 1933 and again in 1978. In light of the translation's initial appearance in *Seitō*, it is interesting to read the book's account of how Sonya's older sister, Aniuta, became a kind of Russian bluestocking, a trend among young upper-class Russian women in the 1860s and 1870s who yearned for the intellectual life of St. Petersburg while their parents wished to keep them home in the country waiting for marriage. Like many young women of her class, Sonya's sister took to wearing simple, almost severe dress, devoted herself to writing, and read romantic fiction. Aniuta also struck up a friendship with Dostoevsky but ultimately rejected his proposal of marriage. Sonya herself received a doctorate in mathematics in Germany at the University of Goettingen and then became the first woman appointed as professor at the University of Stockholm. To her great joy, she was later admitted to the French Academy of Science and respected as an outstanding mathematician. A woman of many parts, Kovalevsky enjoyed writing fiction, engaging in sports, and the conversations of literary salons, but she was unlucky in love. Her marriage failed after her husband squandered the family fortune on various business ventures. Love was also the subject of another work that Nogami translated partially for *Seitō* in 1912 and 1913, namely, the 1836 autobiographical work of Alfred de Musset (1810–57), *La Confession d'un Enfant du Siècle*, in which he discusses his volatile affair with writer George Sand (1804–76). This steamy tale of a wealthy young man's obsession with an older femme fatale is no doubt the kind of decadent writing that made parents want to keep their daughters away from European fiction and *Seitō*.

[6]Ellen Key (1849–1926), the Swedish advocate of the rights of mothers and spiritual role model to Bluestockings Hiratsuka Raichō and Yamada Waka, was a friend of both Sonya Kovalevsky and Anna Leffler. Ellen Key wrote a biography of Leffler and her part in the women's suffrage movement; see Sonya Kovalevsky, *Sonya Kovalevsky: Her Recollections of Childhood*, translated from the Russian by Isabel F. Hapgood, with a biography by Anna Carlotta Leffler, Duchess of Cajanello (New York: The Century Company, 1895), 297.

[7]Iwata Nanatsu, *Bungaku toshite no "Seitō"* (Fuji Shuppan, 2003), 216.

[8]Nogami wrote: "I am once more intrigued by the rather similar features shared by the movement for liberation, which was directed toward a brighter future and gaining knowledge—the whirlwind that swept the Russian intelligentsia of 1860–70 and marked a turning point in the youth of this pioneering woman—and the movement among the new women of Japan, centered at the time around *Bluestocking*, the magazine in which I first published parts of her autobiography"; Keene, *Dawn to the West*, 1116. Keene writes that Nogami wrote separate introductions for each of the three editions of the full translation of Kovalevsky's autobiography, and that her appreciation of Kovalevsky's life and work changed over time. Nogami was struck first and foremost by Kovalevsky's ambition "to achieve recognition in a world dominated by men" and by her desire for romantic love; second, by her Marxist politics; and third, by her and Leffler's ability to capture the flavor of their place and times, a talent that resonated with her own increasing interest in "the importance of the past"; ibid., 1117.

⁹The term I translate here as "woman doctor" is written originally with the character for "woman" (*jo*) and "doctor" (*i*). The other doctor in the story, the man, is referred to in katakana, the Japanese syllabary often used for foreign words, as a *dokutoru*. Both serve as a comment on the state of Japanese medicine in the 1910s: the Japanese man practices a kind of medicine seen as Western, while the woman takes on a professional, modern role still unusual for women.

¹⁰Vera Mackie observes that describing childbirth as a physically and emotionally demanding ordeal, and one that pitted mother against infant, was a theme also taken up by other women associated with *Seitō*. Fukuda Hideko's record of childbirth in her 1904 autobiography, for example, is heroic, making reference to Chinese mythical Emperor Yu and describing dreams of "conflict with supernatural creatures—wolves and dragons—with Fukuda the heroic protagonist who banishes the creatures." Yosano Akiko, who experienced eleven pregnancies, wrote of how absurd it was for men to talk about women "as being physically weak." Hiratsuka Raichō admitted that, in the intense pain of labor, she asked the doctor to stop her suffering "no matter what happened to the baby." Iwano Kiyoko also writes with hostility of the child growing within her. Vera Mackie, *Feminism in Modern Japan: Citizenship, Embodiment and Sexuality* (Cambridge: Cambridge University Press, 2003), 52–54.

¹¹In her 1984 anthropological study of Japanese women, Takie Lebra reports that, though not all women subscribed to the merits of soberly enduring labor pains, "stoicism exhibited at the time of parturition was traditionally regarded as the ultimate test of female discipline." Lebra, *Japanese Women: Constraint and Fulfillment* (Honolulu: University of Hawai'i Press, 1984), 169. Jane Condon gives a similar account: "Few women use any anesthetic during childbirth, and most have such self-control that they do not cry out. When I screamed during my natural childbirth in a Tokyo hospital, I was told politely but firmly, 'Please be quiet.'" Condon, *A Half Step Behind: Japanese Women of Today* (Rutland, VT, and Tokyo: Charles E. Tuttle, Co., 1985), 14.

¹²The overall positive tone of Nogami's story certainly differs from that of the two modern literary sources to which she refers. Wendla is a character in the 1891 German expressionist play *Frühlings Erwachen* (Spring's Awakening) by Frank Wedekind (1864–1918). Wendla begs her mother to tell her the truth about pregnancy and childbirth, and to stop telling her that a stork brings babies, with presents for a baby's sibling. Because Wendla's mother tells her teenaged daughter only that she will become pregnant once she loves and marries, Wendla is surprised to learn that she is pregnant after having sexual intercourse, since she is not married. Her mother brings in a local doctor who arranges to give Wendla an abortifacient. Tragically, the treatment kills Wendla. Frank Wedekind, *Spring's Awakening: Tragedy of Childhood*, translated by Eric Bentley (New York and London: Applause, 1995). "Ann" is most likely a reference to the character Ann Whitefield in the 1903 play *Man and Superman* by George Bernard Shaw (1856–1950). Given the light-hearted reference in Nogami's story to a life force that pushes the protagonist to give birth, it is interesting that Shaw depicts Ann as both a femme fatale and the embodiment of the "life force." In *Man and Superman*, this is a force that ensnares men before they realize what is happening and compels them to play their part in reproduction. The playwright's notes describe Ann as "one of the vital geniuses" who inspires "some fear, perhaps, as a woman who will probably do everything she means to do without taking more account of other people than may be necessary and what she calls right." George

Bernard Shaw, *Man and Superman* (London: Penguin Classics, 2000), 54. There is no mention of Ann Whitefield wanting to give birth to a genius, however. My thanks to John Mertz for suggesting *Man and Superman* as the referent.

[13]"The Heavenly Grandchild and the Sea-God's Daughter," in Ryusaku Tsunoda, Wm. Theodore de Bary, and Donald Keene, comps., *Sources of Japanese Tradition* (New York: Columbia University Press, 1958), 1: 19–20.

[14]Nogami Yaeko, "Nee, Aka-sama" (Isn't that so, Baby Dear?), *Seitō* 4.5 (May 1914): 2–4.

[15]This is most likely a reference to a portrait of George Bernard Shaw, but it might also refer to a portrait painted by the Pre-Raphaelite painter John Byam Shaw (1872–1919). Thanks to Rebecca Copeland and John Mertz for these suggestions.

[16]"Jesus answered and said unto them, 'Though I bear record of myself, [yet] my record is true: for I know whence I came, and whither I go; but ye cannot tell whence I come, and whither I go.'" John 8:14, King James Version.

Chapter 10
Ogasawara Sada (1887–1988)

Her eyes riveted on one spot of her huge stomach, the woman felt uncon-
trollably jealous of the power of the new life within her, which grew and
grew without a second's pause.

The audacity of the Bluestockings' initial pledge to "give birth to the female
genius of tomorrow" reminds us of the ambition, the youthful dreams of
fame and fortune, that inspired *Seitō*. Read against this narrative of hope,
Ogasawara Sada's 1913 short story "Higashi kaze" (Eastern Breeze), a tale of
ambitions dashed by pregnancy, presents a bleak picture indeed.[1] In telling
the tale of a young couple's anxiety at impending parenthood, Ogasawara
creates an overwhelming sense of confinement by describing the couple's
dismal living quarters. She imagines them living in a room as dingy and
airless as a prison cell, a room where scratches covering the walls bear an
uncanny resemblance to claw marks, and suggest a trapped beast trying to
break free. Where once these same walls might have called to mind a kind of
reckless bohemian adventure, and the space itself might have been infused
with the electricity of sexual attraction, all that remain now are disappointment, anger, and poverty.

Ogasawara underscores the extent of her characters' feelings of confinement by allowing the reader to see into each character's unspoken anxieties,
in effect letting us into the space from which the characters cannot escape.
Nameless, the characters become the sum of their frustrations. The woman
might be an educated, middle-class New Woman, especially if we read the
story autobiographically. But she could also be a woman from a much less
privileged background, even a former geisha or maidservant. Ogasawara
does indicate that the man has not always been poor, and had been raised
and educated to expect a much higher status in society. It is his impetu-
ousness, and perhaps the woman's as well—combined with their romantic
desire to abandon propriety—that have brought them face to face with a
harsh reality. Outside, the air is fresh with the promise of spring. Budding
blossoms call to mind the imminent birth of the couple's child. The young
woman identifies with the blossoms, too, clinging to a future full of possibility, while the man sees his youth passing him by as surely as the clouds

traverse the sky. As he says, it is the child who will enjoy the full measure of new beginnings, not the parents. Consequently, the cool breeze outside and other intimations of spring only intensify the stifling quality of the couple's confinement in the dark room, in their no longer passionate relationship, and in their responsibility for a new child.

Ogasawara's attention to the woman's pregnant body and her taut emotions communicates the sense that she is doubly confined. Much like Nogami Yaeko's descriptions of the expectant mother in "New Life" (translated in Chapter 9), Ogasawara's view of pregnancy is anything but romantic. References to the woman's awareness of the man's body and the "feminine plumpness of his skin" develop her as a sensual person. Well into her pregnancy, she retains her sensuality and strong emotion but finds that she is unable to control the physical and mental pain provoked by the changes in her body. Her body and her passions, once the source of her liberated sexuality, have rendered this woman a caged and unhappy beast.

Intriguingly, there is one passage in the narrative where it is impossible to tell in the original Japanese if a certain impulse belongs to the woman or to the man. This is where one of them imagines stabbing the fetus through the woman's body. Positioned between the thoughts of the woman and the thoughts of the man, the passage could represent either a continuation of her frustration or a transition into his. Given the flexibility of subject references in Japanese and Ogasawara's habit of shifting the point of view in her stories, we might wonder how much to make of this. Did the author intend two possible readings, or was the subject so clear to her that she felt no need to make it any plainer for her reader? My translation mirrors the ambiguity I see here. Read in either voice, the image shows deep frustration and a sense of being trapped.

Ogasawara Sada herself was about three months pregnant in April 1913, when this story appeared. She had become pregnant shortly before or after her marriage early that year to Okumura Toyomasa, a friend of her elder brother and the lifelong employee of an insurance company. Unfortunately, the child, a daughter who was born in November 1913, died in 1920, and her second daughter, born in 1921, died in 1926. Ogasawara did have one other child, a son born in 1925, who survived and whom she raised to become an artist. Ogasawara Sada lived longer than any other Bluestocking, celebrating her hundredth birthday in 1987, about six months before her death in June 1988.

"Higashi kaze" (Eastern Breeze) apparently foretold the end of Ogasawara's own brief writing career. The story was the last of her five contributions to Seitō, although she did publish one further story in Shōjo (Girl), a magazine for girls, and served as fiction editor for Seitō in 1913. Ogasawara's stories stand out among others in *Seitō* for the way the point of view shifts among her characters and for her use of color and nature, described in detail, as metaphors for a character's feelings. Two of Ogasawara's stories, "Aru yoru" (One Evening) and "Doromizu" (Muddy Water), are especially interesting for their portraits of the emotionally turbulent lives of young girls' school graduates.[2] Neither Osumi of "Doromizu" nor the "young maiden" of "Aru yoru" wishes to become like her staid mother; both of them long for involvement in a passionate love relationship and creative work. Yet they are at loose ends, unsure of which way to turn. Osumi—who, like her creator Ogasawara, has always enjoyed painting—wants to develop the self-assurance that she sees in a certain young male painter, and thus break free from following her art teacher's instruction to paint in a way that reveals her own vision. Yet when her mother Oichi imagines that one day Osumi will win fame as a painter, Osumi retorts that she is not pursuing art to win her mother glory. She also confesses her fear that her work is simply not very good. The "young maiden" in "Doromizu" envies her boyfriend's absorption in the study of plants he has amassed but feels that he sees her, who has no mission in life, as little more than a curiosity to add to his collection. She, too, needs to find herself before she can enjoy either a mature romantic relationship or a happy relationship with her mother.[3]

After her brief foray into writing and publishing, Ogasawara evidently lost ties with the artistic world. She moved from city to city with her husband, whose company continually transferred him to new locations all over Japan. It was only after his death in 1954, at the age of seventy-one, that Ogasawara Sada, then sixty-six, decided to return to her childhood love of painting. Her first one-woman show took place when she was eighty-four, and she continued to paint until she was ninety-five.

"Eastern Breeze" and the other *Seitō* stories mentioned above make one wonder what ambitions Ogasawara Sada harbored for herself when she came to Tokyo in 1904 as a young woman fresh out of a girls' school in Nagano Prefecture. For example, how were her own ambitions affected by the success her father had enjoyed, and by his death when she was only fifteen? By the time Sada was born in 1887, the family had moved to northeastern Japan, where her father was to preside as judge at the first court in Sendai City. Two years later he moved the family to Fukushima, opened his own legal practice, and became such a prominent leader in the area that he served many terms as a representative to the Lower House of the Diet. After his death in 1903, his wife found herself in financial straits that forced her to try one thing after another to make ends meet. At one point she and Sada operated a rather rundown rooming-house for college men from Waseda University. There Ogasawara must have met many young men who could have served as models for the male characters in "Eastern Breeze" and her other stories.

By the time she was a young woman, Ogasawara had been linked to an elite male world of power and politics through her father, and had also been forced, through her mother's widowhood, into economic insecurity. Despite this insecurity, Ogasawara was able to take advantage of the opportunities open in Tokyo to young women of an artistic bent and ambition: she briefly studied at an art academy for women and took to contributing stories to young women's magazines in 1910. She also worked at a bank in Tokyo before beginning to write for *Seitō* in 1912, at the age of twenty-four.

According to a biographical piece written by Hiratsuka Raichō Association member Inoue Mihoko, when Ogasawara was interviewed in 1978 for a program that aired on Japan's national radio station, she reported that she had vivid memories of her involvement with *Seitō*.[4] Though she had lost contact with other members of the group (indeed, Raichō even wrote in her 1971 autobiography that she thought Ogasawara had died young), Ogasawara Sada expressed pride in having been a part of the Bluestockings.

****

Eastern Breeze
Ogasawara Sada
Seitō 3.4 (April 1913)

The room felt dark and empty. Since the dormer windows faced north, only the palest light filtered in through the one tiny window among them that could actually be opened. The couple had spent half the day cooped up in this gloomy space.

Outside, it was a wonderfully pleasant day. A breeze coming from the east wafted by so softly that one could not hear it at all but only sense its moist warmth. Inside, a dim, murky light passed through the dormers, casting faint shadows over the room's brownish walls and sinking the whole room into a sallow yellowish haze.

Plopping one foot on the low windowsill, the man wearily stretched the full length of his slim body out on the floor. Turning on his side with his back to the woman, the man fixed his gaze on the wall in front of him, staring stone-still at its coldness. Once painted light brown, the wall now had scuff marks everywhere. The marks had been made over some period of time, without either the man or the woman noticing what was happening. Apparently, the corners of a piece of furniture had scraped here and there, scratching the wall and scarring it like so many claw marks. Sad and lonely impressions, he thought.

The old suit the man habitually wore to work was worn out, and so shiny around the shoulders and the lower back that the stripes in the material were no longer visible. His face, even in profile, looked pale and gaunt, and bore an expression of total defeat. All the same, his ears had an aristocratic shape to them and a rosy color, and that, combined with the slenderness at the nape of his neck, gave him the appearance of one still quite youthful somehow.

The man kept staring at the images of claw marks scrawled wildly about the wall.

"What is love? What on earth is it?" The man asked himself the same question over and over. His job was so dull that it had long been parched dry of any fun whatsoever, yet day in and day out, he had been dutifully going to work. Finally, he had come to the point where he could no longer bear the idea of spending another warm, sunny spring day like this having to go out and perform such a lackluster job.

He felt the same way about his relationship with this woman. He no longer sensed any excitement toward her, either. Things had become even more difficult between them this spring, for as her body had changed, she had also become quite anxious. At times she had even become hysterical, and when that happened there was nothing at all he could do to calm her down.

At the time the two of them had begun living together, the man had not felt the slightest bit of regret about all that he had been forced to give up, even though he'd had to sever connections with every influential person he knew and break off with his many friends. The man had, in effect, shattered all his hopes for a prosperous future. His only thoughts had been about the woman's welfare, about how he could take care of her. So even though he'd had to give up his schooling and all his ambitions to devote himself to her, the man had not felt that this was a hardship in any way. Not only had he willingly made such sacrifices, he had also acquiesced to a job he could barely endure. All to take care of her.

But as the years had passed, and while the two of them were quite unaware of it, the gaudy colors painted over their love had peeled away of their own accord. Now the man felt nothing but misery as the lonely, desolate colors of their true relationship appeared plainly to him. It seemed as though he stood at a kind of impasse these days, unable to feel much of anything. Every day was the same as the last, for he could do nothing to overcome the bleak thoughts that gripped him so tightly. Even this morning, the two of them had begun arguing over some trivial matter until the man had been so late for work that he'd ended up not going at all.

A desk had been placed in one corner of the room, and a rather shabby chair set in front of it. The woman sat on this chair, slouching under the weight of her heavy body. Although she was trying to keep her anger in check, she glared in spite at the man's back. For over an hour now, he had stubbornly refused to speak to her.

The breeze from the east came through the tiny space of the one open window, blowing here and there about her face as if flirting with her. The sensation annoyed her to no end, and felt even nastier than when someone deliberately tickled her under the arms. Whenever the moist warmth of the breeze brushed ever so lightly against her cheeks, it made the woman's skin itch. It was as if the breeze were taunting her, driving her to want to scratch and tear at her face. A horrible fever bore down on her like a heavy, hot river of molten lava flowing from her head. It turned her lips a bright blood-red.

Nevertheless, the woman's hands, and her feet, too, had grown as cold as those of a corpse. From time to time a piercing chill emanating from her spine would send shivers throughout her body. These attacks made her so cold that whenever they struck every hair on her body stood on end. Her body was burning up inside with a strange kind of fever that returned swiftly in the wake of each chill. The woman knew that there was no mistaking this.

The woman stared at the reclining figure of the man. He was lying so still that one might wonder whether he had fallen into a deep sleep and would stay that way forever. Suddenly, and for no particular reason, the sight of the soiled suit covering his limp body infuriated her. She had the urge to spring at the man and slap him awake.

But in the end, the woman confined herself to a steely glare. Strangely, as she fixed on that stained and dirty old suit, a powerfully vivid picture of the man's body appeared to her. She could see the beautiful, young male body encased within that suit and recall the feminine plumpness of the touch of his skin. When this vision came to her, the woman could hardly bear the terrible choking sensation that seized her. Only a moment ago she had been consumed with anger, but this vision was wringing all the rage from her body. Cold tears slid down her cheeks, even before the woman realized that she was crying.

The man lying on the floor before her had given up everything in his life for her. Memories of how tenderly affectionate he had once been jolted her emotions. Yet, in an instant, the woman's feelings reversed themselves once again. Strong feelings of regret, deeper than she had ever known before, rooted out the tender memories so intense only moments ago.

The woman sighed tiredly. Abruptly, she got up, determined to make an effort to change her mood. She shook her head briskly, as if to sweep away all the heavy feelings that had been closing in on her, and walked over to the window in a purposeful way. The woman tried to look casual and lighthearted as she flopped down by the windowsill. She peered through the tiny open window in the dormers at the peaceful scene outside, where fleecy, milk-white clouds stretched wide and low in the sky.

The woman looked at the plum tree planted in the middle of the small, boxlike garden running between the wooden fence next door and the storehouse. It was luxuriant with what looked like soft white pearls stuck all over it, like candy. Until now, gazing at this tree had invariably made the woman feel lonely. Little scraps of discarded tissue and such, caught at the tips of its pitiful withered-looking branches, always fluttered so plaintively. But now pearl-like buds had appeared at the tips of these same branches, painting a scene surprisingly full of the energy of life. The woman stared out the window, wondering at the mystery of nature.

Before long these buds would bloom, opening wide like fine, silky angels' robes and giving off a musky fragrance rather like that of an orchid. Recalling their scent made the woman realize that there was no reason she, too, should not feel the sensual warmth of her own youth lingering still, somewhere deep inside her.

"Look, the plum tree is blooming," the woman said suddenly, in a deliberately sweet, childlike voice. She turned around toward the man and, gently shaking one of his legs, tried to rouse him. And then, her face back in the path of the damp breeze, the woman returned to marveling at the quiet scene outside.

"While we have been doing all this arguing, spring has come," exclaimed the woman softly.

As the woman rested her icy palm on his leg, the man felt a chill shoot through his entire body. He couldn't help but recoil from her touch, causing the woman's hand to slip from his leg and fall smack on the windowsill. Instantly, the anger and pain the woman had momentarily forgotten stabbed her anew. Her nerves stood on edge all over again.

"So, even the touch of my hand revolts you now, does it?" the woman cried. Pressing her knees hard into his prone back, the woman scowled at the man. "Well? What about it? Have I really become as repulsive to you as all that? Well, have I?"

Beside herself with anger, her body shaking with rage, the woman kept asking this of the man, all the while pushing her knees into his back. For a moment, however, she stopped her tirade, and in that instant, the woman's eyes happened to light on the beautiful slenderness of the man's neck. But even this sight made her angry, for it ignited feelings of envy in her.

The woman pushed her flushed face into the man's back, and when she did so, tears of regret began to stream down her cheeks.

The heat coming from the woman's feverish face spread into the man's back in an annoyingly ticklish manner. Gently, he pushed the woman away and, sitting up himself, examined her weakened appearance for the first time. Blue veins stood out conspicuously on her hands as she pressed them against her face, her stomach was huge, and she heaved her shoulders painfully when she tried to breathe. All in all she made him feel as if he were looking at some wretched animal. Yet when he thought about the mysterious changes taking place within her body, he felt a strong fatherly love for his unborn child, something he had never experienced before. The thought made him shudder with excitement.

"Come on, now. This is silly. Please stop." Looking intently at the woman, the man stretched his hands out toward her. He took her hands in his and forced them away from her face.

"No! Please don't touch me anymore. You certainly don't want to touch a filthy woman like me!" Sulking like some disobedient child about to throw a temper tantrum, the woman buried her face in her kimono sleeves again.

"What is this?" the man chided. Drawing the woman close to him, the man pulled her head into his chest and held her tightly. "Silly! I only drew back because your hands were so cold. Now stop this stupid crying and pull yourself together."

Embraced in the strong arms of the man, the woman breathed raggedly as she gasped for air. "Well, I thought because . . . ," she said in a flirtatious way, giving him a bit of a smile through her tears.

When he saw her smile, the man quietly pulled away from the woman and went to stand by the window. Trying to soothe her, he asked, "You said the plum tree is blooming? Which one? Where is it?"

Standing with his back to the woman, he asked these questions in a way that clearly showed how much he wanted to win her over. Yet all the while he had the most unbearable feeling that there was some voice inside laughing at him, telling him what a fake he was.

With a sigh, the man put both his hands on his head. He quietly remarked, "Ah, our spring is all gone. No, not just our spring. Everything is lost."

At some point the woman had come over to stand beside the man and was also looking out the window. But at these words, her eyes darted at the man, flinty with anger. "Are you saying that because of me?" she demanded.

"No, I don't mean that this is because of you. Look: spring is gone for both us. But even you . . . you've lost everything, too, haven't you?

The woman was speechless.

"You don't think that there is anything you can actually do now, do you? From now on, we have to live for the child," the man said.

"For the child, you say?" The woman doubted her own ears. She felt as if he were spinning some bizarre fantasy about her. "For the child, you say?! I am not that kind of tired-out old matron yet, you know! Why, there are still plenty of interesting things I intend to do!"

"But don't you see? You can't do them now. It's the child's turn to have fun. That's the whole reason this child is coming!" The man smiled sadly as he said this.

Although the woman had first taken what he'd said as some mean kind of provocation, she gradually began to feel as though a tremendous pressure were weighing against her, as though she could barely breathe. Only a moment passed before she found herself shouting, her tone of voice vicious: "I have absolutely no need for *that* kind of child!"

The man felt he should say something, but kept silent for fear of making the woman even more upset. Then, he deliberately began whistling a song that he had been fond of a long time ago. Her eyes riveted on one spot of her huge stomach, the woman felt uncontrollably jealous at the power of the new life within her, which grew and grew without a second's pause.

Suddenly, the desire came to draw a sword and pierce the spot beneath her breasts, thus destroying the stubborn new creature. Imagine looking down from somewhere while laughing scornfully and watching her body, too, perish along with the new life.

Lost in this sort of fantasy, the man was looking deep within himself. He could see that all the energy and passion of his youth had been consumed by the figure of a cruel love that had all too soon turned its back on him.

The man's love seemed to have been but an endless struggle against insecurity, jealousy, anguish, and passion. He felt as if he had been cast out into a space so empty that it knew no limits. Gazing out the window at nothing in particular, the man looked up at the sky. White clouds were drifting by.

Notes

[1]Ogasawara Sada, "Higashi kaze" (Eastern Breeze), *Seitō* 3.4 (April 1913): 62–71.

[2]Ogasawara Sada, "Aru yoru" (One Evening), *Seitō* 2.7 (July 1912): 42–53; idem, "Doromizu" (Muddy Water), *Seitō* 2.9 (September 1912): 7–27. "Doromizu" is also interesting for its depiction of the mother, a young widow in her thirties, who is feeling free after the death of her overbearing husband. Her daughter Osumi disapproves of the mother's affection for Honda, a young male student who helps the two women with their finances and other business. The mother does not know that Honda has

also been pursuing Osumi. Osumi, however, finds him loathsome and is far more interested in a relationship with a painter.

³Ogasawara's other stories in *Seitō* are "Kyaku" (Guest), *Seitō* 2.6 (June 1912): 100–109, which is told from a man's point of view and concerns his thoughts about having an old flame turn up at his home and becoming good friends with his wife; and "Hina-tori" (Chick), *Seitō* 3.1 (January 1913): 49–64, which describes a young man feeling bored with the young woman whose naïveté once attracted him; he is trying to find out about her past sweethearts as a way to rekindle his own interest in her.

⁴Inoue Mihoko, "Ogasawara Sada," in Raichō Kenkyūkai, ed., *"Seitō" jinbutsu jiten: 110-nin no gunzō* (Taishūkan Shoten, 2001), 58–59. I have drawn on Inoue's biographical notes in writing about Ogasawara's life here.

Chapter 11
Yamada Waka (1879–1957)

Even the slightest contact with a woman who had been badly treated and used by a man would make me feel ready to sacrifice my own life, ready to lead a charge against the demons.

Yamada Waka's 1916 essay "Watashi to sono shūi," translated here as "Myself and My Surroundings," provides the warmest evocations of family harmony, maternal love, and universal sisterhood expressed in *Seitō*.[1] It also includes one of the most heated displays of anger in the magazine. Many *Seitō* essays and stories depict women's sorrow and sense of outrage at the way "being a woman" impinges on their freedom, but none matches the sheer fury seen in "Myself and My Surroundings." What Waka does not tell her reader is that these feelings stemmed from her experience of sexual slavery in North America. Reviewing the trajectory of Yamada Waka's long and eventful life shows how her ideas of women's liberation, so different from the other Bluestockings' views, relate to the abuse she endured. Haunted by memories of a violent past, Waka clung to the ideal of the perfect mother safely embraced in a loving family.

This ideal hardly matched the family of Waka's own birth. Born in the countryside of Kanagawa Prefecture in 1879, Asaba Waka was one of eight children (five sons and three daughters) in a farming family. Waka's maternal grandmother's mood darkened at each of her daughter's pregnancies and the prospect of another mouth to feed. The reality of several children to support was not the only source of conflict in the family. Waka's grandmother did not like her strong-willed son-in-law, whom she had adopted, and her daughter resented her husband's arrogant ways as well. Both Waka's mother and her grandmother appear to have imagined a much grander life for themselves than the one they experienced. They took pride in their reputation for beauty, enjoyed dressing well, and liked to give the impression that they were fine women from the capital. On one occasion, at least, such pretensions led the two women to their rather humorous comeuppance: one day, when they had taken the young Waka on a boat trip with them, they made quite a show of pretending to be from Tokyo, their ruse working until Waka piped up in her countryish dialect, leaving no doubt about the family's rural identity. Waka's early girlhood habit of refusing to wear any clothing at all in the summer must not have sat well with her grandmother, either. The older woman tried to instill a desire for a refined femininity in the girl. She took a particular dislike to Waka's long stride and made her granddaughter practice walking in the pigeon-toed manner suited to wearing a kimono. Waka so internalized her grandmother's admonitions that even years later, when she lived in North America and wore dresses, she continued to walk in this way, even though people often laughed at her for doing so.[2]

As a youngster, Waka had a great enthusiasm for school. To her disappointment, her parents decided that the compulsory four years of elementary school were all she needed, and thereafter kept Waka home to help in the household, as was the custom at the time in this rural area. In 1896, when Waka turned seventeen, her parents, who were facing financial difficulties, pushed her into what became a miserable marriage to an affluent local man, Araki Hichijirō, whom she found to be money-obsessed, stingy, and unwilling to help her family. What seems to have made this match all the more detestable to Waka is that she had enjoyed the flutter of a brief romance, receiving affectionate letters from a young man who sold vegetables. Since his family had even less money than hers, Waka's family put a stop to this relationship. In the end, Waka appears to have achieved what she most wanted, for she managed to obtain a divorce less than a year after her marriage and was able to devote her energies to helping her brother support their large family.

Waka wrote two short stories for *Seitō* that draw on these early experiences: "Ominaeshi" (Primroses) borrows from her unhappy first marriage, while "Tora-san" (Mr. Tiger) describes her feelings for her first love, the vegetable salesman.[3] "Primroses," which appeared in *Seitō* in April 1912, describes the sad fate of Omiyo, a country girl not quite sixteen years old who is forced to marry a man about ten years her senior because her family sees financial rewards in the match. Unlike Waka, Omiyo is not able to divorce her husband. Distraught over her husband's obsession with money, Omiyo has fled back home once but returned to the marriage at her relatives' insistence. Even after they have been married almost twenty years, her husband threatens divorce if Omiyo requests any for money for her family. After her husband dies, Omiyo feels the lack of affection in their long marriage even more acutely than before. Using an image reminiscent of Hiratsuka Raichō's manifesto for *Seitō* (translated in Chapter 4), her younger sister asks Omiyo, "Sister, what would it feel like to use your own strength, absorbing the Sun's very rays directly into you, and living your life that way? Don't you feel like trying to do that?" Omiyo responds only by trembling, as she casts an anxious look at her sister. Quite the opposite of the new, feminist symbolism evoked by the Sun, the title "Primroses" calls to mind the classical Japanese poetic allusion to *ominaeshi* as the "maiden flower," plucked and used for the pleasure of men.[4] The first two characters (pronounced *jorō*) of the three used to write *ominaeshi* mean "prostitute." Far from discovering her modern "hidden Sun," Omiyo has been mistreated in an age-old fashion, as both she and the reader realize.

Waka's May 1912 story, "Mr. Tiger," opens as a woman returning to the rural area of her youth happens to meet an old woman who is the mother of the title character, Tora-san. She now realizes that Tora-san, a poor young man who sold vegetables, was her first love, although at the time she had been confused by his love letters and unable to respond. She remembers how warm memories of Tora-san had comforted her during "difficult times when she'd been away from her family"—perhaps a reference to how Waka used similar memories for comfort during her years in prostitution. On learning from his mother that Tora-san has died, the woman imagines how different life could have been had she and Tora-san been able to marry.

In "Myself and My Surroundings," Waka expresses how strongly committed she was to her brother, describing how, once divorced, she submerged all self-interest in her hopes to help him. Tragically, this devotion led her to those who promised her work in the United States but who kept secret the true nature of this work when they convinced her to set sail for Canada. When Waka went ashore in Vancouver, British Columbia, in 1896, she was immediately sold to a pimp and taken to a brothel in the Japanese community in Seattle. There she was dubbed "The Arabian Oyae" and forced to labor until being rescued by a Japanese journalist, Tachii Nobusaburō (1871–1903), who managed to spirit her away to San Francisco. Because the couple landed in San Francisco with little money, Tachii tried to push Waka back into prostitution there. Fortunately, she escaped to a Christian women's mission later known as Cameron House, a refuge for abused and exploited women. Waka worked at Cameron House for three years, until, in 1905, she met and married Yamada Kakichi (1865–1934). A self-educated man who had lived and worked in Europe and the United States for more than twenty years, Kakichi operated his own foreign-language school in San Francisco. As she discusses in this essay, Waka was always grateful for Kakichi's willingness to help her launch a new life, and for educating and believing in her. His desire to help Waka develop her intellectual talents must have seemed unusual indeed to a woman who had been treated as one more mouth to feed as a girl, as a potential source of financial assistance as a bride, and as a slave in North America. Kakichi's own writing about his relationship with Waka echoes the same pride and affection that Waka describes in "Myself and My Surroundings."[5]

The couple returned to Japan in 1906, in the wake of the San Francisco earthquake. Kakichi set up another language school in Tokyo and, to further his wife's intellectual development, arranged for her to meet the Bluestockings.[6] Waka never became an official member of the Bluestockings, but she was active in her status as a "supporter," contributing short stories, essays, and translations to *Seitō*. Although Waka makes oblique reference in "Myself and My Surroundings" to her years in prostitution and rescue work, she chose not to disclose the full story of her years in the United States. No matter how often women's magazines asked her to write about this period in her life once she had become a well-known writer, Waka demurred, giving only a hint of the hard times she had experienced. Kakichi reportedly also insisted that, for the good of both her career and his, she should not make these experiences public.[7]

In fact, Waka's hard life as an overseas prostitute mirrors the experiences of thousands of poor Japanese girls who were sent to Australia, China, Southeast Asia, Canada, and the United States to fill the brothels established for Chinese and Japanese men already working there. The money they earned provided much-needed capital for the Japanese overseas investment that helped build Japan's modern military-industrial power.[8] Although prostitution in Japan at this time was often a temporary position for impoverished women who eventually made their way into the working classes and into marriage, writer Yamazaki Tomoko claims that the returning overseas prostitutes faced hostility and rejection when they attempted to rejoin their country villages. Her best-selling, semi-fictional 1972 book, *Sandakan hachiban shōkan* (Sandakan Brothel No. 8), later made into a film, brought new attention to this chapter in Japanese women's history. More recent research by historian Bill Milhalopolous, however, argues that among the families on Amakusa Islands off western Kyushu, whose daughters engaged in this form of "migrant labor," as he prefers to call it, sex work was not at all stigmatized.[9] Yet whether or not Waka's own village welcomed her back, as a woman working among the Tokyo intelligentsia and as a writer developing a national reputation as a maternalist, patriot, and conservative intellectual in the late 1910s and 1920s, Waka had good reason to remain silent about her past.[10]

In 1937, however, Waka did choose to confront her past and celebrate her success in overcoming it. In that year she returned to the United States, and did so under circumstances that could not have been more different from those of her first journey forty years before. The Japanese women's magazine *Shufu no tomo* (Housewife's Companion) sponsored this trip, sending Waka on a goodwill speaking tour to advocate the value of motherhood. Despite the tensions between Japan and the United States—or perhaps because of them—Yamada Waka was invited to meet Eleanor Roosevelt and members of Congress.[11] She gave lectures in many places, and on her way back to Japan also paid a visit to Seattle.[12]

According to Yamazaki Tomoko, who followed *Sandakan 8* with a popular biography of Yamada Waka in 1978, Waka's lecture to the Japanese community in Seattle provided an opportunity for her to make peace with her past. Although the event began with welcoming remarks from the president of the Japan Society and other dignitaries, once Waka took the stage the audience jeered at her, yelling out her brothel nickname, "The Arabian Oyae." By remaining calm and silently dignified, she eventually quieted the audience and gave her lecture. Yamazaki interviewed a woman who had been in the audience that night, who remembered Waka saying:

> Once I was not worthy of standing before you. But I have been reborn. Because I have been resurrected from hell, I have plenty to tell you.[13]

Waka never made such a public disclosure in Japan, perhaps out of consideration for her family or concern for her career, or from a desire to avoid voyeuristic curiosity about a period of her life she considered an utter hell. One can also speculate that she had a particular need to face those who knew her history in Seattle as a way of overcoming traumatic memories. If the everprotective Yamada Kakichi, who died in 1934, had been alive to register his opinion, Waka might well not have gone to Seattle again at all.

Waka showed the most interest in using what she saw as her "rebirth" to work on behalf of women as mothers. She fervently advocated for the rights, protection, and esteem she believed motherhood deserved. When the Bluestockings took up the topic of abortion in 1915 (discussed in Chapter 3 above), Waka wrote that people must, above all else, follow the true principles of nature, and that to practice contraception or abortion was fundamentally wrong because both went against nature.[14] Throughout her career, Waka remained adamantly against contraception and abortion in all cases, even counseling that a woman impregnated by rape should proudly carry the pregnancy to term. In 1918, in the famous Motherhood Protection Debate with Yosano Akiko, Hiratsuka Raichō, and Yamakawa Kikue, she reasserted her belief in motherhood as a woman's sacred mission, and one that deserved state support.[15] In 1921, she joined the Aikoku Fujinkai (Japan Women's Patriotic Association) and began writing for their magazine *Aikoku fujin* (Patriotic Women). In 1934, she chaired the Alliance for the Promotion of a Mother and Child Protection Act (Bosei Hogo Hō Seitei Sokushin Fujin Renmei), where her opposition to contraception and abortion brought her into conflict with socialist women in the group.[16] As Vera Mackie puts it, Waka believed in "an idealized family system and gendered division of labor," and once spoke of a mother's love as "the fount of all that is good, the seedbed of human compassion, the source of patriotism—the source of social order."[17] Yamada Waka's position certainly suited the Japanese government's wartime exhortations to women to "be fruitful and multiply." In 1941 Waka was sent as a goodwill ambassador to Italy and Germany, an experience that led her to write a long piece in *Shufu no tomo* about the advance of world war. In 1939, she established the Hatagaya House for Mothers and Children and the Hatagaya Nursery School; both were destroyed in the massive air raid on Tokyo on 25 May 1945. In April 1947, as her way to combat the rise of prostitution in occupied Japan, Waka opened the Hatagaya Girls' School as a kind of rehabilitation and job-training center where women would learn such skills as dressmaking, knitting, and embroidery.[18]

Yamada Waka made twenty-four contributions to *Seitō*, fourteen of which were translations. Waka's translations are excellent—close to the originals in structure and style, and creatively rendered into Japanese. At many points they are as provocative as anything else published in *Seitō*, inviting the magazine's readers into international debates about the New Woman, labor, maternalism, and eugenics. Waka translated short chapters from *Dynamic Sociology* (1883) and *Psychic Factors of Civilization* (1893) by pioneering American sociologist Lester Ward (1841–1913); nearly all of *Dreams* (1891) by South African New Woman Olive Schreiner (1855–1920); and the first two chapters of *Century of the Child* (1900) by the Swedish advocate of the rights of the mother Ellen Key (1849–1926).[19]

In view of Waka's concern over what is now called "domestic violence" in Japan, one of her *Seitō* stories in particular seems out of character and bears recounting here. "Tagusa tori" (Weeding Paddy Fields) opens as a man named Kichizō enjoys a pleasant rest after lunch, following a morning of weeding paddy fields with his wife Okō. When Okō appears, she is carrying a three-month-old smiling infant to whom she is happily devoted. She thanks Kichizō for forgiving her "that time," for if he had been stubborn, she says, who knows what would have happened to the child. Mention of "that time" causes Kichizō to feel a rush of anger as he remembers the evening the previous summer when his "pretty new wife" disappeared at a village festival while he was talking with friends. Concerned that something had happened, Kichizō had looked everywhere for Okō, finally returning home to discover that she was not there, either, and going out again to search. His relief at spotting Okō on a path in the rice fields in her white robe had quickly turned to angry suspicion. Catching up to her, he had slapped her hard and hurried her back to the house. The reader later learns that Hanji, another man in love with Okō, had seen an opportunity to grab her and pull her behind a temple to talk with her. Although Okō had tried to explain this to Kichizō, he had been in no mood to listen. Back home, Kichizō had flown into a rage, "roaring like a lion," calling his wife "a tramp," and, despite protests from his mother and sister, beating Okō until "alas, the bride, her hair in disarray, had blood running from her chin to her knees." The commotion had been loud enough to alarm the neighbors, who had arrived to find Kichizō finally subdued but breathing heavily. The matter had been resolved when Okō won Kichizō's trust by saying that although Hanji might still harbor feelings for her, it was Kichizō, and no other, who was her husband. Even now, the memory of "that time" leaves Kichizō with a mixture of "angry, happy, and strange feelings," though he takes comfort in the realization that Okō is truly his, a fact that gives him great satisfaction. The story ends as the couple, seemingly more in love than ever after having overcome their differences, goes back out to work in the fields. Waka constructs this story in such a way as to lend sympathy to Kichizō, as if to forgive him for loving his wife too much.[20]

Waka was a frequent contributor to *Seitō* and a good friend to several of the Bluestockings. Her experience writing and translating for *Seitō* launched her career as a social critic, and she went on to publish her own magazine, books of translation, and books of her original writing on social problems.[21] By the advent of the Shōwa era, Yamada Waka had established a national reputation and was selected to be an advice columnist for the *Tokyo Asahi shinbun*.[22] In 1934, she began writing a similar column for *Shufu no tomo*. Waka worked through her bereavement after Kakichi's death that same year by continuing to write, travel, and advocate for the protection of mothers and children.

When Yamada Waka died in 1957, at age seventy-seven, she left behind a large body of original essays, translations, and advice columns. The list of organizations and publications in which she had been active document major changes in women's public life from the 1910s through the early postwar period, and span the political spectrum: Shin Fujin Kyōkai (New Woman's Association), Aikoku Fujinkai, *Seitō*, *Shufu no tomo*. Her enslavement in prostitution abroad points to a crucial and still controversial aspect of modern Japanese history, and motivated her work on behalf of exploited and abused women. Yet what gave Yamada Waka's life meaning was, above all, her commitment to an idealized, often sentimental vision of motherhood. Perhaps it was her own physical inability to bear children—likely the result of her years in sexual slavery—that motivated Waka's intense feelings about motherhood. In the several biographies about Waka consulted here, there is very little about her being an adoptive mother of three children. In contrast, chronologies for the other Bluestockings list the birth date, sex, and some-times the name of each child born.[23]

In her essay "Watashi to sono shūi" (Myself and My Surroundings), Yamada Waka employs images of fabric and weaving as metaphors for closeness with others. Whereas other Bluestockings, such as Iwano Kiyoko and Hiratsuka Raichō, emphasize independence and solitude in their search for self-identity, Waka believes that an identity created in relation to oth-ers—both the intimate relations of the family and broader social connec-tions—is far stronger and more satisfying. This emphasis on relationship leads Waka to conclude her essay with a call for women to strengthen their bonds as women in order to overcome "the strength of customs established over thousands of years." Although the Bluestockings were a women-only group, and though they rarely published men's essays, they had banded together as independent-minded women who sought an opportunity for creative self-expression, not sisterhood. Two of the best-known contribu-tors, Yosano Akiko and Hiratsuka Raichō, had even expressed ambivalence about women's abilities and about assuming an openly gendered identity. Imagining the New Woman as one closely bound to other women and work-ing for a common good was a way of thinking that separated Yamada Waka from the other Bluestockings.

****

Myself and My Surroundings
Yamada Waka
Seitō 6.1 (January 1916)

I had been listless with a cold for a few days when it occurred to me that the very next day would be Sunday, and so I should be able to get plenty of sleep and recover completely. As I sipped some hot water mixed with tan-gerine juice before going to bed, I concocted the excuses I would use to sleep late the next morning. What I had in mind was something like, "I have such a terrible headache this morning, Dear. Would you mind getting up first?"

But as things turned out, this plan of mine was entirely undone. The trouble started at about three o'clock the next morning, when I awoke to hear my husband moaning about the chill he felt. His entire body shiver-ing, he kept repeating, "It's so cold. So cold." So I got out every last one of the quilts from the closet, wrapped them about his body, and tucked them in around him. Just when he stopped shaking, however, he broke out in a terrible fever, running a temperature of 104 degrees. What with having to get myself completely dressed at that point and having to get others up to go fetch a doctor, I ended up forgetting all about sleeping or eating while I cared for my husband. As luck would have it, my husband's fever broke after only one day, and he was well out of danger. Once he was feeling better, I thought to myself how funny it was that, in fact, I'd been the one planning to be sick that day.

Afterward, I found myself thinking about this act of forgetting myself. It reminded me of events from my past that were not unlike this. I remembered how, when I was still a child, my brother continually worried over everything. He had the full weight of the declining fortunes of our old, large family on his shoulders, and I sympathized with him to such a degree that my worries gnawed at my own heart. How I wanted to make things easier for him! How I longed to find some way to help him! These were the emotions that gripped me for half my life.

Unfortunately, no matter how noble my motives were, I headed off in the wrong direction more than once. I simply did not know any better. In any case, feeling the way I did in those days, I had no sense whether I belonged to my brother or to myself.

What would happen if now my child were to get sick? Nearly all my attention and energy would be given over to the child. Far into the night, when everyone and everything was quiet, and when I felt as if the only ones awake were the two of us, I would snuggle closer to the child, apologizing for having been distracted by other things during the day. I would swear that, even if it took every last ounce of strength that I had, my child would recover. No matter what I see, no matter what I hear, no matter whom I draw close to, I never feel a more determined or genuine person than in an instance such as this.

There are times in my ordinary dealings with people when I would like to do everything in my own way, whether or not this would please my husband. But when I stop and think about how much consideration I owe him, I put his needs ahead of others. Truly, I do not know whether I belong to my husband and my children or to myself.

Once I broke free of the black hell I lived in, how I hated the people, especially the men, of that world. I was so consumed with hatred that my entire body blazed with the fire of my anger. "How on earth could you do that to me? Demons! You take people at their most vulnerable and exploit them to your own advantage. You take your pleasure by sucking the life-blood right out of another person, and you don't give a second thought to doing this. Watch out for me, because I'd like nothing better than to pour gasoline all over your head and then set the hem of your clothes on fire! I want to see you burn!"

I viewed all men with this same anger. And then the strangest dream began to come to me. While I dreamt that I was hoisting a flag and heading up a brutal charge against men, I imagined that each and every one of the women who had been cruelly abused by men, and even all the dead women who had been exploited by men since the dawn of time, rose together from their graves. Clad in their white shrouds, they stood behind me. Every time this vision came to me, I felt a renewed and vital energy. Even the slightest contact with a woman who had been badly treated and used by a man would make me feel ready to sacrifice my own life, ready to lead a charge against the demons. I continued living like this for just three years, but when I think of it now, I feel as if I were exactly like some small Don Quixote.

It was at that time that I met my present husband. He appeared before me as a man completely unlike any I had ever met before. I was absolutely astonished to see that, among all the people on this earth, there was one such as him. I was frantic with anger, but he admonished me to calm down. He never once said that it was wrong for me to feel this anger, but that the anger itself could never bring me the end I desired. He advised me to "make the opportunities that will enable you to use that anger effectively." He told me that what he meant was that I should acquire knowledge. He said, "For the time being, you must control your anger and you should study."

From that point on he took me under his wing, and even though I began with barely any ability to read or write, he taught me for ten years without ever tiring. He took all the experience he had accumulated and all the knowledge he had achieved and tried to pour every bit of it into me. Occasionally, however, I would be so carried away by my housework that I couldn't even remember where I had placed the book I was in the middle of reading. When this happened my husband would get quite angry with me and lead me right out of the kitchen. It is largely because of him that I am the person I am today. I am his creation. Yet when I tell him, "I am what you have fashioned, I am a doll whose strings you pull," he responds, "I am the instrument that has been used by you."

When I think about who I am, I become confused about where this "me" is supposed to exist. I had nothing to say about being born into this world in the first place. Even after I was born, it was the circumstances of my environment that made me who I was, and so it was that all my actions were determined by my relation to others.

Here is what I think about this.

Although the bodies of human beings do indeed give the appearance of being quite separate and distinct from one another, the essence of humans is quite another thing, for in this area we are most skillfully and finely woven together. We cannot see ourselves as just so many individuals, all separated from one another in a precise way. Take the act of leaving one's relatives to pursue the path of one's own desires. To pursue the other rather than re-maining with one's relatives (whether this means pursuing a sweetheart or even pursuing the entire human race) should not be seen as something done purely out of self-interest, for along this path one arrives at a comparatively more expansive sense of who one is.

To put it simply, think of yourself as the threads in a fabric that run ver-tically, the *tate-ito*. In and of themselves, these threads cannot make a length of fabric. They must be interwoven with the *yoko-ito*—the threads of all sorts that run horizontally—in order to produce cloth. You, the *tate-ito*, will at times be woven together with the *yoko-ito* of your spouse. At other times your parents or your siblings, your children or your friends, or even the entire hu-man race will provide the *yoko-ito* you require. The color of your fabric will continually change, depending on the *yoko-ito* of your weave. Sometimes it will be deep and rich in color, and at other times barely perceptible. That is why the essence of who I am never remains the same. The more numerous the *yoko-ito* that I include in my weave, the deeper the fabric's color grows and the stronger and more splendid I, who am this fabric, become. When I use a loom that is as wide as possible to gather together all these threads, the cloth I weave—this fabric that is me—becomes equally grand.

My greatest happiness comes about when my husband, my children, my siblings, and all the people connected to me melt together as one. When the opposite occurs and I cannot get along well with the people who are closest to me, everything becomes awkward and tense. I feel so constrained that even my breathing becomes labored. This is because I so desire to unify those parts of me that are bound up with my husband, with my older broth-er, and with my children that I cannot abide these parts of myself becoming separated like this.

I have no doubt that people who have a thin cloth with too few *yoko-ito* are lonely and frail. In this sense, because my fabric is always thick with many, many *yoko-ito*, I am a fortunate person indeed.

I, the *tate-ito*, am now trying to weave myself together with the *yoko-ito* that is the Woman Question.

We women, all of us who for so long have lacked the opportunity to nurture our strength, must work as hard as we can to come together and un-derstand one another. Weaving the threads of each other's hearts and minds, we will make a fabric that is thick and strong, and in the weaving itself we will take courage. After creating this beautiful fabric that will be our group, we must advance, removing every obstacle that stands in the way of wom-en's paths as we go. The strength of customs established over thousands of years cannot be overcome with only one or two pairs of weak arms.

Notes

[1]Yamada Waka, "Watashi to sono shūi" (Myself and My Surroundings), *Seitō* 6.1 (January 1916): 107–11.

[2]For these details and more about Yamada Waka's childhood and later life, see Yasukata Misako, "Yamada Waka," in Setouchi Harumi, series ed., *Onna no isshō: Jinbutsu kindai josei-shi* (Kōdansha, 1980–81), 5: 61–104.

[3]Yamada Waka, "Ominaeshi" (Primroses), *Seitō* 4.11 (December 1914): 43–60; idem, "Tora-san" (Mr. Tiger), *Seitō* 5.2 (February 1915): 15–28.

[4]Thanks to Lynne Miyake for informing me of this meaning of *ominaeshi* as used in the famous Heian poetry anthology *Kokinshū* (A Collection of Poems Ancient and Modern, 905).

[5]Yasukata Misako quotes at length from Yamada Kakichi's comments on his wife printed in an article Kakichi wrote for a 1930 issue of *Fujin gahō* (Ladies' Pictorial) entitled "Erai nyōbō o motta otto no hiai wa" (The Sorrow of Husbands Who Have Outstanding Wives). Kakichi writes, "It has now been twenty-five years since I married Waka. I have never felt any sorrow because I have an outstanding wife. Rather I have been filled with gratitude toward my wife." He goes on to describe modestly his role in educating Waka, and how he manages at home so that she is free to lecture and do her other work. He assures readers that their happy relationship is due to their mutual trust, respect, and understanding. Yasukata, "Yamada Waka," 5: 70–71.

[6]On the ship back to Japan, Yamada Kakichi met radical socialist Kōtoku Shūsui (1871–1911), who later introduced him to Ōsugi Sakae (1885–1923). Ōsugi studied with Kakichi, and sent one of Waka's translations to Hiratsuka Raichō, who decided to publish it in *Seitō* immediately. This entrée into the intellectual world of Tokyo put Kakichi in touch with men and women who wanted to study foreign languages (English, French, German) at his new school. Hiratsuka Raichō and Okumura Hiroshi moved near the Yamadas in 1915. Raichō read Lester Ward and Ellen Key with Yamada Waka while Okumura studied French with Yamada Kakichi. Other Bluestockings, such as Ikuta Hanayo, Itō Noe, Iwano Kiyoko, Okada Yuki, and Yoshiya Nobuko, also studied there. Ishizaki Shōko, "Yamada Waka," in Raichō Kenkyūkai, ed., *"Seitō" jinbutsu jiten: 110-nin no gunzō* (Taishūkan Shoten, 2001), 184; Yasukata, "Yamada Waka," 5: 66–69.

[7]Yamazaki Tomoko, *The Story of Yamada Waka: From Prostitute to Feminist Pioneer*, trans. Wakako Hironaka and Ann Kostant (Tokyo: Kodansha International, 1985), 146.

[8]Yamazaki Tomoko, *Sandakan hachiban shōkan: Teihen joseishi joshō* (Tokyo: Chikuma Shobō, 1972); idem, *Sandakan Brothel No. 8: An Episode in the History of Lower-Class Japanese Women*, trans. Karen Colligan-Taylor (Armonk, NJ: M. E. Sharpe, 1999). The 1974 film directed by Kei Kumai is titled *Bōkyō* in Japanese, *Sandakan 8* in English. See the article by Milhalpolous below for a thoughtful critique of Yamazaki's work.

[9]Bill Milhalpolous, "The Making of Prostitutes: The *Karayuki-san*," *Bulletin of Concerned Asian Scholars* 25.1 (1993): 41–56.

[10]When Yamazaki Tomoko first read a note in Raichō's autobiography about Yamada Waka's life in the U.S., she doubted the veracity of the remark. In the course of her research, however, Yamazaki discovered that Waka had in fact been a prostitute, and she went to the Yamada family for help in finding out about this period

in Waka's life. But even in the 1970s, long after Waka's death, the Yamada family was reluctant to make this information known and refused to help Yamazaki in her research. Yamazaki also discovered that Oka Shigeki, publisher of a San Francisco Japanese-language weekly, *Amerika shinbun* (The American Journal), wrote "The Story of the Arabian Oyae" for his publication in 1938, disclosing Yamada Waka's past in the interests of telling "the truth." Yamazaki Tomoko, *The Story of Yamada Waka*, 64–65.

[11]*The New York Times* reported Yamada Waka's attendance at a press conference held on 7 December 1937 in Washington, D.C., at which Eleanor Roosevelt discussed minimum wage laws. "Mrs. Waka Yamada of Tokyo, as a representative of the Shufu-no-Tomo, a Japanese women's magazine attended the conference. Mrs. Yamada told Mrs. Roosevelt that the mothers of Japan and China did not hate each other, earnestly desired to work together to end the conflict between their countries and sought the aid of American mothers to that end." "Mrs. Roosevelt Sees Wage Laws as Bases," 8 December 1937, *New York Times*, 18.

[12]One of Waka's English-language lectures was published in Japan in the late 1930s. See Waka Yamada, *The Social Status of Japanese Women* (Tokyo: Kokusai Bunka Shinkokai [The Society for International Cultural Relations], 1937), the publication of a nineteen-page lecture Yamada Waka delivered on October 15, 1935. The first edition appeared in December 1935; the second edition in May 1937.

[13]Yamazaki, *The Story of Yamada Waka*, 151.

[14]Yamada Waka, "Datai ni tsuite: Matsumoto Gorō-shi '*Seitō* no hatsubai kinshi ni tsuite' o yonde" (On Abortion: To Mr. Matsumoto Gorō upon Reading about "The Ban on the Sale of *Seitō*"), *Seitō* 5.8 (September 1915): 30–38.

[15]In 1925, the April issue of *Fujin kōron* (Ladies' Review) featured a section on Hiratsuka Raichō as "a pioneer of women of a new era." Yamada Waka entitled her contribution to the section "Ryōsai kenbo no Hiratsuka Raichō san" (Ms. Hiratsuka, the Good Wife, Wise Mother), and warmly praised Raichō. Given Raichō's longtime opposition to the notion of *ryōsai kenbo*, one can imagine her surprise at seeing herself portrayed this way. Horiba Kiyoko thinks that Waka's background made it hard for her to view the middle-class ideal of the "good wife, wise mother" as oppressive. To Waka, it was the stuff of dreams. Horiba, *Seitō no jidai: Hiratsuka Raichō to atarashii onna-tachi* (Iwanami Shoten, 1988), 190. For more on the Motherhood Protection Debate (Bosei Hogo Ronsō), see Barbara Molony, "Equality versus Difference: The Japanese Debate over 'Motherhood Protection,' 1915–50," in Janet Hunter, ed., *Japanese Women Working* (London and New York: Routledge, 1993), 122–48; Laurel Rasplica Rodd, "The Taishō Date over the New Woman," in Gail Lee Bernstein, ed., *Recreating Japanese Women, 1600–1945* (Berkeley and Los Angeles: University of California Press, 1991), 175–98; and Hiroko Tomida, *Hiratsuka Raichō and Early Japanese Feminism* (Leiden: Brill, 2004), 221–61.

[16]Vera Mackie writes, "The Mother and Childhood Protection Act (*Boshi Hogo Hō*) was promulgated on 31 March 1937, and became effective on 1 January 1938." Mackie describes the conflict between Yamada Waka and the socialist women in detail. Mackie, *Creating Socialist Women in Japan: Gender, Labour and Activism, 1900–1937* (Cambridge: Cambridge University Press, 1997), 147.

[17]Ibid., 90. Mackie is citing and translating from Yamada Waka, "Fujin no kaihō to wa" (What Is Women's Liberation?), *Fujin to shin shakai*, no. 3 (May 1920): 10.

[18]Yamazaki, *The Story of Yamada Waka*, 155. It is important to note that some wom-

en involved in sex work did not welcome the ministrations of middle-class women, opposing their interventions as naïve and patronizing. See G. G. Rowley, "Prostitutes Against the Prostitution Prevention Act of 1956," *U.S.–Japan Women's Journal*, no. 23 (2002): 39–56. What often got lost in such discussions of women's virtue was the position of the prostitute's patron, both Japanese and foreign, and his ethics.

[19]Chap. 1, "The Right of the Child to Choose his Parents," and chap. 2, "The Unborn Race and Woman's Work," in Ellen Key, *The Century of the Child* (New York: G. P. Putnam's Sons, 1909; originally published in Swedish in 1900); "Female Intuition," in Lester Ward, *The Psychic Factors of Civilization* (Boston: Ginn & Company, 1893), 174–80; "Education of Women," in Lester Ward, *Dynamic Sociology, or Applied Social Science* (New York: D. Appleton & Co., 1883), 1: 614–19; Waka also translated the first ten of the eleven stories in Olive Schreiner, *Dreams* (London: T. Fisher Unwin, 1891).

[20]Yamada Waka, "Tagusa tori" (Weeding Paddy Fields), *Seitō* 4.4 (April 1914), Special Issue on Fiction: 1–8.

[21]Waka's magazine was entitled *Fujin to shin shakai* (Women and the New Society). It was published from 1920 to 1933. Ishizaki, "Yamada Waka," 185.

[22]Waka's advice column in *Asahi shinbun* began on 1 May 1931, and was said to have increased the newspaper's circulation by two million. Yamazaki, *The Story of Yamada Waka*, 124–25.

[23]According to Hiratsuka Raichō, Yamada Waka adopted three children of about the same age. "Two were orphaned relatives, the third, a child of a close friend who had died in the United States." As translated in Hiratsuka Raichō and Teruko Craig, *In the Beginning, Woman Was the Sun: The Autobiography of a Japanese Feminist* (New York: Columbia University Press, 2006), 265; Hiratsuka Raichō, *Genshi, josei wa taiyō de atta: Hiratsuka Raichō jiden* (Ōtsuki Shoten, 1971–73), 2: 561.

Chapter 12
Yosano Akiko (1878–1942)

The day when mountains move has come.

"You see, the mountain *has* moved," exclaimed a beaming Doi Takako, the leader of the Japan Socialist Party. She had just become the first woman to serve as the Speaker of the House of Representatives. The year was 1993, yet this momentous occasion recalled for Doi the celebrated verse penned by Yosano Akiko in 1911 for the inaugural issue of *Seitō*.[1] In "Sozorogoto" (Rambling Thoughts), Akiko had promised that women's energies would erupt in unexpected ways that would shake the very foundations of society.[2] Doi Takako took pride in seeing her own success being in line with Akiko's predictions and knew the kind of resonance her allusion to this verse would inspire. Yet as Yosano Akiko scholars have pointed out, there is much more to this verse than its oft-quoted first, heroic lines. We explore "Sozorogoto" here by looking briefly at Akiko's biography, her involvement with the Bluestockings, and at what critics have said about her famous poem.

As both one of the most celebrated poets in modern Japanese literature and one of the outstanding figures in the history of Japanese feminism, Yosano Akiko, her life, and her work have been much discussed in Japanese, and there is more available in English on her than any other author discussed in this volume.[3] Janine Beichman's 2002 biography, *Embracing the Firebird*, offers a compelling portrait of the young Akiko, which I draw on to provide the short account of her life here.[4] Born in 1878 in Sakai, a provincial city near Osaka, Akiko was raised to become "an ordinary woman" (*tada no onna*) who "could excel in three areas: housekeeping, the everyday management of the family business, and bearing children, especially male ones. Her desired personal attributes were forbearance, self-denial, practicality."[5] Akiko later satirized the "ordinary woman," her lack of intellectual curiosity and drive, in an essay called "The Headless Woman."[6] Akiko was a voracious reader with a sharp mind, a lively imagination, a desire for freedom, and an adventurous, ambitious spirit. Her life choices as well as her forty years of prolific writing made her anything but an "ordinary woman."

Akiko started out life, however, as a disappointment. She was supposed to have been a boy. Instead, she was the first daughter and second child born to Ōtori Sōshichi (1847–1903), whose family owned and operated a confectionary store, and his second wife Tsune (1851–1907); Sōshichi had also fathered two children, both daughters, by his first wife. Sōshichi's distress over the birth of the girl was so great that he stayed away from the house for a week. Akiko was sent to live with a maternal aunt, and did not return until two years later, when the aunt had a baby of her own to care for and Tsune had produced another son. Back with her parents, Akiko grew up to be a difficult child, one who resented the preferential treatment enjoyed by her brothers and later, by her baby sister. Beichman imagines that Akiko never regained the opportunity for closeness with her parents that was lost in her infancy, but asks whether this lack of filial bonding enabled Akiko, as a young adult, to more easily leave her family and community to travel to Tokyo and take up a very different kind of life there.[7]

Other women discussed in this volume—Hiratsuka Raichō, Itō Noe, and Fukuda Hideko—defied feminine codes as physically active girls and were dubbed "tomboys." Akiko resisted in a different way: she countered her mother's insistence on maintaining the appearance of the properly chaste maiden by wearing makeup and fashionable clothing. As an adolescent she was particularly embittered by being locked in her room at night, as many young women in Sakai were, to protect her virtue. As Beichman observes, Akiko also transcended the stifling atmosphere of her environment by developing a double life—a healthy connection to the real world and a vibrant life of the imagination that was fed by her love of reading, a trait she shared with her father. As a girl she read all the major and minor works of classical Japanese literature and discovered the Heian classic *Tale of Genji*, which was to become one of the great passions of her life. But Akiko's reading widened the gulf between her and her mother. The following description that Akiko wrote of her mother in 1915 recalls the kind of sadness Hiratsuka Raichō expresses in her autobiography over the constraints on her own mother's freedom:

> My mother had no education, so she had no way to understand her
> daughter's heart, what books she read, what dreams she dreamed
> or what interests she had. I grieved more for my mother's heart
> than I did over my own situation. To have to look at one's own
> daughter with such base eyes, thinking that one can't let her wear
> makeup, that she'll do anything a man says—there can't be anything crueler than that. In the provinces, many girls are brought
> up in homes like mine.[8]

Like many of the Bluestockings, Akiko was sent to a girls' school and ended up bored with its lack of intellectual rigor. After graduation, she shouldered much responsibility for running the family store and keeping its books, all the while continuing to read as much as she could and to write poetry. Akiko's career in writing took off after 1900, when her poems caught the attention of poet Yosano Tekkan (1873–1935), who had a started a new poetry magazine, *Myōjō* (Venus). Tekkan was taken with Akiko's poetry and with the woman herself. Although he was betrothed to another woman, Hayashi Takino (1878–1966), had agreed to become an adopted son in the wealthy Hayashi family, and had even fathered a child with Takino, he abandoned this life for a new one with Akiko. Akiko fled her family home to live with the man she loved.

In 1901 Yosano Akiko published her most famous collection of tanka poetry, *Midaregami* (Tangled Hair), a work that "boldly explored her personal responses to the world, her youthful sensuality, and her newly awakened feelings of love for the man she was soon to marry."[9] Akiko also attracted notice in 1904, when she published *Kimi shinitamau koto nakare* (My Brother, You Must Not Die), a longer poem in which she pleads with her brother not to die in the Russo-Japanese War.[10] A dynamic writer who needed the income from her publications to support her less financially successful husband and her children, Yosano Akiko also wrote essays on the position of women in Japan and on other social issues. In 1918 she became embroiled in the Motherhood Protection Debate (Bosei Hogo Ronsō), a controversy over whether or not the state should provide welfare for mothers, with former Bluestockings Hiratsuka Raichō, Yamada Waka, and Yamakawa Kikue. Akiko argued strenuously that all women should work to support themselves, whether or not they were mothers.[11] Yosano Akiko spent her later years still involved in one of her lifelong endeavors, a translation of *The Tale of Genji* into modern Japanese. Although her scholarly attention to this classic and others consumed much, if not most, of Akiko's creative energies in the latter half of her career, her fame as a poet has nearly eclipsed her achievement in other areas.[12] When she died in 1942 at age sixty-three, Yosano Akiko left an impressive and voluminous body of writing that continues to inspire writers today.

"Sozorogoto" and *Seitō*

In her 1971–73 autobiography, Hiratsuka Raichō writes that she will never forget visiting Yosano Akiko's home to ask her for a contribution to the first issue of *Seitō*. They had met four years before, when Akiko had lectured on *The Tale of Genji* at the Accomplished Women's Literary Society (Keishū Bungakukai). By the summer of 1911, Akiko, who was then thirty-three, had borne seven of her eleven children, had constant requests for her writing from newspapers and magazines, and had a book of essays coming out in July. Her reputation as a poet had come to overshadow that of her husband

Tekkan; now Akiko was "the famous and prolific 'master' whom everyone clamored to meet."[13] In her recollection of their meeting, Raichō discusses how Akiko, mumbling in her soft-spoken Kansai dialect, expressed her thoughts about the plan for a women's magazine:

> Although I could barely hear her, she seemed to be saying that women were hopeless, that they were inferior to men, and that she had seen many submissions [to *Myōjō*] from all over Japan, but the good poems were invariably by men. I may have misunderstood her, but was she trying to warn us that our bold talk about publishing a women's journal and producing women writers of genius was arrogant and presumptuous? Or was she saying just the opposite—that because of the dearth of female talent, we must put forth the greatest efforts to succeed? In any event, I asked her to be a supporting member and to write something for the inaugural issue, as well as in the future. When I think of it now, I was really asking more of her than was absolutely proper.[14]

Raichō went away unsure of Akiko's feelings on the matter but pleased that she had agreed to be one of *Seitō*'s sponsors. Raichō was even more pleased, and more than a little surprised, when Akiko's contribution to *Seitō* arrived before all the rest:

> Ms. Yosano Akiko's manuscript arrived on August 7th, ahead of the deadline, and what's more, ahead of all other submissions. It was the very first. All of us involved in publishing the magazine were overjoyed. I concluded that what she had told me before must have been intended as encouragement.[15]

Raichō quotes only the first two verses of "Sozorogoto" (translated below as "Mountain Moving Day" and "First Person") in her autobiography, adding how appropriate this powerful poetry was as the first work in *Seitō*'s first issue. She also wonders if the Bluestockings' plans for the magazine and their "Guiding Principles" (translated here in Appendix B) had not actually been the inspiration for the stirring sentiments expressed in Akiko's verse.[16]

By referring to only the first two verses of "Sozorogoto," however, Raichō gives a misleading idea of Akiko's poem. The work is actually a collection of twelve verses of varying length, which do not as a whole form a ringing manifesto. Indeed, what has most struck those who have written about all twelve verses is how the imagery in the final verse—that of a deathly pallid woman, a "moon flower"—differs so dramatically from the descriptions of an emerging female power in the first. In this last verse, the narrator, far from roiling with volcanic energy, appears ready to be absorbed into the mud. Her shelter is about to give way in the rain, her face is pale, and her hair floats out like tentacles in the dirty water. This image also prompts comparison with the emphatic call for women to recover their "hidden Sun" advocated in the *Seitō* manifesto written by Hiratsuka Raichō, which was also included in the inaugural issue of *Seitō* (translated in Chapter 4 above). Since "Sozorogoto" is one of the most famous works to appear in *Seitō*, I translate the twelve verses in full here and mention some ideas that Japanese critics have offered for reading them.

Yosano Akiko gave readers new clues to reading "Sozorogoto" in 1929, when she revised it to give each verse its own title (these are included in the translation below).[17] This, argues Seki Reiko, further directs the reader away from seeing "Sozorogoto" as a manifesto or even as a unified work, and toward attending to its inherent diversity, to the independent coherence of each verse, and to its organization as a series of poems linked by a repetitive and resonating use of images.[18] Seki adds that the overall title calls to mind the ancient Japanese word *suzurugoto* (which can be translated "random thoughts," "rambling thoughts," or even "silly thoughts") and also the classical *zuihitsu* (literally, "following the brush") style of writing, which focused on a stream of images rather than a single message or story. Her interpretation of "Sozorogoto," however, does imply that Seki understands the verses to be connected by virtue of having the same narrator, which she tends to conflate with Yosano Akiko herself. Seki sees the impact of the poem as a whole in the resonance, for example, among such images as the delicate crystal bowl in verse 4, the slim blade of the razor in verse 5, the unraveling sapphire rosary in verse 8, and the grasshopper in verse 9—which to her mind focus on the fleeting and the fragile in order to create an overall sense of ennui that is not unpleasant to the "I" of the verses. Seki reads the list in verse 11 as comprising things that do not appeal to that "I"—a particularly irritating one for Akiko being the art critics who do not understand the work they evaluate.[19] Seki sees the last verse as an embodiment of the internal struggles plaguing the narrator.

Akiko's use of language is also analyzed by Kōra Rumiko, who observes that the character *ao* (which can mean "blue," "green," "pale," "inexperienced," and "unripe") appears seven times in "Sozorogoto." She points to the use of this character in the verses about the *blue* razor, the sapphire (*blue*) gems, the *green* mosquito net and the grasshopper, and the *pale* face of the woman in verse 12. Kōra argues that this frequent use of the character *ao*, which can also be pronounced *sei*, refers to the magazine *Seitō* (Bluestocking) itself.[20] Following Kōra, Nakashima Miyuki notes that the character *ao*, along with variations on the characters *aojiroi* ("pale"; literally, "blue-white"), frequently appears in later *Seitō* writing by other women, too, as a metaphor for the self or for the figure of a woman—and that, as we shall see below, this runs counter to Raichō's appeal for women to associate their creativity with the sun.[21]

Also connecting "Sozorogoto" to the magazine *Seitō*, Muraoka Yoshiko believes that the poem encodes a kind of warning to the Bluestockings. The woman who proudly rises in the first verse and speaks in her own voice in the second may, as the succeeding verses indicate, be laughed at by thoughtless art critics, find her spirit broken by men, and see her dreams unravel like the gems in the great-grandmother's rosary, turned into nothing more than children's toys. I would argue that one can also read in these verses—especially in verses 4 and 6—the charge that it is often a woman's own desire to please the man in her life that renders her fragile and timid. Muraoka also believes that the references to a razor in verse 5 and to "acting like a man" in verse 6 are intended to call to mind the scandal of 1908 involving Hiratsuka Raichō and Morita Sōhei, by alluding to the dagger Raichō took with her and the ensuing spate of bad publicity she endured for, in a sense, "acting like a man" (see the Chapter 4 above). Yet Muraoka reads encouragement in "Sozorogoto," too. Verse 2 tells the Bluestockings to speak honestly in their own voices; Muraoka also sees this as a thinly veiled criticism of the Naturalist writers, whom Yosano Tekkan opposed and whom Akiko is criticizing for their disingenuous use of the first person in their writing.[22]

What about the pale moon flower in the final verse of "Sozorogoto"? Kōra Rumiko interprets the moon flower as a reference to Akiko herself, who continued the narcissistic act of writing poetry while struggling to raise her children and support her husband.[23] Nakashima Miyuki reads the image as a reference to Shakespeare's Ophelia, the madwoman of *Hamlet*, and interprets this as yet another invocation of the "woman in the water" (*mizu no naka no onna*) theme common in Japanese painting and literature at the time. She explains how richly evocative and frequently used the motif was, and its connection to other fictional figures from the West, such as Neptune. The "woman in the water" variously suggested serenity, youthful beauty on the brink of death, premature death, genius, the artist, creativity, and the aestheticization of tuberculosis. Nakashima believes that Akiko's use of the image of a moon flower in the final verse of "Sozorogoto" can signal an association among female creativity, genius, and *Seitō*.[24] Furthermore, Nakashima persuasively argues that the cover art for the initial issue of *Seitō* in which "Sozorogoto" appeared, designed by Naganuma Chieko, is another example of the "woman in the water" theme. On Naganuma's cover, an image that resembles an ancient Egyptian woman is standing in water with bubbles floating upward around her. Nakashima sees this woman as an enigmatic figure who is difficult to locate in time and place, and finds it unusual that she is standing up rather than floating in the water. She cites

Yamasaki Akiko's interpretation of this figure as representing Naganuma's feminist revision of the "woman in the water" icon. Yamasaki imagines that Naganuma's frustration with the misogyny implicit in the familiar image inspired her to redraw the figure for the first *Seitō* cover in a way that suggests a woman "standing on her own" (*jiritsu-teki*).[25] Yet according to Nakashima, it remains difficult to say to what extent this figure can be seen as a reversal of the stereotype of women as passive—and hence as the symbol of a new, liberated woman.[26]

As we can see in Hiratsuka Raichō's 1911 essay "Genshi, josei wa taiyō de atta" (In the Beginning, Woman Was the Sun, translated in Chapter 4 above), which became known as the *Seitō* manifesto, Raichō was one Bluestocking who clearly did not interpret the moon flower as a welcome sign of female creativity. As Nakashima observes, when Raichō discusses the early plans for *Seitō* and her conversations with mentor Ikuta Chōkō in her autobiography, she recalls how taken he was with the image of Ophelia. She writes that men's captivation with this kind of image of female creativity made her want to create something different in her initial essay for *Seitō*, even though she did not consciously consider writing a manifesto or a call for women's rights.[27] Thus in Raichō's 1911 essay, the moon represents illness and the lack of creative power; it is the sun, not the moon, that women must work to recapture. In her 1913 essay "New Woman" (Atarashii onna), Raichō continues this theme, declaring that she is a New Woman and she is the sun.[28]

Nakashima considers that, years later, Yosano Akiko pointedly displayed her own strong sense of self and her resistance to following Raichō's use of sun imagery in her poem "Gaslight" (Dentō), published in *Seitō* in February 1914.[29] In that poem, the narrator sits alone in her narrow study. It is well past midnight, and all is dark save for the wan glow of a single gaslight suspended from the ceiling. She speaks affectionately of the gaslight as her "nocturnal sun," describing it as a kindred spirit that also has a pale (*aojiroi*) face. The gaslight even shares her insomnia and her womanly feelings. Like the gaslight, the narrator, too, comes alive in the darkness, fearing the approach of morning light as a harbinger of other endings as well—the inevitable end of one's genius, one's work, and the end of life. If she listens intently, she can even hear the clock—and her life—ticking away. Whereas Raichō's sun imagery evokes limitless possibility and energy, the narrator of "Gaslight" finds creativity in such melancholy.[30]

Yosano Akiko also wrote several other poems for *Seitō* after "Sozorogoto," including ten long poems and twenty tanka verses, some of which were about her 1912 trip to Paris.[31] For Horiba Kiyoko, one of the most inspiring of these poems is the last one Akiko wrote for the magazine, in May 1915.[32]

"Mori no taiju" (Great Tree in the Forest, published in *Seitō* in September 1915) describes the narrator's feelings for a giant tree, standing tall against a blue sky (*aozora*)—a tree that has long endured and from which she draws energy. Writing in 1988, Horiba sees this tree as a metaphor both for *Seitō* and for the Bluestockings, who, though misunderstood for decades, were finally being fully appreciated by a new generation of Japanese women.[33] Nakashima Miyuki, however, reads the poem in terms of Akiko's enduring love for her husband Tekkan and oft-stated preference for the shade over the sun. The great tree in the poem, "like King David" or "Atlas," holds up the sun while protectively shading the narrator beneath its boughs. The tree, Nakashima argues, is associated with the man from whom the female narrator draws energy and with whom she feels unified. Interestingly, as Nakashima points out, the cover of the September 1915 issue of *Seitō*, edited by Itō Noe, was created by Hiratsuka Raichō's partner, Okumura Hiroshi. It is not known whether Okumura saw Yosano Akiko's poem before deciding on his illustration, although it seems likely he did. The cover shows a woman standing between tree trunks and wearing a flowing dress. Her eyes are closed as if in meditation and there is a halo around her head—the light of the sun or the moon, perhaps? Above the halo around her shoulders, the leaves of the trees are visible. The woman is huge compared to the trees: it is she who is the giant. In fact, Nakashima states, she has become "one with the great tree in the forest" herself.[34] But Nakashima also speculates that featuring the great tree prominently on the cover may have been Okumura's way of signaling that Akiko had won the duel of the metaphors. Raichō, who had earnestly believed in *Seitō* and the sun of genius and self-discovery, had withdrawn from the editorship. There was no longer any need to debate whether it was the sun or the moon that should symbolize women's creativity.[35]

****

Rambling Thoughts
Yosano Akiko
Seitō 1.1 (September 1911)
(Revised by Yosano to give each verse its own title in 1929)

"Mountain Moving Day" (Yama no ugoku hi)
The day when mountains move has come.
Or so I said. But no one believed me.
The mountains have simply been asleep for awhile.

In their ancient past,
the mountains blazed with fire and they moved.
If you don't believe that either, fine.
But trust me when I tell you this—
all the women who were sleeping
are awake now and moving.

"First Person" (Ichininshō)

I desire to write entirely in the first person.
I who am a woman.
I desire to write entirely in the first person.
I. I.

"Tangled Hair" (Midaregami)

Across my forehead, and over my shoulders, too,
stray tendrils of hair.
As though I am being pelted and drenched under a hot waterfall.
Like a flame jumping out of control, a deep sigh of anguish escapes me.
He doesn't suspect any of this.
He praises me now, yet one day soon, I'm afraid,
he will curse me.

"Fragile Bowl" (Usude no hachi)

A brand-new crystal bowl, delicately made. How it delights me!
Fill it with water—flowing tears.
Place a flower inside—burning fire.
What scares me is that if a careless man should break this bowl,
it would shatter more easily than the simplest earthenware pot.
It is infinitely more fragile, more delicate.

"Razor" (Kamisori)

Flickering blue and white,
the blade of a razor has such a refreshing sparkle.
In the stench of hot summer grass, a grasshopper chirps, and
in a rooming house nearby, someone plays the harmonica.
How dull and lazy this makes me feel.
But when I root to the bottom of this oil-stained old comb-box of mine,
what should appear wrapped in crepe paper but the slim blade of a razor!

"Tobacco" (Tabako)

Is it bitter? Or is it pungent? The flavor of tobacco.

The flavor of tobacco is so hard to describe.
If I say that it's sweet,
I bet he'll jump to the conclusion that I find it sweet as sugar.
I've taken up smoking lately,
but I hide my habit from others.
Still, what do I care if gossips malign me for "acting like a man"?
The only thing that does scare me is
how much this man's hasty conclusions matter to me.

"Woman" (Onna)
"Do not forget your whip!"
said Zarathustra.
Women are oxen, they are sheep.
Maybe I should add,
"Let them run to the wilds!"[36]

"Great-Grandmother's Buddhist Rosary" (Daisobo no juzu)
I never knew my grandmother's mother
but I heard that she enjoyed luxury in all things.
She tired of the Buddhist rosary that was crystal, and
even of the rosary that was coral.
They told me she used to roll this sapphire rosary between her thumb and fingers.
I unraveled the sapphire rosary,
and placed the gems one by one in my children's hands.
Destitute, I had no other toys worth giving them.

"My Poems" (Waga uta)
Since my poems are short,
people think that there are some words left out.
There is nothing left out of my verse,
nor is there anything I'd like to add.
Not being a fish, my heart lacks gills.
I simply compose all in one breath.

"Grasshopper" (Suitcho)
Grasshopper! Grasshopper!
Grasshopper who plays the tiny flute of early fall!
Grasshopper who lands atop the mosquito net!
Your trill colors the mosquito net a deeper shade of green.
Grasshopper! Why stop your singing now?

On evenings in early fall, the mosquito net is as chilly as mercury!
Grasshopper! Grasshopper!

"Locust" (Aburazemi)

The locust goes, "Ji ji." This chirp of "ji ji" is—
Alpine Soap bubbles,
a harsh man, his great big mouth opening into a square,
two sen worth of copper coins in the palm of my hand,
art criticism these days,
the infatuations of those young people who speak with such pride.

"Evening Showers" (Ame no yoru)

Downpour on a summer's night,
I imagine my house sagging into the muddy bottom of a sodden rice field,
all its pillars flexing like grass, as
water dribbles through the leak in the roof, just like a snake.
Odor of night-sweat, a sad scent indeed. The grinding teeth of a sickly child.
Green mosquito net, all puffed up like a frog's throat,
hair falling to my shoulders, rustling like grass in a mountain stream.
How pale it makes my face look.
Floating this way on dirty water, it is a Moon Flower.

Notes

[1]This anecdote about Doi Takako comes from Muraoka Yoshiko, "Yosano Akiko," in Raichō Kenkyūkai, ed., *"Seitō" no go-jū-nin* (Raichō Kenkyūkai, 1996), 102. This famous verse was also read in 1975 at the conference in Mexico City that initiated the United Nations Decade of the Woman.

[2]Yosano Akiko, "Sozorogoto" (Rambling Thoughts), *Seitō* 1.1 (September 1911): 1–9.

[3]A bibliography of works in English on Yosano Akiko and translations of several of her poems comprise a special issue of the *Journal of the Association of Teachers of Japanese*, edited by Laurel Rasplica Rodd. For the bibliography, see Rodd, ed., *JATJ* 25.1 (April 1991), Special Issue on Yosano Akiko: 8–9.

[4]Janine Beichman, *Embracing the Firebird: Yosano Akiko and the Birth of the Female Voice in Modern Japanese Poetry* (Honolulu: University of Hawai'i Press, 2002).

[5]Ibid., 51.

[6]Ibid.

[7]Ibid., 27.

[8]Ibid., 31.

[9]Laurel Rasplica Rodd, "Yosano Akiko and the Taishō Debate over the 'New Woman,'" in Gail Lee Bernstein, ed., *Recreating Japanese Women, 1600–1945* (Berkeley and Los Angeles: University of California Press, 1991), 179.

[10]Yosano Akiko's 1904 poem *Kimi shinitamau koto nakare* has been translated by

Laurel Rasplica Rodd as "My Brother, You Must Not Die" and published in Marian Arkin and Barbara Shollar, eds., *Longman Anthology of World Literature by Women, 1875–1975* (New York: Longman, 1989), 189–90. For commentary on this poem, see chap. 5, "Yosano Akiko: To Give One's Life or Not—A Question of Which War," in Steve Rabson, *Righteous Cause or Tragic Folly: Changing Views of War in Modern Japanese Poetry* (Ann Arbor, MI: Center for Japanese Studies, 1998), 107–43.

[11]For more on the Motherhood Protection Debate, see Barbara Molony, "Equality versus Difference: The Japanese Debate over 'Motherhood Protection,' 1915–50," in Janet Hunter, ed., *Japanese Women Working* (London and New York: Routledge, 1993), 122–48; Rodd, "Yosano Akiko and the Taishō Debate over the 'New Woman,'" 189–98; and Hiroko Tomida, *Hiratsuka Raichō and Early Japanese Feminism* (Leiden: Brill, 2004), 221–61.

[12]Yosano Akiko's intense involvement with *The Tale of Genji* is well documented in G. G. Rowley, *Yosano Akiko and The Tale of Genji* (Ann Arbor, MI: Center for Japanese Studies, 2000).

[13]Rodd, "Yosano Akiko and the Taishō Debate over the 'New Woman,'" 179–80.

[14]Teruko Craig's translation. See Hiratsuka Raichō and Teruko Craig, *In The Beginning, Woman Was the Sun: The Autobiography of Hiratsuka Raichō* (New York: Columbia University Press, 2006), 149; Hiratsuka Raichō, *Genshi, josei wa taiyō de atta: Hiratsuka Raichō jiden* (Ōtsuki Shoten, 1971–73), 1: 311.

[15]Ibid., 1: 312. In a 1912 *Seitō* essay on writer Higuchi Ichiyō (1872–96), Raichō quotes only the first two verses of Yosano Akiko's "Sozorogoto" to reflect on how times had changed, arguing that Akiko, as a woman of "new Japan," could take pride in being a woman and proudly proclaim this, whereas Ichiyō, writing in her diary 1896, regarded being a woman as a condition fraught with misery. Hiratsuka Raichō, "Onna to shite no Higuchi Ichiyō" (Higuchi Ichiyō, the Woman), *Seitō* 2.10 (October 1912): 102–28.

[16]Hiratsuka, *Genshi, josei wa taiyō de atta*, 1: 312–13; translated by Teruko Craig in Hiratsuka and Craig, *In the Beginning, Woman Was the Sun*, 149–50.

[17]Seki Reiko, "Bungaku ni okeru jendā tōsō: *Seitō* sōkan-gō no mittsu no tekusuto bunseki o chūshin ni," in Iida Yūko, ed., *"Seitō" to iu ba: Bungaku, jendā, atarashii onna* (Shinwasha, 2002), 18.

[18]Ibid., 18–19.

[19]Ibid., 19.

[20]Kōra Rumiko, "Yosano Akiko to *Seitō*," *Sōzō* 55 (October 1991), as cited in Nakashima Miyuki, "Shi to kaiga ni miru *Seitō* no joseizō," in Iida Yūko, ed., *"Seitō" to iu ba*, 134.

[21]Nakashima Miyuki, "Shi to kaiga ni miru *Seitō* no joseizō," 134–35.

[22]Muraoka Yoshiko, "Shika ni miru shakai to no setten," in Yoneda Sayoko and Ikeda Emiko, eds., *"Seitō" o manabu hito no tame ni* (Sekai Shisō-sha, 1999), 163–65.

[23]Kōra Rumiko, as cited in Nakashima, "Shi to kaiga ni miru *Seitō* no joseizō," 134.

[24]Nakashima believes that, although this image of a moon flower did not appear again in *Seitō*, it gained prominence through the paintings of Takehisa Yumeji (1884–1934) and in a 1918 popular song that tied the moon flower to Takehisa's representations of slender, pale women. Nakashima, "Shi to kaiga ni miru *Seitō* no joseizō," 136–37.

[25]Yamasaki Akiko, "*Seitō* no hyōshi-e: imēji to shite no 'atarashii onna,'" in Shin

Feminizumu Hihyō no Kai, ed., *"Seitō" o yomu: Blue Stocking* (Gakugei Shorin, 1998), 404–8, and as cited in Nakashima, "Shi to kaiga ni miru *Seitō* no joseizō," 132–33.

[26]Ibid., 133.

[27]Hiratsuka, *Genshi, josei wa taiyō de atta*, 1: 333; translated by Teruko Craig in Hiratsuka and Craig, *In the Beginning, Woman Was the Sun*, 159–60.

[28]Hiratsuka Raichō, "Atarashii onna" (New Woman), *Chūō kōron* (January 1913), as cited in Nakashima, "Shi to kaiga ni miru *Seitō* no joseizō," 141.

[29]Yosano Akiko, "Dentō" (Gaslight), *Seitō* 4.2 (February 1914): 61–63.

[30]Nakashima, "Shi to kaiga ni miru *Seitō* no joseizō," 141–42.

[31]For English translations of the poetry Yosano Akiko wrote about her trip to Paris in 1912 and published in *Seitō*, see Janine Beichman, "Akiko Goes to Paris: The European Poems," *JATJ* 25.1 (April 1991), Special Issue on Yosano Akiko: 123–45.

[32]Yosano Akiko, "Mori no taiju" (Great Tree in the Forest), *Seitō* 5.8 (September 1915): 39–42.

[33]Horiba Kiyoko, *Seitō no jidai: Hiratsuka Raichō to atarashii onna-tachi* (Iwanami Shoten, 1988), 257–58.

[34]Nakashima, "Shi to kaiga ni miru *Seitō* no joseizō," 142–45.

[35]Ibid., 144.

[36]Friedrich Nietzsche, "Of Old and Young Women," in idem, *Thus Spoke Zarathustra*, trans. R. J. Hollingdale (New York: Penguin Books, 1961; reprint 1984), 93: "Give me your little truth, woman!' I said. And thus spoke the little old woman: 'Are you visiting women? Do not forget your whip!'"

Appendix A
A *Seitō* Chronology

o   Events in the life of *Seitō*
•   Dates of publications translated in this volume

Meiji 44	1911	June 1	o	First meeting of the five founders of *Seitō* (Hiratsuka Raichō, Yasumochi Yoshiko, Kiuchi Teiko, Nakano Hatsuko, Mozume Kazuko).
		Sep 1	o	*Seitō* debuts, 134 pages; sells for 25 sen; 1,000 copies printed. Ordinary members are to pay 30 sen in dues by the 15th of each month.
			•	"The Guiding Principles of the Bluestockings"
			•	Yosano Akiko, "Rambling Thoughts"
			•	Hiratsuka Raichō, "In the Beginning, Woman Was the Sun"
		Oct	o	Inaugural issue of *Seitō* is sold out.
		Nov	o	Henrik Ibsen's *A Doll's House* plays at the newly opened Imperial Theater.
Taishō 1	1912	Jan	o	*Seitō* includes section of translations of review essays by G. B. Shaw and Janet Lee, as well as several Bluestockings' essays on Ibsen's *A Doll's House*.
			o	Araki Ikuko holds the Bluestockings' New Year's Party.
		Apr	o	The *Seitō* Study Group is initiated.
			•	Araki Iku[ko], "The Letter"; prompts authorities to interrupt the sale of this issue
			•	Katō Midori, "Obsession"

Taishō 1	1912	July	o	The *Seitō* Editors' Notes report that the object of Raichō's affections is a beautiful youth who enjoys five-colored liquor; the "youth" is Otake Kōkichi.
			o	Hiratsuka Raichō, Nakano Hatsuko, and Otake Kōkichi visit the geisha Eizan at the Daimonjirō in the Yoshiwara.
			o	The New Woman becomes a popular media topic. There are sensationalized reports of the Bluestockings' "Five-Colored Liquor Incident" and "Visit to the Yoshiwara"; *Kokumin shinbun* runs the series "The So-Called New Woman."
			o	Bluestockings Hiratsuka Raichō, Otake Kōkichi, Kiuchi Teiko, Yasumochi Yoshiko, Araki Ikuko go on holiday at the seashore at Chigasaki in July and August; Ikuta Chōkō and his wife also there.
		Sept	o	Tōundō Publishing Company becomes the publisher and distributor of *Seitō*; sales increase, eventually to 3,000 issues per month.
		Oct	o	Tōundō assumes responsibility for collecting *Seitō* subscription fees and monthly Bluestockings' membership fees.
			o	Attempts are made to resume the *Seitō* Study Group.
			o	Bluestockings hold an anniversary celebration on 17 Oct at a restaurant favored by literati in Uguisudani, Tokyo.
			o	*Tokyo Nichi Nichi shinbun* runs the six-article series "Women Who Clamor to Be New."

Taishō 1	1912	Nov	o	*Tokyo Nichi Nichi shinbun* runs the ten-article series "Strange Love."
		Dec	o	The *Seitō* Editors' Notes report that journalists are poking fun at New Women and the Bluestockings; it is proposed that the Bluestockings take up the subject themselves.
			•	Kobayashi Katsu, "Anesthetic"
Taishō 2	1913	Jan	o	*Seitō* includes a special section on "The New Woman and the Woman Question."
			o	Hiratsuka Raichō's "I Am a New Woman" is translated in full in *The Japan Times* on 11 Jan.
			o	The major journal *Chūō kōron* runs a special feature on the New Woman.
			•	Itō Noe, "The Path of the New Woman"
			•	Iwano Kiyo[ko], "Men and Women Are Equal as Members of the Human Race"
		Feb	o	*Seitō* Public Lecture takes place 15 Feb (speakers: Baba Kochō, Hiratsuka Raichō, Ikuta Chōkō, Itō Noe, Iwano Hōmei, Iwano Kiyoko, Yasumochi Yoshiko).
			o	Ikuta Chōkō is no longer advisor to the Bluestockings.
			o	Tōundō publishes *A Collection of Seitō Fiction*.
			•	Fukuda Hideko, "The Solution to the Woman Question"—most likely the article that prompts authorities to prohibit the sale of this issue
		Mar	•	Iwano Kiyo[ko], "On Intellectual and Economic Independence"
		Apr	o	*Seitō* produces regular monthly income.
			•	Ogasawara Sada, "Eastern Breeze"
			•	Hiratsuka Raichō, "To the Women of the World"; police warning to Bluestockings to avoid corrupting public morals and order

APPENDIX A

Taishō 2	1913	May	o	Tōundō publishes the collection of Raichō's essays *From the Round Window*, which is quickly banned. Raichō removes "To the Women of World" and successfully publishes the collection in June under the new title *At the Locked Window*.
			o	The *Seitō* Study Group and Public Lectures are halted.
			o	The major journal *Taiyō* features articles on the Woman Question; July issue of *Chūō kōron* takes up women's issues.
		Aug	o	Yasumochi Yoshiko and Hiratsuka Raichō disagree with Tōundō over profits that should accrue to the Bluestockings.
		Oct	•	Revised version of "The Guiding Principles of the Bluestockings"
		Nov	o	Bluestockings transfer publishing and distribution responsibilities to Shōbundō, a bookstore in Kanda, Tokyo; sales decrease; Bluestockings repeatedly try other publishers.
		Dec	•	Itō Noe, "Willfulness"
Taishō 3	1914	Jan	o	Hiratsuka Raichō leaves home 13 Jan to live with Okumura Hiroshi.
		Feb	•	Hiratsuka Raichō, "To My Parents on Becoming Independent"
		Apr	•	Nogami Yaeko, "New Life"
		Sept	o	*Seitō* not published this month.
		Nov	o	Itō Noe assumes temporary responsibility as chief editor and begins discussion with Raichō about making this position permanent; Raichō agrees to this in Dec.
		Dec	o	Debate on chastity begins in *Seitō* with Harada (Yasuda) Satsuki's article "On Living and Chastity," a response to Nishizaki (Ikuta) Hanayo's article "On Eating and Chastity" in the journal *Hankyō* (Echo).

262

Taishō 4	1915	Jan	o	Itō Noe is chief editor of *Seitō*.
		May	o	Special issue of *Seitō* contains several works of fiction, essays, and translation.
		Jun	•	Harada (Yasuda) Satsuki, "To My Lover from a Woman in Prison"; prompts authorities to ban the sale of *Seitō*; debate on abortion follows in *Seitō*
		Aug	o	*Seitō* not published this month.
		Sep	o	Itō Noe vows to maintain *Seitō* despite its financial difficulties and attacks conservative women's groups' anti-prostitution activism.
			•	Iwano Kiyo[ko], "Thoughts on Separation"
Taishō 5	1916	Jan	o	Yamakawa (Aoyama) Kikue and Itō Noe's *Seitō* debate on prostitution begins.
			•	Itō Noe, "Anti-Manifesto: To All of You, My Readers"
			•	Yamada Waka, "Myself and My Surroundings"
		Feb	o	*Seitō* 6.2, the final issue (93 pages; 25 sen), is published. In total, the journal consisted of 52 issues.
			o	Yamakawa (Aoyama) Kikue and Itō Noe's debate on prostitution concludes.
		Apr	o	Itō Noe separates from Tsuji Jun to be with Ōsugi Sakae.
		Nov	o	The Hikage Incident: Itō Noe, Kamichika Ichiko, and Hori Yasuko are all involved with Ōsugi Sakae; Kamichika is arrested after stabbing Ōsugi. Itō and Ōsugi become partners and have five children together before being murdered in Sept 1923.

Appendix B
Declarations: The Bluestocking Bylaws and "Anti-Manifesto"

The story of the Bluestockings, the idea of creating a forum exclusively for women writers, and even the name of the group itself owe their inspiration to one man, Ikuta Chōkō (1882–1936). Essayist, translator, novelist, playwright, and teacher, Chōkō had a fascination with discovering and developing superlative women writers. His role in launching *Seitō* and in shaping the initial direction of the magazine is most evident in "The Guiding Principles of the Bluestockings" (Seitō-sha gaisoku, 1911, translated below), especially in Article One's pledge to promote women's literature and women writers. He was also the person who recommended that the young women form a network of supporters, consisting of women writers who had already made a name for themselves, to help *Seitō* get established; in addition, he evaluated submissions to *Seitō*.[1]

Chōkō remained an advisor to the Bluestockings in the group's first stormy years, strongly encouraging them to respond to public criticism by presenting lectures on the New Woman. He even participated in the lecture event when it took place on February 15, 1913. It appears, however, that the event exacerbated differences in philosophy that had existed between Chōkō and Hiratsuka Raichō since the magazine's inception, for shortly thereafter Chōkō ceased to exert the same influence on *Seitō* policy. His essay was not even included among those lectures reprinted in *Seitō* in March 1913.[2] When "The Guiding Principles" (revised version also translated below) was revised in 1913, Raichō wrote that the group would no longer be "troubling" Chōkō, and Chōkō went on to found a magazine of his own, *Hankyō* (Echo).

At the heart of this rift lay the fundamental difference between Chōkō and Raichō as to the nature of female creativity, which in turn affected their views on *Seitō*'s mission. Chōkō, an avid reader of writing by women, was primarily interested in *Seitō* as a venue in which women writers would be able to display an essentially female voice, one that he believed was too often lost when a woman's writing was placed in a magazine primarily for men writers. As noted in Chapter 12 on the poet Yosano Akiko, Chōkō was also captivated by the notion of female creativity as something ethereal and otherworldly. For Raichō, the modern woman had to be a woman consumed by rigorous introspection and bent on discovery of an essential self that ultimately transcended gender boundaries. Whether or not this led to literary achievements was of little concern to her, and she accepted this part of the *Seitō* mission with little enthusiasm. Her initial proposal for "The Guiding Principles" shows her primary desire to put seeking self-awareness first, and to appeal to all women rather than only those with writing talent:

> This is not the time for women to continue indulging in idleness. We must awaken without delay and fully develop the natural talents that have been given to women as well. Today we launch the Bluestockings, an organization comprised exclusively of women and devoted to women's thought, art, and self-cultivation. We also inaugurate our magazine *Seitō* to give voice to the nameless women who sympathize with these ideas. We hope—and, moreover, we believe—that the outstanding women writers of the future will emerge here.[3]

A segment of the Editors' Notes at the end of the first issue, probably written by Raichō, reiterates these sentiments:

> *Seitō* is for women. Working together on this project, we see its ultimate purpose as the full display of the innate talents of the individual and as an attempt at self-liberation. Because our essential aim is to cultivate ourselves and to publish the results of that effort, we believe that this is not a magazine for its own sake but will always be a magazine for us.[4]

Nevertheless, Raichō accepted Ikuta Chōkō's recommendation to revise Article One of "The Guiding Principles" to emphasize the goal of nurturing women writers.

In 1913, after criticism forced the Bluestockings to take a stand and speak about the New Woman, tensions arose between those members who wanted to proclaim themselves New Women and those who were largely interested in literature and timid about all the controversy. The process of taking stock of the magazine and its direction required revising "The Guiding Principles." The revised version, published in the October 1913 issue of *Seitō*, in the wake of especially hostile public reaction to the escapades of certain Bluestockings, discarded the original mission, envisioned by Chōkō, of developing women's literary talents and building connections with established women writers. The first part of Article One of the 1913 version thus reflects Raichō's original sentiments and "aims to stimulate the awakening of women" rather than to "promote the development of women's literature." One of the other revisions, Article Twelve, shows that while the editors open membership to all women, "only those who agree with the Bluestockings' goals" need apply. Article Thirteen stipulates that an applicant's photograph must accompany application for membership in the Bluestockings. This was added after a young man by the name of Fujii Yoshito (1892–1971) slipped into the ranks by giving his name as Natsu and publishing a tanka entitled "Gem" (Hōgyoku) in Seitō 2.8 (August 1912): 46–49.[5] All current members, including the remaining founders Hiratsuka Raichō (listed as Hiratsuka Haru) and Yasumochi Yoshiko (Yasumochi Hakuu), appear under the heading "New Members," perhaps an indication of the fresh start the group was initiating.

Chōkō's imprint always remained on Seitō because he was the one who had given the magazine its name. Recalling the eighteenth-century London salon led by Elizabeth Montagu (1720–1800), Chōkō suggested adopting the name "Bluestocking." He explained that in this salon women had discussed science and art together with men while wearing blue stockings rather than the usual black ones. Hence "Bluestocking" had become a derisive term associated with a new, often "unfeminine" kind of woman. Since the Japanese public was also likely to receive a woman's literary magazine with derision, Chōkō argued, the group could anticipate this reaction, and in a sense diminish it, by adopting this name in the first place. Raichō had never heard of the Bluestockings but found the idea appealing and agreed with Chōkō's assessment of the situation. Translated into Japanese, the new magazine would be known as Seitō, and the society as Seitō-sha (the Bluestockings).[6]

A final and more radical version of Seitō's mission was penned by Itō Noe during her months at the editorial helm of the magazine. This document is untitled but is headed with the address, "To all of you, my readers" (translated below).[7] Noe had this "anti-manifesto" printed on the cover of the January 1916 issue of Seitō. It reappeared on the cover of the February 1916 issue, which was to be the magazine's last. In this open letter to her readers, Noe vows that the magazine will no longer represent an exclusive group but be open to any and all women who wish to contribute. She declares that each member is to use the magazine as she sees fit, and that if any members need a doctrine, they can create their own. At the same time, Noe expresses more than a hint of defensiveness about her abilities to manage the magazine, despite her resolve to fight on. At this point in the magazine's life, the remaining Bluestockings—and even Hiratsuka Raichō, who had been Itō Noe's mentor in many ways—doubted that Noe could successfully edit Seitō. In fact, the complications of her personal life, the rising costs of producing the magazine, and dwindling support from other Bluestockings made it impossible for Noe to continue publishing Seitō. Yet her "anti-manifesto" ensured that *Seitō* departed with the same kind of utopian dreams and bravura with which it had been born.

****

The Guiding Principles of the Bluestockings
Seitō 1.1 (September 1911)

Article One: This society aims to promote the development of women's literature, to give scope to the innate characteristics of each individual, and to give birth to the female genius of tomorrow.[8]

Article Two: This society shall be named the Bluestockings (Seitō-sha).

Article Three: This society shall establish an office c/o Mozume, 9 Hayashi-chō, Komagome, Hongō-ku [Tokyo].

Article Four: This society shall consist of members, supporting members, and honorary members.

Article Five: Women writers who endorse our goals and young women who would like to become writers in the future or who enjoy literature can all become members without regard to race. Leaders in the women's literary world who endorse our goals can become supporting members. Even men who endorse our goals, as long as they are recognized as meriting the members' respect, can become honorary members.

Article Six: To achieve this society's goals, we will conduct business as listed below:
Once every month, publish the organization's magazine, *Seitō*. *Seitō* should display both the creative and critical work of members and supporting members, and, additionally, criticism by honorary members.
Once every month, hold a members' training and study group. (Supporting members' attendance is voluntary.)
Once every year, hold a general meeting to which supporting and honorary members will be invited and asked to give lectures.
On occasion, arrange excursions.

Article Seven: Members must pay monthly dues of about 30 sen. The society's expenses will include those of both monthly and general meetings.

Expenses will also include providing copies of our magazine *Seitō* to members, supporting members, and honorary members.

Article Eight: The funds for publishing *Seitō* will be disbursed by the founders. These funds will be maintained by donation from members, supporting members, and honorary members.

Article Nine: The chief executives will consist of editors, a general manager, and a treasurer.

Article Ten: These duties will be performed by four people, two of whom will alternate annually. Initially, the founders will assume these duties.

Article Eleven: Chief executives will be elected by the members.

Article Twelve: Chief executives can be reelected.

Founders (in *iroha* order)[9]

Nakano Hatsuko	Yasumochi Yoshiko
Kiuchi Teiko	Hiratsuka Haruko
Mozume Kazuko	

Supporting Members

Hasegawa Shigure	Okada Yachiyo
Katō Kazuko	Yosano Akiko
Kunikida Haruko	Koganei Kimiko
Mori Shigeko	

Members

Iwano Kiyoko	Tozawa Hatsuko
Chino Masako	Ojima Kikuko
Ōmura Kayoko	Ōtake Masako
Katō Midori	Kanzaki Tsuneko
Tahara Yūko	Tamura Toshiko
Ueda Kimiko	Nogami Yaeko
Yamamoto Ryūko	Akune Toshiko
Araki Ikuko	Sakuma Tokiko
Mizuno Senko	Sugimoto Masao

****

The Guiding Principles of the Bluestockings (Revised)
Seitō 3.10 (October 1913)

Article One: This society aims to stimulate the awakening of women, to give scope to the innate characteristics of each individual, and to give birth to the female genius of tomorrow.[10]

Article Two: This society shall be named the Bluestockings (Seitō-sha).

Article Three: This society shall establish an office at 1–163 Sugamo, Tokyo.

Article Four: This society shall consist of executive members, members, and supporting members.

Article Five: To achieve this society's goals, we will conduct business as listed below:

Once every month, publish the organization's magazine, *Seitō*. *Seitō* should carry news about what is going on in the lives of members and supporting members as well as their personal philosophies. (However, this society should also publish the manuscripts of sponsors.)

Publish books.

Occasionally, hold a members' training and study group as well as business meetings. (Supporting members' attendance is voluntary.)

Once every year, hold a general meeting to which supporting members shall be invited and asked to give speeches.

On occasion, arrange excursions.

Article Six: Only women can be executive members, members, and supporting members.

Article Seven: Executive members not only must be those who endorse our society's objectives, they must regard the work of our society as their life's mission. As the leading members, they must devote themselves to the direct management of the affairs of our society. They must assume this responsibility of their own volition. The executive members shall receive *Seitō* every month.

Article Eight: Executive members shall be elected from those members who reside in Tokyo.

Members must pay monthly dues of about 30 sen. The society's expenses will include those of both monthly and general meetings. Expenses will also include providing copies of our magazine *Seitō* to members, supporting members, and honorary members.

Article Nine: There shall be four executive members, two of whom will manage the society's finances while the others take charge of editing and compilation.

Article Ten: Every September there shall be a members' meeting in Tokyo, whereupon executive members will be elected. Reelection is permissible.

Article Eleven: To the extent that the society's finances permit, executive members shall receive some remuneration for their labor.

Article Twelve: Members not only must be those who endorse our society's objectives, they must regard the work of our society as their life's mission. They shall receive our magazine *Seitō*.

Article Thirteen: Those who wish to become members should send us your address, name, age, as well as a general résumé, a description your present circumstances, and your motivation for wanting to join. This should be accompanied by a manuscript of more than ten pages (story, play, impressionistic essay, poetry, criticism, translation; any of these will be fine). All of the above should be sent to our office along with a recent photograph of yourself.

Article Fourteen: Supporters, our superiors (*senpai*), are those who have already established themselves in the literary world, and are also those who endorse the goals of our society and readily consent to contribute to our magazine *Seitō*. They shall receive *Seitō* every month.

Article Fifteen: Sponsors will give financial support to the group's work.

Article Sixteen: We will recruit sponsors through a sponsors' agreement.

Seitō-sha [The Bluestockings]

New Members of the Bluestockings (in *iroha* order)
      Iwano Kiyo[ko]   Itō Noe
      Iwabuchi Yuri   Hayashi Chitose

Nishizaki Hanayo	Ogasawara Sada
Okamoto Kano	Katano Tama
Yasumochi Hakuu[11]	Yasuda Satsuki
Makino Kimie	Kobayashi Katsu
Aoki Jōko	Asano Tomo
Sakamoto Makoto[12]	MikajimaYoshi
Shibata Kayo	Hiratsuka Haru

We would like to ask those of you who have not yet replied to kindly do so at your earliest opportunity. It is time that we prepare for future activities.

Current Executive Members

General Affairs and Accounting Chief	Yasumochi Hakuu
Editor-in-Chief	Hiratsuka Haru
Assistants	Itō Noe
	Kobayashi Katsu

****

Anti-Manifesto: To All of You, My Readers
Itō Noe
Seitō 6.1 (January 1916)

Dear Reader:

I want to make this magazine that I edit as respectable a publication as possible. But no matter how much I try to flatter myself that I can do so, it is just not possible to produce a magazine with anything but the poorest content. Given the limits of my personal influence, I cannot possibly solicit the sort of manuscripts from distinguished writers that would satisfy every reader. Thus, the majority of people included in the Table of Contents have yet to become recognized writers.

Although issue after issue prompts such complaints as "How shabby" or "How boring," I persist in publishing a virtually worthless magazine. To my way of thinking, good reasons for this can, nevertheless, be offered. I do not expect this magazine to possess any merit beyond providing a mere seedbed. At the time I inherited editorial responsibility for this magazine, I warned that I would abolish all its rules and that it would have "no regulations, no policy, no ideology, and no philosophy." As for those of you who want an ideology or who have to have rules, why don't you just make your own? Since I am providing a magazine for all women, a magazine which has no ideology and no philosophy, each of you should feel free to use it any way you wish. Indeed, to enable readers to do what they like with the magazine, I have kept it entirely free of any particular message. This, too, I announced at the time I took charge of *Seitō*. I would like even those who are just glancing at this inadequate magazine to be aware of this. This magazine has absolutely no merit other than to serve as a seedbed. Only to those of you who are intrigued by the plants that have sprouted in this seedbed, only to those who wonder where these plants will be transplanted and how they will grow, only to you will this magazine—this unfinished product—clearly reveal the significance of its existence.

No matter how I may be criticized, using such stubborn protests as my shield, I am publishing this magazine as before, without faltering in my enthusiasm.

Notes

[1]Hiroko Tomida, *Hiratsuka Raichō and Early Japanese Feminism* (Leiden: Brill, 2004), 146–47.

[2]In *Genshi*, Raichō writes, "To compound matters, we had neglected to publish Chōkō's February 15th lecture. Had he been too preoccupied to send back the corrected transcript? Or had he already begun to dissociate himself from Seitō? To this day, I am puzzled." As translated in Hiratsuka Raichō and Teruko Craig, *In the Beginning, Woman Was the Sun: The Autobiography of a Japanese Feminist* (New York: Columbia University Press, 2006), 216; Hiratsuka Raichō, *Genshi, josei wa taiyō de atta: Hiratsuka Raichō jiden* (Ōtsuki Shoten, 1971–72), 2: 453.

[3]Hiratsuka, *Genshi, josei wa taiyō de atta*, 1: 296; Hiratsuka and Craig, *In the Beginning, Woman Was the Sun*, 143.

[4]Editors' Notes, *Seitō* 1.1 (September 1911): 134.

[5]Ikegawa Reiko, "*Seitō*-shi ue yuiitsu no dansei shain? Fujii Natsu," in Raichō Kenkyūkai, ed., *"Seitō" jinbutsu jiten: 110-nin no gunzō* (Taishūkan Shoten, 2001), 145.

[6]Hiratsuka, *Genshi, josei wa taiyō de atta* 1: 298–301; Hiratsuka and Craig, *In the Beginning, Woman Was the Sun*, 144–45. For an interesting explanation of how Raichō chose to render "bluestocking" in Chinese characters, see Tomida, *Hiratsuka Raichō and Early Japanese Feminism* (Leiden: Brill, 2004), 146, n41.

[7]Itō Noe, "Dokusha shoshi ni" (To All of You, My Readers), *Seitō* 6.1 (January 1916): Cover.

[8]The original Bluestocking bylaws appeared in *Seitō* 1.1 (September 1911): 132–33. Brief one- or two-page biographies of most women listed in the original and the revised bylaws can be found in Raichō Kenkyūkai, ed., *"Seitō" jinbutsu jiten*.

[9]The Japanese original states that all names are given in *iroha* order, the equivalent of alphabetical order in English. I have maintained the original *iroha* order. All names are given with family name first and given name last, following the original East Asian naming convention. Raichō appears as Hiratsuka Haruko.

[10]The revised Bluestocking bylaws first appeared in *Seitō* 3.10 (October 1913): 138–39.

[11]In the original bylaws, Yasumochi lists her given name (Yoshiko), but she uses her pen name (Hakuu) in the revised bylaws.

[12]Makoto is commonly a man's first name, but this Makoto was female. Takada Makoto (1889–1954), the first of her parents' six children, took her husband's family name, Shibata, upon their marriage in 1911. Makoto bore five children herself and was active through the early 1930s in movements to expand women's rights. Raichō Kenkyūkai, ed., *"Seitō" jinbutsu jiten*, 112–13.

Bibliography

Ambaras, David R. *Bad Youth: Juvenile Delinquency and the Politics of Everyday Life in Modern Japan*. Berkeley, Los Angeles, London: University of California Press, 2006.

Andrew, Nancy. "The Seitōsha: An Early Japanese Women's Organization, 1911–1916." *Papers on Japan*. Cambridge, MA: East Asian Research Center, Harvard University, 1972, 6: 45–69.

Anderson, Marnie S. "Kishida Toshiko and the Rise of the Female Speaker in Meiji Japan." *U.S.–Japan Women's Journal*, nos. 30–31 (2006): 36–59.

Aoki, Michiko. "Nogami Yaeko." In Chieko I. Mulhern, ed., *Japanese Women Writers: A Bio-Critical Sourcebook*. Westport, CT: Greenwood Press, 1994, 274–83.

Aoyama Kikue. "Nihon fujin no shakai jigyō ni tsuite: Itō Noe shi ni atau" (On the Social Work of Japanese Ladies: A Response to Ms. Itō Noe). *Seitō* 6.1 (January 1916): 142–53.

―――. "Sara ni ronshi o akiraka ni su" (Further Clarification of My Argument). *Seitō* 6.2 (February 1916): 69–79.

Araki Iku[ko]. *Hi no musume* (Daughter of Fire, 1914). Vol. 6 in the series *Sōsho "Seitō" no onna-tachi*. Reprint. Fuji Shuppan, 1986.

―――. *Hi-gami no tawamure* (Frolic of the Sun God). *Seitō* 1.1 (September 1911): 63–89.

―――. "Michiko." *Seitō* 1.3 (November 1911): 27–37.

―――. "Michishirube" (Guidepost). In idem, *Hi no musume*, 180–81. Vol. 6 in the series *Sōsho "Seitō" no onna-tachi*. Reprint. Fuji Shuppan, 1986.

―――. "Tegami" (The Letter). *Seitō* 2.4 (April 1912): 102–6.

―――. "Utsukushiki jigoku" (Beautiful Hell). *Seitō* 4.3 (March 1914): 84–97.

―――. *Yami no hana* (Flowers of Darkness). *Seitō* 2.2 (February 1912): 52–74.

Araki Shigeko. "Uzu" (Whirlpool). *Seitō* 5.10 (November 1915): 70–84 and 5.11 (December 1915): 29–38. [A story that spans two issues.]

Auestad, Reiko Abe. "The Scar, A Story from *Seitō*." *Monumenta Nipponica* 58.2 (2003): 171–92.

Baba Kochō. "Fujin no tame ni" (For the Sake of Women), *Seitō* 3.3 (March 1913), Supplement: 33–45.

Bacon, Alice Mabel. *Japanese Women and Girls*. Boston: Houghton, Mifflin and

Co., 1891.

Barash, Carol, ed. *An Olive Schreiner Reader: Writings on Women and South Africa*. Afterword by Nadine Gordimer. London and New York: Pandora, 1987.

Bardsley, Jan. "Feminism's Literary Legacy in Japan: *Seitō*, 1911–1916." *The Gest Journal*, Princeton University, 5.2 (Winter 1992): 87–102.

———. "*Seitō* and the Resurgence of Writing by Women." In Joshua Mostow, general ed., and Sharalyn Orbaugh, section ed., *The Columbia Companion to Modern East Asian Literature*. New York: Columbia University Press, 2003, 93–98.

———. "Versions and Subversions of a Woman's Life: The Autobiographies of Hiratsuka Raichō." In Janice Brown and Sonja Arntzen, eds., *Across Time & Genre: Reading and Writing Japanese Women's Texts*. Conference Proceedings, Department of East Asian Studies, University of Alberta, 2002, 21–24.

———. "Writing for the New Woman of Taishō Japan: Hiratsuka Raichō and the *Seitō* Journal, 1911–1916." Ph.D. diss., University of California, Los Angeles, 1989.

Beauchamp, Edward R. "The Social Role of Japanese Women: Continuity and Change." *International Journal of Women's Studies* 2 (March–June 1979): 244–56.

Beichman, Janine. "Akiko Goes to Paris: The European Poems." *Journal of the Association of Teachers of Japanese* 25.1 (April 1991), Special Issue on Yosano Akiko: 123–45.

———. *Embracing the Firebird: Yosano Akiko and the Birth of the Female Voice in Modern Japanese Poetry*. Honolulu: University of Hawai'i Press, 2002.

Bowring, Richard. *Mori Ōgai and the Modernization of Japanese Culture*. Cambridge: Cambridge University Press, 1979.

Brownstein, Michael C. "*Jogaku Zasshi* and the Founding of Bungakukai." *Monumenta Nipponica* 35.3 (1980): 319–36.

Buckley, Sandra. "Altered States: The Body Politics of "Being-Woman." In Andrew Gordon, ed., *Postwar Japan as History*. Berkeley and Los Angeles: University of California Press, 1993, 347–72.

———. *Broken Silence: Voices of Japanese Feminism*. Berkeley and Los Angeles: University of California Press, 1997.

———. "A Short History of the Feminist Movement in Japan." In Joyce Gelb and Marian Lief Palley, eds., *Women of Japan and Korea: Continuity and Change*. Philadelphia: Temple University Press, 1994, 150–86.

Coleman, Samuel. *Family Planning in Japanese Society: Traditional Birth Control in Modern Urban Culture*. Princeton: Princeton University Press, 1983.

Condon, Jane. *A Half Step Behind: Japanese Women Today*. Rutland, VT, and

Tokyo: Charles E. Tuttle, Co., 1985.

Copeland, Rebecca. "Fashioning the Feminine: Images of the Modern Girl Student in Meiji Japan." *U.S.–Japan Women's Journal,* nos. 30–31 (2006): 13–35.

———. "Hiratsuka Raichō." In Chieko I. Mulhern, ed., *Japanese Women Writers: A Bio-Critical Sourcebook.* Westport, CT: Greenwood Press, 1994, 132–43.

———. *Lost Leaves: Women Writers of Meiji Japan.* Honolulu: University of Hawai'i Press, 2000.

———. "The Meiji Woman Writer 'Amidst a Forest of Beards.'" *Harvard Journal of Asian Studies* 57.2 (December 1997): 383–418.

———. *The Sound of the Wind: The Life and Works of Uno Chiyo.* Honolulu: University of Hawai'i Press, 1992.

———, ed. *Woman Critiqued: Translated Essays on Japanese Women's Writing.* Honolulu: University of Hawai'i Press, 2006.

Copeland, Rebecca, and Melek Ortabasi, eds. *The Modern Murasaki: Writing by Women of Meiji Japan.* New York: Columbia University Press, 2006.

Craig, Teruko. *See under* Hiratsuka and Craig.

Czarnecki, Melanie. "Bad Girls from Good Families: The Degenerate Meiji Schoolgirl." In Laura Miller and Jan Bardsley, eds., *Bad Girls of Japan.* New York: Palgrave, 2005, 48–63.

Dalby, Liza C. *Geisha.* Berkeley and Los Angeles: University of California Press, 1983.

Danly, Robert Lyons. *In the Shade of Spring Leaves: The Life and Writings of Higuchi Ichiyō, A Woman of Letters in Meiji Japan.* New Haven: Yale University Press, 1981.

Endō Hiroshi. "Shirakaba ha to joryū bungaku" (The White Birch Society and Women's Literature). *Kokubungaku kaishaku to kanshō* (Japanese Literature: Interpretation and Appreciation), (March 1972): 53–57.

Engels, Frederick [Friedrich]. *The Origin of the Family, Private Property and the State.* New York: Pathfinder, 1972.

Enoki Takashi. "Shizenshugi to joryū bungaku" (Naturalism and Women's Literature). *Kokubungaku kaishaku to kanshō* (Japanese Literature: Interpretation and Appreciation), (March 1972): 18–22.

Ericson, Joan E. *Be a Woman: Hayashi Fumiko and Modern Japanese Women's Literature.* Honolulu: University of Hawai'i Press, 1997.

Foreman, Kelly. "The Role of Music in the Lives and Identities of Japanese Geisha." Ph.D. diss., Kent State University, 2002.

Fowler, Edward. *The Rhetoric of Confession: Shishōsetsu in Early Twentieth-Century Japanese Fiction.* Berkeley and Los Angeles: University of California Press, 1988.

———, trans. "Lifeblood" (Ikichi, by Tamura Toshiko, 1911). In Rebecca Copeland and Melek Ortabasi, eds., *The Modern Murasaki: Writing by Women of Meiji Japan*. New York: Columbia University Press, 2006, 348–57.

Frederick, Sarah. *Turning Pages: Reading and Writing Women's Magazines in Interwar Japan*. Honolulu: University of Hawai'i Press, 2006.

Frühstück, Sabine. *Colonizing Sex: Sexology and Social Control in Modern Japan*. Berkeley and Los Angeles: University of California Press, 2003.

Fujii, James A. *Complicit Fictions: The Subject in the Modern Japanese Prose Narrative*. Berkeley and Los Angeles: University of California Press, 1993.

Fujimura-Fanselow, Kumiko, and Atsuko Kameda, eds. *Japanese Women: New Feminist Perspectives on the Past, Present and Future*. New York: The Feminist Press, 1995.

Fujita Kazumi. "*Seitō* dokusha no isō" (Mapping the *Seitō* readers). In Shin Feminizumu Hihyō no Kai, ed., "*Seitō*" *o yomu: Blue Stocking*. Gakugei Shorin, 1998, 466–88.

Fukuda Hideko. "Fujin mondai no kaiketsu" (The Solution to the Woman Question). *Seitō* 3.2 (February 1913), Supplement: 1–7.

Furuya, Tsunatake. "Meiji Women: Landmarks They Have Left." *Japan Quarterly* 14 (July–September 1967): 318–25.

Garon, Sheldon. *Molding Japanese Minds: The State in Everyday Life*. Princeton, NJ: Princeton University Press, 1997.

Gelb, Joyce, and Marian Lief Palley, eds. *Women of Japan and Korea: Continuity and Change*. Philadelphia: Temple University Press, 1994.

Gilman, Charlotte Perkins. *Women and Economics*. Boston: Small, Maynard and Company, 1898. [Translated by Ōtawa Take as *Fujin to keizai*. Dai Nihon Bunmei Kyokai, 1912.]

Hane, Mikiso. *Peasants, Rebels, Women and Outcastes: The Underside of Modern Japan*. Second Edition. Lanham, MD: Rowman & Littlefield Publishers, Inc., 2003.

———, ed. and trans. *Reflections on the Way to the Gallows: Rebel Women in Prewar Japan*. Berkeley and Los Angeles: University of California Press, 1988.

Hanmura Shinobu. "Itō Noe." In Raichō Kenkyūkai, ed., "*Seitō*" *jinbutsu jiten: 110-nin no gunzō*. Taishūkan Shoten, 2001, 40–41.

Harada Satsuki. "Goku-chū no onna kara otoko ni" (To My Lover from a Woman in Prison). *Seitō* 5.6 (June 1915): 33–45.

———. "O-me ni kakatta Ikuta Hanayo-san ni tsuite" (On Meeting Ms. Ikuta Hanayo). *Seitō* 5.2 (February 1915): 66–73.

Hardacre, Helen. *Marketing the Menacing Fetus in Japan*. Berkeley and Los Angeles: University of California Press, 1997.

Hastings, Sally A. "Hatoyama Haruko: Ambitious Woman." In Anne Walthall, ed., *The Human Tradition in Modern Japan*. Wilmington, DE: Scholarly Resources Inc., 2002, 81–98.

Heilmann, Ann. New *Woman Fiction: Women Writing First-Wave Feminism*. New York: St. Martin's Press, 2000.

Hirakawa, Hiroko. "Inverted Orientalism and the Discursive Construction of Sexual Harassment: A Study of Mass Media and Feminist Representations of Sexual Harassment in Japan." Ph.D. diss., Purdue University, 1998.

Hiratsuka Raichō. "Atarashii onna" (New Woman). *Chūō kōron* (The Central Review), (January 1913). Reprinted in Hiratsuka Raichō Chosakushū Henshū Iinkai, ed., *Hiratsuka Raichō chosakushū*. Ōtsuki Shoten, 1983–84, 1: 257–59.

———. "Dokuritsu suru ni tsuite ryōshin ni" (To My Parents on Becoming Independent). *Seitō* 4.2 (February 1914): 102–16.

———. "Genshi, josei wa taiyō de atta" (In the Beginning, Woman Was the Sun). *Seitō* 1.1 (September 1911): 37–52.

———. *Genshi, josei wa taiyō de atta: Hiratsuka Raichō jiden* (In the Beginning, Woman Was the Sun: The Autobiography of Hiratsuka Raichō). 4 vols. Ōtsuki Shoten, 1971–73.

———. "*Hi no musume* o yonde" (Reading *Daughter of Fire*). *Seitō* 4.3 (March 1914): 17–24.

———. "Kojin toshite no seikatsu to sei toshite no seikatsu to no aida no sōtō ni tsuite: Noe-san ni" (On the Conflict Between Life as an Individual and Life as a Sexual Being: To Ms. Noe). *Seitō* 5.8 (September 1915): 1–22.

———. "Onna to shite no Higuchi Ichiyō" (Higuchi Ichiyō, the Woman). *Seitō* 2.10 (October 1912): 102–28.

———. "Sabetsu-teki seidōtoku ni tsuite" (On Discriminatory Sexual Morality). *Fujin kōron* (Ladies' Review) 1.10 (October 1916), as cited in Iwabuchi, "Sekushuaritei no seijigaku e no chōsen: Teiso, datai, haishō ronsō" (Challenging the Politics of Sexuality: Debates on Chastity, Abortion, and the Abolition of Licensed Prostitution), in Shin Feminizumu Hihyō no Kai, ed., "*Seitō*" *o yomu: Blue Stocking*. Gakugei Shorin, 1998, 305–31.

———. "Shojo no kachi" (The True Value of Virginity). *Shin kōron* (New Review), (March 1915), as quoted in Iwabuchi Hiroko, "Sekushuaritei no seijigaku e no chōsen: Teiso, datai, haishō ronsō" (Challenging the Politics of Sexuality: Debates on Chastity, Abortion, and the Abolition of Licensed Prostitution), in Shin Feminizumu Hihyō no Kai, ed., "*Seitō*" *o yomu: Blue Stocking*. Gakugei Shorin, 1998, 305–31.

———. *Watakushi no aruita michi* (The Path I Took). Shinhyōronsha, 1955.

———. "Yajima Kajiko-shi to Fujin Kyōfūkai no jigyō o ronzu" (Comments on the Enterprise of the Women's Reform Society and Ms. Yajima Kajiko). *Shin shōsetsu* (The New Novel), (June 1917).

———. "Yo no fujintachi ni" (To the Women of the World). *Seitō* 3.4 (April 1913): 156–64.

Hiratsuka Raichō, translated with an introduction and notes by Teruko Craig. *In the Beginning, Woman Was the Sun: The Autobiography of Hiratsuka Raichō, Japanese Feminist*. New York: Columbia University Press, 2006.

[Hiratsuka] Raichō, [Katō] Midori, [and Itō] Noe. "Yonda mono no hyō to saikin no kansō" (Comments on Things We've Read and Our Thoughts of Late). *Seitō* 4.5 (May 1914): 110–16.

Hiratsuka Raichō o Yomu Kai, ed. *"Seitō" no go-jūnin* (Fifty People of *Seitō*). Hiratsuka Raichō o Yomu Kai, 1996.

Hiratsuka Raichō Chosakushū Henshū Iinkai, ed. *Hiratsuka Raichō chosakushū* (Selected Works of Hiratsuka Raichō). 8 vols. Ōtsuki Shoten, 1983–84.

Hisamatsu Sen'ichi and Yoshida Sei'ichi, eds. *Nihon joryū bungaku shi* (Japanese Women's Literature). Dōbun Shoin, 1969.

Hogan, Eleanor Joan. "When Art Does *Not* Represent Life: Nogami Yaeko and the Marriage Question." *Women's Studies: An Interdisciplinary Journal* 33.4 (January 2004): 381–98.

———. "A New Kind of Woman: Marriage and Women as Intertext in the Works of Nogami Yaeko and Jane Austen." Ph.D., diss., Washington University, St. Louis, 2001.

Honey, Maureen, ed. *Breaking the Ties that Bind: Popular Stories of the New Woman, 1915–1930*. Norman: University of Oklahoma Press, 1992.

Hopper, Helen. *A New Woman of Japan: A Political Biography of Katō Shidzue*. Transitions: Asian and Asian America. Boulder, Colo.: Westview Press, 1996.

Hori Yasuko. "Watakushi wa furui onna desu" (I Am an Old-Fashioned Woman). *Seitō* 3.1 (January 1913), Supplement: 61–65.

———. "Ōsugi to wakareru made" (Until Separating from Ōsugi). *Chūō kōron* (The Central Review), (March 1917).

Horiba Kiyoko. *Seitō no jidai: Hiratsuka Raichō to atarashii onna-tachi* (The Era of *Seitō*: Hiratsuka Raichō and the New Women). Iwanami Shoten, 1988.

Ibsen, Henrik. *Four Great Plays by Henrik Ibsen*. Trans. R. F. Sharp. New York: Bantam Books, 1959.

———. *Hedda Gabler and Other Plays*. Trans. Una Ellis-Fermor. London: Penguin Books, 1982.

Ide Fumiko. "Araki Iku cho *Hi no musume* kaisetsu" (Comments on *Daughter of Fire*). In Araki Ikuo, *Hi no musume* (1914). Vol. 6 in the series *Sōsho "Seitō" no onna-tachi*. Reprint. Fuji Shuppan, 1986, 1–14.

———. *Hiratsuka Raichō: Kindai to shinpi* (Hiratsuka Raichō: Modernity and

Mystery). Tokyo: Shinchō Sensho, 1987.

———. *Jiyū: Sore watakushi jishin* (Freedom: That Is I). Chikuma Shobō, 1979.

———. *Seitō: Genshi josei wa taiyō de atta* (*Seitō*: In the Beginning, Woman Was the Sun). Kōbundō, 1961.

———. *Seitō no* onnatachi (The Women of *Seitō*). Tokyo: Kaien Shobō, 1975.

Iida Yūko, ed. *"Seitō" to iu ba: Bungaku, jendā, atarashii onna* (The Space Called *Seitō*: Literature, Gender, New Women). Shinwasha, 2002.

Ikari Akira. "Nihon no kazoku seido to joryū bungaku" (The Japanese Family System and Women's Literature). *Kokubungaku kaishaku to kanshō* (Japanese Literature: Interpretation and Appreciation), (March 1972): 53–57.

Ikeda Emiko. "Fūzoku kairan no onna-tachi—hakkin ni kōshite" (The Women who Corrupted Public Decency: Resisting the Bans on Sales). In Yoneda Sayoko and Ikeda Emiko, eds., *"Seitō" o manabu hito no tame ni*. Kyoto: Sekai Shisōsha, 1999, 183–207.

Ikeda Michiko. "Itō Noe." In Setouchi Harumi, series ed., *Onna no isshō: Jinbutsu kindai josei-shi*. Kōdansha, 1980–81, 6: 103–40.

Ikeda Yasuburō and Donald Keene, eds. *Nichi-ei koji kotowaza jiten*. Hokuseidō Shoten, 1995.

Ikegawa Reiko. *"Seitō*-shi no ue yuiitsu no dansei shain? Fujii Natsu" (Fujii Natsu: The Single Male Bluestocking in the History of *Seitō*?). In Raichō Kenkyūkai, ed., *"Seitō" jinbutsu jiten: 110-nin no gunzō*. Taishūkan Shoten, 2001, 145.

Ikegawa Yoshie. "Ikuta Chōkō to *Seitō*" (Ikuta Chōkō and *Seitō*). In Shin Feminizumu Hihyō no Kai, ed., *"Seitō" o yomu: Blue Stocking*. Gakugei Shorin, 1998, 480–513.

Ikuta Hanayo. "Shūi o aisuru koto to dōtei no kachi to—*Seitō* jūni-gatsu-gō Yasuda Satsuki sama no hinan ni tsuite" (On Loving Those Close By and the Value of Virginity: Response to Yasuda Satsuki's Criticism in the December Issue of *Seitō*). *Hankyō* 2.1 (January 1915): 1–17.

———. "Zange no kokoro yori: Hiratsuka Raichō, Itō Noe, Harada-sama ni yosete" (From a Repentant Heart: To Hiratsuka Raichō, Itō Noe, and Ms. Harada). *Seitō* 5.4 (April 1915): 19–28.

Imamura, Anne E., ed. *Re-Imaging Japanese Women*. Berkeley and Los Angeles: University of California Press, 1996.

Inoue, Mariko. "Kiyohata's *Asasuzu:* The Emergence of the *Jogakusei* Image." *Monumenta Nipponica* 51.4 (Winter 1996): 431–60.

Inoue Mihoko. "Kobayashi Katsu." In Raichō Kenkyūkai, ed., *"Seitō" jinbutsu jiten: 110-nin no gunzō*. Taishūkan Shoten, 2001, 92–93.

———. "Ogasawara Sadako." In Raichō Kenkyūkai, ed., *"Seitō" jinbutsu jiten: 110-nin no gunzō*. Taishūkan Shoten, 2001, 58–59.

Inoue Teruko. *Joseigaku to sono shūhen* (Women's Studies and Its Environs). Keisō Shobō, 1989.

Ishigaki Ayako. *Wa ga ai, wa ga amerika* (My Love, My America). Chikuma Shobō, 1991.

Ishimoto, Shidzue. *Facing Two Ways: The Story of My Life*. New York: Farrar & Rinehart, 1935; reprint, Stanford: Stanford University Press, 1984.

Ishizaki Shōko. "Yamada Waka." In Raichō Kenkyūkai, ed., *"Seitō" jinbutsu jiten: 110-nin no gunzō*. Taishūkan Shoten, 2001, 184–85.

———. "Yasuda Satsuki." In Raichō Kenkyūkai, ed., *"Seitō" jinbutsu jiten: 110-nin no gunzō*. Taishūkan Shoten, 2001, 176–77.

Itō Noe. "Aoyama Kikue shi ni" (To Ms. Aoyama Kikue). *Seitō* 6.1 (January 1916): 154–65.

———. "Atarashiki onna no michi" (The Path of the New Woman). *Seitō* 3.1 (January 1913), Supplement: 20–28.

———. "Dokusha shoshi ni" (To All of You, My Readers). *Seitō* 6.1 (January 1916): Cover.

———. "Dōyō" (Turmoil). *Seitō* 3.8 (August 1913): 87–194.

———. "Futatabi Aoyama shi e" (A Second Response to Ms. Aoyama). *Seitō* 6.2 (February 1916): 80–85.

———. "Gōman kōryō ni shite futettei naru nihon fujin no kōkyō jigyō ni tsuite" (Arrogant, Narrow-Minded, Half-Baked Japanese Women's Public Service Activities). *Seitō* 5.11 (December 1915): 1–18.

———. "Henshū-shitsu yori" (From the Editing Room). *Seitō* 4.11 (December 1914): 112–13.

———. "Henshū-shitsu yori" (From the Editing Room). *Seitō* 5.7 (July 1915): 105–6.

———. *Itō Noe zenshū*. 2 vols. Gakugei Shorin, 1970.

———. "Kojiki no meiyo" (Beggar's Honor). *Bunmei hihyō* 3 (April 1918). Reprint. In Itō Noe, *Itō Noe zenshū*. Gakugei Shorin, 1970, 2: 255–81.

———. "Konogoro no kansō" (Recent Thoughts). *Seitō* 3.2 (February 1913): 35–44.

———. "Mayoi" (Perplexity). *Seitō* 4.4 (April 1914): 192–203.

———. "Shishin: Nogami Yae-Sama e" (Private Message to Ms. Nogami Yae). *Seitō* 5.6 (June 1915): 70–81.

———. "Shuppon" (Flight). *Seitō* 4.2 (February 1914): 82–101.

———. *Teihon Itō Noe zenshū* (The Standard Edition of the Complete Works of Itō Noe). 4 vols. Gakugei Shorin, 2000.

———. "Teisō ni tsuite no zakkan" (Miscellaneous Thoughts on Chastity). *Seitō* 5.2 (February 1915): 1–11.

———. "Wagamama" (Willfulness). *Seitō* 3.12 (December 1913): 51–67.

———. "Zatsuon" (Noise). *Osaka Mainichi shinbun*. 3 January–1 April 1916.

Reprinted in Itō Noe, *Itō Noe zenshū*. Gakugei Shorin, 1970, 2: 7–120.

Iwabuchi Hiroko. "Sekushuaritei no seijigaku e no chōsen: Teiso, datai, haishō ronsō" (Challenging the Politics of Sexuality: Debates on Chastity, Abortion, and the Abolition of Licensed Prostitution). In Shin Feminizumu Hihyō no Kai, ed., *"Seitō" o yomu: Blue Stocking*. Gakugei Shorin, 1998, 305–31.

Iwabuchi Junko, ed. *"Danna" to asobi to nihon bunka: Tatsujin ni manabu sui na ikikata* (Patrons, Play and Japanese Culture: A Refined Way of Life Learned from the Masters). PHP Kenkyūjo, 1996.

Iwano Hōmei. "Danshi kara suru yōkyū" (What Men Require). *Seitō* 3.3 (March 1913), Supplement: 8–32.

———. *Hōrō* (Roaming, 1910); *Dankyō* (Broken Bridge, 1911); *Tsukimono* (The Possessed, 1910–18). *Shinchō bunko* series. Tokyo: Shinchōsha, 1955.

———. *Tandeki* (Debauchery, 1909); *Dokuyaku o nomu onna* (The Woman Who Took Poison, 1914). *Kōdansha bungei bunko* series. Tokyo: Kōdansha, 2003.

Iwano Kiyo[ko]. *Ai no sōtō* (Conflict of Love, 1915). Vol. 4 in the series *Sōsho "Seitō" no onna-tachi*. Reprint. Fuji Shuppan, 1985.

———. "Antō" (Secret Feud). *Seitō* 2.4 (April 1912): 82–93.

———. "Bekkyo ni tsuite omou kotodomo" (Thoughts on Separation). *Seitō* 5.8 (September 1915): 23–29.

———. "Binbō no ichi-nen" (A Year of Poverty). *Fujin kōron* (May 1918).

———. "Henshū-shitsu yori" (From the Editing Room). *Seitō* 4.1 (January 1914): 141–48.

———. "Jinrui to shite dansei to josei wa byōdō de aru" (Men and Women Are Equal as Members of the Human Race). *Seitō* 3.1 (January 1913), Supplement: 23–28.

———. "Karekusa" (Withered Grass). *Seitō* 2.2 (February 1912): 43–51.

———. "Kita no kōgai yori" (From a Suburb to the North). *Seitō* 3.11 (November 1913): 73–77.

———. "Kojinshugi to katei" (Individualism and the Family). *Seitō* 4.9 (September 1914): 1–6.

———. "Nikki no dampen" (Odds and Ends from My Diary). *Seitō* 2.5 (May 1912): 65–75.

———. "Omotte iru koto" (Ruminations). *Seitō* 4.5 (May 1914): 105–9.

———. "Otaka" (Otaka). *Seitō* 1.2 (October 1911): 52–63.

———. "Raichō-shi no dai-ni ronshū hakkan ni tsuite" (On the Publication of Raichō's Second Essay Collection). *Seitō* 4.11 (December 1914): 10–14.

———. "Shisō no dokuritsu to keizai-jō no dokuritsu" (On Intellectual and Economic Independence). *Seitō* 3.3 (March 1913), Supplement: 1–7.

———. "Sugamo-mura yori" (From the Village of Sugamo). *Seitō* 4.7 (July 1914): 114–15.

———. "Uranai" (Fortune-telling). *Seitō* 3.9 (September 1913): 99–116.

———. "Wakaretaru otto Iwano Hōmei-shi no shi no kyōgaku o mae ni okite" (Remarks on the Sudden Passing of My Former Husband, Mr. Iwano Hōmei). *Shin shōsetsu* (The New Novel), (June 1920).

———. "Yasukawa naikeiho kyoku-chō no iken ni tsuite" (With Regard to the Opinion of Bureau Chief Yasukawa). *Seitō* 4.9 (September 1914): 150–51.

Iwata Nanatsu. *Bungaku to shite no "Seitō"* (*Seitō* as Literature). Fuji Shuppan, 2003.

———. *"Seitō" no onna: Katō Midori* (A Woman of *Seitō*: Katō Midori). Seikyūsha, 1993.

———. *"Seitō* o shiru tame no kōmoku kaisetsu" (Commentary on Events and Terms Relevant to *Seitō*). In Yoneda Sayoko and Ikeda Emiko, eds., *"Seitō" o manabu hito no tame ni*. Kyoto: Sekai Shisō-sha, 1999, 237–45.

Iwaya Daishi. *Monogatari joryū bundanshi* (Tales of the History of Women's Literary Coteries), vol. 1. Chūō Kōronsha, 1977.

Jimbō Itsuya. "Kinsei bungaku to joryū" (Modern Literature and Women). In Hisamatsu Sei'ichi and Yoshida Sei'ichi, eds., *Nihon joryū bungaku shi*. Dōbun Shoin, 1969, 1–11.

Kamichika Ichiko. "Tegami no hitotsu" (One Letter). *Seitō* 2.9 (September 1912): 100–120.

———. *Watakushi no hansei ki* (Record of Half My Life). Kindai Seikatsu-sha, 1956.

Kanbara Fusae. "Kaetsu jo-shi no seiyō no haibutsu ni tsuite" (With Respect to Mme. Kaetsu's "Obsolescence of the West"). *Seitō* 4.9 (September 1914): 169–70.

———. "Saikin no kansō" (Recent Thoughts). *Seitō* 4.8 (August 1914): 97–100.

Kano, Ayako. *Acting Like a Woman in Modern Japan: Theater, Gender, and Nationalism*. New York: Palgrave, 2001.

Katō Midori. "Atarashii onna ni tsuite" (On the New Woman). *Seitō* 3.1 (January 1913), Supplement: 29–35.

———. "Bokusha no kotoba" (What the Fortune-Teller Said). *Seitō* 4.5 (May 1914): 5–21.

———. "Geijutsu to haru" (Springtime and Art). *Seitō* 3.10 (October 1913): 105–25.

———. "Hoshi no sora" (Starry Sky). *Seitō* 6.1 (January 1916): 116–39.

———. "Kaigi" (Doubt). *Seitō* 2.9 (September 1912): 56–81.

———. "Shūchaku" (Obsession). *Seitō* 2:4 (April 1912): 9–26.

———. "Tada hitori" (All Alone). *Seitō* 5.11 (December 1915): 47–53.

Kawahara Aya. "Hori Yasuko." In Raichō Kenkyūkai, ed., *"Seitō" jinbutsu jiten: 110-nin no gunzō*. Taishūkan Shoten, 2001, 148–49.

Keene, Donald. *Dawn to the West: Japanese Literature of the Modern Era, Fiction* New York: Holt, Rinehart, Winston, 1984.

Kessler, Carol Farley. *Charlotte Perkins Gilman: Her Progress toward Utopia with Selected Writings.* Syracuse, NY: Syracuse University Press, 1995.

Key, Ellen. *The Century of the Child.* New York: G. P. Putnam's Sons, 1909.

———. *Love and Marriage.* New York: G. P. Putnam's Sons, 1911.

Kikuta Shigeo. "Nihon no koten bungaku to kindai joryū no bungaku." (Japanese Classical Literature and Modern Women's Literature). *Kokubungaku to kaishaku to kanshō* (Japanese Literature: Interpretation and Appreciation), (March 1972): 73–78.

Kobayashi Katsu. "Fukeyo kawakaze" (Blow on, River Breeze). *Seitō* 3.2 (February 1913): 45–52.

———. "Kashi" (Riverfront). *Seitō* 3.5 (May 1913): 121–29.

———. "Masui" (Anesthetic). *Seitō* 2.12 (December 1912): 39–46.

———. "O-Fuyu-san no hanashi" (O-Fuyu's Story). *Seitō* 3.4 (April 1913): 93–103.

———. *Onna bakari* (Women Only). *Seitō* 4.7 (July 1914): 54–79.

Kobayashi Tomie. *Hiratsuka Raichō: Ai to hangyaku no Seishun* (Hiratsuka Raichō: A Youth of Love and Rebellion). Ōtsuki Shoten, 1977.

———. *Hiratsuka Raichō: Hito to shiso* (Hiratsuka Raichō: Person and Philosophy). Shimizu Shoin, 1983.

———, ed. *"Seitō" serekushon: Atarashii onna no tanjō* (Selections from *Seitō*: Birth of the New Woman). Jinbun Shoin, 1987.

"Koi no gisei" (Victims of Love). *Tokyo Asahi shinbun.* 26 March 1908: 6.

Kojima Kyōko and Hayakawa Noriyo, eds. *Joseishi no shiza.* Yoshikawa Kōbunkan, 1997.

Kōra Rumiko. "Yosano Akiko to *Seitō*" (Yosano Akiko and *Seitō*). *Sōzō* (Imagination) 55 (October 1991).

Kovalevsky, Sonya. *Sonya Kovalevsky: Her Recollections of Childhood.* Trans. from the Russian by Isabel F. Hapgood, with a biography by Anna Carlotta Leffler, Duchess of Cajanello. New York: The Century Company, 1895.

Kuno, Akiko. *Unexpected Destinations: The Poignant Story of Japan's First Vassar Graduate.* Trans. Kirsten McIvor. Tokyo: Kodansha International, 1993.

Kuramochi Yasuo and Sakata Yukiko, eds. *Kan'yoku kotowaza jiten* (Proverbs Dictionary). Sanseidō, 1983.

LaFleur, William R. *Liquid Life: Abortion and Buddhism in Japan.* Princeton, NJ: Princeton University Press, 1992.

Large, Stephen S. "The Romance of Revolution in Japanese Anarchism and Communism during the Taishō Period." *Modern Asian Studies* 11.3 (1977): 441–67.

Lebra, Joyce, Joy Paulson, and Elizabeth Powers, eds. *Women in Changing Japan*. Boulder, CO: Westview Press, 1976.

Lebra, Takie Sugiyama. *Japanese Women: Constraint and Fulfillment*. Honolulu: University of Hawai'i Press, 1984.

Ledger, Sally. *The New Woman: Fiction and Feminism at the Fin de Siècle*. Manchester and New York: Manchester University Press, 1997.

Levy, Indra. *Sirens of the Western Shore: The Westernesque Femme Fatale, Translation, and Vernacular Style in Modern Japanese Literature*. New York: Columbia University Press, 2006.

Lippit, Noriko. "*Seitō* and the Literary Roots of Japanese Feminism." *International Journal of Women's Studies* 2 (March–April 1979): 155–63.

———. *Stories by Contemporary Japanese Women Writers*. New York: M. E. Sharpe, Inc., 1982.

Lowy, Dina B. "The Japanese 'New Woman': Contending Images of Gender and Modernity, 1910–1920." Ph.D. diss., Rutgers University, 2000.

———. *The Japanese "New Woman": Images of Gender and Modernity*. New Brunswick, NJ, and London: Rutgers University, 2007.

———. "Love and Marriage: Ellen Key and Hiratsuka Raichō Explore Alternatives." *Women's Studies: An Interdisciplinary Journal* 33.4 (January 2004): 361–80.

———. "Nora and the 'New Woman': Visions of Gender and Modernity in Early Twentieth-Century Japan." *U.S.–Japan Women's Journal*, no. 26 (2004): 75–97.

Lublin, Elizabeth Dorn. "Wearing the White Ribbon of Reform and the Banner of Civic Duty: Yajima Kajiko and the Japan Woman's Christian Temperance Union in the Meiji Period." *U.S.–Japan Women's Journal*, nos. 30–31 (2006): 60–79.

Mackie, Vera. *Creating Socialist Women in Japan: Gender, Labour and Activism, 1900–1937*. Cambridge: Cambridge University Press, 1997.

———. *Feminism in Modern Japan: Citizenship, Embodiment and Sexuality*. Cambridge: Cambridge University Press, 2003.

———. "Feminist Politics in Japan." *New Left Review* 167 (January–February 1988): 53–76.

Marukawa Kaseko. "Fukuda Hideko." In Setouchi Harumi, series ed., *Onna no isshō: Jinbutsu kindai josei-shi*. Kōdansha, 1980–81, 6: 57–102.

Maruoka Hideko. *Fujin shisō keisei shi nōto* (Notes on the History of the Formation of Women's Thought), vol. 1. Domesu Shuppan, 1975.

———. "Josei sakka ga kaku onna to otoko" (Women and Men that Women Authors Create). In Kōno Nobuko and Tsurumi Kazuko, general eds., and Okuda Akiko, vol. ed., *Onna to otoko no ji-kū* (Time Space of Gender: Redefining Japanese Women's Writing). Fujiwara Shoten, 1995, 5: 238–77.

Mertz, John Pierre. *Novel Japan: Spaces of Nationhood in Early Meiji Narrative, 1870–88*. Ann Arbor, MI: Center for Japanese Studies, 2003.

Milhalopolous, Bill. "The Making of Prostitutes: The *Karayuki-san.*" *Bulletin of Concerned Asian Scholars* 25.1 (1993): 41–56.

Miller, Laura, and Jan Bardsley, eds. *Bad Girls of Japan*. New York: Palgrave, 2005.

Mitchell, Sally. *The New Girl: Girls' Culture in England, 1880–1915*. New York: Columbia University Press, 1995.

Mitsutani, Margaret. "Renaissance in Women's Literature." *Japan Quarterly* 33 (July–September 1986): 313–19.

Miyamoto, Ken. "Itō Noe and the Bluestockings." *Japan Interpreter* 10 (Autumn 1975): 190–204.

Miyazaki Michiko. *Kindai josei shi* (Modern Women's History). In the *For Beginners* series. Illus. Ichinomon Yōko. Tokyo: Gendai Shokan, 1984.

Molony, Barbara. "Equality versus Difference: The Japanese Debate over 'Motherhood Protection,' 1915–50." In Janet Hunter, ed., *Japanese Women Working*. London and New York: Routledge, 1993, 122–48.

Molony, Barbara, and Kathleen Uno, eds. *Gendering Modern Japanese History*. Cambridge, MA and London: Harvard University Asia Center, 2005.

Molony, Kathleen Susan. *One Woman Who Dared: Ichikawa Fusae and the Japanese Women's Suffrage Movement*. Ph.D. diss., University of Michigan, 1980.

Monnet, Livia. "'In the Beginning, Woman Was the Sun': Autobiographies of Modern Japanese Women Writers." *Japan Forum* 1.1 (April 1989): 55–81, and 1.2 (October 1989): 197–233.

Mori Mayumi, ed. *Fukeyo areyo kaze yo arashi yo: Itō Noe senshū* (Howl, Wind! Rage on, Storm! The Selected Works of Itō Noe). Gakugei Shorin, 2001.

Mori, Ōgai. *The Wild Geese*. Trans. Kingo Ochiai and Sanford Goldstein. Rutland, VT, and Tokyo: Charles E. Tuttle, Co., 1959.

———. *Vita Sexualis*. Trans. Kazuji Ninomiya and Sanford Goldstein. Rutland, VT, and Tokyo: Charles E. Tuttle, Co., 1972.

Morita, James R. "Yosano Akiko." In Chieko I. Mulhern, ed., *Japanese Women Writers: A Bio-Critical Sourcebook*. Westport, CT: Greenwood Press, 1994, 479–90.

Morita Sōhei. *Baien* (Black Smoke, 1909). Vol. 29 in the series *Gendai Nihon bungaku taikei*. Reprint. Chikuma Shobō, 1971.

Mulhern, Chieko I. "A Survey of Japanese Women Writers." In Marian Arkin and Barbara Shollar, eds., *Longman Anthology of World Literature by Women*. New York: Longman Press, 1988, 1152–62.

———, ed. *Japanese Women Writers: A Bio-Critical Sourcebook*. Westport, CT: Greenwood Press, 1994.

Muraoka Yoshiko. "Shika ni miru shakai to no setten" (The Point of Contact with Society as Seen in Poetry). In Yoneda Sayoko and Ikeda Emiko, eds., *"Seitō" o manabu hito no tame ni*. Sekai Shisō-sha, 1999, 159–82.

———. "Yosano Akiko." In Raichō Kenkyūkai, ed., *"Seitō" jinbutsu jiten: 110-nin no gunzō*. Taishūkan Shoten, 2001, 188–89.

———. "Yosano Akiko." In Raichō Kenkyūkai, ed., *"Seitō" no go-jū-nin*. Raichō Kenkyūkai, 1996, 102–3.

Murata Shizuko. *Fukuda Hideko*. Iwanami Shoten, 1959.

Murray, Patricia. "Ichikawa Fusae and the Lonely Red Carpet." *Japan Interpreter* 10 (Autumn 1975): 171–89.

Muta, Kazue. "Women and Modernity in Japan: The New Woman and Moga." Lecture to the Japanese History and Culture Study Group, Asian-Pacific Studies Institute, Duke University, 19 November 2004.

Nagy, Margit. "How Shall We Live? Social Change, the Family Institution and Feminism in Pre-War Japan." Ph.D. diss., University of Washington, 1981.

———. "Middle-Class Working Women During the Interwar Years." In Gail Lee Bernstein, ed., *Recreating Japanese Women, 1600–1945*. Berkeley and Los Angeles: University of California Press, 1991, 199–216.

Nakashima Miyuki. "Shi to kaiga ni miru *Seitō* no joseizō"(Seitō's Images of Women as Seen in Poetry and Pictures). In Iida Yūko, ed., *"Seitō" to iu ba: Bungaku, jendā, atarashii onna*. Shinwasha, 2002, 127–61.

Natsume Sōseki. *Sanshirō*. Trans. Jay Rubin. Seattle: University of Washington Press, 1977.

Nietzsche, Friedrich. *Thus Spoke Zarathustra*. Trans. R. J. Hollingdale. New York: Penguin Books, 1961; reprint 1984.

Nishizaki Hanayo. "Ren'ai oyobi seikatsu-nan ni taishite" (Face to Face with Romantic Love and the Difficulty of Making a Living). *Seitō* 4.1 (January 1914): 70–84.

Nogami Yaeko. "Atarashiki inochi" (New Life). *Seitō* 4.4 (April 1914): 9–27.

———. *Atarashiki inochi* (New Life). Tokyo: Iwanami Shoten, 1916.

———. "Nee, Aka-sama" (Isn't that so, Baby Dear?). *Seitō* 4.5 (May 1914): 2–4.

Noguchi Takenori. "Waisetsukan no hassei" (The Birth of the Concept "Obscene"). *Shisō no kagaku* (Sciences of Thought), no. 18 (1973).

Nolte, Sharon H. and Sally Ann Hastings. "The Meiji State's Policy Toward Women, 1890–1910." In Gail Lee Bernstein, ed., *Recreating Japanese Women, 1600–1945*. Berkeley and Los Angeles: University of California Press, 1991, 151–74.

Nolte, Sharon Hamilton. "Individualism in Taishō Japan." *Journal of Asian Studies* 43 (August 1984): 667–84.

Norgren, Tiana. *Abortion Before Birth Control: The Politics of Reproduction in Postwar Japan*. Princeton and Oxford: Princeton University Press, 2001.

———. "Abortion Before Birth Control: The Interest Group Politics Behind Postwar Japanese Reproduction Policy." *Journal of Japanese Studies* 24.1 (Winter 1998): 59–94.

Notehelfer, F. G. *Kōtoku Shūsui: Portrait of a Japanese Radical*. London: Cambridge University Press, 1971.

Ogasawara Sada. "Aru yoru" (One Evening). *Seitō* 2.7 (July 1912): 42–53.

———. "Doromizu" (Muddy Water). *Seitō* 2.9 (September 1912): 7–27.

———. "Higashi kaze" (Eastern Breeze). *Seitō* 3.4 (April 1913): 62–71.

———. "Hina-tori" (Chick). *Seitō* 3.1 (January 1913): 49–64.

———. "Kyaku" (Guest). *Seitō* 2.6 (June 1912): 100–109.

Ogata Akiko. "Iwano Kiyo cho, *Ai no sōtō*: kaisetsu" (Commentary on Iwano Kiyo's *Conflict of Love*). In Iwano Kiyo, *Ai no sōtō* (Conflict of Love, 1915). Vol. 4 in the series *Sōsho "Seitō" no onna-tachi*. Reprint. Fuji Shuppan, 1985, 1–21.

Ogino, Miho. "Abortion and Women's Reproductive Rights: The State of Japanese Women, 1945–1991." In Joyce Gelb and Marian Lief Palley, eds., *Women of Japan and Korea: Continuity and Change*. Philadelphia: Temple University Press, 1994, 69–94.

Okada Yuki. "Kekkon ni tsuite ryōshin e" (To My Parents on Marriage). *Seitō* 4.10 (November 1914): 109–10.

Okuda Akiko. "Jochū no rekishi" (The History of Maids). In Kōno Nobuko and Tsurumi Kazuko, general eds., and Okuda Akiko, vol. ed., *Onna to otoko no ji-kū: Nihon joseishi saikō* (Time Space of Gender: Redefining Japanese Women's History). Fujiwara Shoten, 1995–98, 5: 376–414.

Okumura Hiroshi. *Meguriai* (Encounter). Tokyo: Gendaisha, 1956.

Ōmori Kaoru. *Hiratsuka Raichō no hikari to kage* (Hiratsuka Raichō's Light and Shade). Daiichi Shorin, 1997.

Orbaugh, Sharalyn. "General Nogi's Wife: Representations of Women in Narratives of Japanese Modernization." In Xiaobing Tang and Stephen Snyder, eds., *In Pursuit of Contemporary East Asian Culture*. Boulder, CO: Westview Press, 1998, 7–32.

Orii Miyoko. "Iwano Kiyoko." In Raichō Kenkyūkai, ed., *"Seitō" jinbutsu jiten: 110-nin no gunzō*. Taishūkan Shoten, 2001, 44–45.

Otsubo, Sumiko. "Engendering Eugenics: Feminists and Marriage Restriction Legislation in the 1920s." In Barbara Molony and Kathleen Uno, eds., *Gendering Modern Japanese History*. Cambridge, MA and London: Harvard University Press, 2005, 225–56.

Otake Kōkichi. "Henshū-shitsu yori" (From the Editing Room). *Seitō* 2.6 (June 1912): 121–25.

———. "Henshū-shitsu yori" (From the Editing Room). *Seitō* 2.7 (July 1912): 110.

Paul, Diana. *Women in Buddhism*. Berkeley, CA: Asian Humanities Press, 1979.

Pflugfelder, Gregory M. "'S' Is for Sister: Schoolgirl Intimacy and 'Same-Sex Love' in Early Twentieth-Century Japan." In Barbara Molony and Kathleen Uno, eds., *Gendering Modern Japanese History*. Cambridge, MA, and London: Harvard University Press, 2005, 133–90.

Pharr, Susan J. *Political Women in Japan*. Berkeley and Los Angeles: University of California Press, 1981.

Powell, Brian. "Matsui Sumako: Actress and Woman." In W. G. Beasley, ed., *Modern Japan*. Berkeley and Los Angeles: University of California Press, 1977, 135–46.

Powell, Irena. *Writers and Society in Modern Japan*. San Francisco: Kodansha International, Ltd., 1983.

Rabson, Steve. *Righteous Cause or Tragic Folly: Changing Views of War in Modern Japanese Poetry*. Ann Arbor, MI: Center for Japanese Studies, The University of Michigan, 1998.

Raichō. *See* Hiratsuka Raichō.

Raichō Kenkyūkai, ed. *"Seitō" jinbutsu jiten: 110-nin no gunzō* (Dictionary of Personalities in *Seitō*: The Group of 110 People). Taishūkan Shoten, 2001.

Reich, Pauline, and Atsuko Fukuda. "Japan's Literary Feminists: The Seitō Group." *Signs: Journal of Women in Culture and Society* 2.1 (Autumn 1976): 280–91.

Rexroth, Kenneth, and Ikuko Atsumi, eds. and trans. *The Burning Heart: Women Poets of Japan*. New York: The Seabury Press, 1977.

Richardson, Angelique. *Love and Eugenics in the Late Nineteenth Century: Rational Reproduction and the New Woman*. Oxford: Oxford University Press, 2003.

Robertson, Jennifer. *Takarazuka: Sexual Politics and Popular Culture in Modern Japan*. Berkeley and Los Angeles: University of California Press, 1998.

Robins-Mowry, Dorothy. *The Hidden Sun: Women of Modern Japan*. Boulder, CO: Westview Press, 1983.

Rodd, Laurel Rasplica. "Yosano Akiko and the Taishō Debate over the 'New Woman.'" In Gail Lee Bernstein, ed., *Recreating Japanese Women, 1600–1945*. Berkeley and Los Angeles: University of California Press, 1991, 175–98.

———, ed. *Journal of the Association of Teachers of Japanese* 25.1 (April 1991), Special Issue on Yosano Akiko (1878–1942).

———, trans. "My Brother, You Must Not Die." In Marian Arkin and Barbara Shollar, eds., *Longman Anthology of World Literature by Women, 1875–1975*.

New York: Longman, 1989, 189–90. [Translation of Yosano Akiko's 1904 poem *Kimi shinitamau koto nakare*.]

Rossi, Alice S., ed. *The Feminist Papers*. New York: Bantam Books, 1981.

Rousseau, Jean-Jacques. *The Social Contract*. Trans. from the French and introduced by Maurice Cranston. Baltimore, MD: Penguin Books, 1968.

Rowley, G. G. "Prostitutes against the Prostitution Prevention Act of 1956." *U.S.–Japan Women's Journal*, no. 23 (2002): 39–56.

———. *Yosano Akiko and the Tale of Genji*. Ann Arbor, MI: Center for Japanese Studies, 2000.

Sasaki Hideaki. *Atarashii onna no tōrai: Hiratsuka Raichō to Sōseki* (The Arrival of the New Woman: Hiratsuka Raichō and Sōseki). Nagoya: Nagoya Daigaku Shuppankai, 1994.

Sato, Barbara Hamill. *The New Japanese Woman: Modernity, Media, and Women in Interwar Japan*. Durham, NC: Duke University Press, 2003.

Sato, Toshihiko. "Ibsen and the Emancipation of Women in Japan." *Orient-West Magazine* 9 (September–October 1964): 73–77.

Schalow, Paul Gordon, and Janet A. Walker, eds. *The Woman's Hand: Gender and Theory in Japanese Women's Writing*. Stanford, CA: Stanford University Press, 1996.

Schierbeck, Sachiko. *Japanese Women Novelists in the 20th Century: 104 Biographies, 1900–1993*. Copenhagen: University of Copenhagen, Museum Tusculanum Press, 1994.

Schreiner, Olive. *Dreams*. Eighth Edition. London: T. Fisher Unwin, 1891.

———. *Woman and Labour*. London: T. Fisher Unwin, 1911. [Translated by Takano Jūzō in *Fujin mondai haya-wakari: Fu: Fujin to rōdō* (Guide to the Woman Question: Appendix: Women and Labor). Keisei-sha Shoten, 1915.]

Scott, W. S. *The Bluestocking Ladies*. London: John Green & Co., 1947.

Seitō (Bluestockings). September 1911–February 1916. Reprinted first in 1969. 6 vols. Fuji Shuppan, 1983.

Seki Reiko. "Bungaku ni okeru jendā tōsō: *Seitō* sōkan-gō no mittsu no tekusuto bunseki o chūshin ni " (Gender Struggle in Literature: Analysis of Three Texts in the Inaugural Issue of *Seitō*). In Iida Yūko, ed., *"Seitō" to iu ba: Bungaku, jendā, atarashii onna*. Shinwasha, 2002, 13–51.

Setouchi Harumi. *Beauty in Disarray*. Trans. Sanford Goldstein and Kazuji Ninomiya. Rutland, VT, and Tokyo: Charles E. Tuttle, Co., 1993. [First volume of Setouchi's novel based on Itō Noe's life, *Bi wa ranchō ni ari*.]

———. *Bi wa ranchō ni ari* (Love in Disarray). 2 vols. Bungei Shunjū, 1966.

———. *Seitō* (Bluestockings). 2 vols. Chūō Kōronsha, 1984.

———, series ed. *Onna no isshō: Jinbutsu kindai josei-shi* (A Woman's Life: Modern Women's History through Personalities). 8 vols. Kōdansha, 1980–81.

Shapcott, Jennifer. "The Red Chrysanthemum: Yamakawa Kikue and the Socialist Women's Movement in Pre-War Japan." *Papers on Far Eastern History*, no. 35 (March 1987): 1–30.

Shaw, George Bernard. *Man and Superman*. London: Penguin Classics, 2000.

———. *Mrs. Warren's Profession*. In *Six Great Modern Plays*. A Laurel Edition. New York: Dell Publishing Co., 1956.

Shimizu Kazumi. "Kanbara Fusae." In Raichō Kenkyūkai, ed., *"Seitō" jin-butsu jiten: 110-nin no gunzō*. Taishūkan Shoten, 2001, 82–83.

Shin Feminizumu Hihyō no Kai, ed. *"Seitō" o yomu: Blue Stocking* (Reading *Seitō*: Blue Stocking). Gakugei Shorin, 1998.

Shinotsuka, Eiko. "Women Workers in Japan: Past, Present, Future." In Joyce Gelb and Marian Lief Palley, eds., *Women of Japan and Korea: Continuity and Change*. Philadelphia: Temple University Press, 1994, 95–119.

Sievers, Sharon L. *Flowers in Salt: The Beginnings of Feminist Consciousness in Modern Japan*. Stanford, CA: Stanford University Press, 1983.

Sōsho "Seitō" no onna-tachi (The Women of *Seitō*). 20 vols. Reprint. Fuji Shuppan, 1985–86.

Stanley, Thomas A. *Ōsugi Sakae, Anarchist in Taishō Japan: The Creativity of the Ego*. Cambridge, MA: Council on East Asian Studies, Harvard University Press, 1982.

Sudermann, Hermann. *Magda: A Play in Four Acts*. Trans. from the German by Charles Edward Amory Winslow. New York : S. French, 1895.

Sugimoto, Etsu. *A Daughter of the Samurai*. Rutland, VT, and Tokyo: Charles E. Tuttle, Co., 1966.

Suzuki, Tomi. *Narrating the Self: Fictions of Japanese Modernity*. Stanford, CA: Stanford University, 1996.

Takamure Itsue. *Josei no rekishi* (Women's History), vol. 2 (1953). Reprint. Kōdansha, 1972.

Takenaka Ranko. *Hiratsuka Raichō monogatari* (Tale of Hiratsuka Raichō). Kamogawa Shuppan, 1996.

Tamanoi, Mariko Asano. "Songs as Weapons: The Culture and History of *Komori* (Nursemaids) in Modern Japan." *Journal of Asian Studies* 50.4 (November 1991) 793–817.

Tanaka Hisako. "*Seitō* to yōroppa no burūsutokkingu ni tsuite" (On *Seitō* and the European Bluestockings). *Kokugo to kokubungaku* (Japanese Language and Literature), (July 1965): 31–54.

Tanaka, Yukiko, ed. *To Live and To Write: Selections by Japanese Women Writers 1913–1938*. Seattle: The Seal Press, 1987.

Tayama, Katai. *Country Teacher*. Trans. Kenneth Henshall. Honolulu: University of Hawai'i Press, 1984.

Tipton, Elise K., ed. *Society and the State in Interwar Japan*. New York:

Routledge, 1997.

Tomida, Hiroko. *Hiratsuka Raichō and Early Japanese Feminism*. Leiden: Brill, 2004.

Toshizawa Yukio. "Joryū sakka ni okeru sei isshiki" (Consciousness of Sexuality in Women Writers). *Kokubungaku kaishaku to kanshō* (Japanese Literature: Interpretation and Appreciation), (March 1972): 73–78.

Tsunoda, Ryusaku, Wm. Theodore de Bary, and Donald Keene, comps. *Sources of Japanese Tradition*, vol. 1. New York: Columbia University Press, 1958.

Tsurumi, E. Patricia. *Factory Girls: Women in the Thread Mills of Meiji Japan*. Princeton, NJ: Princeton University Press, 1990.

———. "Feminism and Anarchism in Japan: Takamure Itsue, 1894–1964." *Bulletin of Concerned Asian Scholars* 17.2 (April–June 1985): 2–19.

Ueno, Chizuko. "The Position of Japanese Women Reconsidered." *Current Anthropology* 28.4 (August–October 1987): 75–84.

Uno Chiyo. "Genius of Imitation" (Mohō no tensai, 1936). Trans. Yukiko Tanaka. In Yukiko Tanaka, ed., *To Live and To Write: Selections by Japanese Women Writers 1913–1938*. Seattle: The Seal Press, 1987, 189–96.

Uno, Kathleen S. "The Death of the Good Wife, Wise Mother?" In Andrew Gordon, ed., *Postwar Japan as History*. Berkeley and Los Angeles: University of California Press, 1993, 293–322.

———. "Womanhood, War, and Empire: Transmutations of 'Good Wife, Wise Mother' before 1931." In Barbara Molony and Kathleen Uno, eds., *Gendering Modern Japanese History*. Cambridge, MA and London: Harvard University Asia Center, 2005, 493–519.

Ushioda, Sharlie C. "Fukuda Hideko and the Woman's World of Meiji Japan." In Hilary Conroy et al., eds., *Japan in Transition: Thought and Action in the Meiji Era, 1868–1912*. Rutherford, NJ: Fairleigh Dickinson University Press, and London: Associated University Presses, 1984, 276–93.

Vavich, Dee Ann. "The Japanese Woman's Movement: Ichikawa Fusae, A Pioneer in Woman's Suffrage." *Monumenta Nipponica* 22 (1967): 402–36.

Vernon, Victoria. *Daughters of the Moon: Wish, Will and Social Constraint in Fiction by Modern Japanese Women*. Berkeley: Institute of East Asian Studies, University of California Press, 1968.

Wakamori Tarō and Yamamoto Fuji. *Nihon josei shi* (Japanese Women's History), vol. 6. Shūeisha, 1975.

Wakatsuki Setsuko. *Netsujō: Itō Noe no seishun* (Passion: Itō Noe's Youth). Shuppan Purojekuto, 1996.

Walker, Janet. *The Japanese Novel of the Meiji Period and the Ideal of Individualism*. Princeton, NJ: Princeton University Press, 1979.

Ward, Lester F. *Dynamic Sociology, or Applied Social Science*, vol. 1. New York:

D. Appleton & Co., 1883.

———. *The Psychic Factors of Civilization*. Boston: Ginn & Company, 1893.

Watanabe Mieko. "*Seitō* ni okeru rezubianizumu" (Lesbianism in *Seitō*). In Shin Feminizumu Hihyō no Kai, ed., "*Seitō*" *o yomu: Blue Stocking*. Gakugei Shorin, 1998, 269–84.

Wedekind, Frank. *Spring's Awakening: Tragedy of Childhood*. Trans. Eric Bentley. New York and London: Applause, 1995.

Yamada Kakichi. "Erai nyōbō o motta otto no hiai wa" (The Sorrow of Husbands Who Have Outstanding Wives). *Fujin gahō* (Ladies' Pictorial), (1930).

Yamada Waka. "Datai ni tsuite: Matsumoto Gorō-shi '*Seitō* no hatsubai kinshi ni tsuite' o yonde" (On Abortion: To Mr. Matsumoto Gorō upon Reading about "The Ban on the Sale of *Seitō*"). *Seitō* 5.8 (September 1915): 30–38.

———. "Fujin no kaihō to wa" (What Is Women's Liberation?). *Fujin to shin shakai* (Women and the New Society), no. 3 (May 1920).

———. *Katei no shakaiteki igi* (The Social Significance of the Family). Tokyo: Kindai Bunmeisha, 1922.

———. "Ominaeshi" (Primroses). *Seitō* 4.11 (December 1914): 43–60.

———. "Ren'ai no jiyū to honnō: Suzuki bōshi ni tou" (Love's Freedom and Instinct: A Response to a Certain Mr. Suzuki). *Seitō* 5.10 (November 1915): 72–79.

———. "Ryōsai kenbo no Hiratsuka Raichō san" (Ms. Hiratsuka, the Good Wife, Wise Mother). *Fujin kōron* (Ladies' Review), (April 1925).

———. *The Social Status of Japanese Women*. Tokyo: Kokusai Bunka Shinkokai (The Society for International Cultural Relations), 1937. [A nineteen-page English-language lecture delivered October 15, 1935.]

———. "Tagusa tori" (Weeding Paddy Fields). *Seitō* 4.4 (April 1914), Special Issue on Fiction: 1–8.

———. "Tora-san" (Mr. Tiger). *Seitō* 5.2 (February 1915): 15–28.

———. "Watashi to sono shūi" (Myself and My Surroundings). *Seitō* 6.1 (January 1916): 107–11.

Yamakawa Kikue. *Nihon fujin undō shōshi* (A Short History of the Japanese Women's Movement). Daiwa Shobō, 1981.

———. *Onna nidai no ki* (The Accounts of Two Generations of Women). Tokyo: Nihon Hyōron Shinsha, 1956.

Yamasaki Akiko. "*Seitō* no hyōshi-e: imēji to shite no 'atarashii onna'" (*Seitō* Cover Art: The "New Woman" as Image). In Shin Feminizumu Hihyō no Kai, ed., "*Seitō*" *o yomu: Blue Stocking* (Gakugei Shorin, 1998), 402–23.

Yamashiroya Seki. "Araki Ikuko." In Raichō Kenkyūkai, ed., "*Seitō*" *jinbutsu jiten: 110-nin no gunzō*. Taishūkan Shoten, 2001, 34–35.

Yamazaki Tomoko. *Ameyukisan no uta: Yamada Waka no sūki naru shōgai* (The Story of Yamada Waka: From Prostitute to Feminist Pioneer). Tokyo: Bungei Shunju, 1981.

———. *Sandakan hachiban shōkan: Teihen joseishi joshō* (Sandakan Brothel No. 8: An Episode in the History of Lower-Class Japanese Women), (Tokyo: Chikuma Shobō, 1972).

———. *Sandakan Brothel No. 8: An Episode in the History of Lower-Class Japanese Women.* Trans. Karen Colligan-Taylor. Armonk, NJ: M. E. Sharpe, 1999.

———. *The Story of Yamada Waka: From Prostitute to Feminist Pioneer.* Trans. Wakako Hironaka and Ann Kostant. Tokyo: Kodansha International, 1985.

Yasuda Satsuki. "Hachijikan" (Eight Hours). *Seitō* 3.9 (September 1913): 60–82.

———. "Ikiru koto to teisō to—*Hankyō* kugatsu-gō 'Taberu koto to teisō to' o yonde" (On Living and Chastity: After Reading "Eating and Chastity" in the September Issue of *Hankyō*). *Seitō* 4.11 (December 1914): 1–10.

———. "Sayonara" (Goodbye). *Seitō* 2.12 (December 1912): 117–23.

Yasukata Misako. "Yamada Waka." In Setouchi Harumi, series ed., *Onna no isshō: Jinbutsu kindai josei-shi.* Kōdansha, 1980–81, 5: 61–104.

Yasumoro Yasuko. "Katō Midori." In Raichō Kenkyūkai, ed., *"Seitō" jinbutsu jiten: 110-nin no gunzō.* Taishūkan Shoten, 2001, 74–75.

Yoneda Sayoko. "Hiratsuka Raichō." In Raichō Kenkyūkai, ed., *"Seitō" jinbutsu jiten: 110-nin no gunzō.* Taishūkan Shoten, 2001, 142–43.

———. "Hiratsuka Raichō's Idea of Society: Nature, Cooperation and Self-Government." Trans. Hiroko Tomida. In Hiroko Tomida and Gordon Daniels, eds., *Japanese Women: Emerging from Subservience, 1868–1945.* Folkestone, Kent: Global Oriental, 2005, 21–39.

———. *Hiratsuka Raichō: Kindai Nihon no demokurashii to jendā* (Hiratsuka Raichō: Modern Japanese Democracy and Gender). Yoshikawa Kōbunkan, 2002.

———. "Ikuta Hanayo." In Raichō Kenkyūkai, ed., *"Seitō" jinbutsu jiten: 110-nin no gunzō.* Taishūkan Shoten, 2001, 36–37.

Yoneda Sayoko and Ikeda Emiko, eds. *"Seitō" o manabu hito no tame ni* (For People Who Study *Seitō*). Kyoto: Sekai Shisō-sha, 1999.

Yosano Akiko. "Dentō" (Gaslight). *Seitō* 4.2 (February 1914): 61–63.

———. "Mori no taijū" (Great Tree in the Forest). *Seitō* 5.8 (September 1915): 39–42.

———. "Pari zatsuei" (Miscellaneous Poems on Paris). *Seitō* 2.9 (September 1912): 133–37.

———. "Sozorogoto" (Rambling Thoughts). *Seitō* 1.1 (September 1911): 1–9.

Yoshida Sei'ichi. "Kindai joryū bungaku" (Modern Women's Literature). *Kokubungaku kaishaku to kanshō* (Japanese Literature: Interpretation and Appreciation), (March 1972): 10–17.

Index

home, as a space of entrapment, 150–51, 222–23, 225–30
homosexuality: 80; lesbianism, 86; same-sex love (*dōseiai*), 81, 85, 86, 116n30
Hori Yasuko, 17; in Hikage Incident, 126–27, 144n15; and Ōsugi Sakae, 126; Texts: "Watakushi wa furui onna desu" (I am an Old-Fashioned Woman), 144n15
Horiba Kiyoko, 34n4, 244n15, 252–53
Hototogisu (Cuckoo, journal), 204, 206
housework: 28, 183, 241, 246; as onerous, 44, 89, 97, 150, 164

Ibsen, Henrik: *Doll's House, A*, 3, 12, 17, 122, 179; Nora (character), 122, 179; *Hedda Gabler*, 3, 34nn5, 8, 107, 179
Ide Fumiko, 14, 21n31, 26, 34nn5, 8, 143n1
Ikuta Chōkō: 30, 31 fig. 5, 148, 159; as advisor to Bluestockings, 149, 177, 264; choice of name *Seitō* (blue stocking), 18n2, 266; as editor of *Hankyō* (Echo), 51, 77n23, 264; fascination with Shakespeare's Ophelia, 252, 264; involvement in Shiobara Incident, 82; rift with Bluestockings, 82, 264–66; as teacher, 82, 264; as translator, 89, 264
Ikuta (Nishizaki) Hanayo: 82, 126; family background, 52–53; Hiratsuka Raichō's praise for, 53; and Iwano Kiyoko, 157, 170; marriage to Ikuta Shungetsu, 53–54, 55, 56, 58; pen name Chōsakabe Kikuko, 53; study at Yamada Kakichi's language school, 243n6; Texts: *Mibojin* (Widow), 23; "Ren'ai oyobi seikatsu-nan ni taishite" (Face to Face with Romantic Love and the Difficulty of Making a Living), 54; "Taberu koto to teisō to" (On Eating and Chastity), 54–55; "Zange no kokoro yori" (From a Repentant Heart), 58. *See also* chastity, Bluestockings' debate of; Harada (Yasuda) Satsuki
impressionistic essay (*kansō*), 4, 45n2, 171n18, 193n9

incest, 36n18
individualism, 11, 38, 39, 58, 59, 60, 64, 66, 67, 68, 73, 102, 104, 105, 106, 147, 151, 154, 155, 157, 158, 159, 161, 164, 166, 169, 175, 180, 207, 241
infertility, 61, 238
Inoue, Mariko, 19n20
Inoue Mihoko, 202n3, 225, 231n5
I-Novel. See *watakushi shōsetsu* (personal fiction)
Ishigaki Ayako, 1, 3, 18n1
Ishizaki Shōko, 49, 76n2, 76n5
Itō Noe: 4, 8, 9, 16, 24, 38, 49, 92, 152, 176, 178, 253; on abortion, 48, 61–63, 66, 67, 68, 69, 79n42; admiration of Emma Goldman, 125, 126, 144n11; advocacy of self-assertion, 83, 91, 127–28; on chastity, 51, 57, 58; as editor of *Seitō*, 119, 120, 125, 126; family background and girlhood, 38, 81, 120–21; Hikage Inn Incident, 126–27; 144n15, 144n16; and Hiratsuka Raichō, 80, 120, 123, 124, 125, 131; as mother, 119, 120, 124, 126, 131; murder of, 119, 127; and Nogami Yaeko, 61, 67, 68, 79n39, 124, 205; and Ōsugi Sakae, 17, 78nn27, 32, 119, 120, 126–27, 143n2, 144nn14, 15; 205, 243n6; photographs of, 120; on prostitution, 50, 128–31; on Raichō-Kōkichi relationship, 85–86; study at Yamada Kakichi's language school, 243n6; and Suematsu Fukutarō, 122, 124; translations of, 120; and Tsuji Jun, 17, 63, 119, 122, 123–24, 125–26, 127, 144n11; works about Noe, 14, 119, 143n1; Texts: "Aoyama Kikue shi ni" (To Ms. Aoyama Kikue), 143n3, 145n18; "Atarashiki onna no michi" (The Path of the New Woman), 41, 124, analysis, 127–28, translation, 131–33; "Dokusha shoshi ni" (Anti-Manifesto: To All of You, My Readers), 17, 120, 121 fig. 6, 126, translation, 266; "Futatabi Aoyama shi e" (A Second Response to Ms. Aoyama), 145n18; "Gōman kōryō ni shite futettei naru nihon fujin no kōkyō jigyō ni tsuite" (Arrogant,

88–89, 94, 96, 102, 252; moonflower, 89, 249–52, 256, 257n24; compare with sun imagery in Hiratsuka Raichō, "Genshi, josei wa taiyō de atta" (1911 *Seitō* manifesto)

morality: 4, 6, 7, 24, 41, 57, 60, 64, 66, 71, 85, 86, 87, 91, 114, 127, 130, 131,145n16, 149, 159, 160, 183; "beautiful virtues" (*bitoku*), 1, 6, 12, 100–106, 152. *See also* censorship; educators; girls' schools; Naturalism

Mori Ōgai, 18n2, 26, *Wild Geese* (Gan), 35

Morita Sōhei, 22, 35n12, 51, 82, 115n1, 150, 251. *See also* Hiratsuka Raichō; Ikuta Chōkō

motherhood: Bluestockings' concerns about combining motherhood and careers, 13, 67–68, 70, 83, 119, 126, 176, 178, 179, 180, 182, 192, 193, 196; concepts of, 4, 59, 60, 61, 64, 65, 66, 83, 90, 104, 151, 158, 164, 180, 219n6, 232, 235, 236, 237, 238, 244n11. *See also* adoption, Alliance for the Promotion of a Mother and Child Protection Act, good wife, wise mother; Motherhood Protection Debate; mothers; mythology

Motherhood Protection Debate (Bosei Hogo Ronsō), 94, 117n51, 236, 244n15, 248, 257n11

mothers: expectant, 67, 69, 151, 220n16, 223; mythic, 89, 204, 211, 212–13; of Bluestockings, 22–23, 35, 38, 39, 48, 81, 82, 107, 108, 109, 111, 114, 148, 176, 195, 204, 224–25, 232, 246–47. *See also* abortion, contraception, infertility, pregnancy

Mozume Kazuko, 28, 85, 115n9

Muraoka Yoshiko, 251

mythology: Greek, Roman, 206, 207, 212–13; Japanese: Amaterasu, Sun Goddess, 89; Sea Princess, 207; *Kojiki* (Records of Ancient Matters), 207–8

Naganuma Chieko, *Seitō* cover art by, 2 fig. 1, 251–52

Nakano Hatsuko, 5 fig. 2, 84, 92, 115n9

Nakashima Miyuki, 89, 117n40, 250, 251, 252, 253, 257n24

Naruse Jinzō. *See* educators

Natsume Sōseki, 20n22, 204

Naturalism, 4, 183; Naturalists, 6, 90, 100, 101, 147, 148, 164, 251

nature, idealization of, 43, 90, 91, 98–99, 100–102, 154, 190, 191

New Man, 60, 94, 174, 208

New Woman [New Women], 3, 4, 6, 7 fig. 3, 9, 12, 13, 14, 16, 22, 26, 30, 35n13, 41, 46n5, 49, 51, 53, 54, 55, 56, 59, 60, 66, 67, 68, 80, 82, 83, 84, 86, 87, 91, 92, 94, 105, 106, 107, 110, 119, 120, 123, 127–28, 131–33, 144n15, 145n16, 150, 151, 152, 154, 155, 157,159, 176, 219n8; and eugenics, 116n13; scholarship on, 14, 15, 20n27; as transnational phenomenon, 14, 18. See also *atarashii onna*

Nietzsche, Friedrich, *Thus Spoke Zarathustra*, 89, 97, 118n53, 255, 258n36

Nishizaki Hanayo. *See* Ikuta (Nishizaki) Hanayo

Nogami Yaeko: career, 16, 204; on childbirth, 204–18, 223; family background and girlhood, 204–5; and Itō Noe, 61, 67, 68, 79n39, 124, 205; and Natsume Sōseki, 20n22, 204, 218n4; and Nogami Toyoichirō, 204–6, 208; Texts: "Atarashiki inochi" (New Life), analysis, 204–8, translation, 208–18; "Enishi" (Ties That Bind), 204; "Machiko," 218n4; "Meian" (Light and Dark), 218n4; "Mori" (The Forest), 204; translation of *Sonya Kovalevsky*, 205–6, 219nn5, 6, 8. *See also* Kovalevsky, Sonya

Nogi Shizuko, 12, 144n15; and General Nogi Maresuke, 13

noh theater, 204; *Hagoromo* (noh play), 90, allusion to, 96

nuns, 185, 196

Ogasawara Sada: career, 16, 223–25; childbirth, 223; family background and girlhood, 224–25; and Okumura Toyomasa, 223; painting talent, 224;

ABOUT THE AUTHOR

Jan Bardsley is Associate Professor of Japanese Humanities in the Department of Asian Studies, and affiliated with the Curricula in American Studies and Women's Studies, at the University of North Carolina at Chapel Hill, where she was the 2001 recipient of the J. Carlyle Sitterson Teaching Award for Excellence in Freshman Teaching. With Joanne Hershfield, she is co-director of the 2002 documentary film *Women in Japan: Memories of the Past, Dreams for the Future*, and is co-editor with Laura Miller of *Bad Girls of Japan* (New York: Palgrave, 2005).